PRAISE FOR *INVISIBLE NO MORE*

"*Invisible No More* deserves a standing ovation. It's a passionate, incisive critique of the many ways in which women and girls of color are systematically erased or marginalized in discussions of police violence. The stories told here will haunt, inspire, and challenge you to reimagine justice by moving the experience of Black women and girls from the margins to the center."

—Michelle Alexander, author of *The New Jim Crow*

"*Invisible No More* is a necessary intervention in the literature on policing. Ritchie moved me from page one with layered, thoughtful, and well-researched storytelling describing the multiple ways women of color are impacted by criminalization, begging the question of how their stories have been neglected and calling on all of us to make them visible. The insights revealed by these experiences, if heeded, will undoubtedly transform the course of history."

—Opal Tometi, cofounder of Black Lives Matter
and executive director of Black Alliance for Just Immigration

"With a profound sense of urgency and deep compassion, combining her keen instincts as a legal scholar and her work as an antiviolence activist, Andrea Ritchie brings long overdue attention to the policing of Black women and other women of color such that their stories are indeed invisible no more. All of us must recalibrate our activist responses to the pernicious state violence used to maintain structural racism, heteropatriarchy, transphobia, class oppression, and other manifestations of injustice in ways that reflect our now deepened understanding of how police violence affects Black women and women of color."

—Beth E. Richie, author of *Arrested Justice:
Black Women, Violence, and America's Prison Nation*

"*Invisible No More* is a pathbreaking, timely, and powerful exposé of police violence against Black women and women of color written by a leading advocate for race, gender, and queer justice. Andrea Ritchie not only explains with clarity why this policing constitutes systemic and structural violence that is at once racialized and gendered but also shows that resisting it requires centering the experiences of marginalized women. Essential reading for everyone committed to working for a world free of state violence."

—Dorothy Roberts, author of *Killing the Black Body: Race, Reproduction, and the Meaning of Liberty*

"*Invisible No More* is the most recent book by the brilliant Black feminist legal scholar, writer, and activist Andrea Ritchie, in which she maps the brutal history of police violence against Black, Indigenous, and other women of color in what is now the United States, countering the erroneous notion that men are the only or primary victims of such violence. From settler-colonial atrocities and the school-to-prison pipeline to the experiences of transgender women, Ritchie confronts us with a set of realities too vivid to ignore. *Invisible No More* is a hard book to read, but it is a necessary read, combining cutting-edge analyses with stories, including the author's, that will anger, educate, and inspire you to act."

—Barbara Ransby, historian, activist, author of *Ella Baker and the Black Freedom Movement*, and president of the National Women's Studies Association

"This is a terrifying book, not only because it exposes the startling number of Black women whose lives were cut short by state-sanctioned violence or the fatal consequences of policing Black women's bodies. What is most disturbing is how little we know about these women and their stories. It is astounding how quickly women of color disappear when we memorialize the 'many thousands gone.' But thanks to Andrea Ritchie's thorough research and raw storytelling—capturing both the horrors and the resistance—we can finally begin to #sayhername and end the state's war on women of color once and for all."

—Robin D. G. Kelley, author of *Freedom Dreams: The Black Radical Imagination*

"This long-awaited book from Andrea Ritchie, the leading expert on police violence against women of color, is well worth the wait. This book is quite simply stunning. Ritchie's analysis deeply challenges both antipolicing and antiviolence movements to expand the scope of their work to address how policing operates through gender, race, disability, and colonialism. Offering a rich genealogy of police violence, Ritchie demonstrates that, both historically and today, gender violence is central to policing. Her attention to the myriad ways policing impacts Black women and women of color is brilliant. A crucial and paradigm-shifting book."

—Andrea Smith, author of *Conquest:*
Sexual Violence and American Indian Genocide

"With *Invisible No More*, Andrea Ritchie has produced a work of great scope and depth, tightly documented and deeply moving. Ritchie spans multiple centuries, nations, issues, and identity lenses to lay bare the effects of violent policing on women of color. She authentically and skillfully centers Black women while seeding the ground for alliances among women of color, and she gives us a thorough consideration of the experiences of women with disabilities. Most importantly, she introduces us to a generation of fighters we can follow, support, and lift up."

—Rinku Sen, executive director of Race Forward

"Andrea Ritchie's *Invisible No More* is a powerful affirmation of why our movement has to be rooted in exposing and advocating for Black women and girls who experience state brutality. We saw with cases such as those of Sandra Bland, Gynnya McMillen, Kayla Moore, and Joyce Curnell how mainstream media and policymakers ignore police brutality against Black women. *Invisible No More* is a powerful tool that analyzes our criminal justice system's practices and patterns that maintain this problem. Through her writing, Ritchie has created the opportunity to do more than amplify police violence against Black women and to enable Color of Change and other movement organizations to also identify the intervention points where we can make real change happen in order to create a just and safe society for all Black people, especially cis and trans women and girls."

—Rashad Robinson,
executive director of Color of Change

"Andrea Ritchie's work is a vital contribution to our understanding of policing and criminalization, exposing how women, trans, and gender-nonconforming people are targeted. Ritchie's intersectional analysis exposes how policing operates off racialized-gendered structures that target people with disabilities, Black mothers, Indigenous women, and others made hypervisible and/or invisible by white gender norms. This is the tool we need in this exact moment, as grassroots resistance to police violence grows alongside an increasing emboldenment of racist law enforcement."

—Dean Spade, author of *Normal Life:*
Administrative Violence, Critical Trans Politics, and the Limits of Law

"*Invisible No More* is more than a book about police accountability; it is an important read that interrogates policing practices at the intersections of race, gender, sexuality, and ability. By examining how culpability has been constructed to facilitate the dehumanization and criminalization of women and girls of color, Ritchie skillfully presents the transgenerational trauma produced by centuries of overt and covert state violence against cis and transgender women and girls of color in the United States."

—Monique W. Morris, author of *Pushout:*
The Criminalization of Black Girls in Schools

"*Invisible No More* is not only a hard testament to the true nature of policing in the United States upon Black, Indigenous, and other women of color but also to our foremothers' relentless resistance; to their gifts of truth, kinship, and radical love; and to their will to see us and our own freedom dreams come to fruition."

—Paulina Helm-Hernandez,
former codirector of Southerners on New Ground

"*Invisible No More* is a thorough and compelling documentation of police abuses against and human rights violations experienced by Black, Latinx, and Indigenous women, other women of color, and trans women and men that should pierce the conscience of even those most resistant to calls for police accountability. Most importantly, it serves as a powerful call to action to all who care about women—that we must demand a complete rethinking of what justice is for those who have been denied, and that we must commit to fighting for that vision together. I'm grateful to Andrea Ritchie for her personal courage in telling the stories of these women and her own story, and assuring that none will be forgotten."

—Margaret Huang,
executive director of Amnesty International

"*Invisible No More* thoroughly demonstrates why we must radically reframe the criminal justice stories that too often present the myopic view that the torture and inhumane deprivation of life of men of color are the only pressing issues in the criminal (in)justice system and prison industrial complex. Andrea Ritchie's meticulous documentation and masterful writing emphasize why it is imperative that we examine the roles of race, gender, gender identity, and sexuality when we talk about and work on eradicating racial profiling, police brutality, mass incarceration, and other forms of state-sanctioned violence in the United States. *Invisible No More* is an invaluable organizing resource that is required reading for anyone interested in violence against women, criminal justice, and radical social change."

—Aishah Shahidah Simmons,
producer/writer/director of *NO! The Rape Documentary*

"This compelling, essential, and deeply informed book exposes the impact of policing, criminalization, and violence on the lives of Black women and women of color in the United States. Ritchie is at once eloquent and forensic in centering the experience of Black women of all genders and colors to build an urgent argument to reconstitute the policing function itself."

—Urvashi Vaid, attorney and author of *Irresistible Revolution: Confronting Race, Class, and the Assumptions of LGBT Politics*

"Reading this book is hard but critically important—and essential for our political education. The stories and timeline are both well researched and needed, and they taught me things I wasn't aware of and am grateful to learn. If Andrea Ritchie hadn't documented these histories, I'm afraid no one else would have."

—Coya White-Hat Artichoker (Lakota),
founding member of the First Nations Two Spirit Collective

"In *Invisible No More*, Andrea Ritchie draws from her experiences as an organizer, researcher, activist, agitator, immigrant, and survivor to paint a tear- and blood-splattered portrait that illustrates with depth and clarity the shared struggles of women of color in the United States of America. Ritchie, however, doesn't rest on that commonality. With painstaking care, she explores difference, privilege, and the layers of oppression that often mask the specific struggles of Indigenous, immigrant, and Black women in a country that hates us for our freedom. Ritchie speaks unapologetically from the margins, tackling white supremacy, police brutality, gender, and class with a deft hand and a full heart. She makes it abundantly clear that women of color are under constant threat of violence from all corners and always have been. Ritchie's work is invaluable to me as a journalist, and with this book, she continues to show that writing is resistance and that if liberation is our true goal, then Black women and girls can be invisible no more."

—Kirsten West Savali,
senior writer and editor at TheRoot.com

INVISIBLE NO MORE

Police Violence Against
Black Women and Women of Color

ALSO BY ANDREA J. RITCHIE

Queer (In)Justice: The Criminalization of LGBT People in the United States (with Joey L. Mogul and Kay Whitlock)

Say Her Name: Resisting Police Brutality Against Black Women (with Kimberlé Williams Crenshaw)

INVISIBLE NO MORE

POLICE VIOLENCE AGAINST
BLACK WOMEN AND WOMEN OF COLOR

ANDREA J. RITCHIE

BEACON PRESS
BOSTON

BEACON PRESS
Boston, Massachusetts
www.beacon.org

Beacon Press books
are published under the auspices of
the Unitarian Universalist Association of Congregations.

20 19 18 17   8 7 6 5 4 3 2 1

This book is printed on acid-free paper that meets the uncoated paper
ANSI/NISO specifications for permanence as revised in 1992.

Text design and composition by Kim Arney

"For the Record," from *Our Dead Behind Us*, by Audre Lorde. Copyright © 1986
by Audre Lorde. Used by permission of W. W. Norton & Co., Inc.

Cover photo: Janae Bonsu, Black Youth Project 100,
by Sarah Jane Rhee, Love and Struggle Photos

Some passages were adapted from the following articles and chapters: Andrea J. Ritchie,
"Black Lives over Broken Windows: Challenging the Policing Paradigm Rooted in
Right-Wing 'Folk Wisdom,'" *Public Eye*, Political Research Associates (Spring 2016);
Andrea J. Ritchie, "Crimes Against Nature: Challenging Criminalization of Queerness and
Black Women's Sexuality," *Loyola Journal of Public Interest Law* 14, no. 355 (Spring 2013); and
Andrea J. Ritchie and Kay Whitlock, "Criminalization and Legalization," in *The Routledge
History of Queer America*, Don Romesburg, ed. (New York: Routledge, forthcoming).

Library of Congress Cataloging-in-Publication Data
Names: Ritchie, Andrea J., author.
Title: Invisible no more : police violence against black women
and women of color / Andrea J. Ritchie.
Description: Boston : Beacon Press, [2017] | Includes bibliographical
references and index.
Identifiers: LCCN 2016056081 (print) | LCCN 2017014635 (ebook) |
ISBN 9780807088999 (e-book) | ISBN 9780807088982 (pbk. : alk. paper)
Subjects: LCSH: Police brutality—United States. | Police misconduct—United States. |
African American women—Violence against. | Minority women—Violence against—
United States. | Police-community relations—United States.
Classification: LCC HV8141 (ebook) | LCC HV8141 .R57 2017 (print) |
DDC 363.2/32—dc23
LC record available at https://lccn.loc.gov/2016056081

*For all the Black and Indigenous women, girls,
and gender-nonconforming people*

*and all the women, girls, and
gender-nonconforming people of color*

who have survived and resisted police violence,

for all who haven't, their families, and loved ones,

*for all who have struggled in the shadows
to ensure they would not be forgotten,*

and for all who have resisted in their names

CONTENTS

FOREWORD

Invisible No More: Police Violence Against Black Women and Women of Color is a very important twenty-first-century document. It reminds us how little in the way of material progress has been made during the last century in purging our societies of officially condoned racist violence. At the same time, Andrea Ritchie's multifaceted and unrelenting antiviolence practice over the last decade, to which her book bears witness, reveals extraordinary progress in the way we conceptualize state violence and antiviolence strategies. She does not urge us simply to add women of color to the list of targets of police violence—a list that is already longer than anyone would wish. She asks us to consider what the vast problem of state violence looks like if we acknowledge how gender and sexuality, disability, and nation are intermeshed with race and class. In other words, Ritchie's feminist approach reminds us that the job of purging our worlds of racist violence is far more complicated than advocates of simple police reform would have us believe. It is not only Black women and women of color who are "invisible no more" but also the immensity and complexity of the problem of rooting out the nexus of racist violence.

Reading Ritchie's text, I was immediately reminded of *We Charge Genocide*, the petition presented to the United Nations in 1951 by William L. Patterson and Paul Robeson. *We Charge Genocide* also documented hundreds of cases of racist violence, both legal and extralegal, in order to solidify the argument that if one took seriously the UN definition of genocide, then people of African descent in the United States would certainly be considered the targets of a genocidal strategy. This petition against genocide reflected a broader approach forged by the Civil Rights Congress and anchored in the development of international solidarities against US racism. Ritchie's work also calls forth Ida B. Wells's 1895 *The Red Record*, which documented countless descriptions of lynchings in the aftermath of slavery. In each of these efforts, the unifying theme is the impossibility of eradicating racist violence without radical transformation of the social, economic, political, and cultural contexts that produce it.

Like its antecedents, this is a difficult book to read. Because we encounter case after case of excessive, traumatic force, including systemic sexual violence, this is a book that dares us not to turn away. It challenges us to acknowledge the human dimension of this violence, which should not be effaced in abstract statistical accounts. A close-up account from the person who litigated many of these cases, has engaged in activist work with various antiviolence organizations and agencies, and authored or coauthored central policy reports, this book is testimony of a life devoted to collective struggle and radical social transformation.

—Angela Y. Davis, Distinguished Professor Emerita
of History of Consciousness and Feminist Studies,
University of California, Santa Cruz

FOREWORD

and I am going to keep writing it down
how they carried her body out of the house
dress torn up around her waist
uncovered
past tenants and the neighborhood children
a mountain of Black Woman

—AUDRE LORDE, "For the Record"

Eleanor Bumpurs's 1984 killing by Officer Stephen Sullivan didn't make a strong impression on me as a thirteen-year-old Black girl growing up in New York City. I know that there was press coverage and some local organizing seeking justice for her death, and that when I was fifteen, Stephen Sullivan was tried and acquitted for killing Bumpurs. The more things stay the same, the more they stay the same.

As I was becoming politicized in my teenage years and began to pay attention to the violence of policing, I understood and interpreted oppressive policing primarily through a Black masculinist lens. All the victims who shaped my consciousness were men—specifically, Black men like Michael Stewart, Edmund Perry, and Mark Davidson, to name a few. At the time, I didn't realize policing also disproportionately negatively impacted Black women. It wasn't until I began working with survivors of rape and domestic violence that I gained a greater understanding of racialized gendered violence (both interpersonal and institutional). Though my personal consciousness was raised over the course of organizing and work, I'm sad to say that more than thirty years since Bumpurs was shot and killed, police violence against Black women remains under-examined and too often invisible in public discourse.

I spent more than two decades living and organizing in Chicago, a city known for one of the most brutal and corrupt police forces in the country. Chicago is, after all, the city where Commander Jon Burge and his fellow officers tortured at least 120 Black people from 1972 to 1991. It is also, as I learned while doing research for a zine, the city where Jessie Mae Robinson, owner of the New South Park Record Store, recounted a story of violence at the hands of Chicago police from her hospital bed in 1959. Mrs. Robinson was arrested, along with nearly fifty others, during a warrantless police raid of a party at a private home. The partygoers were taken to the Englewood police station. The officers helped themselves to some beer during the raid and started drinking when they arrived at the station. Mrs. Robinson said that the eight women among those arrested "were subjected to indignities" including racial epithets and physical assaults, in Mrs. Robinson's case, severe enough to cause her to be hospitalized. None of the officers who assaulted her and the other partygoers were disciplined. This is by now a familiar outcome to twenty-first-century readers. What historian Sarah Haley has termed "the absence of a normative gendered subject position" for Black women explains (in part) how Chicago police could so cavalierly brutalize Mrs. Robinson.

In Chicago, I spent time organizing with and on behalf of girls and young women of color. Their stories of being "catcalled" and "hassled" by cops on the street, being sexually harassed by police stationed in their middle and high schools, and living in fear that their brothers, fathers, boyfriends, and friends would be shot or killed by law enforcement are seared in my memory. When narratives about police violence are written, though, most often these young women's voices are still missing.

Yet young women of color have been and are speaking out to pierce the silences around the impact(s) of state violence on their lives. *Invisible No More* mentions, for example, the Young Women's Empowerment Project, an organization that Andrea Ritchie and I both spent several years supporting as a board members, donors, and allies. YWEP documented, through participatory-action research, girls and gender-nonconforming young people's encounters with the police in their Bad

Encounter Line report and in zines. In *BEL Zine* #3, YWEP researchers share the following story:

> I was walking to the bus when a police officer called out and said, "Hey you come here girl with all of that ass." I ignored the comment unaware of where it was coming from until he pulled up on the curb to block my path in his undercover cop car. He jumps out and yells "Didn't you hear me calling you girl?" I replied by simply saying "No, my name isn't aye girl with all that ass." He got really mad and slapped me saying that I was very disrespectful and do I know who he is and what he can do to me?

The incident escalated, with the officer sexually assaulting the young woman, then arresting and jailing her when she tried to report him. Collecting and sharing such stories is a critical form of resistance led by marginalized young women of color. We need more such efforts, grounded in our communities, to document police violence against women and girls of color.

In 2011, as Ritchie briefly recounts, I supported a young woman named Tiawanda Moore. Tiawanda, who was twenty at the time, reported that she had been sexually assaulted by a police officer and was then herself charged with two counts of eavesdropping on police after she recorded internal affairs officers discouraging her from filing a complaint. If she had been found guilty at trial she would've faced up to fifteen years in prison. After she was—thankfully—acquitted, she filed a lawsuit against the City of Chicago. The fact that Tiawanda was sexually assaulted by a police officer in her own apartment and then found herself on trial and facing prison while the officer was not even reprimanded was a terrible injustice. I'm grateful that more people will learn about Tiawanda's bravery in standing up to the officer who assaulted her, to the Chicago Police Department, and ultimately to Cook County. To read about how Tiawanda refused to be intimidated and pressed forward to lodge her complaint is to draw strength from her courageous actions for our own fights. We need more people to center women of color targeted by police in their freedom campaigns.

———————

There are countless stories of other women of color and of gender-nonconforming people who have suffered police violence up to and including death. Yet, writing in the mid-1990s in *Resisting State Violence*, Dr. Joy James explained: "The death of women in police custody by means of law enforcement's measures to discipline and punish is an issue rarely raised in feminist explorations of women and violence or masculinist explorations of racism and policing." *Invisible No More* is a long overdue corrective to this neglect and erasure, comprehensively documenting, for the first time, a long history of police violence against women of color.

By centering the experiences of girls and young women of color, *Invisible No More* extends and enlarges the carceral landscape, insisting that we consider the streets, the schools, and the home as sites of oppressive policing. Previously obscured, sexual and reproductive violence also come into view. *Invisible No More* argues that paying attention to these issues expands and transforms how we consider policing. As more people address the ever-expanding prison-industrial complex (PIC), this book finds itself in dialogue with others addressing the history and impacts of mass incarceration on women of color (particularly Black women and girls). After all, the police are the gatekeepers of the PIC. Racialized gender violence doesn't stop with police but extends to other forms of state violence, including the violence of prisons, the medical-industrial complex, and economic violence, all of which require our attention and organizing.

This book doesn't just document police violence against women of color, nor does it simply offer policy prescriptions to reduce the harms of oppressive policing. *Invisible No More* is also an invitation to resistance to each of us and will serve as a long overdue and invaluable resource to anchor and inform the efforts of young people organizing today against state violence in all its forms.

I've been protesting police since I was a teenager. Back then, I called it anti–police brutality activism. Thirty years later, I've retired the term "police brutality." It is meaningless, as violence is inherent to policing. *Invisible No More* underscores that Black women like Jessie Mae Robinson, as well as women and gender-nonconforming people of color like those whose experiences were documented by YWEP, have never had the benefit of protection by and from the state. In fact, one of the projects I currently play a leadership role in, Survived and Punished, challenges the ways women and gender-nonconforming people are punished for survival and self-defense.

Today, my organizing work is focused on abolishing police, prisons, and surveillance. It took a long time for me to embrace abolition as praxis. I bought into the idea that more training, more transparency, better community oversight, and prosecuting killer cops would lead to a more just system of policing. I was wrong. The origin story of modern American policing is slave patrols and union busting. A system created to contain and control me as a Black woman cannot be reformed. *Invisible No More* provides ample evidence about the endemic violence of policing against women of color (particularly those who are Black and Indigenous). Abolitionists can use this information in our campaigns to build new life-giving and life-affirming institutions. For me, abolition is the way forward.

This book has been years in the making, and I know that Andrea Ritchie has lived with many ghosts and spirits during that time. That takes an emotional toll. But I can imagine the ghost of Eleanor Bumpurs watching over her as she wrote this important and critical book, giving her fortitude and maybe some comfort, whispering the names of Eulia, Aiyanna, Duanna, Rekia, Hattie, and so many more in her ear, saying: "Don't forget us. Tell our stories. Say our names." And because Audre taught her well, Andrea kept writing it all down. We are all the beneficiaries.

—Mariame Kaba, founder, Project NIA,
and co-organizer, Survived and Punished

INVISIBLE NO MORE

Police Violence Against
Black Women and Women of Color

INTRODUCTION

Pulled over in a traffic stop and beaten by the side of the road.
Placed in a banned choke hold by a New York City police officer.
Violently taken into police custody, never to come out alive.
Shot first, questions asked later.

The stories and images that immediately leap to mind in connection with these scenes are those of Black men—Rodney King, Eric Garner, Freddie Gray, Philando Castile.

But these are also the stories of Black women.*

Women like Sandra Antor, pulled over and brutalized on Interstate 95 in 1996 by a South Carolina State Trooper in an incident captured on video five years after images of Rodney King's beating sparked a national uprising.

Women like Rosann Miller, placed in a choke hold in 2014 by a New York City police officer when she was seven months pregnant, just weeks after police choked Eric Garner to death on camera using one.

Women like Alesia Thomas, repeatedly kicked and beaten by a Los Angeles police officer in 2012 while handcuffed in the back of a police cruiser. Like Freddie Gray's, the injuries she sustained in police custody proved fatal.

Women like Mya Hall, a Black trans woman shot dead by police after making a wrong turn onto National Security Agency property outside of Baltimore, just weeks before Freddie Gray's case rocked the city and the nation.[1]

---

* As used throughout this book, the terms "woman" and "women" are emphatically inclusive of transgender women.

Yet Black women's experiences of profiling and often deadly force remain largely invisible in ongoing conversations about the epidemic of racial profiling, police violence, and mass incarceration in the United States.

Since the Ferguson Uprising of 2014, the Black Lives Matter movement and the call to lift up Black women's stories of police violence under the rubric of Say Her Name have forced increased attention to these experiences. In the words of Black Lives Matter cofounder Alicia Garza, "Black Lives Matter affirms the lives of Black queer and trans folks, disabled folks, Black-undocumented folks, folks with records, women and all Black lives along the gender spectrum. It centers those that have been marginalized within Black liberation movements."[2]

In this context, Black women, long the backbone of efforts to resist state violence, are insisting that we will no longer only play the role of aggrieved mother, girlfriend, partner, sister, daughter, or invisible organizer, and demanding recognition that we, too, are targets of police violence.

Nevertheless, Black women's experiences of racial profiling, the use of deadly and excessive force, sexual violence at the hands of police, and mass incarceration remain largely uncharted territory. In some ways, the experiences of Indigenous, Latinx,* Asian, Arab, Middle Eastern, Muslim, and South Asian (AMEMSA) women are even further off the map. *Invisible No More* brings them all to the center, placing individual women's stories into broader contexts, and identifying commonalities and distinctions between experiences of Black women and other women of color, and with those of Black men and men of color. It also explores the ways in which women's experiences of policing take forms short of fatal force, and how they are uniquely informed by race, nation, gender, gender identity and expression,† sexual orientation, poverty, disability,

---

* The term "Latinx" (pronounced La-teen-ex) is a gender-neutral alternative to "Latino/a" that moves beyond gender binaries to make room for the infinite possibilities of gender in a gendered language.

† The term "gender identity" is used to refer to a person's understanding of that person's own gender. The term "gender expression" is used to refer to the ways in which people represent or present gender identity to others, through clothing, hairstyles, or other characteristics.

and mental health.³ Drawing on individual stories and existing research, *Invisible No More* identifies broader patterns and paradigms of policing that drive police violence against Black women and women of color, unmasks the continuing operation of controlling narratives of Black women and women of color rooted in colonialism and slavery in police interactions,⁴ and asks what these experiences teach us about manifestations of structural racism. Finally, it pushes us to consider what it would mean for women to no longer be invisible in the discourses of racial profiling, police brutality, mass incarceration, violence, and safety.

Invisible No More is also the story of the evolution of my own understanding of policing and criminalization of Black women, Indigenous women, and women of color over the past twenty years, as well as the evolution of a movement.

Scene I. I am fourteen or fifteen, walking down a deserted street of a strange city alone, when a group of young men start catcalling. "Hey baby hey baby hey baby," they yell out, increasingly insistent, describing what they would like to do with, and to, me as I speed up without responding. I breathe a sigh of relief when a pair of police officers come into view ahead at the corner. I hurry in their direction, as the young men's commentary becomes more graphic and more angry, as it so often does if your initial response is not to their liking. Somewhat out of breath, I tell the officers, "I need help—those guys are harassing me." The officers laugh, leer, and start their own stream of ribald commentary as they slowly surround me. Panicking, I slip out from between them and walk away briskly, frantic now that it is clear that those who are supposed to protect me are in on the game . . .

Scene II. I am fifteen or sixteen, wandering the streets of another strange city late at night. I have just escaped the clutches of a young man who thought that the dinner he bought me entitled him to more than I was prepared to give that night. I discover that the train station I had planned to sleep in is closed. I walk to another station and see lights on in a small office—the railway police station. I walk in, tell the officers I am on the first train out in the morning, and ask if I can sit in the office until then. They pause, then slowly point me to a room, cautioning that I cannot sleep there. I gratefully agree, enter the room, close the door, pull out a book and begin reading, prepared to while the night away in a novel, as I often did at that time of my life. Within an hour, one of the officers opens the door, closes it behind him, strikes up a casual conversation, works his way closer to me, and, eventually, sexually assaults me.

I got the message. The police are not here to protect me. They are just as likely as anyone else to commit violence against me.

I am a light-skinned Black woman, with curly hair and green eyes, and features more reminiscent of my Scottish ancestors than my African Jamaican ones, making it possible for me to pass as white. I am often recognizable to members of my community as Black, and it is clear to most that I am at least an indeterminate woman of color. For police officers, that was apparently enough to also read me as "sexually available" and "unworthy of protection." This reality is exponentially starker for my darker-skinned sisters.

There were other moments, even when I was older and more privileged. As an undergraduate at a protest encampment calling for divestment of university holdings from apartheid South Africa, we heard that campus police had pictures of women protesters on their lockers who were regularly the subject of sexual commentary. After law school, I was assigned to a ride-along with a police officer in Los Angeles during research for a human rights report on police misconduct. He drove me to a deserted spot in Griffith Park—where he brings his girlfriend, he said—and his questions began to take a distinctly personal turn as he moved closer. Here we go again, I thought, feeling powerless to stop what I felt increasingly certain was about to happen, panic rising as I saw no escape or rescue in sight. Just as he put his hands on me, he got a call for a robbery in progress, and we careened through the streets of LA to respond, his adrenaline pumping, my relief palpable.

These are stories I have never told, even as I spent the past two decades researching, documenting, agitating, advocating, litigating, and organizing around police violence against Black women, women of color, and lesbian, gay, bisexual, transgender, and queer people of color.

I recognize that I have been able to do this work from a place of privilege—of skin color/passing privilege, cisgender privilege, educational privilege, Global North privilege, and fluctuating economic privilege.[5] Simultaneously, I have been called to this work as a Black woman, a survivor of police and interpersonal violence, a lesbian, an immigrant (albeit from Canada), and a woman living with invisible disabilities. My intention in writing this book is to amplify the experiences, voices, work, and perspectives of Indigenous women, Black women, and women of color, not to take the place of or to supplant the voices of my darker-skinned sisters, my trans and gender-nonconforming siblings, the Indigenous peoples whose land I am complicit in settling, or immigrants who have been subject to much harsher enforcement of the nation's borders. I write as an act of love, of mourning, of honoring, of commemoration, of liberation, as a contribution to our shared struggles, wrestling with the meanings of Blackness, privilege, solidarity, and co-struggling; of "survivor" and "ally."

Ironically, it was not my personal experiences that sparked my passion to shine light on women's experiences of policing. Like many Black women and women of color, I had been engaged in struggles against racial profiling and police brutality for years, yet I had never seen my own experiences, or experiences of sexual violence by police, for that matter, as part of the conversation.

My initial awareness of police violence against women of color came when I was twenty-one, in the summer of 1990 during the Oka Crisis, a siege laid by the Canadian army just outside Montreal against the Kanien'kehá:ka (referred to by settlers as "Mohawk") community of Kanehsatá:ke, who were fighting to protect their ancestral lands and burial grounds from development into a golf course. As events unfolded, I learned with horror about verbal, psychological, physical, and sexual abuse by police and army officers against women leading blockades and fighting for their land throughout the siege. I later learned, from Andrea Smith's *Conquest: Sexual Violence and American Indian Genocide*, that women of Chicago's Women of All Red Nations were arrested as they attempted to videotape the crisis, held for eleven hours in a location covered with pornography, and denied access to the bathroom unless male officers could watch them.[6] My immediate response at the time was to join efforts to get food and supplies behind army lines to the community, and to join the camp acting as a human shield outside the perimeter and bearing witness to those trapped inside by tanks, soldiers armed to the teeth, and choppers flying incessantly overhead. These events rammed home for me, a settler who grew up just across the river from Kanehsatá:ke, on what is clearly also Kanien'kehá:ka land, the continuing violence of colonialism—and the central role of police and military violence against Native women and their communities in maintenance of the settler state.

This reality was again laid bare as I was completing this book, as police repeatedly attacked Native women on the front lines of the struggle to stop the construction of the Dakota Access Pipeline on unceded land of the Standing Rock Lakota, a pipeline that would destroy ancestral burial grounds and potentially contaminate the water supply of the Standing Rock Sioux Nation and millions beyond. Native women water protectors—including a seventeen-year-old pregnant woman and a seventy-eight-year-old elder—were repeatedly subjected to pepper spray, batons, water cannons, concussion grenades, Long Range Acoustic Devices (LRADs), dogs, fists, and Tasers by police, private security personnel, and the National Guard with tanks and riot gear. They were singled out for arrest on the front lines, and subjected to humiliating strip searches during which they were forced to bend over and expose themselves, cough, and jump up and down, held in dog kennels, and denied water, food, and medication while in police custody.[7] On November 20, 2016, a Morton County sheriff's officer intentionally shot Vanessa Dundon, a Diné warrior woman, in the eye with a tear-gas canister, causing her to suffer a number of injuries, including a detached retina (see photo insert). Vanessa, also known as Sioux Z, is unlikely to regain full sight in that eye.* She later said of the incident, "They knew.

---

* Throughout the book I use women's first names in order to restore some of the humanity stolen from them in accounts of violence perpetrated against them, intending the utmost care and respect.

They knew they were directing that towards my head. There were seven other women [including a thirteen-year-old girl] that got shots to the head that night. They were just picking on the women." Later that night, authorities turned water hoses on others in the area, as temperatures hovered in the midtwenties.[8] The water protectors at Standing Rock are not alone—state violence against Indigenous land defenders is an everyday occurrence across the United States.

One year after the Oka Crisis of 1990, I watched in horror as the video of Los Angeles police department officers beating Rodney King filled my television screen, and the following year when the officers responsible were acquitted, I took to the streets with the thousands whose outrage I shared. But it was not until 1993, when I first learned of the late-night street-corner strip search of a Jamaican woman named Audrey Smith, that I embarked on a mission to document women's experiences of policing and bring them to the center of movements for police accountability. I read, horrified, about how two Toronto Police Service officers approached Audrey, who was visiting relatives in Toronto—where I was living at the time—as she stood on a busy corner late one night. They demanded to know her name and where she was hiding the drugs. Shocked, she told them she had no drugs and asked why they thought she did. They told her she "looked like a drug dealer" and proceeded to strip-search her right there on the street, in full view of protesting passersby. The officers found no drugs. The Special Investigations Unit found no wrongdoing.

Later, I learned the name of Sophia Cook, a twenty-three-year-old Black Jamaican single mother who one day in October of 1989 had caught a ride after missing her bus in a car that was subsequently alleged to be stolen. A Toronto police officer shot her in the back while she was sitting, seat belt on, unarmed, in the passenger seat. She was paralyzed by her injury. The officer responsible was charged with careless use of a firearm but was acquitted.

Both of these women, Jamaican like my mother, could have been my sister, aunt, or cousin.

Yet, while many of the Black women and women of color I knew recognized all of these incidents as police violence, the rest of the world spoke only of Rodney King. Police and military violence against Indigenous women and Black women, as well as sexual violence by police, remained invisible.

In 1997, I was serving on the board of directors of Nellie's, a shelter for homeless women and survivors of violence in Toronto, when I was asked to join an advisory board of antiviolence advocates who would guide the City of Toronto's auditor in a review of the police department's responses to sexual assault. The audit had been ordered as part of the settlement of a suit brought by a woman known as Jane Doe, who essentially had been used as bait by police to catch a serial rapist.[9] As we reached out to sexual assault survivors to better understand their experiences of police responses to sexual assault, another story began to surface: one of police as perpetrators of sexual assault—whether through strip searches, such as the one Audrey Smith was subjected to; extortion of sexual services from women engaged in the sex trades; or rape or sexual assault using the power of the badge.

In the end, it was stories of the women who came forward—and the reality that very few people were paying attention to them, much less expanding their analysis of policing issues to make room for their realities—that drove what has become a lifelong journey. Since then I have been moved to search out and unearth the largely invisible experiences of profiling, police brutality, and criminalization of Black women and women of color and, later, LGBTQ people of color, and to insert them into debates about racial profiling, police brutality, criminalization, and mass incarceration, as well as discussions about violence against women and LGBTQ people.

The journey to this moment and to this book has been a long one, collectively and personally. Over the past two decades, I have done this work in many capacities, primarily as a researcher, writer, litigator, and policy advocate, supporting organizing efforts behind the scenes with factsheets, legal information, legislative analysis, legal observation at protests, criminal defense for protesters, and continuing support for community Cop Watch teams. Until 2009, the vast majority of my work on policing of women of color was unpaid, a labor of love and struggle. For much of that time, INCITE! both housed and deeply informed my evolving analysis. My tenure on INCITE!'s national collective culminated in the release of the INCITE! *Law Enforcement Violence Against Women of Color and Transgender People of Color: Organizer's Resource and Tool Kit* at the Critical Resistance Tenth Anniversary Conference in 2008. In the years following 9/11, when domestic discourse on policing was deeply suppressed, I engaged in international advocacy before the United Nations, coauthoring *In the Shadows of the War on Terror: Persistent Police Brutality and Abuse in the United States*, a report endorsed by more than one hundred national, state, and grassroots organizations working toward police accountability, for racial justice, and against gender-based violence. My research and writing has also focused on the experiences of queer and trans people of color, both as an expert consultant and coauthor of Amnesty International's 2005 report *Stonewalled: Police Abuse and Misconduct Against LGBT People in the United States*, and as coauthor of *Queer (In)Justice: The Criminalization of LGBT People in the United States*. In 2015, I coauthored, with Kimberlé Crenshaw, the African American Policy Forum report *Say Her Name: Resisting Police Brutality Against Black Women*. Ultimately, *Invisible No More* is the culmination of this life's work, drawing deeply on the work of many Black women, Indigenous women, and women of color who came before me, and of the survivors, organizers, and visionaries I have had the privilege of learning from and struggling alongside.

———————

In July 2015, the dash-cam video of the stop and verbal and physical abuse of Sandra Bland, coupled with lingering questions about her death in police custody, catapulted one Black woman's experience of profiling and police brutality into national headlines and public consciousness, at the height of a summer of protest against police violence across the country. Doubtless there are many reasons Sandra's story gained national traction when so many other women's had not. Prior to her death, she recorded a series of Facebook videos, "Sandy Speaks," in which she talked about white privilege, racial profiling, police brutality—in particular the killing of Walter Scott—and our responsibility to resist. Sandra was a member of a Black sorority, leading her story to

be lifted up by a powerful network of organizations that have historically played a pivotal role in civil right struggles. In many ways, Sandra Bland came to stand for every Black woman who has ever changed
lanes without using a turn signal, expressed frustration at getting a
traffic ticket, or experienced depression—so much so that the hashtag
#IfIdieinpolicecustody, under which Black women of all backgrounds
expressed their fears of, and resistance to, sharing Bland's fate, trended
on social media. For all these reasons and more, Sandra Bland's name
and story became an integral part of the broader movement challenging racial profiling and police violence sparked by the August 2014 killing of Michael Brown by Ferguson police officer Darren Wilson. But
she is not alone.

Sandra's traffic stop was not an isolated incident, an unusual case
of driving while Black that happened to snag a Black woman instead of
the usual, male target. Racial profiling studies analyzing the experiences
of women of color separately from those of men of color conclude that
there is an *identical pattern of racial disparities in police stops for both men
and women*.[10] In New York City, one of the jurisdictions with the most
extensive data collection, racial disparities in stops and arrests among
women are the same as they are among men.[11] The year before Brown
was killed, Black women in Ferguson were subjected to traffic stops
more frequently than any other category of motorist.[12] They also reported similar experiences of arrest and police violence as Black men.[13]

Black women are not immune to the perceptions of Black people
that drive these policing practices. In June 2015, just a month before
Sandra Bland was stopped in Plainview, Texas, elementary school-
teacher Breaion King was pulled over four hundred miles south in Austin. Dash-cam video shows officers repeatedly throwing Breaion to the
ground and then onto the hood of their patrol car (see photo insert). Although she was stopped for speeding, the officers justified their behavior by saying they believed she might have a weapon (she was unarmed)
and claiming that she had an "uncooperative attitude." Illustrating what
really drove the abuse, one of the officers later told Breaion as she sat in
the back of the police car on the way to the precinct that people are afraid
of Black people because of their "violent tendencies." As evidenced by

Breaion's experience, such perceptions drive officers' interactions with Black women as much as they do those with Black men.[14] Indeed, Black women, and their responses to white male authority, have been policed in brutal and deadly ways ever since the formation of slave patrols in the mid-eighteenth century, which were among the first police departments in the United States.

The war on drugs is the context in which Black women's experiences of policing have been most widely discussed: for instance, racial profiling and unlawful strip and cavity searches of Black women at airports were the subject of a well-known 2000 study by the General Accounting Office.[15] Yet this was just the tip of the iceberg—pervasive profiling of women of color as drug users, couriers, and purveyors persists and extends into highways, streets, and communities across the country.[16] It's also well known that enforcement of drug laws has driven an 800 percent increase in the population of predominantly Black, Indigenous, and Latinx women in US prisons since the 1980s.[17] Yet existing research, discourse, and debate about women's experiences of the criminal legal system have primarily focused on the impacts of mandatory minimum sentences imposed in the war on drugs, the criminalization of drug use among pregnant women, and women's gendered experiences of prison, from sexual assault to shackled childbirth. Strikingly, the police interactions that kick off the chain reactions that land women in court to face a stiff drug sentence, or in prison to be raped, or to give birth in chains have garnered very little attention, erased within broader discourses surrounding the drug war, racial profiling, police violence, and mass incarceration.

Invisible No More seeks to undo this erasure; to deepen, broaden, and provide context to the discussion of Black women's experiences of policing and criminalization; to expand the frame to bring the experiences of Indigenous, Latinx, Asian, and AMEMSA women into view; and to illuminate the historic and present-day role of policing of gender and sexuality in the criminalization of communities of color. It begins with and centers the experiences of Black women, because that is the community I am a part of, and to contribute to the current conversation and movements challenging anti-Black racism, state violence, and Black liberation.

It also highlights the experiences of my Indigenous sisters and Two Spirit siblings as an act of solidarity and accountability for my complicity in the continuing colonization of this land.[18] Although this book touches on experiences of non-Black and non-Indigenous women of color, it offers a limited examination of the unique historical and present-day contexts informing the experiences of distinct groups of women of color. While emphatically inclusive of transgender women in the discussion of women's experiences of policing, it does not fully address the experiences of transgender men and gender-nonconforming people of color, many of whom are read as feminine by law enforcement officers. Trans men's experiences of policing are largely absent from both mainstream discourses of police violence focused on men, and from efforts to lift up the experiences of women—trans and non-trans—in broader debates around policing. This book attempts to strike a balance between addressing these realities and respecting the gender self-determination of trans men by not attempting to shoehorn their experiences into a discussion explicitly focused on women, taking full responsibility for the resultant contribution to the invisibility of trans men's experiences of policing and reification of the gender binary. These and other areas require more attention, research, and organizing. This is by no means intended to be a definitive, exhaustive, or comprehensive treatment of the issue of police violence against women and gender nonconforming people, but simply one of many to be written.

The term "woman of color" is inclusive of Black women and Indigenous women, yet I also speak of Black women, Indigenous women, and other racialized women separately in an effort to avoid erasing or sublimating anti-Black racism, the unique relationship of Indigenous women and Two Spirit people to this land and its colonizing forces, or the unique historical relations of each group of immigrants to the US nation-state.[19] When using "women of color," I do so in the hopes of gesturing toward common ground and sites of shared struggle, while simultaneously honoring difference.

For instance, the same month Sandra Bland died in police custody, Sandra Lee Circle Bear, a twenty-four-year-old Indigenous mother of two, also died in police custody hundreds of miles north of Plainview,

Texas, in South Dakota. Although the trajectories that brought the two women into contact with police were strikingly different, as were the stated reasons for their deaths, both women were casualties of a criminal legal system that responds to minor traffic infractions by locking people behind bars, and then exhibits, at best, callous indifference to their well-being. In the end, both deaths were the product of coming into contact with police in the first place, and of the subsequent denial of the women's humanity and medical needs while in police custody. In Sandra Bland's case, officials denied her medication and lied about performing required regular welfare checks at fifteen-minute intervals. In Sandra Lee Circle Bear's case, her complaints of excruciating pain were met with demands that she "quit complaining." In both cases, the women were dehumanized by their jailers, their pain ignored, their lives treated as if they were of no value.

For Bland and Circle Bear, death came inside a cell. However, *Invisible No More* focuses primarily on the police encounters that brought them and other women to those cells, stopping short for the most part of tackling the violence visited on Black and Indigenous women and women of color in jails, courts, and prisons, as well as when they are on probation and parole, which has been the subject of greater inquiry and discussion. Constraints of time and space also preclude an in-depth examination of other forms of state violence, including economic, reproductive, and environmental violence, although, where possible, their intersections with police violence are explored. Nevertheless, *Invisible No More* takes a broad approach to policing, exploring the widespread, systemic, and structural nature of police violence against Black women, Indigenous women, and women of color by local, state, and federal law enforcement agents, including immigration enforcement and Customs and Border Patrol, school resource officers, and private security officers nationwide, throughout the country's history.

In chapter 1, we begin at the beginning—with the notion that physical, sexual, cultural, and spiritual violence against Indigenous women and gender-nonconforming people at the hands of military authorities and law enforcement agents, and the control of their movements on and off reservations, is a central mechanism of the continuing colonization of this land. The slave trade, "plantation justice," and the evolution of slave patrols produced brutal violence against women of African descent, as well as continuing police violence and violation of Black women through the Reconstruction, Jim Crow, and civil rights eras to the present. Through successive waves of migration, the borders of the settler state have been enforced on the bodies of Asian, Latinx, AMEMSA, and African immigrant women through exclusion and physical and sexual violence. Laws and policing practices evolved to explicitly police the lines of gender and gender identity and to control women's behavior, sexuality, and agency; such practices include the enforcement of sumptuary laws, designed to control gender expression, and "common nightwalker" laws, used to control women's movements and sexual transactions. Simultaneously, deeply entrenched "controlling narratives"—archetypal stories shaping how the actions and existence of Indigenous women, Black women, and women of color are perceived—evolved in service to colonization, slavery, and the establishment and enforcement of the nation's borders, and continue to operate in everyday police interactions.

Shifting to the present, chapter 2 examines current policing paradigms such as the war on drugs, broken windows policing—the aggressive enforcement of low-level offenses—immigration enforcement, and the "war on terror" through the lens of women's experiences, both bolstering and expanding the case against them. Chapter 3 uncovers the role of police in driving the pushout of young Black women, Indigenous women, and women of color from public schools and public spaces, deepening our understanding of the school-to-prison pipeline and the surveillance, abuse, and criminalization of young people. Chapter 4 focuses on police interactions with people with mental and physical disabilities, which frequently prove deadly, and explores the ways in which, as theorized by law professor Camille Nelson, disability is racialized and race is disableized in these encounters.

Expanding our analysis of policing along the axes of gender and sexuality brings into view gender-specific *forms* of police abuse such as sexual harassment, assault, and rape by law enforcement agents, which are explored in chapter 5. It also elucidates the continuing role police play in enforcing the gender binary in day-to-day police interactions taking place within the broader context of policing race and poverty, as discussed in chapter 6. Additionally, it illuminates gender-specific *contexts* of policing, such as policing of prostitution, covered in chapter 7. In this context, images of the monstrous and licentious "Jezebel," the drunk and promiscuous Native woman, the "hot-blooded" Latinx, and the highly sexualized and degraded Asian woman—elaborated in service of the establishment and maintenance of the settler state, chattel slavery, and national borders—continue to produce surveillance and punishment by police as enforcers of white supremacy disguised as morality. Often invisible forms of police violence against, and criminalization of, pregnant and parenting women are described in chapter 8, highlighting a central contradiction—police officers commit violence against mothers of color with impunity, while simultaneously criminalizing them for the slightest actual or perceived harm to their fetus or child.[20] The harmful consequences for women of color of reliance on police to respond to domestic violence and sexual assault are discussed in chapter 9. These gender-specific forms and sites of police violence are neither anomalies nor aberrations; they are central weapons in the arsenal of police brutality, integral to systems of policing and instrumental to establishing and maintaining structures of power along axes of race, gender, sexuality, class, and nation.

Expanding our understanding of the forms and contexts of police violence experienced by women and gender-nonconforming people of color enables us to better understand the full shape and reach of state violence in ways essential to countering it. Additionally, confronting systemic violence against women of color at the hands of a system that so frequently justifies its existence by taking on the mantle of "protecting" women also brings racial profiling and police violence against women of color squarely and directly within the frame of movements against gender- and sexuality-based violence. In so doing, it calls into question our approaches to violence and safety, and demands that we radically reimagine them.

There is a great deal of violence of all kinds described in the pages that follow. I have struggled, both in writing this book and whenever I speak about these issues, with striking a balance between countering the invisibility of police interactions with women of color and the violence they reflect, but not reproducing it. I attempt to include enough information to incontrovertibly undo the elision of these experiences, emphatically assert their systemic nature, illustrate the many forms they take, and push through erasure and silencing to affirmatively insert women's stories into a conversation they keep sliding out of because its narrative paths have been so well worn around them. In a tradition of radical honesty, I seek to honor our truths by showing the full range, breadth, and depth of our experiences, without euphemizing or sugarcoating them. At the same time, I strive to avoid reproducing and normalizing violations through what essentially amounts to a parade of Black, Indigenous, and "othered" death and a pornography of abuse. I have not always gotten it right, and I continue to grapple with how to speak these truths in the least harmful and most generative and honoring ways. Where possible, given how little information is available about these cases and the women at their center, I have made every effort to breathe life into women's stories beyond the moment of their violation, using their own words or those of their loved ones.

Each chapter, and the book itself, concludes by exploring what's next, beyond simply including the names and stories of women in the roll call of victims of police violence. *Invisible No More* not only gathers what we know about police violence against women of color; it also tells the story of a movement that has been building for decades, largely in the shadows of mainstream movements for racial justice and police accountability, and only recently gaining visibility. This evolution is chronicled in the conclusion. Angela Y. Davis, whose visionary theorizing and praxis drive and inform so much of this work, squarely places these movements in their historical context in her foreword. Mariame Kaba, director of Project Nia and a longstanding and visionary activist against state violence against women of color, and Charlene Carruthers, the national director of Black Youth Project 100, an organization that has played a leadership role in grassroots organizing around Black women's experiences of policing, shine a light on the way forward in their foreword and afterword, respectively.

It is not only the experiences of women of color with racial profiling and police violence that must be invisible no more but also our
long-standing resistance. This book is ultimately a celebration of the
roles that Indigenous women, Black women, and women of color
have played in movements to resist racial profiling and police violence
against communities of color, and in challenging antiviolence movements' investment in criminal legal systems to demand safety on our
terms. At the same time, *Invisible No More* interrogates dynamics that
have contributed to the erasure of our experiences of police violence in
spite of our leadership in both movements. It confronts the reality that
existing resistance and accountability measures are not designed to de-
tect or address gender-specific forms of law enforcement violence, and
explores how placing Black women and women of color at the center of
the conversation shifts demands, analysis, and approaches.

Thanks in large part to the invisible labor, radical imaginations, and
creative doggedness of Black women, Indigenous women, and women-
of-color-led movements, as we approached the end of 2016 we found
ourselves at a crossroads in our nation's approach to policing, safety,
and the criminal legal system. In 2017, the terrain shifted dramatically.
Nevertheless, as we continue to challenge and resist police violence
and mass incarceration under an explicitly more violent regime, and
to grapple with visions of safety in the context of this latest iteration
of the long history of white supremacy in the United States, the stories of Black women, Indigenous women, and women of color deserve
to be at the center of the conversation. As we contemplate the future,
there are a number of questions we must ask ourselves, particularly as
we enter a period of heightened policing, immigration enforcement,
surveillance and militarization, in which manifestations of anti-Black
racism, the targeting and exclusion of Muslim and Latinx immigrants,
and violations of the sovereignty and spirituality of Indigenous peoples
are dramatically increasing. How does centering women's experiences
of racial profiling and police violence shape, shift, and expand our understanding of the operation of white supremacy? How does it inform
our understanding of gender-based violence and its relationship to

state violence? How does it fuel our struggles for reproductive justice? What does it mean for the organizing strategies we employ and the systemic changes we pursue? What are the meanings of and requirements for "sanctuary" and safety for Black women, Indigenous women, and women of color? Perhaps the greatest challenge of all lies in asking how our reliance on police, prosecution, and prison to prevent and respond to violence has contributed to the experiences of police violence described in these pages, and what it would mean to build structures and strategies beyond police that will produce genuine safety for women of color, especially in hostile terrain.

The road ahead is uncertain. But this book represents my commitment to my sisters and gender-nonconforming siblings that our lives, our violations at the hands of police, and our experiences of punishment rather than protection will be invisible no more.

CHAPTER 1

ENDURING LEGACIES*

The history I learned in school rarely mentioned Indigenous women's experiences of colonial violence, Black women's encounters with slave patrols and Jim Crow policing, or immigrant women's experiences with policing at and beyond the border. These stories must be searched out between the lines of a historical record in which men are the main protagonists on all sides of the equation. Indigenous and Black feminist historians have made significant inroads in undermining this framework, highlighting the instrumental role of state-sponsored violence, particularly sexual violence, against women and gender-nonconforming people through colonial genocide, chattel slavery, and the continuing enforcement of racially drawn boundaries of gender, sexuality, motherhood, and nation. I am not a historian, and what follows is by no means an exhaustive examination of this literature. Rather, it represents an initial effort to understand how policing has manifested with respect to women of color throughout US history, and how persistent historical patterns and perceptions permeate present-day police interactions with Indigenous women, Black women, and women of color.

COLONIAL VIOLENCE

The earliest manifestations of policing in the United States took the form of military violence, as European colonizers seized and stole land

---

* This chapter is based in part on my 2002 unpublished law review article, "Invisible Crimes, Inadequate Remedies"; chapter 1, "Setting the Historical Stage: Colonial Legacies," in Joey L. Mogul, Andrea J. Ritchie, and Kay Whitlock, eds., *Queer (In)Justice: The Criminalization of LGBT People in the United States* (Boston: Beacon Press, 2011); and a forthcoming essay, "Criminalization and Legalization," coauthored with Kay Whitlock, in *The Routledge History of Queer America*.

by exterminating or relocating many of the ten to twelve million Indigenous inhabitants of this land.[1] Relatively little information exists
about the specific experiences of Native women during the "Indian
Wars," but there is no doubt that colonization required the slaughter,
rape, maiming, kidnapping, policing, and imprisonment of Indigenous
women, gender-nonconforming people, and children alongside men,
and that Native women and Two Spirit people were central to Indigenous resistance.[2]

Colonial armies and settlers did not "distinguish between male and
female, [nor] even discriminate as to age" in their genocidal practices.[3]
Women and children were often taken as hostages and killed when resisting Indigenous peoples refused to meet settlers' demands. As Roxanne Dunbar-Ortiz describes in *An Indigenous Peoples' History of the
United States*: "In the beginning, Anglo settlers organized irregular units
to brutally attack and destroy unarmed Indigenous women, children,
and old people using unlimited violence in unrelenting attacks" aimed
at displacing and removing Indigenous peoples from their lands. Far
from the peaceful image portrayed in depictions of Thanksgiving, Pu-
ritans waged "a hideous war of annihilation" against the Pequot people
for their territory in Connecticut, routinely entering Indigenous villages
"killing women and children or taking them hostage." As the Continen-
tal Congress met to draft the Declaration of Independence proclaiming all men to be equal, "Rangers," members of settler militias roused
to take and defend land for settler armies, tortured, killed, and scalped
women and children of the Delaware and Cherokee nations, "sparing
no one in their blood-drenched raids on Indigenous villages."

State-sponsored and -condoned violence against Indigenous women
by militias continued well into the next century. In 1864, 105 captive
Cheyenne and Arapaho women and children at the Sand Creek military
reservation in southeast Colorado were massacred by Colorado Volun-
teers, who then butchered, scalped, and mutilated the corpses, decorat-
ing their "weapons and caps with body parts—fetuses, penises, breasts
and vulvas."[4] According to Native Studies scholars Andrea Smith and
Luana Ross, "The history of mutilation of Indian bodies, both living
and dead, makes it clear to Indian people that they are not entitled to

bodily integrity. . . . [Desecration was an] attempt not only to defeat Indian people, but also to eradicate their very identity and humanity . . . to transform Indian people from human beings into tobacco pouches, bridle reins, or souvenirs—an object for the consumption of white people."[5] Militias engaged in such war crimes had the full endorsement of the state, and throughout the eighteenth and nineteenth centuries, the murder of Indigenous people, deemed subhuman "bucks" and "squaws," was not a crime at law.[6]

Regular army forces committed similar atrocities. For instance, George Armstrong Custer, the infamous commander of the US Army Seventh Calvary, waged an attack in November 1868 on the Washita reservation, in what is now known as Oklahoma, murdering more than 100 Cheyenne women and children, whose bodies were also mutilated for "ghoulish trophies."[7] Twelve years later, the Seventh Cavalry struck again, this time at Wounded Knee, attacking a group of 350 surrendering Lakota, including 230 women and children, and slaughtering 300.[8]

These are but a few explicit mentions of Indigenous women's experiences of colonial violence in the historical record—no doubt representing just a fraction of the instances in which women were among those slaughtered, maimed, and tortured in the name of establishing the United States on stolen land. Even though there were no doubt myriad moments of individual and collective resistance by Indigenous women throughout US history, few were recorded. Among the few that were was one instance in which the last person captured in a battle against Indigenous resisters was described by conquistador Nuño de Guzmán as "a man in the habit of a woman" and as having "fought most courageously."[9] Another involved Lozen, a member of the Mescalero Apache nation, who accompanied her brother into battle against the US Army. He described her as "strong as a man, braver than most, and cunning in strategy, Lozen is a shield to her people."[10] Many more stories of Indigenous women's resistance to colonial violence remain to be uncovered.

As Andrea Smith argues in *Conquest*, "Issues of colonial, race, and gender oppression cannot be separated," and sexual violence is an instrumental tool of colonization.[11] Sexual violations of Native women during massacres not only signified that both the land and the bodies of Indigenous women were invadable; they also represented efforts to control Native women's sexuality and prevent Native women from continuing to reproduce Indigenous people designated for extermination.[12] Such violations were not limited to the battlefield: "In eighteenth century California, priests often complained that soldiers "seduced" and raped neophyte women" at missions.[13] Along the Trail of Tears, the forced relocation of the Cherokee nation to Oklahoma in the 1830s, soldiers similarly targeted Cherokee women for sexual violence.[14] Another historian notes, "In 1856, the San Francisco *Bulletin* carried a story of a reserve where 'some of the agents, and nearly all of the employees' were 'daily and nightly . . . kidnapping the younger portion of the females, for the vilest purposes.'"[15] Criminologist Cyndi Banks describes interactions between Alaska Natives and missionaries and government officers:

> For the military, the civilizing mission was often treated as an opportunity to promote alcohol abuse among the natives, sexually exploit native women, and practice . . . immorality and depravity. . . . Thus, while the administration and the army officially attacked native customs they deemed depraved and uncivilized, they permitted native women to be preyed upon, abused, and vilified.[16]

The construction of gender hierarchies, and their violent, sexualized enforcement, was also instrumental to the colonization of this continent.[17] Andrea Smith, citing Two Spirit scholar Paula Gunn Allen, submits that violent imposition of a binary gender system was essential to establishment of the US nation-state on Indigenous land, rather than a mere side effect of the importation, imposition, and evolution of European cultures and moralities. Rigid and immutable gender categories were required to establish the hierarchies necessary to colonial logics.[18] Sociologist Maria Lugones points out that, much like the invention of the concept of race was central to colonialism, creating an entrenched and seemingly intractable axis of domination—gender—far from being biologically determined, is "constituted by and constituting" of colonial relations of power, establishing binarily opposed and hierarchical social categories.[19]

Colonialism thus established and enforced a binary, oppositional, and hierarchical gender system dividing people into two rigidly defined genders—privileging one over the other and engaging in deeply gendered violence to punish any digression.[20] It also created persistent notions of white femininity and masculinity, which in turn were based on and required oppositional narratives of Black, Native, Latinx, and Asian masculinities and femininities. Only white women could access "true womanhood," characterized by "piousness, purity, submissiveness, and domesticity."[21] Conversely, women of color were denied access to these same perceptions and privileges.[22] Simultaneously, as we described in greater detail in *Queer (In)Justice*, colonizers projected "deviant" sexualities onto Indigenous peoples, enslaved Africans, and immigrants of color as a tool of dehumanization, effectively criminalizing and condemning entire populations on the basis of actual or perceived deviation from normative sexualities. As Andrea Smith puts it, the "U.S. empire has always been reified by enforced heterosexuality and binary gender systems."[23]

Policing and punishment of perceived sexual and gender deviance among Indigenous peoples was often explicit and harsh. Deborah Miranda describes Spanish conquistadors' practice of literally throwing gender- and sexually nonconforming Indigenous people to their hunting dogs as part of what she terms "gendercide"—the intentional eradication of anyone who departed from European conventions of gender and sexuality, and a tool to terrorize entire Indigenous populations.[24] Through corporal punishment and "re-gendering" practices at state-sponsored missions, churches played an active role in punishing actual or perceived gender and sexual nonconformity among Indigenous peoples well into the early twentieth century.[25] In the early nineteenth century, the US government created additional locations of gender-based violence by mandating forced attendance for Native youth at state-run or state-sponsored residential schools aimed at assimilation. Mothers who tried to resist their children's kidnapping were subjected to violence, first at the hands of soldiers and later at the hands of Indian agents and police.[26] The theft of Native children by child-welfare authorities was similarly often achieved through police violence specifically against Indigenous women.[27]

Over time, policing of Indigenous peoples shifted from armies and militias to regular police forces with the explicit goal of targeting Indigenous people. For instance, the St. Louis, Missouri, police force was founded in 1808 to "protect" residents from Native Americans.[28] In the nineteenth century, special regulations to control the movements of Native people off reservations, including a pass system, were implemented.[29] Laws specifically targeting alleged vagrancy among Native people allowed police to arrest any "Indian found 'loitering or strolling about'" to be "hired out to the highest bidder for up to four months."[30]

Over time, writes Roxanne Dunbar-Ortiz, "Natives joined African Americans, Mexican Americans, and Chinese immigrants as targets of individual racial discrimination between the end of the Reconstruction in the South in the 1880s to the mid-twentieth century. . . . The virulent and organized racism of the 1920s spilled over to other peoples of darker hue.[31] The ongoing operation of the confluence of these forces, which Luana Ross describes as "neocolonial racism," shapes present-day policing of Indigenous women and Two Spirit people.[32]

Dunbar-Ortiz elaborates that for Indigenous women, presumed absence or invisibility is the norm. In order to render invisible the continuing colonial violence required to establish and sustain the United States, Indigenous peoples must simply tragically disappear in our collective imaginations. Under this logic, the continued presence of Indigenous peoples is an inherent breach of the natural order of things, a "dirty" and unwanted blemish on the otherwise pristine fiction of this country's history.[33] Through the myth of absence, "Native women have been reduced to the depraved squaw or the Indian princess. . . . The princess is noble, virginal; the squaw is savage, whorish."[34] The princess has vanished, and the "squaw" is to be punished. Any Indigenous people who remain are framed as "savage," divested of any pretense of nobility, deviant, irresponsible, backward, and in need of "civilization."[35] As a result, in the late nineteenth century, "All Indigenous individuals and groups living outside designated federal reservations were deemed 'fomenters of disturbance'" by the US War Department.[36]

The imperative to disappear thus creates the context for violence against Indigenous women, producing controlling narratives framing them as inherently dangerous and violent, heartless, promiscuous, unclean, drunk and disorderly, "inherently rapeable," incapable of feeling pain, and irresponsible.[37] As Salish sociologist Luana Ross writes, "Good Indians, the silent ones, know their place[;] bad Indians are shiftless, savage, drunk, immoral, dumb, criminal."[38] Such logics inform the perception of threat and complete disregard for the lives of Native women in police interactions and in custody.

SLAVERY AND BEYOND

African-descended women have been subject to—and have resisted—brutality by state-sponsored police forces and state-condoned extralegal violence throughout American history. In *Ain't I a Woman: Black Women and Feminism*, bell hooks describes rape as a common form of torture in the Middle Passage, the horrific conditions under which enslaved women gave birth on slave ships, and slavers' torture and ridicule of enslaved mothers through abuse of their children.[39] African women who resisted being stripped naked for branding were subjected to torturous punishments, and those who engaged in more sustained overt forms of resistance were even more severely punished. For instance, one woman who incited a mutiny onboard a slave ship was hung by her thumbs, whipped, and slashed with knives by the ship's captain until she died.[40]

Once on US soil, African women were subject to a system of "plantation justice." According to the historian David Baker,

> Slave law enforcement mostly took place on plantations since it was relatively expensive and time-consuming to prosecute slaves publicly. . . . Planters often branded, stabbed, tarred and feathered, burned, shackled, tortured, maimed, mutilated, crippled, whipped, hanged, beat and castrated slaves.[41]

Additionally, in most Southern states, "slave codes" were enacted to strictly control the movements and behaviors of the enslaved population in an effort to prevent rebellion. They "permitted *any* white to punish a slave who stepped out of line," without fear of criminal sanction.[42] William Craft, who escaped slavery with his wife, Ellen, in 1848, wrote,

> The lowest villain in the county, should he be a white man, has the legal power to arrest, and question, in the most inquisitorial and insulting manner, any coloured person, male or female, that he may find at large, particularly at night and on Sundays, without a written pass, signed by the master or someone in authority; or stamped free papers, certifying that the person is the rightful owner of himself.[43]

In the 1930s, the Federal Writers' Project of the Works Progress Administration gathered more than 2,300 first-person accounts from people born into slavery. Many of these accounts were replete with references to plantation-based policing of enslaved African women and girls. Elizabeth Sparks, a formerly enslaved woman, recounted that slave owners "beat women jes' lak men."[44] Linda Brent tells of her mother, who worked as a cook, being whipped or having her cooking forced down her throat when their master, or even their master's dog, didn't like it.[45] Elizabeth Keckley witnessed her mother's beating at her master's hands for grieving the loss of her son, who had been sold away.[46] Often, punishment came for no reason at all.[47] Annie Hawkins describes their slaveholder beating her grandmother to death for no particular reason.[48]

Enslaved African women perceived to be resisting in any fashion were summarily and brutally punished. For instance, Elizabeth Keckley's mistress hired the local schoolmaster to "subdue what he called [her] stubborn pride" through sexual violence.[49] Sylvia DuBois describes "severe floggings" from one of her slaveholders for being "a little obstinate,"[50] and being severely whipped on numerous other occasions for being "saucy."[51]

Enslaved women also experienced unique forms of "plantation justice." For instance, the "modesty" afforded white women was denied to African-descended women, who were routinely stripped naked when at auction or as part of punishment.[52] Additionally, as historian Gerda Lerner notes,

In general, the lot of black women under slavery was in every respect more arduous, difficult, and restricted than that of the men. Their work and duties were the same as that of the men, while childbearing and rearing fell upon them as an added burden. Punishment was meted out to them regardless of motherhood, pregnancy, or physical infirmity. Their affection for their children was used as a deliberate means of tying them to their masters. . . . Additionally, the sexual exploitation and abuse of black women by white men was a routine practice.[53]

Black women's motherhood in particular served as an instrument of punishment. One narrative of a formerly enslaved person provides a graphic image of the treatment of pregnant enslaved women: "A woman who gives offense in the field, and is large in a family way, is compelled to lie down over a hole made to receive her corpulency, and is flogged with a whip or beat with a paddle, which has holes in it; at every stroke comes a blister. . . . Overseer, Mr. Brooks, killed in this manner a girl named Mary."[54]

Another account describes the treatment of nursing mothers: "On the estate I am speaking of, those women who had sucking children suffered much from their breasts becoming full of milk, the infants being left at home. They therefore could not keep up with the other hands: I have seen the overseer beat them with raw hide, so that the blood and milk flew mingled from their breasts."[55] Linda Brent recalls her mother being locked away from her nursing baby for a day as punishment.[56] And the threat of selling a child was a powerful instrument of punishment, employed against Linda herself to force her sexual submission to her master.[57]

Angela Y. Davis emphasizes that sexual abuse of Black women during slavery was a systemic instrument of repression:

Slavery relied as much on routine sexual abuse as it relied on the whip and the lash. Excessive sex urges, whether they existed among individual white men or not, had nothing to do with this virtual institutionalization of rape. Sexual coercion was, rather, an essential dimension of the social relations between slavemaster and slave. In other words, the right claimed by slaveowners and their agents over the bodies of female slaves was a direct expression of their presumed property rights over Black people as a whole.[58]

Accordingly, the rape of a Black woman was not a crime under most slave codes,[59] or at common law.[60] Linda Brent recounts her experience of sexual abuse by her slaveholder within this legal context: "He told me I was his property, that I must be subject to his will in all things. . . . No matter whether the slave girl be as black as ebony or as fair as her mistress, in either case there is no shadow of law to protect her from insult, violence, or even from death. . . . The mistress, who ought to protect the helpless victim, has no other feelings towards her but those of jealousy and rage."[61]

At the same time, Black women's exercise of sexual and emotional autonomy were heavily policed. For instance, Mary Prince describes being horsewhipped for intending to marry a freedman. Linda Brent was beaten and abused by her slaveholder for meeting her lover, a free man, in a public street.[62]

By the mid-eighteenth century, all Southern states had enacted statutes expressly establishing slave patrols, which were among the first state-sponsored police forces in the United States.[63] The "'new police' were given power to break into Black people's homes, punish enslaved people or runaways, whip enslaved people who challenged their authority, and apprehend any enslaved person suspected of a crime."[64] Patrol members, appointed by justices of the peace, were required to "carry a pistol while on duty" and "arrest all slaves found outside their master's domain without a pass," and were empowered to "search for offensive weapons and fugitive slaves."[65] Lizzie Williams, a formerly enslaved woman, described: "De niggahs hab' to get a pass from massa or de missus if dey go ennywhar. De paddyrollers jes lik' police. 'Bout dozen of dem ride 'long togedder. Fus thing dey say: 'Whar yo' pass?' Den iffen yo' hab one dey lets you go but iffen you don' hab one dey strips yo' to de waist and dey lams yo' good till de blood comes."[66]

In addition to physical abuse, Black women routinely experienced sexual violence at the hands of slave patrols, in the community and during searches of their homes.[67] Ida Henry described an assault by a slave patrol against his mother: "De patrollers wouldn't allow de slave to hold night services, and one night dey caught me mother out praying. Dey stripped her naked and tied her hands together and . . . dey pulled her up so dad her toes could barely touch de ground and whipped her."[68]

African-descended women resisted enslavement at every turn, from work slowdowns to arson to poisoning and killing those who would enslave them, to outright rebellions and active leadership in the movement to abolish slavery.[69]

The end of chattel slavery did not bring an end to violations of Black women. In fact, "emancipation" was characterized by violence and rape of Black women, including those snatched up, robbed, and jailed by Union troops during the 1865 occupation of Richmond, Virginia.[70] During the Reconstruction era, "Black codes" replaced slave codes. Like their predecessors, the Black codes controlled the movements of formerly enslaved Black people, severely restricted liberty in employment and conduct, and continued to empower state police forces and the white population at large to enforce them. Black codes in several states prohibited formerly enslaved African women employed as domestic workers from leaving their employer's property. Those who left their employment while under contract were arrested and returned.[71] Under Mississippi law, any free Black woman over eighteen years of age without lawful employment or business could be declared a vagrant and subject to a fine of up to fifty dollars and imprisonment for up to ten days; those unable to pay would be hired out by the sheriff to anyone willing to pay the fine.[72] Historian Talitha LeFlouria attributes these provisions in part to planters' reaction to newly freed Black women's decisions to withdraw their labor in order to care for their families.[73]

According to historian Sarah Haley, "Police arrested hundreds of black women annually in [Atlanta] after the Civil War."[74] "By 1888 . . . black women were 5.8 times more likely to be arrested than white women" and were "disproportionately charged with public quarreling and using profane language" and "drunk and disorderly conduct and occupying/keeping a house of ill repute." Black women were also arrested for vagrancy, though not as often as their male counterparts.

Sometimes these charges actually referred to prostitution. In these ways, "Black women's perceived unruliness, propensity to fight, inability to control their children, and general vulgarity were policed as an infringement on their ability to perform their natural duties as washerwomen and domestic servants." Haley further theorizes that "the sight of black women on the streets, in black neighborhoods, perhaps with their voices raised, was an assault on the model of a docile black woman in the white domestic sphere, and therefore subject to punishment." Records reveal that in Atlanta, "in each year between 1893 and 1900 more black girls and young women between the ages of fifteen and twenty were arrested than white boys and white girls in the same age group combined." In 1893, Black women were 6.4 times as likely as white women and Black girls 19 times as likely as white girls to be arrested. In comparison, Black men were 1.4 times as likely to be arrested as white men, and Black boys were three times as likely to be arrested as white boys. Haley describes one Black girl's arrest during this period. Twelve-year-old Lucinda Stevens had recently lost her mother when, passing a rail yard in Atlanta, she picked up a few pieces of coal. She was immediately arrested by police and held in the city stockade, despite her father's petitions on her behalf.

Before and after the Black codes were struck down by the Civil Rights Act of 1866, Black women were also subject to arrest for any actual or perceived transgression reported by their employers.[75] At times, Black women supplemented their meager salaries by taking food, clothing, money, or other basic necessities. Police called by employers broadly interpreted "theft" to include taking leftover food scraps or using an employer's table and chair, interpretations that provided unmitigated support of whites' complete control over the lives of Black women.[76] As a result, LeFlouria notes, "Larceny was the most prevalent offense committed by freedwomen in the post-Emancipation South."[77] Upon conviction, the Thirteenth Amendment allowed Black women "duly convicted of a crime" to be subject to forced labor in state prison camps, on chain gangs, and in indentured servitude.[78] One woman employed as a "Negro nurse" in Atlanta described her employment situation as "as bad as, if not worse than, it was during the days of slavery," but the alternative—arrest, jailing, and free labor on the state farm—was even worse.[79]

During this period, anxiety around "Negro crime" was constructed to "promote and rationalize the mass incarceration of ex-slaves and their progeny after the Civil War."[80] Late-nineteenth-century scientific racism framed Black women, at best, as "prostitutes" and, at worst, as "savage beast[s]" or "true monster[s]" genetically inclined to "barbaric acts of cruelty."[81] Newspapers promoted stories of "crazy negresses" prone to attacking white men, women, and children, acting in immoral, deranged, and atrocious ways, "luring young white girls into sex work and stealing and brutally whipping 'blue-eyed' white babies." In addition, "More frequent allegations of black female deviance [involved] their inclination to kill their own children."[82] These images fueled the arrest, incarceration, and lynching of Black women, and the constitution of Black women "as subjects outside of the protected category 'woman.'"[83]

Moreover, within this framework, "their excessive reproduction of nefarious black children was a threat, a divergence from their primary function, maintaining the white domestic sphere and the sanctity of the white home."[84] Accordingly, Haley concludes, "Beneath the vague charges was the goal of making them good domestics but dissociating them from femininity by presenting them as bad mothers and aggressive beings who were dangerous because they might produce more of their kind."[85]

From the early 1900s to the late 1960s, Jim Crow segregation laws[86] effectively replaced the slave codes and Black codes.[87] In 1951, the Civil Rights Congress, an organization formed to challenge the House Un-American Activities Committee and to support unionizing workers in the South, filed a historic petition with the newly formed United Nations. It charged the United States with genocide against African Americans as a people under the 1948 Convention on the Prevention and Punishment of the Crime of Genocide.[88] The petition presented voluminous evidence of acts falling within the convention's definition of genocide, gleaned from newspaper articles in the Black press and from reports of civil rights groups, labor organizations, and occasional hearings by city, state, and federal government agencies. Even though the drafters of the petition limited themselves to incidents that occurred between January 1, 1945, and June 1951, the document is replete with examples of police brutality against Black women.

The petition describes how, in many cases, police officers abused Black women for failure to display what they considered appropriate deference. For instance, when Mrs. Lena Fausset inadvertently bumped into a policewoman on the streets of Jamaica, New York, the policewoman responded by beating her. Police officers were also called upon by whites to intervene in disputes with Black women. In February 1947, Mrs. Billie Moton Holmes ordered her landlord from her home in Flint, Michigan. The landlord returned with a police officer, who served a summons on Mrs. Holmes, struck her in the face, and dragged her down a stairway to his police car. When Mrs. Lena Thomas got into an argument with a food checker at a supermarket in Harlem, the store manager called the police. They resolved the dispute by beating Mrs. Thomas. The incident prompted outrage in the predominantly Black community, in response to which "hundreds of police were rushed into the area." Mrs. Thomas sued the New York Police Department for $10,000 in damages.

The petition also documented the brutal enforcement of antimiscegenation laws. On May 4, 1950, Mrs. Charles Turner, the well-known owner of Mom's restaurant in New York City, left her restaurant after closing with a "very fair-complected Negro man." Police officers who noticed the couple beat Mrs. Turner, believing her companion to be white.

As under the slave codes and Black codes, police officers continued to serve as instruments of enforced employment. In 1946, Margaret DeGraffenried, a mother of four children, joined other workers in striking against a North Carolina tobacco company for a wage of sixty-five cents an hour. She was brutally beaten by police and sentenced to three months on a road gang.

Police officers also used their authority to sexually abuse Black women on a regular basis. Danielle McGuire's groundbreaking *At the Dark End of the Street: Black Women, Rape, and Resistance* documents a number of cases. In 1945, a committee initially organized around the gang rape of Recy Taylor by a group of white men in Abbeville, Alabama, later issued a flyer announcing that "two Negro girls were forced into a police car, taken for a ride in the country, and criminally assaulted by two uniformed policemen." In 1946, Nannie Strayhorn, a thirty-two-year-old mother, accepted a ride home with two officers in Richmond, Virginia, who instead "drove to an isolated area outside town and took turns raping her at gunpoint."[89]

Even when police officers' sexual predations against Black women came to light, they often went unpunished, based on the continued presumption that Black women were "unrapeable." For example, on August 3, 1945, in Memphis, Tennessee,

> two young Negro women were raped by uniformed police officers. They were waiting for a street car to take them home from work, when the officers took them into custody. They were then driven to an isolated spot where the officers raped them. The officers warned them that they would be killed if they reported the incident. A complaint to the Chief of Police from the mother of one of the young women brought the advice that she keep her mouth shut. The two officers were acquitted by an all-white jury.[90]

Women who challenged Jim Crow segregation laws were singled out for particularly violent police abuse. In one case, documented in "We Charge Genocide," from July 9, 1945, "PFC [Private First Class] Helen Smith, PVT [Private] Tommie Smith, and PFC Georgia Boson, all members of the US Women's Army Corps, were brutally beaten in the Elizabethtown, Kentucky bus terminal for sitting in the 'white' section when the 'colored' section was full." They were certainly not alone.[91] According to Danielle McGuire, "There were plenty of stories . . . about black women who had been arrested and beaten by policemen after protesting mistreatment on buses." For instance, one day in 1942 in Montgomery, Alabama—thirteen years before Rosa Parks's legendary stand on the same bus route—Ella Ree Jones refused to give up her seat to a white man on a segregated bus. Two police officers pulled her out of her seat at the behest of a bus driver, who said, "I'm going to teach you to do what the white man tells you to do." The officers twisted her arms until she screamed, threatened to kill her when she resisted, and then beat her with a pipe behind city hall until she was unable to get up, kicked her as she attempted to do so, slammed her head into a brick wall, and then picked her up off the ground by the hair and threw her in a jail cell. She was charged with "suspicion." After spending the day reading about Harriet Tubman and Sojourner Truth, fifteen-year-old Claudette Colvin protested when ordered to give up her seat on the bus, citing a finer point of law that allowed her to keep it. The arresting officer, calling her "that thing" and "black whore," yanked her out of her seat and kicked her down the aisle as she sobbed in protest. When one of the officers summoned to the scene joked about her breasts and bra size, Claudette said, "I was afraid they might rape me."[92]

As resistance grew, so did police violence against Black women. On Bloody Sunday, during the historic march from Selma to Montgomery, "Images of policemen clubbing women as they struggled to stand and mounted officers flattening children . . . sent a powerful message about the brutality of Jim Crow."[93] Police also engaged in harassment of women civil rights activists, such as following women who cooked for Montgomery bus boycott participants and giving them traffic tickets, and pouring acid on boycott mastermind and leader Jo Ann Robinson's car. Additionally, sexual violence continued to be wielded by police against Black women protesters. Angela Y. Davis cites reports from civil rights organizers that Southern white policemen raped Black women activists arrested during the civil rights struggle,[94] and Danielle McGuire chronicles efforts by Dorothy Height, the National Council of Negro Women, and the Delta Sigma Theta Sorority to document and organize around rape, sexual abuse, and assaults of female freedom fighters in Southern jails.[95] Fannie Lou Hamer and several other women were severely beaten and sexually assaulted while under arrest for daring to defy Jim Crow laws and customs (see arrest photo in insert). One officer yelled at Fannie Lou, "You bitch, we going to make you wish you was dead," as others beat her, felt under her clothes, and pulled her dress over her head, leaving her naked in front of five men. June Johnson, a sixteen-year-old arrested with Fannie Lou, was also brutally beaten and stripped naked. Even though Fannie Lou told her story on national television during the 1964 Democratic National Convention, the sexual nature of police violence against Black women in the civil rights movement has largely been erased from public discourse.[96]

Much as present-day perceptions of Indigenous women are rooted in colonial legacies, according to the sociologist Patricia Hill Collins, "society continues to view Black women through a series of controlling narratives constructed during slavery," Reconstruction, and Jim Crow, shaping conscious and unconscious reactions and understandings of Black women's personhood, conduct, and experiences of violence, as well as police responses to Black women.[97] For instance, during slavery, Black women were expected to reproduce and expand the population of enslaved people and care for white families. Slavery was predicated on the notion that Black women experience no pain—and can thus be worked beyond exhaustion, give birth in the fields and return to work immediately, have their children taken from them without compunction, and undergo surgeries without anesthesia, despite its availability to white women.[98] This system of constructed categorizations of Black women's behavior and possibilities for existence persists to the present day: the ideal Black woman conforms to the image of the "mammy"— submissive, maternal, domestic, religious, and devoted to both her family and the white people for whom she works, and tolerant, if not deserving, of all forms of imposition, violation, pain, and abuse.[99] Such narratives inform police perceptions of what conduct is appropriate and permissible toward Black women.

Black women who deviate from the "mammy" role are framed through two other controlling narratives. The first, the "Jezebel" narrative, is the myth of the Black woman whose out-of-control sexuality seduced white men, justifying systematic rape during slavery and the continued presumption of universal sexual access to Black women's bodies.[100] Additionally, as Cathy Cohen argues, Black women, excluded from the dominant norms of white womanhood, are thus "queered" through projection of non-normative and deviant sexualities in service of "institutional racism, patriarchy and class exploitation," which drives the criminalization of Black women of all sexual orientations.[101] Patricia Hill Collins points out that over time, the "Jezebel" image has framed Black women as

> the freak on the border demarking heterosexuality from homosexuality. . . . On this border, the hoochie participates in a cluster of "deviant female sexualities," some associated with the materialistic ambitions where she sells sex for money, others associated with so-called deviant sexual practices such as sleeping with other women, and still others attached to "freaky" sexual practices such as engaging in oral and anal sex.[102]

Collins goes on to suggest that the projection of oversexualization onto Black women also contributes to "masculinizing" them, thereby removing them from protective spheres.[103]

Alternately, Black women become "Sapphires," the image of the domineering, emasculating Black woman that emerged in the century following slavery when Black women entering the workforce were perceived to be usurping men's roles.[104] Author bell hooks describes Sapphires as "black women . . . depicted as evil, treacherous, bitchy, stubborn and hateful, in short all that the mammy figure was not."[105] Black women perceived as Sapphires are conceived of as "super-women," aggressive and prone to violence, requiring swift and forceful submission.

Under both Jezebel and Sapphire stereotypes, Black women are perceived as subhuman, animalistic, to be violated, feared, and punished.[106] Any departure from the mammy role in a police interaction therefore becomes dangerous for a Black woman, her stance presumed to be unacceptably aggressive, the physical threat she poses drastically overblown, her sexuality automatically deviant, her body devoid of feeling, her personhood undeserving of protection.[107] The criminalization of Black women through such imagery served to reestablish hierarchies of bodies after slavery and Reconstruction, writes Sarah Haley. Depictions as "excessive, disfigured, and incorrigible" and "monstrous meant not only that [Black women's] political and economic power would be limited, but also that they would be subject to disproportionate arrest and imprisonment."[108]

BORDERS AND BEYOND

As successive waves of immigrant women arrived in the United States, they too became subjects of policing at the border and beyond. Noting that "women's bodies historically serve as the iconic sites for sexual intervention by state and nation-making projects,"[109] historian Eithne Luibhéid chronicles the operation of the "immigration control apparatus as a key site for . . . the regulation of sexual norms, identities and behaviors."[110] According to Luibhéid, in addition to constructing the US nation-state along racial lines, "Immigration laws and procedures . . . differentiated women into categories such as wife, prostitute and lesbian . . . regulating admission based on sexuality," preferring the former, and excluding the latter.[111] Beyond the explicit ban on entry of individuals considered "homosexuals," immigration officials also used prohibitions on entry for "lewd and immoral purposes," as well as a prohibition of individuals labeled with psychiatric conditions, deemed "likely to become public charges," or "arriving in a state of pregnancy" to exclude women at the border.[112] Luibhéid emphasizes that immigration authorities not only were charged with "discovering" such identities but also "contributed to constructing" them in ways that "reconstructed racialized, class-differentiated forms of patriarchy."[113] In so doing, they evaluated women immigrants both as "individual bodies to be disciplined" and on their suitability to contribute to the larger national identity, including by giving birth to large numbers of children or intermarrying with "Americans."[114]

Among the regulations governing immigration to the United States were Chinese exclusion laws and laws barring "prostitutes." Both targeted Asian women, who were presumed to be both. Luibhéid submits that the Page Act of 1875, which prohibited the "importation to the United States of women for the purposes of prostitution,"[115] was intended to exclude and applied primarily to Chinese and Asian women "because their intersecting gender, class, ethnic and racial identities led to suspicion that they were likely to engage in prostitution, offer[ing] a paradigmatic example of how racialized gender identities were treated as presupposing particular sexual acts. Even when these acts had not actually taken place, the fear that they might occur was the grounds for exclusion."[116] The law not only significantly interfered with Chinese women's ability to cross the border, but also set a precedent for gender- and sexuality-based exclusions aimed at preventing certain groups of immigrants of color from settling in the United States. Luibhéid proposes that attitudes toward "Chinese women laid the groundwork for the subsequent delineation and surveillance of a whole host of other 'dangerous' peripheral sexual figures," including the "racialized prostitute, the amoral and despotic pimp, the fecund woman whose reproduction was uncontrolled, the gold digging hussy intent on snaring an American husband, and the foreigner who threatened miscegenation."

Luibhéid emphasizes "the centrality of sexuality as an axis of power through which immigration admission and exclusion have been organized," describing how categories of lesbian, "prostitute," and "immoral women" who "fail to conform to the heterosexual imperative, emerge as figures that particularly threaten the nation and have to be disciplined" by being refused entry. This was the case for Sarah Harb Quiroz, a Mexican mother, domestic worker, and lawful US permanent resident who in 1960 was stopped at the US-Mexico border. A US immigration officer with a reputation for detecting "sexual deviates" perceived Quiroz, who wore "trousers and a shirt" with "hair . . . cut shorter than some other women's," to be a lesbian. Ultimately, Quiroz was deported despite her status as an authorized immigrant. In subsequent appeals, her condition of being an alleged lesbian was pathologized and conflated with "a disorder of the personality which has brought her in conflict with 'the prevailing culture,'" confirming that immigration enforcement was to operate as if there was no place in the United States for gender or sexual nonconformity, as gender and sexual norms were defined by whiteness. Indeed, cross-dressing and gender nonconformity served as an unofficial independent basis of exclusion, regardless of whether they were read to signify nonheteronormative sexuality. In another example documented by Luibhéid, Alejandra Veles, a woman described as "boyish in appearance" and "dressed in men's clothes," was threatened with arrest "for her defiance of the rules"—presumably the rules of gender—and was released by immigration officials only on condition that she leave the country immediately.

Other pathologized bodies have been excluded under laws denying entry to "idiots" and "lunatics," and later to individuals infected with "loathsome and contagious diseases," such as tuberculosis, syphilis, gonorrhea, and, later, HIV. Individuals deemed to have engaged in "crimes of moral turpitude," extending beyond prostitution to any sexual offense, have been banned since 1891. Pregnant women, married or not, have also been excluded on the grounds that they were likely to become public charges, demonstrating that childbearing by immigrant women, even in the context of marriage, has continually been framed as problematic. In the wake of World War I, Japanese women's childbearing, characterized by "too many children and [inappropriate] mother[ing]," was framed as a threat of Japanese conquest of the United States, leading to a 1920 agreement barring Japanese women—including those who were wives of Japanese men in the United States—from entry.

Within borders, criminal and immigration law were similarly deployed to police perceived deviance and citizenship. Historian Clare Sears details how perceived gender nonconformity in both appearance and behavior among Asian women and men rendered them "problem bodies" requiring surveillance within the United States, when not excluded outright.[117] As a result, prostitution-based policing of Chinese women, framed as threats to white families and as purveyors of disease and immorality, was rampant within the nation's borders. Even before prostitution was generally prohibited, police targeted Chinese prostitution as a "public nuisance," and brothel laws in San Francisco were "enforced . . . mainly against Chinese and Mexican brothels." As of 1907, any woman who began practicing prostitution within three years of entry was subject to deportation.[118]

Through exclusion, policing, and deportation of immigrant women, a heteronormative, gender-conforming, and intrinsically white national identity was constructed and enforced. At the same time, controlling narratives of immigrant women as importers of vice, disease, and uncontrolled reproduction were mobilized to justify state violence.

Because immigrant women are largely not supposed to be here, it therefore becomes permissible for law enforcement agents to violently exclude them or to eradicate them through killing, rape, or deportation.[119]

Within this context, racialized perceptions of immigrant women have developed to justify their continued exclusion and subordination in the United States. For instance, Asian women continue to be profiled as being engaged in prostitution and as immoral; "dishonest, tricky, and sneaky"; and ultimately unassimilable. Asian women have also been stereotyped alternately as "the servile, oversexed Asian female," as "superfeminine" (the "China Doll"), or as "castrating" (the "Dragon Lady").[120] They are therefore imagined to be sexually available, subservient, and devoted, and if they deviate from this image, they are framed as scheming, duplicitous, tyrannical, and dangerous. Latinxs have been portrayed as "hot blooded" and as "wetbacks, junkies, knife-wielding Puerto Ricans, promiscuous Latinas, revolutionaries, terrorists and Mexican thieves." The "latest among these images is the Latina gang member living her *vida loca* and that Latin American mula ["mule"] transporting drugs into the United States and Europe. Combined, these images depict . . . Latinas, as immoral, criminal, and violent."[121] Additionally, immigrant Latinxs' sexuality and motherhood are portrayed as a threat to the nation's safety net.[122] In recent years, Haitian, Arab, Middle Eastern, Muslim, and South Asian immigrants have also increasingly been framed as threats in economic, health, and terrorist terms. For each of these groups, these archetypal representations play out in police interactions.

GENDER POLICING

Actual or perceived deviation from gender and sexual norms has served as a basis of criminalization since the colonial period. The first recorded law targeting gender nonconformity was a 1696 Massachusetts statute banning cross-dressing "to curb the possibility of same-sex sexual encounters."[123] Historian Clare Sears traces the evolution of cross-dressing laws in forty-five cities in more than twenty-one states during the late nineteenth and early twentieth centuries. According to Sears, such laws were explicitly intended to regulate racialized boundaries of gender, "construct a gender-normative nation," and impose a moral order in municipalities in order to make them safe for "good" white middle- and upper-class citizens by excluding gender "outlaws" from public spaces. Prohibitions against cross-dressing were often found within broader indecency laws targeting "lewd" conduct and prostitution, "one part of a broader legal matrix centrally concerned with the boundaries of race, sex, citizenship and city space."[124]

The post–World War II era is perhaps the most well-known period in which sodomy and anti-cross-dressing laws, in conjunction with laws prohibiting vagrancy, sedition, lewd conduct, and prostitution, were deployed to criminalize gender- and sexually nonconforming women. Nan Alamilla Boyd chronicles the ways in which military police, liquor control authorities, and local law enforcement collaborated to mark places and people for routine raids, arrests, convictions, and court-martial across the country, increasingly cracking down on lesbian bars and gathering places, and charging lesbians under antiprostitution laws, regardless of whether they were trading sex at the time. Both Joan Nestle and Boyd describe the conflation of cross-dressing among women with prostitution, and the shared experiences of policing and survival within often-overlapping lesbian and sex working communities.[125]

As discussed in greater detail in subsequent chapters, the existence of laws against cross-dressing through the late twentieth century branded gender-nonconforming individuals, particularly people of color and low-income people, as embodiments of "disorder" and "fraud," leading to continuing criminalization by other means, such as broken windows policing and policing of prostitution.

ENDURING LEGACIES

Far from being mere echoes of a distant past, the historical context of state violence against women and gender-nonconforming people of color in the United States deeply informs present-day interactions with police and systems of law enforcement. Beyond individual acts of violence at the hands of colonial soldiers, whites, slave patrols, immigration officers, and urban police forces, patterns of law enforcement violence across time have served to structure and reinforce present-day perceptions of Indigenous women, Black women, and women of color, and have fossilized into what Patricia Hill Collins terms "controlling narratives."[126] These racially gendered and sexualized myths conjured to justify the brutal social control used to maintain racially gendered hierarchies persist to this day, having transformed, solidified, and mutated over time to fit shifting realities. They pervade daily law enforcement interactions with women and transgender people of color, structuring police and public perceptions of women's appearance and behavior, and dictating the terms of policing and police violence against women's bodies in the context of present-day policing paradigms.

CHAPTER 2

POLICING PARADIGMS
AND CRIMINALIZING WEBS

There are multiple "wars" being waged within the United States that serve as both backdrop and driving forces for present-day racial profiling, police violence, and mass incarceration. Volumes have been written about each of them: the war on drugs, broken windows policing, heightened immigration enforcement, the war on terror. Yet there has been relatively little analysis of women's experiences of policing under any of these paradigms, and few connections have been made between individual incidents of police violence against women of color and their relationship to these larger frameworks of profiling and policing. Over the past two decades, as each of these paradigms has evolved, I have found myself searching for women's stories and asking myself, fellow organizers, researchers, advocates, and policymakers, "How does this affect women of color? What do we learn about the operation of these policies from women's experiences? What would it take to make their experiences more visible within this broader discussion?" These questions—often met with uncomfortable silences—largely remain unanswered.

Since the mid-1970s, several strands of criminal legal policy have woven a net that has increasingly ensnared women of color in systems of surveillance, control, and punishment, producing, in 2008, the highest rates of incarceration of women in history.[1] Between 1980 and 2014, the number of women in federal, state, and local prisons and jails in the United States increased by more than 700 percent.[2] Half of all women incarcerated are in a city or county jail, generally held because they previously failed to appear, are not afforded, or cannot afford to post bail.

And more than half of these women are imprisoned in small county jails, such as those where Sandra Bland and Sandra Lee Circle Bear died.[3] Although women still represent a relatively small fraction—10 percent—of the more than two million people incarcerated in the United States, the rate at which the number of women in prison has grown has outpaced men's by 50 percent.[4] Since 1970, the number of women in jail* has increased fourteenfold—as a result, "the number of women in jail nationwide is growing at a faster rate than any other incarcerated population."[5] Another million-plus women are under the supervision of the criminal-legal system, on probation, or on parole.[6]

The vast majority of women impacted by mass incarceration and criminalization are Black, Indigenous, and Latinx, though the shape of racial disparities has shifted somewhat over the past decades. Between 1986 and 1991, the number of Black women in state prison for drug offenses nationwide increased by more than 800 percent. This was nearly double the increase for Black men and more than triple that of white women, making Black women the fastest-growing population of prisoners during this period.[7] By 2003, Indigenous women were being incarcerated at 6.7 times the rate of white women.[8] Although the rate of incarceration for Black women declined between 2000 and 2014, Black women continue to be incarcerated at twice the rate of white women on average, and at rates vastly disproportionate to their representation in the general population.[9] Meanwhile, the incarceration of Latinx women has increased by 7 percent over the same period. Additionally, two-thirds of women in local jails are women of color: 44 percent Black, 15 percent Latinx, and 5 percent other women of color.[10]

Of course, women don't just show up in jail or prison—someone puts them there. The path to punishment usually begins with a police encounter. More than 2.2 million women were arrested in 2014, making up a quarter of all arrests.[11] According to criminologists, arrest rates are more related to "public attitudes and police practices than actual

---

* Jails are local facilities run by cities or counties where individuals are held pre-trial or to serve sentences of a year or less. Prisons are state- or federally run facilities where individuals are incarcerated for a year or more.

behaviors."[12] For women, most relevant are attitudes toward—and increased policing of—poverty, violence, and drug and alcohol use. In 2014, the majority of women's arrests were for theft and other property crimes, followed by assaults and drug- and alcohol-related offenses.[13]

Though it is well known that the enforcement of drug laws is one of the top three pathways to prison for women, crimes of poverty and "public order" offenses targeted by broken windows policing have also driven women's mass incarceration: 28 percent of women in state prisons across the nation have been convicted of property offenses, including larceny, theft, and fraud (including "welfare fraud"), and 9 percent have been locked up for public-order offenses such as "disorderly conduct."[14] Together, drug, property, and public-order offenses are responsible for 60 percent of the women in state prisons; the remaining 38 percent have been convicted of violent offenses, often committed in self-defense in the context of family or gender-based violence.[15] Meanwhile, in local jails across the country, 32 percent of women are being held for property offenses, 29 percent for drug offenses, and 21 percent for public-order offenses.[16] Barbara Bloom and Meda Chesney-Lind describe the latter as "deportment offenses," which are increasingly the subject of broken windows policing: "Under current punishment philosophies and practices, women are also increasingly subject to criminalization of noncriminal actions and behaviors. For example, large numbers of poor and homeless women are subject to criminalization as cities across the nation pass ordinances prohibiting begging and sleeping in public places."[17]

Black women and women of color are disproportionately impacted by the policing of poverty simply by virtue of making up a significant proportion of the population of low-income and homeless people of color: the national poverty rate for African American women is 28.6 percent, compared to 10.8 percent among white women, and 21 percent among working-age Black men.[18] It jumps to 46 percent for Black families with children headed by single Black women.[19] Poverty rates are similarly high for Latinx women, at 24.8 percent, and at 48.6 percent for Latina-headed household with children.[20] Of households headed by Native women, 42 percent live in poverty.[21] Presence in public spaces, reliance on public benefits or health care, and general elision of privacy rights of poor people combine to increase criminalization of low-income women.[22] As law professor Priscilla Ocen puts it, "Poor Black women are vulnerable to surveillance as a result of the presumed criminality that flows from the intersection of race, gender, and poverty."[23]

Heightened border and interior enforcement of immigration laws—often in collaboration with local law enforcement—have similarly contributed to increased rates of arrest, incarceration, and deportation for immigrant women. The "war on terror"—commonly understood to specifically target Arab, Middle Eastern, Muslim, and South Asian men—has had devastating effects on women from the same communities, whether they have been profiled on the basis of religious or culturally specific attire or subject to coercion to get them to inform on men in their communities.

An in-depth exploration of each of these phenomena warrants a volume of its own. What follows is a brief introduction to the ways in which predominant present-day paradigms frame the policing and criminalization of women of color.

THE WAR ON DRUGS

Drug laws and their enforcement in the United States have always been a deeply racialized project. In 1875, San Francisco passed the country's first drug law criminalizing "opium dens" associated with Chinese immigrants, though opium was otherwise widely available and was used by white Americans in a variety of forms.[24] Cocaine regulation at the turn of the twentieth century was colored by racial insecurities manifesting in myths that cocaine made Black people shoot better, rendered them impervious to bullets, and increased the likelihood that Black men would attack white women.[25] Increasing criminalization of marijuana use during the early twentieth century was similarly premised on racialized stereotypes targeting Mexican immigrants, fears of racial mixing, and suppression of political dissent.[26]

The "war on drugs," officially declared by President Richard Nixon in 1971, has come to refer to police practices that involve stopping and searching people who fit the "profile" of drug users or couriers on the nation's highways, buses, trains, and planes; saturation of particular neighborhoods (almost entirely low-income communities of color) with law enforcement officers charged with finding drugs in any quantity through widespread "stop and frisk" activities; no-knock warrants, surveillance, undercover operations, and highly militarized drug raids conducted by SWAT teams. It also includes harsh mandatory minimum sentences for drug convictions, which contribute to mass incarceration, and a range of punitive measures aimed at individuals with drug convictions.[27]

Feminist criminologists assert, "The war on drugs has become a largely unannounced war on women, particularly women of color."[28] According to the Drug Policy Alliance, "Drug use and drug selling occur at similar rates across racial and ethnic groups, yet black and Latina women are far more likely to be criminalized for drug law violations than white women."[29] Black, Latinx, and Indigenous women make up a grossly disproportionate share of women incarcerated for drug offenses, even though whites are nearly five times as likely as Blacks to use marijuana and three times as likely as Blacks to have used crack.[30] According to sociologist Luana Ross, although Native Americans make up 6 percent of the total population of Montana, they are approximately 25 percent of the female prison population. These disparities are partially explained by incarceration for drug offenses.[31] These statistics are not just products of targeting Black, Latinx, and Indigenous communities; they are consequences of focusing on women of color in particular. From 2010 to 2014, women's drug arrests increased by 9 percent while men's *decreased* by 7.5 percent.[32] These disparities were even starker at the height of the drug war. Between 1986 and 1995, arrests of adult women for drug abuse violations increased by 91.1 percent compared to 53.8 percent for men.[33]

However, there continues to be very little information about the everyday police encounters that lead to drug arrests and produce racial disparities in women's prisons.[34] For instance, less well known in Sandra Bland's case is the fact that before her fateful July 2015 traffic stop, she was twice arrested and charged for possession of small amounts of marijuana. After her first arrest a $500 fine was imposed. After the second, she served thirty days in Harris County jail, a facility criticized by the Department of Justice (DOJ) for its unconstitutional conditions of confinement.[35]

One notable exception to the lack of information with respect to women's experiences of drug law policing was a General Accounting Office investigation, which found that Black women were more likely to be subject to searches of their bodies and personal effects by US Customs and Border Protection agents than any other group. In fact, Black women were nine times as likely as white women to be X-rayed after being frisked or patted down, and two to three times as likely to be strip-searched, even though they were less than half as likely as white women to be found to be carrying contraband. Black women were also searched at a rate one and half times that of Black men and Latinx people, and were less likely to be found with contraband than any other group.[36] The report also found that Asian and Latinx women were strip-searched three times as often as men of the same race, and were 20 percent less likely than white women to be caught with contraband.[37]

Amanda Buritica, a fifty-two-year-old school-crossing guard born in Colombia, landed in San Francisco in 1994 on her way back from Hong Kong. She was strip-searched, forced to drink laxatives, repeatedly kicked by a US Customs officer, and held more than twenty-four hours before she was returned to the airport, sick and dehydrated from her ordeal.[38] Across the country, shortly after landing in Fort Lauderdale following a trip to Jamaica, Janneral Denson found herself handcuffed to a bed at Miami Jackson Memorial Hospital by US Customs inspectors; she was forced to drink laxatives, her bowel movements were monitored, and she was held without contact with the outside world for two days, all because she allegedly fit the profile of a drug courier.[39] She was seven months pregnant and experienced severe diarrhea and vaginal bleeding upon release. One week later, she delivered by C-section a three-and-a-half-pound baby who required prenatal intensive care for a month. These stories are just a few of the many behind the statistics that reflect pervasive stereotyping of Black and Latinx women as drug couriers.[40]

In the late 1990s, these violations came to a head through litigation and congressional hearings. In both contexts, Black women described abusive frisks during which inspectors yelled at them, kicked their legs apart, and touched their breasts and vaginas through their clothes. They were subjected to strip searches and visual body-cavity searches during which inspectors insisted that women, including menstruating women, bend over and spread their buttocks, and, at times, inserted their fingers into women's vaginas and anuses. No contraband was found on any of the women who came forward.[41] The women described their experiences as "humiliating," "sexually degrading," and "like slavery."[42] Indeed, the sociologist Yvonne Newsome links these experiences of the war on drugs to the enforcement of slave codes, Black codes, Jim Crow laws, and other historic forms of policing of Black women's movements and social mobility. She submits that "like the slave patrols of the past, Customs officers serve as gatekeepers who contain African American women's freedom of movement,"[43] and elaborates:

> African American women who exit and reenter the United States cross two types of boundaries: a geographic boundary that marks the territorial limit of the nation-state and social boundaries that demarcate the power relations between race, gender and social class group. . . . International travel by African American women challenges normative expectations about the appropriate social and spatial locations for their race-gender group. Thus, Customs agents may perceive them as transgressors who—because they are "out of their place"—require scrutiny or other reprisals.[44]

Newsome links the "highly subjective" criteria used by Customs agents in surmounting the relatively low legal bar to conducting searches at the border to specific aspects of controlling narratives shaping how Black women's movements and actions—however innocent—are perceived.[45] Newsome goes on to connect Customs agents' perceptions of Black women to controlling images that "depict them as masculine, crafty, promiscuous, sexually inviolable, pathological and criminally inclined." In so doing, she relies heavily on the revelations made by

Cathy Harris, a Black US Customs inspector-turned-whistleblower who shared both the official and "unwritten rules" used to determine which passengers to target for searches.[46] Newsome concludes that "the drug courier profile seems to have been constructed primarily around stereotypical notions of African American women and other people of color. This profile seems to assume that the only reason African American women travel internationally is to engage in criminal misconduct."[47]

Sadly, attention to women's experiences of profiling and discriminatory and abusive searches motivated by the war on drugs largely subsided into the annals of history after the initial outcry. Yet, profiling at the border is just the tip of the iceberg: pervasive profiling of women of color as drug users, couriers, and purveyors extends into highways, streets, and communities across the country, motivating ongoing strip searches and visual and physical body-cavity searches. In just one example, in 2007, a twenty-seven-year-old Black woman social worker was pulled over on an Arizona highway for making an improper right turn and was strip-searched in full view of male officers on suspicion that she was concealing drugs. She told the American Civil Liberties Union (ACLU) of Arizona, "I was visually raped, unconstitutionally violated, and racially profiled."[48] Yet Black women's continuing experiences of violation in the context of drug law enforcement rarely make national headlines, nor are they highlighted in analyses of the drug war's impacts.

The same is true of Latinxs. According to sociologist Juanita Díaz-Cotto, "The community-wide surveillance of Chicana/o barrios intensified under the war on drugs and made it virtually impossible for Chicanas/os to escape police harassment and brutality. This was regardless of Chicanas/os' gender, age, sexual orientation, where they lived or socialized, and whether or not they engaged in illegal activities." She notes that many Chicanxs she interviewed "experienced routine surveillance, harassment, arrests and excessive use of force in the streets, at police stations, and/or during raids of their homes. Almost half . . . were brutally beaten at least once, and sometimes by more than one officer." One woman interviewed by Díaz-Cotto, Linda, described, "Wherever you got arrested...you could hear words like 'fucking Mexicans,' 'dirty Mexicans' . . . 'fucking whore' . . . 'bitch,' 'slut.' . . . That was routine."

Another said, they "put us on the street, faced down, spread eagles. They didn't care if you had a dress. . . . They didn't care if you were pregnant. . . . That's just the way they're gonna treat you." Searches conducted for the ostensible purpose of locating weapons or drugs "were also frequently part of a pattern of sexual harassment and intimidation to which women suspects were routinely subjected [by male officers] . . . regardless of who conducted the searches and where, they were always invasive and humiliating."[49]

Despite disproportionate rates of incarceration, Native women are even less frequently recognized as targets of the war on drugs and police profiling. Yet, Lori Penner, a Native woman living in Oklahoma, testified at a 2003 Amnesty International hearing about a raid on her house by law enforcement officers claiming to be searching for drugs. According to Lori, police pulled her fifteen-year-old daughter "out of the shower and forced [her] to stand naked in front of three male officers. . . . One police officer had the audacity to tell my daughter she cleaned up nice and looks good for a fifteen-year-old girl."[50] Like colonial wars, the war on drugs clearly features gendered degradation of Native women.

Women's experiences of policing in the war on drugs are thus highly gendered and sexualized. As explored in other chapters, the war on drugs also drives gendered forms of police violence, such as extortion of sexual favors under the threat of a drug arrest that could lead to the loss of a job, a home, or children to child-welfare authorities, or to a long mandatory-minimum sentence, or to policing of pregnancy and motherhood. In just one case that came to light in 2016, two Los Angeles police officers were found to have coerced or extorted sex from at least four women arrested on drug-related charges.[51]

The war on drugs can also prove deadly, as it did for Frankie Perkins, Tarika Wilson, Alberta Spruill, Kathryn Johnston, and Danette Daniels—the roll call of female casualties of the war on drugs is both hidden and long.[52]

Racial disparities in rates of arrests and convictions, and the incarceration of women of color, are connected to the considerable discretion exercised by law enforcement agents waging the war on drugs when they decide who to stop and who to search.[53] Law enforcement interactions with women of color are informed by perceptions of their bodies as vessels for drugs ingested, swallowed, or concealed and of women of color as "out of control" unfit mothers, community members dependent on drugs and men, or coldhearted "gangsta bitches" prone to inhuman violence.[54] They are also informed by profound notions of the disposability of Black women, Indigenous women, and women of color. This was evident, for instance, in the case of Treasure, a Black trans woman brutally killed and dismembered after Detroit police, who had arrested her for prostitution, set her up as an informant in a drug transaction without any protection whatsoever.[55]

Additionally, "Occupational hierarchies within the drug economy serve to reproduce the gender, race and class relations that structure social relations on a more general level."[56] Because police focus enforcement on street-based drug markets in low-income communities of color, women of color, relegated to these lower rungs of the trade, are therefore at greater risk of arrest than users and sellers operating in private spaces such as penthouses, fraternity houses, suburban basements, and boardrooms.[57] While at one time the perception was that women were less likely to be stopped or searched by police on the streets, officers' tactics shifted over time to proactively engaging in public strip searches. According to one Black woman interviewed by Rebecca Maher, "Now these cops around here starting to unzip girls' pants and go in their panties."[58] Once caught in the maw of the system, women are subject to criminal sanctions far greater than their actual role in the drug trade.[59]

While rates of arrest and incarceration of women of color in the context of the war on drugs have abated somewhat over the past decade from the levels in the 1980s and 1990s, the drug war continues to shape policing practices and devastate the lives and families of women of color—and is poised to intensify once again. It also serves as the backdrop against which broken windows policing and the policing of prostitution, poverty, and motherhood are superimposed.[60] The ways the drug war is waged in day-to-day police interactions with women of color—and its role in the violation, incarceration, and deaths of women of color—therefore continue to demand our attention.

"BROKEN WINDOWS" POLICING

Federal drug enforcement policies of the 1980s were premised on the concept of "zero tolerance," which promoted allocating additional law enforcement resources to areas where crime was said to be endemic, and mandated immediate and harsh responses to the most minor violations with little or no consideration for individual circumstances.[61] "Zero tolerance," particularly of possession of guns and drugs, is most frequently practiced in school settings, as discussed in greater depth in the next chapter. It also informed the simultaneous evolution of broken windows policing.

The "broken windows" theory of policing was outlined by neo-conservatives George Kelling and James Q. Wilson in a 1982 *Atlantic Monthly* article. It goes something like this: if signs of disorder (like broken windows) and minor offenses (like loitering, panhandling, and graffiti) are left unchecked, then it's only a matter of time before a community descends into chaos and violence.[62] According to Kelling and Wilson, the only effective form of crime prevention is aggressive enforcement and prosecution of minor offenses—in other words, zero tolerance. The theory evolved to incorporate the premise that individuals who commit minor offenses such as fare evasion on public transit will, if not caught and punished, eventually commit more serious offenses: a sort of slippery slope of criminality.[63] As with earlier vagrancy and indecency laws, broken windows policing focuses not so much on behaviors as on what Clare Sears terms "problem bodies" and their racially gendered presence in the public sphere. Indeed, the article presenting the theory explicitly names particular types of people—youth, homeless people, people perceived to be engaged in prostitution—as embodied signs of disorder.[64] Precursors to Kelling and Wilson's 1982 article were much more explicit about the racial and gender makeup of signs of neighborhood disorder: "young Black men, young women in short shorts hanging out on corners, interracial couples, and gay folks."[65]

Even Kelling and Wilson acknowledged in 1982 that it is "not inevitable that serious crime will flourish or violent attacks on strangers will occur" if signs of disorder are left unchecked. Indeed, the two wrote that their entire premise is drawn from what they themselves call "folk wisdom" rather than objective data, based on a belief that perceived disorder somehow renders an area more "vulnerable to criminal invasion" such that "drugs will change hands, prostitutes will solicit, and cars will be stripped."[66] In a comprehensive review of the literature and summary of his own research, Columbia law professor Bernard Harcourt concludes, "Taken together, the wealth of research provides no support for a simple disorder-crime relationship as hypothesized by Wilson and Kelling in their broken windows theory. . . . What I have come to believe is that the broken windows theory is really window dressing, and it masks or hides more profound processes of real estate development and wealth redistribution."[67]

Key to implementation of broken windows policing is the proliferation of "quality of life" regulations criminalizing an ever-expanding range of activities in public spaces, including standing or walking (recast as "loitering"), sitting, lying down, sleeping, eating, drinking, urinating, making noise, and approaching strangers, as well as a number of vaguer offenses such as engaging in "disorderly" or "lewd" conduct. This broad range of potential offenses gives police almost unlimited license to stop, ticket, and arrest, and facilitates targeting homeless people and others who exist largely in public spaces. A 2014 study by the National Law Center on Homelessness and Poverty found that over half of cities in the United States ban sitting or lying down in particular public places, and 18 percent of cities completely ban sleeping in public. In 43 percent of cities it is illegal to sleep in a car. A quarter of cities ban begging citywide, and 76 percent ban soliciting for money in certain public places. Thirty-three percent of US cities ban loitering anywhere, while 65 percent ban it in particular places.[68] According to one researcher, enforcement of such low-level offenses has become the "most common point of contact between the public and the criminal justice system."[69] In New York City alone, the NYPD issued almost two million summonses for quality-of-life offenses between 2010 and 2015, not including arrests for such offenses.[70]

What is deemed disorderly or lewd is often in the eye of the beholder, an eye that is informed by deeply racialized and gendered perceptions. When I speak at universities or conferences about broken windows policing, I often ask how many members of the audience have ever fallen asleep on a train or in a park at some point in their lives. Dozens of hands shoot up. When I ask how many have ever been ticketed or arrested for it, almost all hands come down. If I am at a drop-in center for homeless youth or adults, or in a low-income Black neighborhood, and ask the same question, many hands remain in the air.

For instance, Giselle, a twenty-year-old Latinx lesbian from New York City was taking a nap on the train as she was going home with her girlfriend. An officer woke her up and ordered her off the train, frisked her, demanded her ID, and then roughly arrested her. Giselle felt that she was targeted based on her race and sexual orientation—and not for the first time. Nevertheless, she says, "I refuse to be victimized."[71]

Police officers are afforded almost unlimited discretion when determining who and what conduct is deemed disorderly or unlawful.[72] More specific regulations, such as those criminalizing sleeping, consuming food or alcohol, or urinating in public spaces, criminalize activities so common they can't be enforced at all times against all people. As a result, both vague and specific quality-of-life offenses are selectively enforced in particular neighborhoods and communities, or against particular people, including people who, due to poverty and homelessness, have no choice but to engage in such activities in public spaces.

Scratching the surface of broken windows policing reveals that, ultimately, the paradigm is nothing more than a repackaged and sanitized version of enforcement of age-old vagrancy laws and municipal codes criminalizing cross-dressing, common night walkers, and "lewd" conduct that were explicitly created to criminalize and control the movements of people deemed undesirable throughout US history. In a defense of broken windows policing published in 2015, a year after

Michael Brown was killed in Ferguson by an officer who was engaged in it, Kelling acknowledged the lineage directly:

> Given the subject of our article, the Black Codes—vague loitering and vagrancy laws passed in the South immediately after the Civil War— were of special concern for us. Under these laws police arrested African Americans for minor offenses and, when they could not pay the fines, courts committed them to involuntary labor on farms—in a sense, extending slavery for many into the 20th century.

Without offering a means of distinguishing broken windows policing from enforcement of Black codes, Kelling submitted that he and Wilson were simply arguing for "doing a better job at maintaining order."[73] Yet in their 1982 article, Kelling and Wilson acknowledge that there are "no universal standards . . . to settle arguments over disorder . . ." and that charges of being a "suspicious person" or vagrancy have "scarcely any legal meaning."[74]

Yet, "disorder" has economic and racial meanings. Broken windows policing advances the interests of corporations, businesses, and wealthy residents—and "disorderly people" has come to mean low-income and homeless people displaced into public spaces by a lack of affordable housing and cuts to social programs. The "community" broken windows policing purports to protect became the wealthier, white professionals and businesses moving into urban neighborhoods previously occupied by low-income people and people of color, who fear the presence and existence of the people they are displacing.

Indeed, fear is the undercurrent of broken windows policing—fear of "disorderly people," "addicts," people living with mental illness, and "aggressive panhandling, squeegee cleaners, street prostitution, 'boombox cars,' public drunkenness, reckless bicyclists, and graffiti," all of which allegedly contribute to "the sense that the entire public environment is a threatening place."[75] Anti-Blackness, including its specific manifestations with respect to Black women, is embedded within this fear of disorder: a 1994 internal police memorandum entitled "Reclaiming the Public Spaces of New York," by Republican mayor Rudolph

Giuliani and Police Commissioner William Bratton, cited both Kelling and Wilson's *Atlantic* article and Daniel Patrick Moynihan's controversial report, *The Negro Family: The Case for National Action*, which blamed social dysfunction on Black families, in particular, Black mothers—"Sapphire"-like "matriarchs."[76]

Broken windows policing has always self-consciously been about promoting a particular type of community. A desirable community is one of "families who care for their homes, mind each other's children, and confidently frown on intruders."[77] According to Kelling and Wilson, society "wants an officer to have the legal tools to remove undesirable persons from a neighborhood."[78] Broken windows policing is thus posited as the last bulwark against a "frightening jungle" (a term fraught with racial meaning) in which "unattached adults"—that is, adults operating outside of hetero-patriarchal families—replace traditional families, teenagers gather in front of the corner store, litter abounds, and panhandlers stalk pedestrians.[79] Ultimately, broken windows policing isn't about reducing crime; it's about assuaging white fears, however irrational or racist, of poor and homeless people, Black people, people of color, and queer and gender-nonconforming people.

The result: dramatically increased frequency and intensity of police interactions with Black and Latinx youth, low-income, and homeless people; public housing residents; people who are—or who are perceived to be—engaged in street-based prostitution; street vendors (many of whom are immigrants); and anyone else who is hypervisible in public spaces. This includes—as highlighted by the Audre Lorde Project's (ALP) Working Group Against Police Violence—lesbian, gay, bisexual, trans, and gender-nonconforming youth and adults.[80] Quality-of-life provisions that are associated with congregating in and using public spaces or with living on the streets disproportionately impact homeless, precariously housed, and low-income women and trans people of color, as well as those providing vital outreach services to those communities.[81] Broken windows policing not only increases the number of law enforcement officers on the streets; it also increases the likelihood that women and trans people of color will be approached by police, sometimes with deadly consequences.

This was the case for Margaret Mitchell, a homeless, 102-pound, fifty-four-year-old Black woman described by authorities as "mentally ill." In 1999, she was confronted by two LAPD officers enforcing a quality-of-life law allowing them to ticket people using shopping carts without a store's permission and to confiscate the carts, a law almost exclusively enforced against homeless people. Margaret tried to walk away from the police, with her shopping cart full of her possessions. When someone driving by recognized her, they pulled over to try to talk the cops out of hassling her. Margaret began to run, pulling the cart behind her as the cops chased her. The next minute, the police shot her dead.[82]

Even when not fatal, broken windows policing can escalate to the brutal use of force in the most mundane of police encounters. For instance, the year after Margaret Mitchell was killed, in 2000, a police officer in Sioux Falls, South Dakota, violently arrested Sharon Gullikson, a homeless Native woman, for disorderly conduct, panhandling at a grocery store, and trespassing. Witnesses describe the officer approaching Sharon, grabbing her, and slamming her to the ground. Sharon says, "The next thing I knew, I was face down. My glasses broke, and my head hit the pavement. He kneeled on my kidney. . . . A lot of homeless people are scared of him."[83] Broken windows policing was the excuse for officers to stop Stephanie Maldonado in New York City's West Village for "jaywalking" and then slam her to the ground, injuring her face, just days before Michael Brown was killed in August 2014 following a similar stop.[84] Some months earlier, in June 2014, another jaywalking incident escalated into physical violence when a police officer stopped Arizona State University English professor Ersula Ore as she walked in the street to avoid construction. When she questioned why she was being singled out, noting that she had never seen anyone else stopped for walking in the street on a university campus, the officer responded by handcuffing her and threating to "slam" her. In the end, that is exactly what he did, causing her skirt to ride up as she hit the ground, exposing her.[85] On video, Ersula can be heard telling the officer, "This entire thing has been about your lack of respect for me."

Broken windows policing also facilitates racialized policing of gender and sexuality.[86] According to Tanya Erzen, broken windows policing "enables officers to act upon racial and gender biases they may have when they enter the police department—under the guise of enforcement of . . . 'lewd' or 'disorderly' conduct [laws]."[87] All too often, as discussed in chapter 6, officers read actual or perceived gender disjuncture as disorderliness, resulting in stops, harassment, and arrests of transgender, gender-nonconforming, and queer people of color for disorderly conduct.[88]

Broken windows policing is also a driving force behind aggressive policing of street-based prostitution, leading to documented racially disparate impacts on women of color, trans and not trans, as discussed in chapter 7. Street vendors, many of whom are immigrant women, are also marked as signs of disorder and harbingers of crime under broken windows policing. Veronica Garcia of Esperanza del Barrio of New York City testified at a 2003 Amnesty International hearing:

> Most of the street vendors in the barrio, we are women, we are immigrants, and we are mothers and we are victims of abuse…and harassment on behalf of the police. . . . They tell us that we are illegal, that we have to go back to Mexico, and that we don't have rights. They also threaten us to take away our children…they have used excessive force…they throw away food and merchandise.[89]

Immigrant women thus find themselves drawn into the criminal legal system through arbitrary arrests for minor violations, which in turn can lead to deportation.

More than thirty years after Kelling and Wilson's article, this unproven theory remains a dominant policing paradigm in urban areas. This reality requires that we pay particular attention to how controlling narratives inform broad exercises of police discretion and fuel police stops, harassment, violence, extortion, and arrests of women of color in the context of broken windows policing across the country.

IMMIGRATION ENFORCEMENT

Since the turn of the twenty-first century, the United States has dramatically increased spending on immigration enforcement, which, as of 2016, totaled nearly $18 billion per year—$3.5 billion more than the cost of all other federal law enforcement combined, and fifteen times as much as in 1986.[90] President Barack Obama, in addition to making history as the country's first Black president, was also its "deporter in chief," deporting the greatest number of immigrants in the nation's history.[91] The tactics used to achieve this milestone included militarization of the US-Mexico border, now patrolled by more than 21,000 Border Patrol agents (up from four thousand in the 1990s, making Border Patrol the second-largest law enforcement agency in the United States after the New York City Police Department); heightened interior enforcement through raids; and increased collaboration between federal immigration enforcement and local police agencies.[92] All have dramatically increased immigrant women's vulnerability to policing, criminalization, and deportation.[93]

Women living in the US-Mexico borderlands suffer constant harassment, stops, and threats of violence from Border Patrol agents in what the Border Action Network describes as "low intensity warfare." Grandmothers step out of their homes to find rifles pointed at them by officers, and women cannot drive to and from work without being stopped and harassed, regardless of their citizenship status.[94] Border Patrol and other law enforcement agents also engage in widespread sexual violence (discussed in greater detail in chapter 4).

Policing of immigrants at the border includes policing of Indigenous peoples whose ancestral lands have been bisected by an artificial border, and whose movements across it are routinely punished. In one instance documented by Tucson's Coalición de Derechos Humanos, in June 2004, a grandmother, mother, and son who are members of Tohono O'odham Nation, which straddles the US-Mexico border, were traveling within their federally recognized reservation when they were stopped by two Border Patrol officers who held them at gunpoint and threatened to call ground and air forces to detain and deport them.[95] Also, according to journalist Roberto Rodriguez, "Border Patrol officers . . . specifically target Spanish-speaking people with Indigenous features such as brown skin, brown/black hair and brown/black eyes: people who are racialized as Brown, unwanted, 'enemy others.' Immigration enforcement, in effect, amounts to modern-day Indian removal."[96]

Additionally, since passage of the Illegal Immigration Reform and Immigrant Responsibility Act (IIRIRA) in 1996, the US government has engaged in a "comprehensive interior enforcement strategy" to identify and deport individuals violating immigration laws in non-border areas through raids at schools, shopping centers, and workplaces, sweeping for undocumented immigrants and creating additional opportunities for profiling and abuse.[97] Although the majority of immigrants removed under this strategy so far have been men, women and children are increasingly being swept into the net.[98] In 2016, immigration raids in Georgia, Texas, and North Carolina resulted in 121 arrests and deportations, all of women and children, subjecting them "to terrifying and unnecessary police encounters."[99] In her 2001 paper "Whose Safety? Women of Color and the Violence of Law Enforcement," Anannya Bhattacharjee describes several violent immigration raids in the 1990s in Washington State and Texas, in which immigrant women were subject to abuse and threats of separation from their children. In one 1993 case, an agent told a mother that he would rape her thirteen-year-old daughter unless she signed voluntary departure papers, while calling her a "fucking bitch" and "daughter of a whore." He also threatened to physically harm the mother if the daughter didn't convince her to sign.[100]

Heightened interior enforcement has also involved increased collaboration with local law enforcement: since the mid-2000s, the federal government has entered into what are known as 287(g) agreements, after the section of the federal statute that authorizes them, whereby local law enforcement officers are deputized to enforce federal immigration laws.[101] Additionally, in 2014, the federal government adopted the Priority Enforcement Program (PEP), which requires local law enforcement agencies to notify immigration authorities if fingerprints of individuals in their custody match those of individuals flagged as deportable in immigration databases.[102] Funding for these programs increased from $23 million to $690 million between 2004 and 2011.[103] States also began to enact their own legislation encouraging local law enforcement officers to enforce immigration laws, such as Arizona's infamous SB 1070 law.

Enforcement of immigration law by local law enforcement agents both promotes and exacerbates the consequences of racial profiling and discriminatory enforcement. Within this context, undocumented Black immigrants are detained and deported at higher rates than their non-Black immigrant counterparts.[104] Collaboration with federal immigration authorities by local law enforcement also disproportionately targets Latinx people who are "driving while Brown." For instance, a 2012 US DOJ report found that deputies in one North Carolina county pulled Latinx people over four times as often as non-Latinx people, consistently stopped Latinx people at checkpoints, and arrested Latinx people for minor traffic violations—thereby placing undocumented people at risk of detection through PEP—while issuing citations or warnings to non-Latinx people.[105] South Asian immigrants also come within the crosshairs of police collaborating with immigration enforcement. For instance, Terwinder, a Sikh mother of two US-born children, was arrested and subject to deportation after police officers helping her with a flat tire ran her information and found out, thanks to information-sharing programs, she had an outstanding deportation order. She had lived in the United States for twelve years with her family, running a small business.[106] Collaboration with immigration authorities can extend to officers stationed in schools, hospitals, and other community-based institutions. In one such case, a school-based police officer arrested eighteen-year-old Karina Acosta, who was five months pregnant, in her high school classroom and held her until ICE (Immigration and Customs Enforcement) agents came to take her away. She had been cited for a parking violation and not having a driver's license three days earlier.[107] Such collaboration has not only led to violence and deportation; it also has increased people's fear of seeking help from police or social services, as discussed in greater detail in chapter 9.[108]

Additionally, the criminalization of immigrants contributes to perceptions of immigrant women as threats, thus creating additional contexts and opportunities for violations of women of color. Such perceptions and realities inform police violence against Latinx women such as Alicia

Sotero Vásquez, whose roadside beating by police was televised in 1996, five years after the Rodney King incident. Alicia was traveling in a pickup truck with nineteen other undocumented immigrants in Southern California when Immigration and Naturalization Service (later ICE) officers began following the truck. Once the truck crossed county lines, Riverside county sheriffs took over. When they eventually stopped the truck, officers grabbed Alicia by the hair, although she was completely compliant, "dragged her out of the truck, smashed her face against the hood of the car, threw her on the ground, and continued beating her on her back and legs. Televised across the nation, this image immediately traveled around the world." Alicia later said, "I didn't do anything wrong. I merely came here to find work. . . . They beat me. I thought they were going to kill me." The beating, accompanied by racial slurs, was described by one officer at the scene as "whaling on." Professor Rita Urquijo-Ruiz concluded, "Sotero Vásquez, as a brown Mexican woman, was brutalized because her body represented that of a dangerous and unwanted Mexican criminal; the 'other' who cannot be seen as a desired or needed worker or potential citizen."[109] The same could be said of many Latinxs, whose stories are described throughout this book. Ultimately, as Martha Escobar puts it, "(Im)migrant women's violability is cemented through their assumed violation of the nation-state, constructing them as a public enemy who needs to be disciplined, and, in some cases, killed."[110]

THE WAR ON TERROR

The September 11, 2001, attacks marked the official start of the "war on terror," when more than 1,200 Muslim, Arab, and South Asian men were rounded up by local and federal law enforcement agents and detained indefinitely, although not one was ultimately found to be connected to any terrorist-related activity.[111] The ripple effects were felt by many more than those detained. In the following months, the FBI visited and interviewed up to 11,000 men and women of Muslim, Arab, and South Asian descent.[112] According to Tram Nguyen, former director of Colorlines, "FBI agents began showing up at their early-morning visits bearing extra headscarves for the women of the house, to save them time as they got ready to be questioned and searched."[113]

As in other contexts, women's experiences as targets of the war on terror are hidden within the broader discourse. In 2005, Tashnuba Hayder, a sixteen-year-old Bangladeshi Muslim youth in Queens, New York, was the subject of the first terrorism investigation to involve a minor. FBI agents monitored her visits to an Internet chat room where sermons by a London-based Islamic cleric believed to encourage suicide bombings were posted. They then showed up at her home without a search warrant or other legal basis, one posing as a youth counselor pretending to follow up on a missing-persons report filed five months earlier when Tashnuba briefly left home. The agents immediately began rifling through her diary, papers, and home-schooling materials, and asked her about her views on jihad and why she had no posters on her walls. They focused on an essay she wrote discussing the positions taken on suicide by various religions, and another about the Department of Homeland Security, in which she stated that she felt that Muslims had been targeted and "outcasted" by the government since 9/11. Three weeks later, on the basis of a "secret" declaration, a dozen federal agents raided her home at dawn, citing the expiration of her mother's immigration papers as justification for taking Tashnuba into custody. Without providing her parents with any information as to her whereabouts for two weeks, federal agents transferred Tashnuba to a juvenile detention center in Pennsylvania where she was interrogated, without a parent or a lawyer present, by the members of the FBI Joint Terrorism Task Force, and repeatedly questioned about her friends, young women she had met at mosques. She was released only upon her mother's agreement to a "voluntary departure" to Bangladesh.[114]

The *New York Times*'s Nina Bernstein later spoke to her from there and reported: "Tashnuba says that she opposes suicide bombing, that her interest in the cleric was casual, and that the government treated her like a criminal simply for exercising the freedoms of speech and religion that America had taught her. . . . F.B.I. agents tried to twist mundane details of her life to fit the profile of a terrorist recruit, and when they could not make a case . . . covered their tracks by getting her out of the country." According to documents obtained by the *Times*,

"The F.B.I. asserted that the girls presented 'an imminent threat to the security of the United States based upon evidence that they plan to be suicide bombers.' The document cited no evidence."[115]

Another sixteen-year-old Muslim girl, Adama Bah, was also detained as part of the investigation. Adama came to New York when she was two years old from Guinea with her mother to join her father. According to news reports, she was a popular high school student in Manhattan until one morning in March 2005 when FBI agents raided the family home, screaming, "We're going to deport you and your whole family." They took Adama to the same juvenile detention facility where Tashnuba was being held. There, Adama was isolated, subjected to strip searches, and interrogated for six and a half weeks until an attorney was able to obtain her release. She was required to wear an ankle bracelet and observe a 10 p.m. curfew for three years until her claim for asylum was granted. After her father was deported as a result of the investigation, she dropped out of high school to work three jobs to support her family. Adama was never offered any explanation for what happened to her. Now married with two children and living in the Bronx, she told the *New York Times*, "I was definitely cheated of a future."[116]

Adama Bah's case illustrates that Black people, too, are targeted in the war on terror and subject to profiling as potential terrorists. This can be the case even if they are not Muslim. For instance, when Mya Hall, a Black trans woman, made a wrong turn onto National Security Agency property, she wasn't seen as a motorist who had lost her way, like so many people before her have done at the same highway exit, but was immediately shot as a potential terrorist.[117] When Miriam Carey drove into a barrier near the Capitol in Washington, DC, with her baby girl in the backseat of her car, she wasn't seen as a mother trying to get to safety, but as a potential "terrorist."[118] And, of course, Black organizers from Assata Shakur to Black Lives Matter have been framed as "terrorists" by law enforcement and the public alike, contributing to often brutal police violence.[119]

Beyond direct targeting in terror investigations, women who wear the hijab or otherwise appear to be Muslim were routinely subject to discriminatory and abusive policing practices after 9/11, from verbal abuse and discriminatory arrest to airport profiling and unwarranted searches violating religious precepts.[120] For instance, a South Asian woman who was a member of Desis Rising Up and Moving (DRUM) testified in 2003 at an Amnesty International hearing in New York City about being stopped by police officers as she was walking down the street, asked what religion she practiced, and given baseless tickets for jaywalking. Emira Habiby Browne of the Arab American Center testified at the same hearing: "We have certainly seen a lot of profiling for the women in terms of . . . dress, and targeted and stopped and questioned and harassed, and just everything, on the street, in the schools, in the airports."[121] Non-Muslim Arab and Middle Eastern women were targeted too. For instance, on the day of the attacks, security officers stormed the classroom of an Arab woman teaching in a Chicago public school, ordered her out of the room, and searched her and her purse. She later discovered she was the only person at the school subjected to this treatment.[122]

Heightened profiling of Arab, Middle Eastern, Muslim, and South Asian women is now a fact of life. Chaumtoli Huq, a Bangladeshi Muslim law professor, described her 2014 arrest (see photo insert):

> Last summer, during the Muslim holy month of Ramadan, I stood on the sidewalk in Times Square while my husband took my kids to use a restroom in a nearby restaurant. We had just left a rally for Palestinian children killed in Gaza. As I waited alone, a police officer monitoring the rally ordered me to move. I did, stepping back toward the restaurant wall. This was not good enough for him. In seconds, he flipped me, pushed me against the wall, pressed his body on mine and while I was handcuffed, said I was resisting arrest. Photos later revealed his arms bulging with the ferocity of the arrest.
>
> As a lawyer, I have done know-your-rights trainings on this very police tactic: bootstrapping charges to justify arrest. As I was being arrested, I began to repeat in a monotone voice, "I am not resisting arrest," to which the officer responded, "Shut your mouth." When I objected to him going through my purse and pulling out my photo

I.D., he said, "I can do whatever I want, because you are my prisoner." At that moment it was true. It didn't matter that I had been appointed in January 2014 as top counsel to New York City's public advocate, the first Bangladeshi-American to reach that level of city government and one of few Muslim Americans in the newly elected administration.

The command "Shut your mouth" stuck out for me, because it is symbolic of how our legal and political system views and expects people of color to behave: quietly. Sandra Bland asked why she was being arrested. Asserting her rights as a woman of color to a white male officer was seen as disruptive and met with an aggressive response. Wearing my traditional South Asian tunic, visibly an immigrant, my mere presence was disruptive as well.[123]

Chaumtoli's experience also starkly illustrates the ways in which broken windows policing is used to target immigrant and Muslim women's bodies in public spaces. If you have ever been to Times Square, you know how many white tourists and theatergoers *actually* block the sidewalk, impeding other pedestrians' progress without *ever* getting arrested. Adding insult to injury, Chaumtoli was later told at the police station when she gave a different last name than her husband's that "in America, wives take the names of their husbands."[124] She sued and won a settlement from the NYPD, yet the City was unwilling to implement any policy or systemic change.

A year later, on July 4, 2015, Itemid "Angel" Al-Matar, a young Saudi student, was transferring from one Chicago subway line to the next, anxious to get home to her family in time to break her daily fast during Ramadan. As she climbed the stairs to the second train platform, four Chicago police officers tackled her, slamming her down on the stair landing and ripping off her hijab and niqāb. Once at the police station, she was forced to strip naked.[125] The police report indicated that the officers had profiled Itemid as a "lone wolf" terrorist based on her attire, her "suspicious behavior," including walking at "a brisk pace, in a determined manner," and the fact that she was carrying a backpack and had what they believed were "incendiary devices" around her ankles—which turned out to be weights. "They asked me why I put my food inside my bag, why I'm Muslim, why I'm fasting, why I'm wearing these clothes, why I cover my body," Itemid later reported. Although they found no evidence of wrongdoing, they still charged her with reckless misconduct and resisting arrest. She was acquitted at trial, and filed a lawsuit challenging the officers' violations of her rights.[126]

Police treatment of Tashnuba, Adama, Chaumtoli, and Itemid reflects the narrative of the "'mad Muslim terrorist' who threatens the white social order, and therefore must be incarcerated, eliminated, or banned from entry into the United States."[127] Arab women have been constructed and demonized alternately as violent agents of terror, "the nameless veiled woman," an anonymous figure envisioned crying and screaming, being out of control, or passively accepting her oppression.[128]

Obvious parallels exist among the profiling associated with the war on drugs; broken windows and "gang" policing, and the fear-mongering and targeting of people who are perceived to embody disorder; immigration enforcement and its focus on excluding and removing an imagined threatening other; and the war on terror.[129] Marqueece Harris-Dawson, an activist in South Central Los Angeles, observes, "What they're doing to Arabs and Muslims, it's like how they do us out here in South Central. And it's about who you know and who you hang around with."[130]

As Michelle Alexander put it in 2001, when she worked at the ACLU on racial profiling, "The war rhetoric is giving license to law enforcement to engage in racial profiling, just as it did in the war on drugs. Both wars create a 'by any means necessary' attitude that encourages law enforcement to target people based on race."[131] Nguyen concurs:

> The profiling and policing within suspect communities done in the name of the war on terror is remarkably similar to that which has been done to African American communities in the name of the war on drugs. . . . For noncitizens, the entry points into this security–policing system are numerous: a routine traffic stop, a domestic-violence incident, a neighbor's tip to the FBI . . . chewing of a traditional stimulant called *khat* . . . urinating in public.[132]

As Anannya Bhattacharjee cautioned in "Whose Safety?":

Law enforcement is increasingly a seamless web, in which authorities may move without hindrance between a traffic stop and deportation, or a hospital visit and a prison, or the airport and a maximum security cell. . . . The logic of such policies is similar, whether the specific language refers to "quality of life" policing, drug interdiction, counter-terrorism or national security. The major difference is that some such measures purport to protect the national borders of the United States, while others seek to defend the interior borders based on institutionalized racism and economic privilege.[133]

Ultimately, whether a woman of color is read as a drug user, courier, or distributor, a disorderly person, an undesirable immigrant, a security threat, or some combination of these, the war on drugs, broken windows and gang policing, immigration enforcement, and the war on terror weave a web of criminalization that ensnares women in devastating ways.

CHAPTER 3

POLICING GIRLS

In the months following the 2014 Ferguson uprising, two stories, both illustrative of current trends, brought national attention to policing of Black girls in communities and in schools. In May 2015, Dajerria Becton was assaulted by a Texas police officer responding to a complaint about Black youth attending a private pool party in a predominantly white suburb. His violent response was both reminiscent of the Jim Crow era and characteristic of broken windows policing. Six months later, a young Black woman was assaulted in her own classroom by an officer stationed at South Carolina's Spring Valley High School, dramatically illustrating the perils of zero-tolerance policing.

Nineteen-year-old Tatyana Rhodes and her family were hosting a graduation cookout for her school friends at a community pool in their neighborhood, the majority-white Craig Ranch subdivision in McKinney, a suburb of Dallas. A dispute arose about the number of young people in the pool. White residents approached Tatyana and other Black youth at the party, called them "Black fuckers," and told them to "go back to Section 8 housing where you belong and get out of my neighborhood." When the youth protested that these comments were racist and wildly inappropriate, a white woman slapped Tatyana in the face, prompting two young Black women to come to her defense. A scuffle broke out.[1] Someone called the police to complain about youth in the area who "refused to leave," claiming that they neither lived in the area nor had permission to be there—although, in fact, the young people either lived in the neighborhood or were there at the invitation of people who did.[2]

A dozen armed police officers responded. By the time they arrived, the scuffle had already been broken up by a security guard. While a bystander's video shows some officers attempting to calmly engage those present, others, including Officer Eric Casebolt, can be seen on video randomly chasing and grabbing Black youth. A white youth described the scene to a reporter: "Everyone being put to the ground was Black, Mexican, Arabic. The cop didn't even look at me. It was like I was invisible." All youth handcuffed were people of color, the one exception a white woman who attempted to explain to Officer Casebolt what had transpired.

Casebolt is then seen yanking fourteen-year-old Dajerria Becton by the back of the head and shoving her violently toward the ground. When two teens approached to reassure the distraught young woman, telling her they would call her mother, Casebolt unholstered his weapon, pointed it at them, and began chasing them until his fellow officers stopped him. Dajerria screamed for her mother as the officer turned back to her, gun still out, holstering it only to grab her arm and throw her to the ground, yelling, "On your *face!*" He then knelt on top of her, putting his full weight on both his knees as she lay facedown, sobbing. For weeks after the assault, Dajerria had trouble sleeping and eating and rarely left her aunt's house.[3] The white women who initiated the fight over the presence of Black youth in a pool in a white neighborhood left without consequence.[4] Jim Crow policing is alive and well; "order" was restored.[5]

The sight of a two-hundred-pound, armed white police officer kneeling on top of a sobbing, slight young Black woman in a bikini shocked the nation as video of the incident went viral. MSNBC host Chris Hayes exclaimed to Tara Dowdell, a Black woman correspondent on his show, "If you did that in a park to your own kid, you would have DCFS [department of children and family services] called on you faster than anyone could snap a finger. . . . And if there was video like that, good luck keeping your kid." "If you did that to a dog . . . ," Dowdell responded wryly, and went on to emphasize the importance of the case in drawing attention to police violence against Black women.[6] Their conversation highlighted a contradiction further explored in chapter 8 of this book: aggressive police treatment of Black children is condoned, while Black parents are harshly criminalized for any actual or perceived harm to their children.

Black women were quick to vehemently criticize the incident as a sexualized assault by a police officer on a young Black girl.[7] Protests erupted in McKinney, bringing together Black Lives Matter activists, New Black Panther Party members, and parishioners of local Black churches.[8] Casebolt resigned after the local chief of police launched an investigation, later calling the officer's conduct "indefensible" and "out of control."[9] When a grand jury refused to indict, Becton's family, represented by my Howard University School of Law classmate Kim T. Cole, filed a civil suit in June 2016.[10]

Six months after the McKinney incident, on October 26, 2015, Shakara, a sixteen-year-old Black girl recently placed in foster care after her mother's death, briefly pulled out her phone in a classroom at Spring Valley High School in Columbia, South Carolina. When she didn't put it away fast enough for the teacher's liking, the teacher told her to leave the classroom. Shakara refused, believing it to be unfair punishment for such a minor offense. The teacher called an administrator, who in turn called Ben Fields, an armed officer of the Richland County Sheriff's Department stationed in the school as a "school resource officer." What happened next, caught on video taken by a student, like the McKinney incident, shocked the nation. Fields walked over to where Shakara can clearly be seen calmly sitting at her desk, and told her to leave. When she didn't, he suddenly grabbed her by the neck in an attempt to pull her out of her desk. When that failed, he flipped the desk upside down with the girl still in it, slamming her head to the ground. Fields then dragged both girl and desk toward the door, causing injuries to Shakara's neck, shoulders, and arm, and leaving a carpet burn on her forehead, then placed her under arrest. Another young Black woman, eighteen-year-old Niya Kenny, protested the brutal treatment of her classmate, only to be placed under arrest herself. Both girls were charged with "disturbing school," an offense carrying a $1,000 fine and the possibility of spending ninety days in jail.[11]

The student who filmed the Spring Valley High incident later tweeted that the "officer came in because she wouldn't leave the class when the teacher told her to. I still don't know what she did to be asked to leave." In the next tweet he added, "Just to be clear, before the video, she was sitting quietly at her desk. Did nothing to provoke the officer." He also said that she was "apologetic" when ordered to leave the classroom.[12] Both Fields and the sheriff claimed Shakara was resisting arrest. Niya later described her arrest on national news: "I was crying, literally screaming crying like a baby. . . . I was in disbelief. I know this girl don't got nobody, and I couldn't believe this was happening. I've never seen nothing like that in my life, a man use that much force on a little girl. A big man, like three hundred pounds of full muscle? I was like, 'No way, no way.' You can't do that to no little girl. I'm talking 'bout, she's like five foot six."[13]

Again, outrage erupted on social media, and organizations from the NAACP to the Black Parents' Association issued statements condemning the violent assault.[14] In July 2016, Kenny, Girls Rock Charleston, and the ACLU filed suit to strike down the offenses of "disturbing the schools" and "disorderly conduct," on the grounds that both are unconstitutionally vague, inappropriately used to handle minor issues previously addressed by school administrators, and discriminatorily used against Black students.[15] The sheriff fired Fields and asked the US Attorney's Office and the FBI to investigate the incident.[16] Charges against Niya and Shakara were ultimately dropped—but none were brought against the officer.[17]

These two cases are representative of decades-long trends in policing Black girls and girls of color across the country, in and out of school. The violence directed at Dajerria Becton and her friends illustrates how broken windows policing is driven by notions that youth of color "don't belong" in particular neighborhoods, their presence signifying "disorder" which must be eliminated, by force if necessary. Fields's attack on Shakara in her classroom exemplifies how zero-tolerance policies—the school-based counterparts of broken windows policing—place disagreements between students and teachers, regulation of classroom behavior, and enforcement of school rules in the hands of armed police officers stationed in public schools, creating opportunities for violation and criminalization of young Black women.

———

I had been documenting police violence against adult women of color for almost a decade when I learned about the case of Jaisha Aikins, in

2005. Jaisha, a five-year-old Black girl, was handcuffed and arrested at her St. Petersburg, Florida, school for essentially throwing a temper tantrum—as every five-year-old has done at some point. The school's administrators and some media commentators justified putting a five-year-old in handcuffs on the grounds that she "punched" the school's vice principal, as if the little girl had hauled back and clocked her, rather than flailing at her with tiny hands while in the throes of a tantrum, with the force of a child. It was clear from video taken of the incident that the vice principal was not hurt and that Jaisha eventually calmed down. In fact, like Shakara, Jaisha was sitting calmly in a chair when police arrived in response to the vice principal's call to arrest an unruly student. Even after discovering the student was a kindergartener, three white armed officers nevertheless proceeded to pull the little girl's hands behind her back to put them in handcuffs as she cried and begged them not to. Jaisha was taken to the police station in a patrol car, but released to her mother's custody when prosecutors refused to file charges against her.[18]

Jaisha's story illustrates just how deeply entrenched controlling narratives of Black women and girls are—no matter how young and small they are. The video of the incident was also one of the first depicting police violence against a Black girl to be widely broadcast and generate outrage across the country. In her groundbreaking book *Pushout: The Criminalization of Black Girls in Schools*, Monique Morris tells the stories of several other Black girls as young as six and seven arrested in school in similar incidents over subsequent years, some as recently as 2013. In some cases, the little girls were held in police cars and stations for extended periods of time after arrest.[19]

Policing of girls extends beyond instances where officers are summoned by school administrators. As evidenced by Shakara's arrest, police are increasingly stationed inside schools, leading to increased police contact with girls, and increased police violence as officers enforce school rules. For instance, the New York Civil Liberties Union (NYCLU) reported several cases where young women of color were slammed against the wall, thrown to the floor, and arrested by officers stationed in their schools for leaving class a few minutes late ("roaming the hallways"), asking for return of a confiscated cell phone ("threatening an officer"), or cursing in the hallway ("disorderly conduct").[20]

As on the streets, police in schools don't just apply the rules; they make them up as they go along and often enforce them in deeply racialized ways.[21] In the INCITE! *Organizer's Tool Kit on Law Enforcement Violence*, we tell the story of Pleajhai Mervin, a sixteen-year-old girl slammed onto a table by a school safety officer stationed at her Palmdale, California, high school, when she failed to pick up pieces of spilled cake from the cafeteria floor to his satisfaction. As he held her down, the officer yelled, "Hold still, nappy head."[22]

What happens behind school doors often mirrors what happens on the streets in the context of broken windows and gang policing in the community. In 2010, I represented three young Black women pulled off a New York City subway train by officers who believed they had gotten on without paying—a classic broken windows offense that was the number-one arrest charge in New York City in 2015.[23] In fact, as part of an after-school program, they had entered as a group with the stationmaster's permission. The officers also acted on the assumption that the young women were involved in a purportedly gang-related fight on a completely different platform. One officer yelled at one seventeen-year-old girl to "get the fuck off the train, bitch!" Even though she was complying, he grabbed her by the neck and slammed her down onto a bench, choking her. As her twin approached, alarmed, she too was thrown down and hit her head and face on the floor as an officer began striking her. Officers slammed the third young woman, the twins' friend, to the ground and pepper-sprayed her in the face before handcuffing her. Afterward, they left her in a cell for thirty minutes with no means of removing the burning spray from her eyes, despite her desperate pleas for relief. Throughout the violent encounter, the officers referred to the young women as "bitch" and "Shaniquah," making explicit the racially gendered perceptions driving their violent behavior within the broader framework of broken windows and gang policing.

Over the past several decades, since the myth of the young Black "superpredator" took hold in the 1990s, broken windows policing, gang policing, and the growing presence of police in schools have dramatically increased the criminalization of youth. Although much has been written about each of these phenomena, there has been little examination of the experiences of young Black women and girls, Indigenous youth, and women and girls of color in these contexts.

————

In 1995, ten years before Jaisha's arrest, the Gun-Free Schools Act was passed as a response to more than fifty school shootings across the country, imposing dramatic penalties for possession of a firearm on school property. By 1997, 94 percent of public schools had implemented zero tolerance policies banning guns in schools, and many had adopted harsh "school safety" policies.[24] Despite the fact that incidents prompting these policies primarily took place in majority-white, wealthy suburban high schools, the most punitive measures were adopted in urban schools attended by low-income youth of color. Over time, schools were outfitted with metal detectors and surveillance cameras, and were subjected to an influx of armed police officers empowered to enforce school discipline codes by means of summons and arrests. Taken together, the measures have created what has become known as the "school-to-prison pipeline."[25] As Sheba Remy Kharbanda and I wrote in *Education Not Deportation*:

> Under the "broken windows" theory, "zero tolerance" policies quickly extended beyond firearms possession on school premises to minor infractions of school disciplinary policies such as tardiness and truancy, schoolyard scuffles and even verbal disagreements and cursing in school, contributing to dramatic increases in the frequency and level of school discipline imposed for what is essentially routine youth (mis)behavior.[26]

In this context, according to Morris, "Black girls have become the fastest growing population to experience school suspensions and expulsions, establishing them as clear targets of punitive school discipline."[27]

The presence of law enforcement officers in schools has driven increased student referrals to police and arrests in schools,[28] often "for actions that would not otherwise be viewed as criminal . . . such as refusing to present identification, using profanity with a school administrator, or 'misbehaving.'"[29] One study found that the rate at which students are referred for lower-level offenses more than doubles when a school has regular contact with a "school resource officer."[30] The result is a "net-widening" effect expanding surveillance of youth of color and infusing policing and prison culture into schools across the country, with predictable effects.[31] Kathleen Nolan, a former New York public school teacher, describes "considerable subjectivity in determining whether a behavior was actually a violation of the law," and notes that everyday items—box cutters used for after-school jobs, razors used to style hair, Mace or pepper spray carried by young women for protection—were met with "zero tolerance" in a school populated by youth of color.[32]

Indeed, a 2005 report issued by the Advancement Project the same month Jaisha was arrested concluded, "Across the board, the data shows that Black and Latino students are more likely than their White peers to be arrested in school . . . [despite the lack of] evidence that Black and Latino students misbehave more than their White peers." Black students are "punished more severely for less seriously and more subjectively defined infractions" such as "disturbing school" or "disorderly conduct."[33] A 2011 Texas study found that, after controlling for eighty other variables, race remained a reliable predictor of discipline for subjective violations like disruption.[34] In South Carolina, Black students like Niya and Shakara are nearly four times as likely to be charged with "disturbing school" as white students.[35]

Today Black girls make up approximately 33 percent of girls referred to law enforcement or arrested on school grounds but only 16 percent of the female student population.[36] Yet the discourse around the policing of youth and the "school-to-prison pipeline" continues to focus nearly exclusively on boys and young men.

Behind the facts and figures, schools represent a site in which Black femininity is deeply regulated and severely punished. Monique Morris theorizes the polarized frames that set up Black girls as "nonconforming":

> Historic representations of Black femininity coupled with contemporary memes—about "loud" Black girls who talk back to teachers, "ghetto" Black girls who fight in school hallways, and "ratchet" Black

girls who chew dental dams like bubble gum in classrooms—have rendered Black girls subject to a public scrutiny that affects their ability to be properly situated in the racial justice and school-to-confinement narrative. They are rendered invisible or cast as deserving of mistreatment because of who they are misperceived to be. [37]

These perceptions translate to tickets and arrests for being "insubordinate," "disrespectful," or "uncontrollable" or for engaging in "willful" or "oppositional" "defiance," a vague discretionary offense that can mean anything from "having a verbal altercation with a teacher to refusing to remove a hat in school or complete an assignment," even if the behaviors pose no threat whatsoever to the safety of anyone at the school.[38] Building on bell hooks's concept of the "oppositional gaze," Morris effectively reframes the behavior punished in schools as Black girls' critical response to erasure, invisibility, unfair treatment, and systemic oppression within and beyond schools.[39] Often Black girls are policed, punished, and pushed out for "having the audacity to demand being treated with dignity," Morris concludes.[40] She also points out the dynamic of "age compression": an inability on the part of adults (including law enforcement) to see Black girls like Jaisha Aikins as children, and their propensity to treat them as they would Black adults.[41]

Much of the discussion of the school-to-prison pipeline has focused on Black youth, yet Native youth also suffer significant disparities in referrals and arrests. Nationally, in 2011, Native students were three times as likely as white students to be referred to law enforcement.[42] In Utah, Native students from kindergarten to sixth grade were referred to law enforcement more frequently than *any* other group. They were also four times as likely as other students of color to be arrested at school and six times as likely as white students.[43] Native young women are nearly five times more likely than white girls to be detained in juvenile facilities, largely the result of arrests for minor and family offenses.[44] The statistics clearly reflect ongoing perceptions of Native people as inherently disorderly and subject to removal.

In South Dakota, members of the Rosebud Sioux nation filed a successful lawsuit challenging school arrest practices affecting Native girls such as Mindi, a thirteen-year-old who struck a white girl at her school who had scratched and cursed at her Native friend. The principal had the two Native girls arrested, but not the white girl who had committed the initial assault. Police took Mindi to jail, where she was charged with "disturbing school" and "disorderly conduct." The principal had her arrested two more times, each time making her write an affidavit used against her in court without allowing access to a parent, guardian, or lawyer, even though he knew Mindi had cognitive disabilities requiring accommodations throughout her school life. Fifteen-year-old Josie Traversie was similarly arrested when defending herself against students who pushed and spit on her, as well as for cutting class; she was placed on probation for twelve months and eventually was held in a juvenile detention center.[45]

Latinx youth are also subject to presumptions of violence and disorder that are rooted in prevailing stereotypes that they are "hot-tempered" and "volatile." In March 2016, a police officer stationed at twelve-year-old Janissa Valdez's San Antonio school assumed she was approaching another girl to start a fight. Instead of calmly intervening, he immediately grabbed Janissa from behind, pinned her arms behind her back, and threw her to the floor from chest height, causing her to land on her face with an audible crack and momentarily lose consciousness. The officer responsible in this case was later fired; nevertheless, such extreme forms of violence in response to actual or perceived infractions, which should never occur in the first place, are all too commonplace.[46]

Alarmingly, among the violent policing tactics that have migrated from the streets to schools is indiscriminate use of Tasers, which are used to subdue people by firing barbs into them that deliver a jolt of electricity. While researching a 2006 report on the US government's failure to comply with the UN Convention Against Torture, I discovered a 2004 case in which a Miami-Dade police officer used a Taser against a twelve-year-old girl, shocking her with fifty thousand volts of electricity—for skipping school.[47] Between late 2003 and early 2005, at least twenty-four Central Florida students, some as young as twelve, were shocked with Tasers by police officers in public schools. A typical scenario involved officers wading in through a crowd to break up a fight and using Tasers to "get them to move."[48] As of 2005, 32 percent of police departments interviewed by the weapon's manufacturer, Taser International, had used Tasers in schools.[49] An August 2016 *Huffington Post* investigation uncovered at least eighty-four incidents of Taser use against students since 2011.[50]

Beyond the discriminatory arrests and excessive force, police sexual harassment and violence also takes place inside the schoolhouse gate. Inappropriate commentary about young women's bodies and appearance by police officers stationed in or near schools is commonplace. At one New York City school, "school safety agents . . . would degrade students with comments like 'That girl has no ass.'"[51] I witness similar harassment on a daily basis as young women travel back and forth on my Brooklyn street to attend one of three schools on my block.

Daily pat-downs and mandatory passage through metal detectors before entering schools are also experienced by young women as violative and degrading, especially when conducted by male officers. Jacquia Bolds, a Syracuse, New York, high school student, testified to a UN committee in 2008, "It is more uncomfortable for girls because sometimes they check you around your most private areas."[52] The New York Civil Liberties Union reports that in New York City schools in the 2000s:

> After being pushed against the wall for frisking, many girls were ordered to squat for intrusive searches with handheld metal detectors. After forcing one child to squat, a male officer repeatedly traced his handheld metal detector up her inner thigh until it beeped on the button of her jeans. "Is there something in your pants?" he asked repeatedly. The frightened girl repeated that there was not, but the officer kept at it, making her fear a cavity search, until he finally let her go.[53]

The girl's fears were not baseless: "routine" frisks and scans can quickly escalate to strip searches. Girls whose underwire bras set off metal detectors have been forced to lift up their shirts or unbuckle or unzip their pants to prove that they are not concealing weapons, or cell phones.[54] One fourteen-year-old Chinese girl who was interviewed in New York City stated: "The security guard accused me of having a knife. . . . They took me to a room and made me take off my shirt and pants to check my bra. They didn't call my parents or let me talk to a teacher I know. I didn't have a knife just like I told them."[55] Maksuda, a seventeen-year-old South Asian high school student, stated, "School safety agents pick on those they perceive to be religious, particularly those who wear scarves and hijab."[56] A Muslim youth, sixteen-year-old Fariha, explains in a video made by grassroots group Girls for Gender Equity, "For some of us it's about you're not covered up enough; for us it's like you're covered up too much."[57] The searches these girls were subjected to appear to have been motivated at least in part by controlling narratives framing Asian women as knife-wielding assassins, Latinxs and Black girls as drug "mules," and Muslim women as potential terrorists. They also often produce racially gendered humiliation, as officers rifling through young women's belongings find tampons, birth control pills, and condoms.

Schools, like streets subject to broken windows policing, are also sites of explicit and implicit policing of sexual and gender nonconformity by law enforcement agents. For instance, an advocate working with youth at three Los Angeles high schools predominantly attended by youth of color described harassment and differential treatment of LGBTQ students by school police on the basis of sexual orientation. Some officers would seek to discipline students who were displaying affection toward other students of the same gender while the same behavior among students of different genders went unpunished. Trans students also face discriminating policing in schools: Jewlyes Gutierrez, a trans teen, was arrested after a fight prompted by bullying by classmates at a Hercules, California, school. Yet, police only charged Gutierrez. Thankfully, the charges were ultimately dropped, and the youth were referred to a restorative justice program.[58] Many other trans, queer, and gender-nonconforming teens suffer similar harassment and criminalization across the country.

The presence of law enforcement agents in schools can also have unique impacts for immigrant students. In 2006, Sheba Remy Kharbanda and I, working as RFR Researchers, had the privilege of joining with the Youth Power Project of DRUM to explore the impacts of police presence in schools on South Asian youth. Overall, over half of South Asian students surveyed by their peers in Queens, New York, had experienced or seen harassment by school police and authorities; 85 percent believed the harassment was based on actual or perceived race, ethnicity, religion, or immigration status. Young South Asian women reported gender-based and sexual harassment by police and school safety agents, who made lewd or inappropriate comments during security checks or when stopping them in the halls. Almost half had been asked about their immigration status by police or school authorities. Undocumented immigrant students described their fear that "if the police ask for their identification and find out they don't have papers or if they get picked up by cops for any reason at all, including being late, being in the hallway, or just 'looking suspicious,' they could ultimately be detained in immigration detention and deported." Sadia, a seventeen-year-old Pakistani woman who described her school as "filled with school safety agents," told us, "I am in constant fear that my immigration status will be revealed."⁵⁹

Black girls and young women of color emphasize that as they move between school, streets, and home, they experience similar forms of policing. For instance, fifteen-year-old Monique Tillman and her brother Eric Branch were having a typical teen afternoon in May 2014, taking some clothes to a consignment shop, eating a hamburger and fries, and then biking home through a mall parking lot in Tacoma, Washington, when a police car pulled up behind Monique's bike, lights flashing, air horn blaring. When she asked the officer why he was following her, he told her he was going to write her up for trespassing on mall property. She repeatedly asked him what they had done wrong, arguing that they had just come from the mall and often took the same shortcut to get home. As she began to ride away, the officer grabbed her, yanked her off her bike, threw her against a nearby car, and began choking her, pushing his arm against her chest. As she struggled to breathe, he pulled her off the car, grabbed her hair, and repeatedly body slammed her on the pavement like a rag doll before shoving her to the ground, holding her by the neck, using a Taser on her, and putting her in handcuffs. Monique later said, "I feel like I was targeted because I am a person of color. It was frustrating because I knew I didn't do anything wrong, but I couldn't stop them."[60] Adding insult to injury, Monique was charged with resisting arrest and assaulting an officer; both charges were later dismissed at her criminal trial based on video evidence from a security camera.[61] In addition to illustrating the police violence young Black women face in their communities, Monique's case highlights the blurring between public police officers and private security: although the officer involved worked for the Tacoma Police Department, was in full uniform, and was using his department-issued vehicle, Taser, and handcuffs on Monique, he was actually off-duty, working as a private security officer for the mall at the time of the incident. Monique has since filed a civil lawsuit against the officer and the mall that employs him.

Monique's and Shakara's cases exemplify the reality that, in school or out, the slightest question or perceived challenge to an officer can easily lead to punitive and outrageous uses of force against Black girls, much as they do for adult Black women.

And, as with adult women, when it comes to policing of girls, "few studies have considered how gender intersects with race and neighborhood context in determining how police behaviors are experienced."[62] As a result, "the theoretical models used to explain discriminatory patterns of policing . . . display a presumption of gender neutrality or an uncritical focus on men." In one 1999 study examining young women's experiences of street policing, criminologists Rod Brunson and Jody Miller surveyed and interviewed twelve-to-nineteen-year-old Black youth in St. Louis, Missouri—fifteen years before and just a few miles from where Michael Brown was killed. Researchers found that young men reported experiences of mistreatment by police more often than young women. One young woman, Destiny, said, "It's little stuff they be saying to us [girls], but like with the dudes, they'll try to lock them up and try to take them to jail." While police stopped young men at all times of the day, police stopped young women most frequently at night, asking questions about what they were doing and where they were going, on the pretext of enforcing truancy or curfew violations—"status" offenses, which are crimes only for people under eighteen. Although young women reported that overall they experience police violence at lower rates and lower intensity than young men, the types of incidents they reported were similar: one told of being thrown to the ground during an arrest for a curfew violation; another of being thrown onto a car and having her arm wrenched behind her because she was not "sufficiently deferential"; a third of being told to "assume the position," because she "fit a description." A young woman named Janelle notes, "The police harass the guys a little bit more than the girls, but there's always certain females that they'll pick to harass."

Sexual and gender nonconformity play significant roles in determining which young women the police target. In a 2011 national long-term study, nonheterosexual girls were found to experience disproportionate punishment by police, school, and other law enforcement authorities.[63] One of the most severe instances of police violence reported in the Brunson and Miller study involved a young woman, described by her cousin as "a tomboy," who was sitting on her grandmother's porch when officers pulled up. They ordered her to put her hands up, then threw her against the wall to search her. Finding nothing, they threw her to the ground, kicked her, and put a gun in her mouth, telling her that if she told anybody, they would "blow her Black brains out" or would "take her away and rape her, and she won't be found."

Police harassment of young women in their communities continues to take place in the shadows of larger conversations around policing. For instance, a number of young women came forward to testify during 2012 citywide hearings on New York City's "stop and frisk" practices—widely described as exclusively targeting young Black and Brown men. Shannara, a seventeen-year-old member of Black Women's Blueprint, testified, "I have been stopped and frisked by the police at least six times. I organize with at least twenty other young women who have been sexually harassed by the police and felt they were touched inappropriately, plus the one who was beaten by six officers, slammed to the ground after that." Manny Yusuf, a fourteen-year-old Bangladeshi youth leader at DRUM, testified about being stopped and frisked on her way home from school. She believed she was singled out from a group of friends because she had the darkest skin. On another occasion, an officer called her over to his car to ask her for her number. She asked City Council members, "How do you think it feels to be stopped and searched by an officer when all you are doing is going home from school?" Another fourteen-year-old girl described being stopped with a cousin and two friends and frisked because officers thought they had weed on them— which is not sufficient legal justification for a frisk, and certainly not for a male officer to frisk a fourteen-year-old girl.[64]

RESISTANCE

When challenging the school-to-prison pipeline and policing of youth in our communities, how can we better center the experiences of young women and girls of color? At the most basic level, we can show up to advocate for girls as protesters did in McKinney and Columbia, incorporate their stories and their analysis of their experiences into research and advocacy around the presence of police in schools and communities, and most importantly, support and lift up their leadership.[65]

In the days following what was known on social media as #AssaultatSpringValleyHigh, Vivian Anderson of New York City could not rest. She wrote, "After days of outrage, no sleep and an overwhelming sense of sadness for these girls I could no longer sit. I traveled to South Carolina . . . to offer assistance in ensuring both girls were receiving emotional support for the trauma they had experienced."[66] Before Vivian left, Black Lives Matter New York City chapter cofounder Nakisha Lewis coined #EveryBlackGirl in response to the incident and drafted a letter from the leaders of Black Lives Matter to Shakara and Niya Kenny. Together, they secured more than 15,000 signatures. The letter emphasized that "Black girls in schools like yours all over the country are criminalized, suspended unfairly, and are introduced to the system for the most minor of infractions." The letter went on to affirm in no uncertain terms that Black Lives Matter is for girls like Niya and Shakara, committing to combating the long legacy of violence against Black girls, and to lifting up the Black girl magic and resilience of Black girls throughout the centuries.[67] When Vivian arrived in North Carolina, she presented Niya with the letter at the official launch of #EveryBlackGirl alongside Efia Nwangaza, a longtime civil rights and human rights activist and former organizer for the Student Nonviolent Coordinating Committee

(SNCC). The EveryBlackGirl campaign not only focuses on securing justice for Shakara and Niya and on removing police from schools, but it also works to identify what Black girls do, and don't, need in order to be successful and safe at school and in all aspects of their lives, and organizes to ensure that these needs are met.[68] In October 2016, a year after the assault on Shakara and Niya, EveryBlackGirl hosted a national conference, the State of Black Girls, to envision a future with safety.[69]

"We are the forgotten voices. Listen, I got a story to tell!" are the opening lines of the Sadie Nash Leadership Project video *Revealing Women's Voices Under a Police State,* which challenged the erasure of young women in the debate about New York City's stop-and-frisk practices.[70] The video highlights the pervasive sexualization of young women of color during police stops, sexual intimidation, and extortion of sexual favors in exchange for their freedom. A young Black woman describes her experience: "Walking down the street being cat-called. . . . He was New York's 'finest,' police badge, blue suit." Vivian, a young woman involved with CAAAV: Organizing Asian Communities, talks about frisks conducted to assign gender to gender-nonconforming women, as well as profiling of women, particularly women who are trans and gender-nonconforming, as being involved in prostitution. "You thought I was a prostitute. You stripped me of my dignity," a seventeen-year-old girl named Sade says in the video. "You have judged me because of the accent in my throat. You have assumed that because my hips are a little wider, and my curls are little tighter, that I am promiscuous. Officer, I'm just trying to get to church," she protests. With this video, young women broke important silences in an ongoing conversation around racial profiling and discriminatory stops and arrests of young people.

In 2016, the New York City Council Young Women's Initiative, cochaired by Girls for Gender Equity, the YWCA, and the New York Women's Foundation, outlined a blueprint for action to improve the lives of young women through a participatory process bringing together hundreds of young women, organizers, service providers, and policymakers. We called for policies regulating stops, frisks, and searches of women and explicitly prohibiting police sexual harassment and assault, as well as an audit of policies governing police interactions with trans women and gender-nonconforming people. But we didn't stop there. We also asked ourselves what brings young women into contact with police in the first place, whether it is police presence in schools, broken windows policing, or police responses to violence. Like the community organizing hundreds of miles south in Columbus, South Carolina, we asked ourselves what young women need to be safer, and allowed our imaginations to roam free. The answers ranged from removing police from schools and decriminalizing the offenses young women were most frequently arrested for, to closing Rikers Island, New York City's notorious jail, and funding youth-designed safe spaces to support young women who experience violence.

Ultimately young women of color experience every form and context of police violence discussed in this book, and their stories—and examples of their leadership—are found throughout. And, there are unique settings (such as schools), offenses (such as "status" offenses), and paradigms (such as broken windows policing) that are particularly used as tools to police young women and girls of color. It is our responsibility to create spaces in which girls' and young women's experiences of policing can be seen and heard, and to support their leadership and their demands to get police out of schools, stop the use of status offenses and low-level offenses to criminalize young women of color, end broken windows policing, and promote conditions under which young women of color can be safe and thrive.

CHAPTER 4

POLICING (DIS)ABILITY

One of the first stories of police violence against a Black woman in the United States that I became aware of was that of Eleanor Bumpurs. I was taking a course on Black feminism at the Toronto Women's Bookstore taught by my dear sisterfriend and mentor Beverly Bain in the mid-1990s, in which we read an essay by Angela Y. Davis entitled "Violence Against Women and the Ongoing Challenge to Racism." Writing in 1985, Davis called on activists challenging violence against women to incorporate police violence into their agendas and "defend, for example, the memory of Eleanor Bumpurs, the sixty-seven-year-old black woman from the Bronx who was murdered in 1984 by New York Housing Authority policemen because she dared resist an attempted eviction."

Seven years before the national uprisings sparked by Rodney King's beating, Eleanor, a Black grandmother who had arthritis and diabetes, fell behind on her rent of less than $100 a month for her public housing unit. Eventually, the New York City Housing Authority sent police—armed with a shotgun—to evict her. As they slammed her door with a battering ram, Eleanor, who had been diagnosed as psychotic and was described as standing naked in her kitchen, reached behind her for something to defend herself with and came up with a knife. The officers charging her used a Y-shaped stick to push her back, and then an officer pumped two shotgun blasts into her. The first hit the hand that held the knife, the second, her chest, killing her instantly.[1]

The case prompted marches in New York City, editorials, and demands for improved police responses to people in mental health crisis. The officers were indicted but eventually acquitted. Over time the case receded from New Yorkers' memories and was rarely, if ever, mentioned in mainstream writings, protests, and debates about racial profiling and police brutality in the 1990s. When speaking publicly, I often speculate that if Eleanor Bumpurs's case had become iconic in the same ways as Rodney King's, perhaps, in addition to talking about "driving while Black," we'd also be talking about "living while elderly, disabled, Black, female, and poor"[2] and the role that controlling narratives of "deranged" Black women of inhuman or superhuman strength played in Eleanor's senseless killing would be central to our understanding of racial profiling and police violence.

Two and a half decades after the 1991 beating of Rodney King was broadcast on TV, another bystander captured video of a different beating by the side of a Los Angeles freeway, featuring another Black grandmother (see photo insert). Marlene Pinnock, diagnosed as bipolar, had been homeless off and on for several years. She was walking along Interstate 10 in Los Angeles, headed to a location where she felt safe to sleep that was only accessible by freeway. A California Highway Patrol officer stopped her, eventually tackled and threw her to the ground, and proceeded to punch her in the head ten times as he straddled her body on the side of the freeway. Marlene later said, "He grabbed me, he threw me down, he started beating me. . . . I felt like he was trying to kill me, beat me to death." Adding insult to injury, during the assault Marlene's skirt began to ride up. When she attempted to pull it down, the officer ripped her dress, displaying her naked buttocks to surrounding traffic. She was subsequently hospitalized for several weeks for injuries to her head, which left her with slurred speech, and experienced ongoing nightmares about the incident. The officer also claimed that Marlene was mentally unstable, causing the hospital to hold her longer, against her will, for observation.

The officer later claimed that he stopped Marlene because she was walking barefoot on a highway talking to herself, presenting a danger to herself and motorists, and that she told him she wanted to walk home and called him "the devil." He also claimed that she was resisting arrest. The man who captured the beating on video told Reverend Al Sharpton that after the officer first approached her, Marlene walked away, off the highway. The officer re-engaged her and escalated the situation; the witness observed no resistance whatsoever. Once the video went viral, civil rights leaders began to speak out about Marlene's beating, using the video to counter the officer's justifications for the violence. "Without the video my word may have not meant anything," Marlene said.

The Los Angeles County District Attorney's Office investigated the incident and concluded that the officer's "use of force was legal and necessary."[3] The report quotes officers describing Marlene as "strong"—again invoking racially gendered narratives of Black women with superhuman strength, immune to pain. The officer admitted that he donned gloves before taking her down because she was homeless, and that he was "fucking wailing [*sic*] away" on her.[4] Highlighting the role of public perceptions of Black women in fueling police violence, the report also documented statements by individuals who reported Marlene's presence on the freeway to police based on assumptions that Marlene might have a gun or pose a threat, and which describe her as "looking psycho." A civil suit resulted in a $1.5 million settlement, and the officer responsible agreed to resign from the force.[5]

On October 18, 2016, things came back full circle when, thirty-two years after the killing of Eleanor Bumpurs, history repeated itself. NYPD officers, responding to a call about an "emotionally disturbed person," shot to death sixty-six-year-old Deborah Danner, who had been diagnosed as schizophrenic, in her Bronx apartment. Police claimed that Danner had advanced on them with a baseball bat.[6] The connection to the Bumpurs case was quickly made by protesters and media—and, most strikingly, by Danner herself, who wrote about deadly police responses to people labeled with mentally illness four years before she was killed: "We are all aware of the all too frequent news stories of the mentally ill who come up against law enforcement instead of mental health professionals and end up dead. . . . They used deadly force to subdue her [Bumpurs] because they were not trained sufficiently in how to engage the mentally ill in crisis. This was not an isolated incident."[7] City officials quickly admitted that, in Danner's case, responding officers had not followed NYPD policies governing responses to calls about people in mental health crisis, which had been changed following Bumpurs's killing.[8]

At least half a dozen cases of police shootings of Black women documented in *Say Her Name*, the report I coauthored with Kimberlé

Crenshaw, arose from police interactions with women in actual or perceived mental health crisis: Shereese Francis, killed in New York City in March 2012; Miriam Carey, shot in Washington, DC, in October 2013; Pearlie Golden, shot in Hearne, Texas, in May 2014; Tanisha Anderson, killed in Cleveland in November 2014.[9] Although no official statistics exist, based on my experience tracking cases over the years, it appears that police responses to mental health crises make up a significant proportion of Black women and women of color's lethal encounters with police. As was the case for Eleanor and Deborah, these encounters often reflect police perceptions of Black women as volatile and violent, portrayed, in the words of historian Sarah Haley, as "daft," "imbecilic," "monstrous," "deranged subjects," "lacking essential traits of personhood and normative femininity,"[10] to be met with deadly force rather than compassion, no matter their condition or circumstance.

Indeed, disability—both mental and physical—is socially constructed in ways comparable to, and mutually constitutive of, the construction of race and gender.[11] As disability justice and transformative justice activist Mia Mingus points out, women of color are *already* understood as "mentally unstable," regardless of whether or not they are actually "disabled." "This kind of racialized able-ism inherently informs how police (and society at large) interact with Black and Indigenous women, and women of color."[12] Actual or perceived disability, including mental illness, has thus served as a primary driver of surveillance, policing, and punishment for women and gender-nonconforming people of color throughout US history.

Scientific racism has been fundamental to conceptions of mental health and disorder.[13] According to Vanessa Jackson, the first asylums for "lunatic slaves" were created in response to a case of a Black woman found to be insane after she allegedly killed her child. Indeed, resistance to slavery was pathologized as mental illness inherent in African-descended people.[14] The same resistance-equals-insanity trope was projected onto Indigenous people. In her pamphlet *Wild Indians*, Pemina Yellow Bird, a member of the Three Affiliated Tribes and psychiatric survivor activist, describes how, from 1899 to 1933, Indigenous people who resisted reservation agents, refused kidnapping of their children to Indian Residential Schools, or violated laws that criminalized traditional spiritual practices were sent to the Hiawatha Asylum for Insane Indians in Canton, South Dakota. There, "Indian defectives" were incarcerated and subjected to torture and physical, cultural, and spiritual abuses.[15]

Urban policing also evolved in part around a mandate to remove both gender-transgressing and disabled bodies from public spaces. According to Clare Sears, "Within nineteenth-century municipal code books, for example, cross-dressing, prostitute, and disabled bodies appeared alongside one another as (il)legal equivalents in public space, through general orders that banned the public appearance of a person wearing 'a dress not belonging to his or her sex,' in 'a state of nudity,' or 'deformed so as to be an unsightly or disgusting object.'"[16] As a result, in the first half of the twentieth century, disabled women—as well as lesbian, bisexual, and transgender women labeled as having a psychiatric disability because of their sexual or gender nonconformity—were forced into institutions, often following interactions with law enforcement.[17]

Today police continue to target people who have, or who they perceive to have, psychiatric or cognitive disabilities for violence, arrest, and commitment in institutions of various kinds. National statistics indicate that the majority of people who experience police violence are labeled as mentally or physically disabled; one study estimates that "roughly a third to a half of all people killed by police are disabled" and that the "most common type of killing" involves a person who is in "a mental health crisis" and is holding an item described as a weapon (from firearms to household implements or tools) when shot by law enforcement.[18] According to the Treatment Advocacy Center, "The risk of being killed during a police incident is 16 times greater for individuals with untreated mental illness than for other civilians approached or stopped by officers."[19]

The risk of deadly police encounters for people labeled mentally ill has increased significantly since the 1970s in the wake of deinstitutionalization. A severe shortage of community-based services has produced disproportionate levels of homelessness and unemployment among people with mental illness and other disabilities, resulting in increased police contact in the context of the criminalization of poverty in public spaces, housing, and services.[20] Additionally, in the absence of alternatives, the police tend to be the people called to assist people in the midst of a mental health crisis; in New York City, for example, the police department receives approximately four hundred mental health-related calls a day.[21] Arrest rates among recipients of public mental health services are four and a half times those in the general population; most of these arrests are for "public nuisance" offenses.[22] Officers exercise significant discretion when determining whether to respond to calls involving people in mental health crisis with violence, arrest, involuntary commitment, or nonpunitive responses. Arrests are more likely when individuals are perceived as "disrespectful" or use offensive language, especially in public situations.[23]

Not surprisingly, race and gender continue to frame perceptions of disability and police responses.[24] Police are more likely to criminalize and use excessive force against people of color with psychiatric disabilities through a process that law professor Camille A. Nelson terms the "disabling of race and the racing of disability."[25] Nelson described the case of Rosie Banks, a thirteen-year-old autistic junior high student who reacted to teasing by fellow students in "an aggressive manner." When brought to the administrative office, an officer who, thanks to the increased presence of police in schools described in chapter 3, "just happened to be there," immediately confronted her. When she became "more aggressive," he pepper-sprayed her in the face. In so doing, and in a subsequent incident in which he handcuffed Rosie, the officer immediately circumvented de-escalation options typically used with white students, even when they pose a greater objective threat. Nelson posits that race, gender, and disability all played mutually reinforcing roles in this exercise of discretion.[26] Rosie Banks's treatment was no doubt also informed by her failure to display the passivity expected of people with disabilities.

The odds that Black women and women of color who are or are perceived to be in mental health crisis will experience violence, arrest, or involuntary commitment are compounded by perceptions of mental instability based on gender, gender nonconformity, and sexuality. Trans people and gender-nonconforming people have long been treated by medical professionals and law enforcement as mentally unstable, leading police to respond based on presumptions of volatility and irrationality that must be subdued with force.[27]

For Kayla Moore, all of these factors were at play. In 2013, Berkeley, California, police responded to a call from Kayla's roommate, who told police that Kayla, a Black trans woman labeled as schizophrenic, had been drinking and using drugs and had locked him out of their apartment. According to her sister Maria Moore, Kayla was calm and cooking when the officers arrived, but they claimed that she was "speaking incoherently." A subsequent investigation revealed that instead of asking her or her caregiver, who by then was also on the scene, what she needed, the officers misgendered Kayla, and told her there was a warrant out for her arrest. In fact, the warrant was for a person who was twenty years older than Kayla who bore the male name she had been assigned at birth. Confident that there was no warrant in her name, Kayla said she would call the FBI to prove it. The two officers forcefully took her down to the floor, where Kayla landed on her stomach. Eventually eight officers piled on top of Kayla, putting two sets of handcuffs on her and wrapping her legs together. Minutes later they realized that she had stopped breathing, but refused to give her CPR because they didn't have a device that would keep their lips from touching hers. Her sister believes their actions were motivated by transphobia, noting that officers referred to Kayla as "it" as her body lay on the ground, partially uncovered. Kayla died at thirty-two years of age while on her way to the hospital. The cause of death was given as a combination of drugs and an enlarged heart, but in truth Kayla was a victim of police perceptions of Black women, trans women, people labeled with mental illness, and drug users.[28]

Kayla Moore's killing prompted protests in city council and Police Review Commission meetings and on the streets of Berkeley. Organizing led by Kayla's sister has seamlessly lifted up the many identities and experiences that played a role in Kayla's deadly encounter with police—as a Black woman, a trans woman, and a person labeled mentally ill and characterized as having a physical disability. I first learned of Kayla's case from Andrea Pritchett, a long-standing Berkeley Copwatch organizer who attended the first workshop on police violence against women and LGBTQ people of color I had conducted in 2004. In the fall of 2013, we were both at a national Cop Watch conference organized by People's Justice and the Justice Committee in New York City when she handed me a copy of Berkeley Copwatch's independent report on Kayla's case. At one of the breaks in the conference, Andrea sang a song in Kayla's honor. Maria Moore continues to organize for justice for Kayla as part of the Say Her Name movement and with other families of people killed by police.[29]

Ultimately, following Kayla's death, more officers in the Berkeley police department received crisis intervention training. A commission of inquiry unanimously found that officers had violated policies against keeping arrestees prone on their stomachs for prolonged periods of time. Additionally, the Berkeley Independent Police Review Commission found that officers failed to monitor Kayla's vital signs after piling on top of her as she lay facedown and binding her hands and feet. Despite these findings, no officer was disciplined.[30] The family filed a civil suit, the bulk of which was dismissed in October 2016, on the grounds that the force used was not excessive and did not cause Kayla's death.[31] Berkeley Copwatch made a series of policy recommendations, including increased funding for psychiatric treatment and the development of alternative, nonpolice responses to mental health crises.

On August 14, 2014, just days after Michael Brown was killed in Ferguson, Missouri, Michelle Cusseaux was at home in Phoenix, Arizona, fixing her door when a police officer, Percy Dupra, came to execute a "pickup order" to bring her to a mental health treatment facility.[32] When officers arrived at her home, Michelle spoke with them through the door and refused to leave her home or consent to their entry. She said she did not trust them, and believed they would shoot her. Both Michelle and her mother told officers that she did not have a weapon in the house. According to the complaint filed in a civil suit brought by Michelle's mother, Fran Garrett, "Rather than give Michelle space and more response time, attempt to deescalate the situation, engage in additional communication with Michelle in a calm manner in order to build trust or alleviate her fears, or seek the involvement of appropriately trained personnel, Dupra instructed an Officer Anderson to pick the exterior locked door of Michelle's residence."[33] When they entered, Officer Dupra saw Michelle standing near the door holding a hammer, interpreted it to be a weapon, and shot her. He later said that something about the look on her face—"eyes wide open, mouth wide open. . . . She had that anger in her face that she was going to hit someone with that hammer"—caused him to fear for his safety.[34] Fran Garrett later questioned the officer's response: "What did the police see when they pried open that door? A Black woman? A lesbian? He said it was just a look on her face. What look would you have on your face if the police broke into your house? Could that have been the look of fear? I would have been in fear for my life too, especially if I already felt like they were going to kill me." Once again, perceptions of Black women as "deranged subjects" prone to violence colored an officer's response to a Black woman standing with a hammer, with deadly results.

In the wake of Michelle's killing, her mother organized with community members, marching her casket to the US Attorney's Office to demand an investigation into her death. In October 2014, in response to Michelle's shooting, the Phoenix Police Department announced the creation of a Mental Health Advisory Board to guide the department's policies. The department also instituted mobile crisis teams and crews of behavioral-health specialists, and mandated a decreased focus on arrest in favor of providing needed services and increased supervision by trained officers when executing "pickup orders" like the one that brought officers to Michelle Cusseaux's home.[35] Ultimately, the Phoenix Police Department found that Officer Dupra violated departmental use-of-force policies, and he was subsequently demoted but not prosecuted or fired.[36] "That was like a smack in the face—to find someone responsible and put him back out in the community with no evaluation, no additional training, no other consequence for taking a life," Fran Garrett said.

As in Kayla's and Michelle's cases, police violence against people in mental health crisis often occurs in homes and facilities away from public view—and cop-watching cameras. One winter day in 2012, one such incident took place in a Rosemead, California, community mental health clinic, where Jazmyne Ha Eng, a forty-year-old Asian woman who was a regular patient, was waiting in the lobby of Pacific Clinic's Asian Pacific Family Center, when she was shot to death by Los Angeles County sheriffs. Clinic staff had called 911 to get someone to take Jazmyne in on an involuntary psychiatric hold. The deputies claimed that Jazmyne, who was four feet nine inches and weighed ninety-three pounds, had waved a hammer over her head and charged at them. Yet clinic staff had described her in the 911 call as "sitting calmly," patiently waiting for hours. While it is unclear what exactly transpired, no doubt historic perceptions of Asian women who do not fit the "China doll" image as masculinized and dehumanized "others" played a role in transforming Jazmyne, in the officers' eyes, from a tiny woman sitting quietly, in need of help, into a raging threat that must be met with lethal force. They no doubt also played a role in the district attorney's office ruling that the shooting was lawful. Nevertheless, Jazmyne's family's litigation seeking review of police responses to people in mental health crisis resulted in a $1.8 million settlement, and investigation of the shooting resulted in "administrative action" against two deputies involved.[37]

Controlling narratives often frame nonsubmissive Asian women as being out of control and deranged, even where no disability exists. In April 2016, Ok Jin Jun, a sixty-two-year-old Korean woman, was followed into her church parking lot by LAPD officers after she honked at them to move their SUV, which was blocking the entrance. As she exited the car, they demanded to see her registration. Because she speaks little English, she called 911 for a translator. The officers responded by calling for backup, summoning two additional cars to the scene. Surveillance video shows them charging at the woman, pushing her up against her car, and slamming her to the ground; then, three officers piled on top of her before handcuffing her, leaving bruises and scrapes on her face.[38] The officers' response not only punished Jin Jun for seeking language assistance but also reflected rage at perceived failure to display the deference expected of an Asian woman, transforming an elder on her way to pray who had committed no offense whatsoever into a threat that must be met with force. The police department later claimed a "mental health" issue may have prompted the response, projecting disability onto Jin Jun where none existed and responding with violence.

As is the case in school settings, children are unfortunately not immune from police projections of deranged threat—even a seventy-pound, eight-year-old Lakota girl in distress in her own home. In October 2014, officers responded to a call for help from a babysitter because the girl was threatening to hurt herself with a knife. Upon the officers' arrival, the girl pointed the knife at her own chest except for a brief moment when it was pointed at one of the officers. They responded by using a Taser on her; the weapon's fifty thousand volts of electricity lifted the little girl's body and threw it against the wall, causing her physical and emotional injuries. Subsequently, the South Dakota Division of Criminal Investigation found no wrongdoing by the officers.[39] Her attorneys protested, "These are trained professional law enforcement officers and there were four of them. . . . Not one of them thought to reach out and grab her, or talk her down. . . . They came in there and dealt with her like she was a thirty-year-old. . . . 'Drop the knife or else!'"[40]

Controlling narratives framing Indigenous women as violently "insane" if they resist authority in any way, as well as expendable and to be eradicated, also contributed to the death of Loreal Tsingine, a twenty-seven-year-old Navajo mother who had been prescribed medication for psychosis. In March 2016, an officer responding to a call about a disturbance in a store killed Loreal within thirty seconds of approaching her on the street. The officer forcefully took her to the ground, spilling the contents of her purse, which included a pair of scissors friends say she used to cut split ends from her hair. Loreal got up immediately. The officer's body-camera video shows Loreal walking toward him, holding the scissors pointed to the ground, with the officer's partner behind Loreal, ready to assist in taking her into custody.[41] Instead of working with his partner to physically restrain her, the first officer shot Loreal five times, killing her instantly. It later came to light that the officer had incurred thirty violations during his training, including falsifying evidence and being "too quick to go to his gun," leading training officers to recommend against his hiring. He also had a history of violence toward women: he had been found to have made vulgar comments to a fifteen-year-old girl and had used a Taser on another fifteen-year-old girl with her back to him.[42] The DOJ opened an investigation and the officer eventually resigned.[43] Loreal's aunt, Floranda Dempsey, mourned the young woman at her funeral, saying, "Even with a broken heart that never recovered from devastation, she showed us what love should be about. We will miss her tight hugs and beautiful smile and love."[44]

As Dara Baldwin of the National Disability Rights Network emphasizes, it is not only people with mental disabilities who are at increased risk of physical and lethal violence by police; women of color with physical disabilities are also subject to police brutality, including police sexual violence and sometimes deadly force. Lisa Hayes, a Black school counselor living in Rehoboth, Delaware, who is quadraplegic and has a speech impediment caused by cerebral palsy, is one of them. A tactical team trained to combat "domestic terrorism" conducted a drug raid at her mother's house. They drove up in an armored personnel carrier, armed with assault rifles, and burst into the family home at 6 a.m. Lisa's husband, Ruther, a disabled veteran, was giving her a sponge bath, and tried to cover her with a sheet because she was naked from the waist down when the officers broke down the door. The officers threw Ruther to the ground and pointed their assault rifles at Lisa as she lay half naked on the bed, screaming at her to "get the fuck up"—which she was physically unable to do. The officers were clearly on notice of this fact: her wheelchair was next to the bed; officers had stormed up a wheelchair ramp before breaking down the door; and Lisa, as well as Lisa's mother and son, repeatedly told the officers that she couldn't move. After being held at gunpoint for an extended period of time while officers beat and tasered her husband, Lisa told the officers she was experiencing chest pain and believed she was having a heart attack. The officers stopped beating her husband and called for medical assistance. Instead of dressing her and taking her out of the house in her wheelchair, the officers wrapped the top half of Lisa's body in a sheet, leaving the bottom exposed, and carried her out by the arms and legs, half naked in front of her neighbors. After the incident Lisa said, "I feel not only degraded, humiliated; I feel like they didn't treat me as a human being. I relive that day when they came in on me and them yelling at me to get up when they knew that I couldn't get up."[45] She continues to suffer flashbacks of the raid, depression, panic attacks, and chest pain. The ACLU filed a lawsuit on the couple's behalf.[46]

Police interactions with deaf people are notoriously dangerous because in the absence of interpretation, deaf people are perceived to be "noncompliant." Lashonn White, a Black deaf woman, called 911 to report that she was being abused by another woman in her home, and repeatedly pleaded for help. Throughout the call, she emphasized that she required a sign-language interpreter in order to communicate with hearing people. After she followed the dispatcher's instructions to go out her front door to meet police, Lashonn was immediately Tasered in the ribs and stomach by the officers, causing injuries to her cheek, chin, ribs, neck, and arms and leaving her bloody. She later said, "All I'm doing is waving my hands in the air, and the next thing I know, I'm on the ground and then handcuffed. It was almost like I blacked out. I was so dizzy and disoriented." Hearing Lashonn screaming in pain, her neighbor yelled down to officers that the woman was deaf and couldn't speak and criticized them for not signaling her to stop using hand signals instead of verbal commands. One officer later said he thought that Lashonn, who was running toward him for help as instructed, was "charging at him," and describing her as "making a loud grunting noise, [having] a piercing stare in her eyes and . . . a clenched right fist in the air." Police also claimed that they mistakenly believed she was the assailant, despite having been given a detailed description, which did not match what Lashonn was wearing. As with Michelle Cusseaux, all it took was a "look" to transform Lashonn from a person desperate for police intervention into a dangerous threat in the eyes of officers. Officers charged Lashonn with assault and obstruction of justice, invoking images of her as animalistic—"deranged" and "grunting"—to justify their actions. Lashonn was taken to jail and held for sixty hours without medical treatment or an interpreter, in violation of state law, until the prosecutor dropped the charges.[47] While a jury in a civil case brought by Lashonn believed that her rights had been violated during the arrest, they awarded her only one dollar in damages, making clear how much value they placed on her Black deaf life.[48]

RESISTANCE

The editors of the anthology *Disability Incarcerated* point out, "Disability, situated alongside other key lines of stratification such as race, class nationality, and gender, is central to understanding the complex, varied and interlocking ways in which incarceration occurs."[49] A March 2016 white paper on disability and police violence calls for increasing visibility of disability in police encounters, pointing out that many of the cases of police brutality that have been the subject of resistance since 2014—Eric Garner, Tanisha Anderson, Freddie Gray, Sandra Bland— have involved people with disabilities, a reality too often erased from media coverage. Garner, Anderson, Gray, and Bland had asthma, bipolar disorder, lead poisoning, and epilepsy, respectively.[50] The paper posits that Bland's disability may have played a role in her death, noting that deprivation of the anti-epileptic drug Bland was prescribed can lead to suicidality.[51] It also highlights the ableist terms used by media to describe people with disabilities, and the ways in which the media paints white disabled victims of police violence in sympathetic terms but depicts Black disabled victims as deranged and dangerous.[52] Although a significant number of women killed by police were in mental health crisis at the time, discourse around police responses to people with disabilities have focused on the experiences of men. This is exemplified by a June 2015 *Washington Post* exposé entitled "Distraught People, Deadly Results," which fails to mention any of the forty-two cases of women with mental illness killed by police in 2015.[53]

Also invisible is organizing around police violence by women of color with disabilities. Dara Baldwin describes loose networks of disability activists who regularly listen to police scanners, and when they hear of a person with a disability in police custody, quickly dispatch an advocate to the station.[54] In New York City, RIPPD (Rights for Imprisoned People with Psychiatric Disabilities), a group of psychiatric survivors with histories of contact with the criminal legal system, along with their friends and family members, have long led advocacy around police responses to mental health crises. Led by Lisa Ortega, a Latinx single mom targeted by police on many occasions, the group emphasizes that the police mindset—"subdue, control and contain" —fuels police violence against people in mental health crisis.[55] Ortega and RIPPD call for alternative responses involving peer counselors, mental health professionals, and diversion programs, and emphasize the importance of involving people with psychiatric disabilities in developing them.[56]

In the wake of Deborah Danner's killing, there was a renewed chorus of calls to eliminate police involvement in responses to people in mental health crisis. Anti–police brutality activists aren't the only ones calling for change; the Treatment Advocacy Center has posited that "reducing encounters between on-duty law enforcement and individuals with the most severe psychiatric diseases may represent the single most immediate, practical strategy for reducing fatal police shootings in the United States."[57] Given how mental health crises and diagnoses intersect with racially gendered controlling narratives framing women of color as inherently mentally unstable threats with superhuman strength, there is no doubt that such a move would improve the life chances of women of color with and without disabilities in police encounters.

As Candice Bernd describes, the town of Eugene, Oregon, has been experimenting with nonpolice responses to mental health crises since 1989.[58] The city's CAHOOTs (Crisis Assistance Helping Out on the Streets) program enables dispatch of a mobile crisis unit consisting of a nurse or EMT and a crisis worker in response to nonemergency police calls related to drug use, poverty, and mental health—with no police officers.[59] However, the program still runs through the police department, and the decision about whether to involve police remains with the police dispatcher.[60] Nevertheless, CAHOOTs now responds to nine thousand calls a year, providing counseling instead of cops in 64 percent of calls, and is expanding to a nearby town. It could potentially serve as an intermediate model in cities across the country, although advocates caution that a program developed in a small, predominantly white community may not operate in the same way in larger urban departments policing communities of color.[61]

In the end, nothing short of completely uncoupling police from mental health crisis responses will achieve safety for people with disabilities. Mia Mingus also cautions that medically based alternatives must be evaluated in light of the long history of violence, abuse, and incarceration of people who have been labeled as mentally or physical disabled by medical authorities.[62] In this context and others, eliminating police doesn't necessarily eliminate policing or violence. The challenge of finding solutions that genuinely promote the safety, security, and self-determination of people with disabilities is great, but one that we must rise to meet.

CHAPTER 5

POLICE SEXUAL VIOLENCE

"What is the first image that comes to mind when I say police brutality?" It's a question I started asking in 2004 when I began facilitating workshops on the policing of women and LGBTQ people of color, which I developed with Sheba Remy Kharbanda, a South Asian artist, activist, and former colleague at Amnesty International. Years later, I still ask that question and, years later, the answer continues to be something along the lines of a white cop beating a Black man (almost always imagined as heterosexual and cisgender) with a baton. Rarely has sexual violence been the first response. If it does come up, the image of the person targeted is Abner Louima, a Haitian man who was sodomized by NYPD officers in 1997. It is not the daily sexual harassment, assault, and violation experienced at the hands of police by women of color across the United States. Yet once it is named as a form of police brutality, invariably, at least one person at my workshops shares a story of sexual violence by a police officer, often one that they have never told a soul about.

At the 2004 National Coalition on Police Accountability conference, a man who identified himself as a former member of the Black Panther Party approached me at the end of the workshop. He said that his sister had been raped by a police officer "back in the day," but he had never understood what happened to her as police brutality until he had heard it framed that way in the workshop. I asked him how he and his sister had described her experience. He answered, somewhat bewildered, that it was "just something bad that happened." He then thanked me for opening his eyes as to how his sister's experience fit into the work he had been doing all his life to challenge state violence against Black people.

At my next workshop, a daylong gathering in post-Katrina New Orleans, when the issue of police sexual violence was raised, a middle-aged

Black woman stood up and told the group that she had been raped by a cop when she was fourteen years old but before that very moment had never spoken to anyone about it. Everyone sat stunned, unsure how to respond. There were no resources to point her to, no campaign she could join, and, frankly, none of us even knew how to comfort her in that moment of remembering her raw pain, violation, and betrayal by an armed agent of the state, and of breaking a silence held too long. When I asked her afterward why she had chosen that moment to disclose her assault, she simply said it was the first opportunity that had presented itself. She had never before been in any space where the story "fit" into the conversation; she had never heard anyone talk about sexual violence as part of the fabric of police violence, or about police as perpetrators of sexual violence.

Similarly, as we were conducting research for the 2005 Amnesty International report *Stonewalled: Police Abuse and Misconduct Against LGBT People in the United States*, many of the trans, lesbian, and queer survivors who courageously came forward to share stories of sexual violence at the hands of police had never reported their violations to the authorities out of shame or fear that they would not be believed, fear of exposure of their sexual orientation or gender identity, of retaliation, of deportation, or of being charged with a crime because they were engaged in sex work or the use of controlled substances.

Almost a decade later, Oklahoma City police officer Daniel Holtzclaw's rape and sexual assault of at least thirteen Black women and girls came to light. I first learned of the case from two grassroots organizations, Black Women's Blueprint (BWBP) and Women's All Points Bulletin (WAPB), which, in September 2014, a month after Holtzclaw was indicted, drafted a shadow report to the United Nations Committee on the Elimination of Racial Discrimination that highlighted the case as a compelling example of ongoing state-sponsored sexual violence against Black women in the United States.[1] The submission argued, as did submissions I and others made to the UN in 2006 and 2008, that sexual violence by state actors such as Holtzclaw amounts to torture.[2] Early on, bloggers such as Kirsten West Savali placed the Holtzclaw case in the larger context of mounting protest over police killings of Mike Brown and Eric Garner.[3] As word of Holtzclaw's assaults spread, outrage grew among local activists, Twitter users, and bloggers, first at the news that Holtzclaw had been released on bond and that a Facebook page in support of him had been set up, and later at mainstream media, local and national anti–police brutality groups and antiviolence organizations for not paying more attention to the case.[4] Holtzclaw's trial and conviction eventually garnered national coverage when an all-white jury was selected to hear his case. Many asked whether Holtzclaw wouldn't more quickly have become a household name had he assaulted thirteen white women.

Holtzclaw's pattern of sexual violence came to light when Jannie Ligons, a fifty-seven-year-old Black grandmother who runs a day-care center in Oklahoma City, was driving home from a late-night domino game at a friend's house through the Eastside, a low-income Black neighborhood. Holtzclaw pulled her over and ordered her to step out of her car, put her hands on the hood of his car while he patted her "all over," and then sit in the backseat of his patrol car. Eventually, he forced to lift her shirt and expose her breasts, and later her genitals, then perform oral sex on him. Jannie described the scene: "I was out there alone and helpless, didn't know what to do."[5] She later said, "I was looking at that gun in his holster and I'm saying to myself . . . he's going to shoot me in the head. I was really afraid."[6] But, as Jannie told *Democracy Now* listeners, "He just picked the wrong lady to stop that night."[7] After Holtzclaw left her at her daughter's house, she immediately went to a police station to report what had happened to her. This kicked off an investigation in which Detective Kim Davis of the sexual assault squad tracked down women Holtzclaw had been in contact with, and used the GPS tracking device on his car to corroborate their stories of sexual violence. Thirteen Black women eventually came forward to participate in his prosecution.[8]

Most women Holtzclaw targeted said he stopped them as they were walking down the street and questioned them about what they were doing and where they were going. He often forced them to expose their bodies to show that they weren't hiding drugs in their bras or pants, much as Audrey Smith was ordered to on a Toronto street corner. Often

Holtzclaw would go further, opening his fly and demanding oral sex, sometimes taking the women home or to deserted areas to rape them— in his patrol car, on their front porch, or in their bed. In some cases, like that of his first victim, Sharday Hill, whom he first assaulted while she was handcuffed to a hospital bed, he would show up at their houses again and again. Sometimes he targeted "working girls"—people he believed to be engaged in the sex trades. He often used the fact that women had outstanding tickets or warrants to pressure them. Even if they didn't have any, the threat that he could charge them was enough. One victim, T.M., testified, "I felt like even though I didn't have no warrants that he might make up something on me and send me into jail anyway." He clearly targeted women he thought would never come forward and accuse him. T.M. said later, "I didn't think nobody was going to believe me anyway. . . . I'm a drug addict." Another victim, C.J., asked "Who are they going to believe? It's my word against his because I'm a woman and, you know, like I said, he's a police officer."

Holtzclaw was tried and convicted in December 2015. His defense consisted of denying the abuse and claiming that his accusers were lying, untrustworthy, inconsistent, high, and women with "an agenda" based on past criminal histories.[9] Ultimately, the jury found Holtzclaw guilty of eighteen of thirty-six charges involving eight of the thirteen women who came forward, and he was sentenced to 263 years in prison.[10]

The case prompted the Associated Press to conduct a yearlong investigation, which revealed that one thousand officers nationwide lost their licenses between 2009 and 2014 as a result of their sexual violence.[11] Two earlier studies of revocations of law enforcement licenses in Missouri and Florida found that sexual misconduct was the basis for revocations in almost 25 percent of cases.[12] And those are only the officers who were caught and held accountable—law enforcement officials and advocates alike will tell you these numbers are just the tip of the iceberg. Holtzclaw's case and his targets were unusual only in that he was caught, convicted, and sentenced to 263 years. Sadly, the experiences of the Black women who had the courage to come forward to testify against Holtzclaw are all too similar to those I have heard over the past two decades in countless workshops, "know your rights" trainings, and public forums—stories that rarely see the light of day, let alone command national headlines or animate our organizing.

Daniel Holtzclaw is far from the first police officer to have used the power of the badge to violate those he is sworn to serve and protect. And unfortunately, he won't be the last. In fact, Holtzclaw's predatory ways are eerily reminiscent of those of Eugene, Oregon, police officer Roger Magaña, convicted in 2004 of sexual assault and rape of a dozen women over an eight-year period. Like Holtzclaw, he preyed on women criminalized through the "war on drugs," broken windows policing, and the policing of prostitution, as well as survivors of violence and women labeled as mentally ill. Magaña would threaten arrest and then trade leniency for sexual acts. In some cases, Magaña used the pretext of conducting "welfare checks," unscheduled visits where officers gain entry into private homes by simply stating that they believe a person's well-being is at risk. In other instances, he conducted invasive and abusive searches of women on the side of the road. Magaña also threatened to retaliate against women if they reported him: one woman described Magaña putting his service weapon against her genitals and saying he would "blow her insides out" if she told anyone. This intimidation, along with indifference to the problem in the police department, allowed Magaña to engage in this conduct with impunity for almost a decade before his assaults came to light. Like the Holtzclaw survivors, many of the women who eventually came forward said they initially did not report the assaults because they feared they would not be believed. And their fears proved to be founded: police files indicate that at least half a dozen officers and supervisors heard complaints about Magaña's sexual violence over the years but dismissed them as the "grumblings of junkies and prostitutes."[13]

Echoes of the Magaña case resonated again in 2016 when the DOJ investigation of the Baltimore Police Department revealed a number of instances in which officers had extorted sex from women in the sex trades in exchange for leniency, and that the department had conducted shoddy and incomplete investigations that had led to no consequences for the officers involved.[14] In the intervening decade, researchers have consistently documented patterns of inadequate investigations of police sexual violence.[15]

The widespread, systemic, and almost routine nature of police sexual violence remains largely invisible to the public eye, though it chronically festers on the streets and in alleys, squad cars, and police lockups. A 2015 investigative report by the *Buffalo News* cataloguing more than seven hundred cases concluded, "In the past decade, a law enforcement official was caught in a case of sexual abuse or misconduct at least every five days."[16] A national study of officer arrests for sexual misconduct between 2005 and 2011 found that one-half of the cases involved on-duty sexual offenses, one-fifth forcible rape, and almost one-quarter forcible fondling, and that almost one-half targeted minors.[17] The study further notes that "distinctions between on- and off-duty police crime are often difficult to make" and that off-duty sexual offenses are often facilitated by the power of the badge or the presence of an official service weapon.[18] According to the Cato Institute, sexual misconduct is the second most frequently reported form of police misconduct, after use of excessive force. Yet it is clearly not the second most frequently talked about.[19]

The reasons for the seemingly impenetrable veil shrouding sexual abuse by officers are many and complex. One is a lack of data. As of 2016, there are no official statistics regarding the number of rapes and sexual assaults committed by police officers in the United States. To the extent that sexual assault by state actors has been documented at all, it has been in detention facilities such as jails and prisons.[20] The limited data gathered by federal and state governments on the use of excessive force by law enforcement officers do not include information on the number of allegations, complaints, or incidents of rape, sexual assault, or coerced sexual acts. Similarly, data gathered by the federal government on overall prevalence of rape and sexual assault do not include information concerning the number of perpetrators who are police officers and other law enforcement agents. In the absence of official data, law enforcement authorities can continue to sweep the issue under the rug—and, when it does come to light, claim that it is dealt with swiftly and decisively through discipline and criminal prosecution.[21] Likewise, government can continue to act as though the issue doesn't exist: when I testified before the Prison Rape Elimination Commission, one of the commissioners told me it was hard to take action against police sexual violence without concrete data. Thus, sexual violence by police remains what former Seattle Police Chief Norm Stamper dubs a "nasty little secret."[22]

Invisibility is also perpetuated in part because, in the absence of official data, our understanding of police violence is shaped by research studies based on complaints and media reports. It is estimated that only one-third of rapes and sexual assaults are ever reported.[23] This rate is no doubt far lower among women who are raped by the very law enforcement agents they would have to report to.[24] As Penny Harrington, former Portland chief of police, points out, "The women are terrified. Who are they going to call? It's the police who are abusing them."[25] Many survivors—like the woman I met in New Orleans, like the Holtzclaw survivors, like me and many others who have told me their stories over the years—don't report incidents out of shame or fear that they will not be believed. Some survivors fear exposure of their sexual orientation or gender identity, retaliation by police officers, or criminal charges or deportation because they are undocumented, are involved in sex work, or are using controlled substances. Some may fear coming forward in isolation, in the absence of support from anti–police brutality or anti-violence advocates. Or, as Joo-Hyun Kang, director of Communities United for Police Reform, once suggested to me, maybe sexual violence by the police just becomes part of a seamless web of sexual harassment, assault, and violence that begins for women of color in the morning when they take the garbage out and are whistled at by their neighbor, continues with endemic sexual harassment at work or school, and ends when they are propositioned or groped during a stop by a cop on the way home. Simultaneously ordinary and out of the ordinary.

Even when a woman takes the risk to lodge a complaint, there is the question of whether it will be recorded, taken seriously, and covered by the media, particularly given that officers are known to target individuals whose credibility will be challenged. By its very nature, sexual violence is hidden away from public view, witnesses, and cop-watching cameras, making it more likely that complaints will be deemed unsubstantiated. Because officers can often rely on threats of force or arrest, there are often no injuries requiring immediate medical attention and therefore no "evidence" beyond a woman's word.[26]

As a result, researchers almost universally caution that because of these limitations, documented cases "may represent only the tip of the iceberg."[27] Yet, even in the absence of official data and the limitations of other sources, sexual violence by law enforcement is one of the areas in which the greatest amount of social science research on women's experiences of policing exists.

A STRUCTURAL PROBLEM

Following a rash of reports in 2009 and 2010 of cases of sexual assault by police, in 2011 the International Association of Chiefs of Police (IACP) issued guidance defining the problem of "police sexual misconduct" for local law enforcement agencies.[28] According to the IACP, the term is intended to encompass a broad spectrum of activity:

- Sexual behavior while on duty, including "voyeuristic actions"[29]
- Unnecessary contacts or actions taken by officers for personal or sexually motivated reasons such as unwarranted callbacks to crime victims or making a traffic stop to get a closer look at the driver for nonprofessional reasons
- Inappropriate touching during stops, searches, and detention
- Sexual "shakedowns"—extortion of sexual favors in exchange for not ticketing or arresting someone
- Forcible or coercive sexual conduct, including rape[30]

Others have included within the definition of police sexual misconduct the following:

- Pressuring individuals to provide their phone number or other contact information in order to contact them for non–law enforcement purposes
- Inappropriate or sexual comments made to passersby, during traffic or street stops, in the context of searches, including strip searches, or while an individual is in police custody
- Inappropriate questions or conversation about individuals' sexual orientation

Researchers emphasize the importance of viewing police sexual violence as a continuum in order to counter "the tendency to view the more extreme forms of sexual violence as aberrations, which severs them from their common structural and cultural bases."[31] It is important to include sexual harassment on this continuum, because police officers have "the state-sanctioned power to detain, arrest and use physical force . . . [and] can invoke operational necessity, sometimes with institutional support, to engage in a range of potentially abusive behaviors, most significantly the legitimate use of violence."[32] And police sexual harassment can be a precursor to more serious forms of violence.

Researchers also emphasize that police sexual violence is a structural issue, facilitated by the nature of police work. Much like other professions in which sexual misconduct is particularly prevalent, officers work alone or in pairs, often late at night or in private locations, "often in situations with little or no direct accountability," with considerable access to women and young people.[33] A review of the Eugene, Oregon, police department conducted in the wake of the Magaña case concluded that lack of direct supervision was a "major problem."[34] According to Penny Harrington, "There is this culture in law enforcement . . . you don't tell on your buddies. . . . You get so bought into this police culture . . . you don't see anything wrong with it. It's like as a badge of honor, how many women in the community you can have sex with, and the younger the better."[35]

Using media reports, arrest records, and civil and criminal court opinions, researchers have pulled together a more detailed picture of how police sexual violence happens, and to whom. The targets of reported police sexual violence are overwhelmingly women, and typically women of color who are or are perceived to be involved in the drug or sex trades, or using drugs or alcohol, as well as people with prior arrest records, immigrants, people with limited English proficiency, people with disabilities, and people who have previously been targeted for police sexual violence.[36] Some researchers theorize that women who are targeted for police sexual violence are considered "police property" and therefore fair game for sexual extortion or assault.[37] Additionally, young women are particularly at risk: in a 2003 study of young women in New York City, almost two in five young women described sexual harassment by police officers. Thirty-eight percent were Black, 39 percent Latinx, and 13 percent Asian or Pacific Islander. As one young Black woman put it, "They say they are protecting us, but they only make us feel more at risk."[38]

SITES OF POLICE SEXUAL VIOLENCE

Police sexual violence takes place in locations ranging from police cars to private homes, from the streets to police detention facilities, and in contexts including immigration enforcement, "Explorer" programs designed to engage youth from the community, responses to calls for assistance, and the policing of prostitution and so-called lewd conduct.[39] Traffic stops, the war on drugs, stop-and-frisk practices, broken windows policing, and regulation of people on probation and parole, who live at the mercy of officers who can violate them on any or no pretext at any time—all serve as facilitators of police sexual violence.[40] According to the *Buffalo News* investigation, "In more than 70 percent of the cases, officers wielded their authority over motorists, crime victims, informants, students and young people in job-shadowing programs."[41] Two studies conducted by Samuel Walker and Dawn Irlbeck found that 40 percent of cases of police sexual misconduct reported in the media involved teenagers, and 34 percent took place in the context of a traffic stop.[42]

The pattern of officers targeting women during traffic stops is so prevalent that Walker and Irlbeck coined the term "driving while female" to describe the pattern, though they problematically represented it as "parallel" to, rather than a central feature of, racial profiling.[43] Their 2002 report documented over four hundred cases of sexual harassment and abuse by law enforcement officers in the context of traffic stops across the United States, yet only a quarter resulted in any kind of sanction of the perpetrators.[44]

A 2003 update to *Driving While Female* takes readers beyond the context of traffic stops, featuring page after page of incidents of police sexual violence that quickly overwhelm the reader, with stories from all over the country of officers raping, assaulting, and extorting sex from women and girls under a variety of circumstances.[45] From these cases, the authors identify a second pattern of police sexual violence, targeting young women in Explorer programs. In one case, Diana Guerrero of Las Cruces, New Mexico, was a high school police intern when she was sexually assaulted during a ride-along with an officer. She sued the city for violation of her constitutional rights, and in March 2016, by then twenty-one, was awarded a $3 million settlement by the city. Diana reflected on her experience: "It had never occurred to me that a person who had earned a badge would do this to me or anybody else. . . . I lost my faith in everything, everyone, even in myself." She went on to say, "I am most happy and satisfied that this lawsuit brought to light a cesspool of sexual violence and harassment that exists in police departments across this country. I'm living proof that you can speak out against sexual violence and win justice."[46]

Another frequent site of sexual violence by law enforcement is the border between Mexico and the United States, where Latinx immigrants, both documented and undocumented, report routine rape by both local law enforcement and Border Patrol agents, sometimes working together.[47] In September 2010 the *Los Angeles Times* reported, "In the last 18 months, five Border Patrol agents have been accused or convicted of sex crimes, including one agent who pleaded guilty in January to raping a woman while off duty, and another who is accused of sexually assaulting a migrant while her young children were nearby in a car."[48] More recently, in March 2014, Border Patrol agent Esteban Manzanares picked up a Honduran woman and her two girls near the Rio Grande, raped the woman and slashed her wrists, and sexually assaulted her fourteen-year-old daughter and then tried to break her neck until she lost consciousness. The mother and one daughter escaped; Manzanares took the other daughter back to his house, where he raped her. He killed himself when police summoned by her mother closed in; the woman and both daughters survived the incident. Juanita Valdez Cox of La Union del Pueblo Entero later said, "While some may say it is an isolated case, there are too many of these isolated cases of abuse by Border Patrol agents, and Border Patrol has done too little to address the problem."[49] Accountability is rare, due to the isolated locations in which abuse by Border Patrol agents takes place, the immediate detention and deportation of survivors, and women's undocumented status, which deters them from coming forward.

The issue of sexual violence in the context of immigration enforcement is not limited to the Border Patrol. Immigration agents have also extorted sex from women seeking legal status. According to a 2008 *New York Times* investigation, a New York agent demanded oral sex from a Colombian woman in exchange for overlooking an arrest that could have resulted in denial of her green card application. Across the country, in California, an immigration adjudicator was charged with extorting sexual favors from a Vietnamese woman in exchange for approving her citizenship application. One immigration official testified before Congress in 2006 that such corruption is "rampant."[50]

Additionally, local law enforcement officers target women they believe or know to be undocumented. For instance, in 2011 a Georgia deputy was found guilty of kidnapping, raping, and falsely imprisoning an undocumented Salvadoran woman, threatening to deport her, and "using the power of his badge to force her to his nearby apartment," where he raped her at gunpoint. As officers often did during the Jim Crow era, he defended himself by claiming that the woman was a "prostitute."[51] Similarly, an Anaheim, California, officer was charged with stopping an undocumented woman, asking if she had papers, and forcing her to perform oral sex.[52] A quarter of Latinx immigrant trans women surveyed by the Los Angeles organization Bienestar, the majority of whom were undocumented, reported sexual assault by law enforcement agents, primarily police officers and undercovers.[53]

Eithne Luibhéid argues that because their presence in the United States is framed as an illegal act, immigrant women are "constructed as inherently criminal, imbued with negative qualities, and positioned outside the conventional boundaries of society . . . [and] rapable."[54] She elaborates, "Initially in my research, I assumed that rape functioned as a form of crude, violent, border defense strategy. Like barbed wire and canine units, it kept women out."[55] While this remains true, she also notes that many women are not deported by the officers who assault them but rather released within the United States. As noted above, sometimes officers even solicit sex in exchange for assisting with immigration issues. The borders produced by such acts are thus

> not reducible to the nation's territorial borders. . . . Instead they involve social, economic, political, psychological and symbolic borders within the United States that connect to sexuality, gender, race, and class inequalities. Yet, at the same time, the reproduction of these internal borders articulates with practices for controlling the territorial border. . . . Rape inscribes undocumented women within US-based hierarchies of gender, sexuality, race and class.[56]

Often when I speak about police sexual violence, people are most disturbed by its prevalence in the context of police *responses* to violence (discussed in detail in chapter 9). Yet sexual assault in this context is simply another manifestation of power and opportunity. One North Carolina sheriff's domestic violence investigator bragged that "finding dates working with victims of domestic violence is like shooting fish in a barrel."[57]

Beyond targeting survivors of domestic violence, officers like Holtzclaw, Magaña, and countless others target women seeking other forms of assistance or use their power of "protection" to gain access to women. A Syracuse, New York, police officer, Chester Thompson, was eventually charged with sexually assaulting Black, Latina, and Middle Eastern women he was supposed to help, or "protect," over a ten-year period. Maleatra Montañez called 911 for help in February 2015 to report her daughters missing. She later testified that as soon as Thompson responded to the call, he immediately "told her she was 'pretty,' her butt was big, and that her 'lips looked like it can hold . . . a penis.'"[58] The next thing she knew, Thompson forced her to perform oral sex on him, and then turned her around to face her newborn son as he raped her.[59] When she heard about Montañez's case, Kim Fletcher, a thirty-five-year-old mother of five, came forward to report that when she called police for assistance with her daughter in June 2013, Thompson, who responded to the call, assaulted her, and then continued to call her and show up at her house. She later described feeling powerless: "He's a cop. . . . They're not going to believe me so I'll just deal with it until he decides to go away."[60]

Shakina Thompson read about the case and remembered that she had called 911 during a dispute with her girlfriend ten years earlier, only to have Chester Thompson tell her that he would file aggravated assault charges against her girlfriend if Shakina had sex with him. Shakina later told reporters, "I didn't know what to do. . . . I felt violated." He came back on at least two more occasions and assaulted her again each time. She, too, had not come forward because she didn't think she would be believed.[61] Six years before Thompson assaulted Shakina, he approached eighteen-year-old Liz ElBayadi at an outdoor concert where she had been drinking. She later said, "I remember him making a comment about him being an officer and me being drunk and underage, then he forcibly bent me over the port-a-potty and raped me." Liz came forward when others did, she said, because "I want to stitch my story next to theirs because very little has changed in this patriarchal society."[62] Thompson was fired and pled guilty to "official misconduct," a misdemeanor, and was given probation, prompting protests outside the courthouse at his sentencing.[63]

Police holding facilities are also prevalent sites of sexual violence by police. In 2006 I testified before the Prison Rape Elimination Commission about sexual violence in police "lockups," sharing the story of Denise Almodovar, Sarah Adams, Candace Ramirez, Becki Taylor, and Lindsey Valsamaki. In November 2002, the group was picked up, allegedly for public intoxication, by Officers Dwaun Guidry and Rolando Trevino of the Balcones Heights, Texas, police department, taken to the police station, booked, and placed in a holding cell. The officers then removed the five women from the cell and brought them into the patrol workroom—where there is no video surveillance—and ordered them to dance to music. They then sexually assaulted the five women, forcibly kissing them, forcing their hands down the women's pants, and exposing their penises and masturbating in front of the women. One of the women later testified that she felt unable to resist or run away because "he had his gun and I was singled out. I was by myself. I didn't know what door led out. I couldn't go anywhere."[64]

SEXUAL VIOLENCE AS A TOOL OF ENFORCING GENDER NORMS

Within and beyond these specific sites of police sexual violence, researchers note that officers often target women who are perceived to be deviating from "norms of feminine sexuality" and "their proper place" by being out late at night (as opposed to "home with their boyfriends") or who may have been drinking.[65] For example, in March 2013, Kim Nguyen, a twenty-seven-year-old graduate student, had been out drinking with friends in Los Angeles's Koreatown, and was standing in a parking lot waiting for a ride home when Officers David Shin and Jin Oh pulled up and began questioning them. Eventually they arrested Kim—but neither of her companions—for public intoxication, handcuffed her, and put her in the patrol car. One officer stayed in the backseat with her and began forcefully groping her, pulling up her skirt, forcing her legs apart, and grabbing her chest. Then, suddenly, the door behind her opened as the officers sped through a green light. Nguyen was thrown to the pavement, and can be seen on video captured by a nearby surveillance camera lying on the street with the top of her dress pulled down, her skirt hiked up, and severe injuries to her head. She filed a lawsuit that settled on the eve of trial.[66]

Consistent with the notion that police use sexual violence to enforce gender norms, as further explored in chapter 7, women working in the sex trades report rampant sexual abuse by law enforcement officers.[67] Both studies by Walker and Irlbeck reported a number of instances in which police extorted sex from people in the sex trades by threatening arrest.[68] Also consistent with use of sexual violence as a weapon of gender policing, as discussed in greater detail in the next chapter, trans and queer people report high levels of sexual violence at the hands of police. For instance, according to a 2014 study by New Orleans' BreakOUT!, a grassroots organization working to end criminalization of LGBTQ youth, 59 percent of transgender respondents were asked for a sexual favor by police, compared with 12 percent of cisgender respondents, and 43 percent of respondents of color had been asked for a sexual favor by police, compared with 11 percent of white respondents.[69] One respondent described feelings of powerlessness in the face of such demands:

Would he be angry if I rejected him? He could easily have forced me to have sex with him and who would have believed me if I told anyone— a transgender woman of color in New Orleans? . . . I continue to feel less and less protected by the police but now, not only do I feel unprotected, I feel threatened. I can walk in an area with cops on every corner and rather than feeling safe, I am in fear of losing my life, my dignity, or my freedom.[70]

In October 2012 in El Monte, California, just outside of Los Angeles, "Jane Roe," a Mexican trans woman, was crossing the street on the way home from a friend's house when an officer pulled up in a patrol car and asked what she was doing. The officer then groped her breasts and "asked [her] if she was 'a nasty she-male.' [She] responded that she was transsexual." He then ordered her through an alley into a deserted parking lot where he forced her to perform oral sex and raped her over the trunk of his car. He threw away the condom he used and told her to leave. Jane later went back to get it and turned it over to police as evidence, prompting an investigation which led to the officer being placed on unpaid administrative leave.[71] Jane's case is strikingly similar to the case of a Navajo trans woman that I documented in Los Angeles more than a decade earlier and which is described in greater detail in chapter 8. Both are part of a continuing epidemic of police sexual violence against trans women.

Police also enforce gender norms by using sexual violence against lesbians, who report "being forced to describe or engage in sexual acts with other women while in police custody, and threatened with rape by other detainees or law enforcement officers to 'cure' or punish their sexual orientation."[72] For instance, in *Stonewalled* we documented the case of a Black lesbian raped by a Georgia officer who said the world needed "one less dyke."[73] In some cases, the sexual violence is more subtle, but still traumatic. In a 2017 study, Tiffany, a young Black woman in her twenties, describes an arrest in her New York City public-housing project in which a group of officers, guns drawn, screamed at her and a friend to put their hands up as they walked down a staircase from the roof. When Tiffany told them she did not consent to a search, one officer responded by saying, "Oh, so you think you're smart, girl?" and proceeded to grope her breasts for an extended period of time as Tiffany told him to stop and eventually began screaming and crying, while other officers looked on but did nothing. When Tiffany later tried to report the officer's assault at the precinct, the officer mocked her and told her he knew where she lived, placing her in fear of further sexual assault in police custody and beyond. Tiffany describes being targeted by police often based on gender nonconformity and presumptions about her sexual orientation, saying, "Y'all think that like I wanna be a man . . . like those stereotypes are, like those things that people say about gay women who dress tomboyish." Sadly, she is not alone.[74]

LACK OF ACCOUNTABILITY

Much of the information about police sexual violence is based on cases in which criminal charges were brought, creating the false impression that police sexual violence is effectively handled by the criminal legal system. Yet in most cases, even officers who are eventually indicted operate with impunity for years. Ernest Marsalis was ultimately terminated from the Chicago Police Department for kidnapping and raping a nineteen-year-old Black woman he arrested. Before the case came to light, he had been accused of violent or threatening behavior, in most cases against women, in more than twenty cases, without any consequence.[75] A decade-long study of newspaper reports of police sexual violence in the Midwest confirms he is not an anomaly: 41.5 percent of cases involved a repeat offender, who had targeted four people on average, and had between two and twenty-one prior allegations of police sexual violence.[76] In an investigation of civilian complaints against the Chicago police department, Adeshina Emmanuel, an Ida B. Wells Fellow at the Nation's Investigative Fund, found a number of poorly investigated and incorrectly catalogued cases of police sexual violence. In several cases, police union contracts and state law precluded a full investigation.

Unlike incidents of excessive force, where there may be witnesses and, if the survivor is lucky, video footage, often, because of the private nature of sexual violence, it's entirely a woman's word against an officer's. Accountability is rare, and officers are frequently able to resign without consequence, and move on to another jurisdiction in what researchers call the "police officer shuffle," enabling them to continue patterns of abuse.[77]

SEARCHES AS SEXUAL ASSAULT

Beyond rape and sexual assaults as conventionally understood, "police can engage legally in many behaviors that would be considered criminal if performed in a different context."[78] Strip and cavity searches are normalized policing practices, permitted by law under certain circumstances, such as when there is "reasonable suspicion" to believe that a person is concealing a weapon, or "probable cause" to believe they are concealing evidence or contraband. Yet even a federal appeals court has described them as "demeaning, dehumanizing, undignified, humiliating, terrifying, unpleasant, embarrassing, repulsive, signifying degradation and submission."[79] Women often experience such searches as rape and sexual assault, regardless of legal justification. In other words, they constitute "state-sanctioned sexual assault,"[80] rendering sexual violence an inherent part of policing.[81] Searches conducted to assign gender on the basis of anatomy, although not permitted by law, are also experienced as sexual assaults and are often accompanied by racialized sexual commentary, homophobia, and transphobia. Of course, race, gender, and other factors shape how these legal standards are applied—and violated.

In the context of the war on drugs, cavity searches are often justified on the basis of a deeply racialized, "sexist, culturally based belief . . . that women are capable of carrying drugs and weapons inside their body cavities, and do so regularly."[82] Such notions harken back to the theories of scientific racism positing that Black women's deviant sexual organs made us more prone to criminal or deviant acts. In 2015, a series of roadside body-cavity searches conducted by officers who claimed to believe that women were concealing marijuana came to light in Texas: Charnesia Corley, a twenty-one-year-old Black woman, was subjected to a strip search and visual cavity search at a gas station in full view of passersby. Two other Black women, Brandi Hamilton and Alexandria Randle, were subjected to a roadside cavity search by officers during a traffic stop as they drove home from the beach.[83]

Similar perceptions of Indigenous and Latinx women's bodies produce similar results. In 2006, the American Friends Service Committee and members of the Passamoquoddy tribe in Maine reported that Native women were routinely subjected to visual body cavity searches by local sheriffs as a matter of policy, whereas similarly situated white women were not, and that women were required to remove one article of clothing at a time in a way that simulated a striptease. If searching officers were not satisfied, they would order the woman to start over.[84] Researchers describe a case in which officers showed up at Shirley Rodriquez's home late at night, forced the door open, and, finding her sleeping in bed with her husband, told her that they had a warrant to search her vagina for drugs and insisted that she reach in and "take out the stuff." When she refused, police took her to a local hospital and forced the physician on duty to forcefully conduct an invasive search of Shirley's vagina, during which no drugs were found.[85] Her civil case was dismissed on the grounds the officers were acting pursuant to a lawful warrant, but the basis for issuing a warrant to search a woman's vagina was never questioned.

At other times, strip and cavity searches are simply deployed as another tool of police violence. In a case described in detail in Beth Richie's *Arrested Justice: Black Women, Violence, and America's Prison Nation*, Diane Bond, a fifty-year-old Black woman, was forced into her apartment at gunpoint by Chicago police officers who then ordered her to undress, bend over, expose her genitalia to the male officers, and reach inside her own vagina under threat of having her teeth removed with needle-nose pliers unless she complied. Although she successfully sued them, none of the officers have been disciplined or prosecuted for their torture and terrorization of Diane.[86]

RESISTANCE

What can and should we be doing to prevent police sexual violence? At a minimum, we need to collectively commit to challenging its continuing and seemingly intractable invisibility, even in moments of heightened awareness and discussion of police violence. As Ahmad Greene-Hayes, who works with Black Lives Matter NYC and Black Women's Blueprint, put it in an article by Darnell Moore critiquing the movement's unilateral focus on police shootings to the exclusion of sexual violence, "Safety, in light of police brutality, means organizing against racial-sexual violence. . . . Police officers can be killers, but they can also be rapists."[87] Experience and research demonstrate that naming the issue increases the likelihood that survivors feel safe(r) in coming out of the shadows.[88]

As an initial step, we need to create space for survivors to come forward that do not require them to turn to the very institution that perpetrated sexual violence against them. In the vast majority of jurisdictions, survivors of police sexual violence are pointed in a single direction for redress: the police. Even where civilian oversight mechanisms exist, the vast majority are neither equipped nor empowered to receive complaints of police sexual violence; instead, they refer cases to local prosecutors, who in turn refer them to the police. In October 2016, while finishing this manuscript, I testified before the New York City Civilian Complaint Review Board, urging the entity—one of the first and largest civilian oversight bodies in the country—to set an example and play a leadership role by launching a public awareness campaign and creating an infrastructure, complete with supports for survivors, that would enable them to collect, analyze, and publish data about complaints of police sexual violence. Doing so could inform prevention efforts, as well as promote accountability without requiring women to go to the police.[89]

In light of the many obstacles survivors face to come forward, particularly high for populations targeted for police sexual violence, we also need to move away from strategies reliant on receiving and adjudicating individual complaints, whether in criminal, civil, or administrative venues, and move toward proactive and systemic approaches.[90] The most effective measure is to reduce opportunities for law enforcement officers to engage and hold power over women of color. This would mean, for instance, ending the war on drugs and broken windows policing, decriminalizing prostitution and poverty-related offenses, developing alternate responses to domestic violence and mental health crises, and creating community supports and safety mechanisms. Law enforcement officers particularly leverage their power to demand sexual acts in exchange for avoiding charges carrying long sentences and multiple collateral consequences, including the possibility of losing housing or custody of children if convicted of a drug- or prostitution-related offense.[91]

Until we are able to take police out of the equation altogether, we need harm reduction strategies. Researchers emphasize that comprehensive written policies setting forth clear accountability processes are essential to preventing and addressing police sexual violence.[92] Of course, policies alone are never enough—prevention, implementation, independent oversight, and accountability are essential. Once caught, officers shouldn't be able to simply move from one jurisdiction to the next.[93] Yet, as a Soros Justice Fellow, I found that more than half of thirty-six police departments among the top fifty in the US *had no policy whatsoever* explicitly prohibiting police sexual violence against members of the public.[94] A 2016 *Al-Jazeera* investigation found that only three in twenty police departments had any policy explicitly prohibiting police sexual misconduct.[95] The International Association of Chiefs of Police has no information on how many departments have followed its 2011 Guidance.[96] Departments clearly aren't taking action on their own. But, the IACP notes, "we don't see a groundswell from people who are protesting their police departments for this kind of activity."[97] It's clearly time that they did.

We need to fully integrate the issue of police sexual violence into our policy advocacy agendas. In 2014, bolstered by more than seventy-five antiviolence, racial justice, and police accountability organizations and advocates who signed on to my submission on police violence against women to the President's Task Force on 21st-Century Policing, convened by President Obama in 2014 in the wake of outrage and resistance in the streets of Ferguson and across the country, I called for national action on police sexual violence. In response, the task force recommended that the DOJ develop and disseminate a model policy for law enforcement agencies, and that the federal government collect data on the issue.[98] It's now up to us to reduce the harms of policing by integrating demands relating to police sexual violence into police reform agendas.

Antiviolence advocates must also take up the charge. As far as I know, I was also the only person to speak on the issue of police sexual violence at the United State of Women, a day-long White House summit covering a broad range of violence and structural issues affecting women, held in June 2016. While waiting in line to enter, I was asked what I would be speaking about; when I answered, I was met with blank stares from mainstream antiviolence advocates. After a three-year process, the DOJ issued a *Guidance on Gender Bias in Policing* in 2016 that makes reference to police sexual violence, giving antiviolence advocates ammunition to call on local police departments to take action on the issue. As I said when concluding my remarks at the Summit, no survivor of rape or sexual assault should be left out in the cold, out of the conversation, or out of the solution just because her rapist or perpetrator was a police officer.

Beyond policy advocacy, what does it look like to stand with survivors of police sexual violence? Oklahoma City Artists for Justice was founded by Grace Franklin and Candace Liger in response to the arrest of Daniel Holtzclaw.[99] Franklin described the reasons for the group's founding: "We are Black women. It could have been us. . . . We had to speak up."[100] The two founders frequently tell the story of how they reached out to the local YWCA for support when the case first broke, only to be told that the nonprofit's relationship with law enforcement precluded it from taking a stand. OKC Artists for Justice forged ahead without them, becoming a regular presence outside the courthouse at each hearing and in discussions across the country, challenging Holtzclaw's sexual violence, his efforts to discredit the women he targeted, and the institutions that lined up to support him (see insert for protest photo). As the case gained national attention, OKC Artists for Justice were joined by BWBP, which organized a caravan to travel to Oklahoma City to stand with the survivors during trial and sentencing, and by Barbara Arnwine of the Transformative Justice Coalition and Kimberlé Crenshaw of the African American Policy Forum in an effort to bring national media attention to the case.

Although local and national women's groups called for Holtzclaw to be held without bond and subjected to the heaviest possible sentence upon conviction—263 years—BWBP highlighted the limitations of criminal legal responses to police sexual violence after Holtzclaw's conviction and sentence, issuing a call

> for sustainable justice strategies and a call to envision justice for ourselves, survivors, and future generations; a visioning of justice beyond what the prison system and criminal justice system offers. One conviction does not end rape. . . . Historically the criminal justice system has seldom represented a safe space or answer for Black women. . . . Beyond reactionary prison system responses that fail to prevent rape from happening in the first place and don't stop it from happening again, we ask your response to this question: What would justice really look like to Black women survivors of sexual assault?[101]

That is the question we are called to answer.

CHAPTER 6

POLICING GENDER LINES*

Although the role of law enforcement in policing lines of race and class is generally recognized, until more recently their role in constructing and enforcing racialized borders of gender has been less visible. When gender has been addressed in the context of policing, discussion has largely focused on the targeting of men of color *by* law enforcement and the role of women *in* law enforcement.[1] Yet, throughout US history, police have consistently targeted women and gender-nonconforming people and used harassment, physical and sexual violence, arrest, lethal force, and denial of protection to produce, maintain, and reify racially constructed gender norms, even as the legal landscape of gender has shifted over time. Gender represents a central axis around which policing takes place, and gender policing is embedded in, operates in conjunction with, and furthers policing of race, class, and nation.

The lines of gender are drawn most literally between a false gender binary that tolerates no deviation in appearance, behavior, or expression from characteristics associated with the gender assigned at birth, leading to suspicion and presumptions of instability, criminality, fraud, and violence in police interactions with transgender and gender-nonconforming people, particularly of color.[2] Additionally, as feminists of color have taught us, the lines of gender are also drawn around idealized notions of white womanhood developed in service of white supremacy, which implicitly exclude and punish nonwhite women. This is often accomplished through deployment of controlling narratives constructing women of color in opposition to characteristics imputed to pure and innocent white women: chastity, motherhood, domesticity, piety,

---

* This chapter is based in part on a draft coauthored with Z. Gabriel Arkles in 2010.

and meekness. These narratives, and the structural relations of power they serve, inform daily police interactions and exercises of discretion. Finally, throughout US history, women who departed from chaste and domestic gender roles—for instance, by traveling unaccompanied on the streets at night, being "drunken and disorderly," or engaging in "lewd and lascivious behavior"—have been criminalized.[3] This chapter focuses primarily on the policing of the gender binary, while other forms of racialized gender policing are explored throughout the book.

CLOTHING

Although the terms "trans," "transgender," and "gender nonconforming" evolved relatively recently, individuals and societies whose expressions of gender transcend rigid binary constructions have long existed. As described in chapter 1, imposition of a binary gender system was essential to the project of colonization, justifying violence against Indigenous peoples framed as existing beyond European-imposed understandings of gender.[4] Gary Bowen, a trans man of Native descent, author, and organizer, emphasizes that Native people "have been murdered, burned, beaten, hanged, imprisoned, flogged, stripped, humiliated, and otherwise forced into compliance with dominant standards of gender and sexuality or exterminated when they resisted."[5] Coercive enforcement of binary and hierarchical notions of gender has continued throughout US history through punishment of individuals who fail to meet racialized ideals of gender.

Enforcement of sumptuary laws—laws designed to regulate habits on moral or religious grounds—is one of the more recognized forms of gender policing.[6] Law professor I. Bennett Capers explains that such laws supplemented and replaced laws prohibiting enslaved people and people of lower classes from wearing clothing associated with ruling classes:

> Between 1850 and 1870, just as the abolitionist movement, then the Civil War, and then Reconstruction were disrupting the subordinate/ superordinate balance between blacks and whites, just as middle class women were demanding social and economic equality, agitating for

the right to vote, and quite literally their right to wear pants, and just as lesbian and gay subcultures were emerging in large cities, jurisdictions began passing sumptuary legislation which had the effect of reifying sex and gender distinctions.[7]

Historian Clare Sears describes the passage of laws prohibiting cross-dressing in San Francisco as a formalized expression of "[state] interest in defining and policing normative gender as part of the work of governance . . . pushing previously tolerated cross-dressing and commercial sex practices to the margins, as acts that no longer belonged in everyday public life."[8] Enforcement focused on "feminist dress reformers, 'fast young women' who dressed as men for a night on the town, female impersonators, and people whose gender identifications did not match their anatomy in legally accepted ways." Police drew lines not only between men and women but also around "gender appropriate" behaviors, attempting to neutralize "threats to male dominance posed by dress reform feminists who defied women's confinement in the private sphere, threats to sexual morality posed by cross-dressing 'degenerates' who caroused in bars . . . and threats to the cultural imperative of gender legibility posed by people with a gender identity that diverged from their legal sex."

Enforcement required police to scrutinize bodies in the public sphere for any "ostensible disjuncture of gendered clothing and sexed body." San Francisco officers used "the size of a suspect's hands and feet, the presence or absence of facial hair, the . . . way he or she walked" as markers of gender in the nineteenth century. These means of enforcement have not changed much over the past century and a half: present-day police officers have listed these exact characteristics when I've deposed them around how they interpret gender for purposes of arrest processing in litigation challenging unlawful searches of trans and gender-nonconforming people.[9] "Gender searches"—whether through the "removal of a wig or veil" or "jailhouse medical examination"— were endemic to enforcement of cross-dressing laws in nineteenth- century San Francisco, and remain pervasive today.[10]

When enforcing cross-dressing laws, police both produced and reinforced white normative gender.[11] In the nineteenth century, the majority of reported arrests under cross-dressing laws in San Francisco involved white women, presumably because women of color, already excluded from the bounds of "womanhood," could not transgress them by cross-dressing. Normative gender was thus inscribed as "the exclusive property of whites."[12]

Nevertheless, people of color, particularly immigrants, were occasionally targeted for the enforcement of sumptuary laws. Geraldine Portica, a light-skinned Mexican who had been raised and lived as a woman all her life, was arrested in 1917 "for wearing women's clothing on a body the police classed as male." A police officer inscribed a photograph of her with the caption "This is not a girl, but a boy," in so doing "reinscribing maleness on her body," writes Sears.[13] Portica was deported to Mexico.[14] In 1908 a Chinese youth named So Gitwho was arrested on the belief that, despite a feminine gender expression, So Gitwho was male. Newspapers claimed that So Gitwho was part of a larger criminal enterprise and framed the "Chinese cross-dressing criminal as indicative of an undifferentiated, all-consuming threat."[15] Across the country, in mid-nineteenth-century New York City, Mary Jones, also known as Peter Sewally, a Black person, was repeatedly arrested for "perambulating the streets in woman's attire."[16] Lawrence Jackson, described as a "brazen faced darky," was arrested in Chicago for "promenading on Clark avenue wearing female attire" in 1881.[17] Such arrests were not confined to urban environments: Babe Bean, a gender-nonconforming Latinx person described as a "passing woman," was arrested in Stockton, California, in 1897 for cross-dressing.[18]

Immigration authorities and the public both projected gender nonconformity wholesale onto Chinese migrants within the broader context of the Chinese Exclusion Act of 1882.[19] Proponents of Chinese exclusion "deployed cross-dressing imagery in their constructions of national belonging, linking Chinese immigrants in particular to gender deviance and deceit."[20] In this context, according to Sears, "masculinizing accounts of Chinese women joined feminizing accounts of Chinese men to produce an image of Chinese gender as utterly illegible," a kind of "foreign and pathological formation," deployed "to produce and police the racialized borders of the nation-state," justifying exclusion and informing policing of Asian women both as presumed "prostitutes" and as masculinized threats.[21]

For much of the twentieth century, police used sumptuary laws to punish gender nonconformity among drag queens, transgender women, and butch lesbians of color.[22] Piri, a self-described "Black stud"—a term used by lesbians of color on the masculine end of the gender spectrum—who experienced police brutality and arrest for wearing men's clothing in the 1940s and 1950s, said, "At the time, when they pick you up, if you didn't have two garments that belong to a woman, you could go to jail . . . and the same thing with a man. . . . They call it male impersonation or female impersonation and they'd take you downtown. . . . It would give them the opportunity to whack the shit out of you."[23] Poet and activist Audre Lorde similarly wrote that "there were always rumors of plainclothes women circulating among us, looking for gaygirls with fewer than three pieces of female attire."[24] Trans women and self-identified drag queens of color were often rounded up and arrested on the basis of cross-dressing laws.[25] Sylvia Rivera, a Puerto Rican revolutionary and veteran of the Stonewall Uprising in New York City in 1969, remembers: "When I was growing up, if you walked down Forty-Second Street and even looked like a faggot, you were going to jail. I went to jail a lot of times."[26] At times, perceived violations of cross-dressing laws proved fatal: in 1970, police shot a young Black person in Chicago in the back eight times after seeing the person on the street wearing women's clothes; the person had previously been arrested and charged with "impersonating the opposite sex."[27]

While enforcement continued through the twentieth century, courts began striking down sumptuary laws in the 1970s. Yet formal changes in the law have not translated into an end to policing of perceived violations of gender norms in clothing, particularly for women and trans people of color. For instance, in 2002, a Black lesbian reported that Washington, DC, police officers unbuttoned her trousers during a street search, asking her, "Why are you wearing boys' underwear? Are you a dyke? Do you eat pussy?"[28] Latinx lesbians report increased police harassment when they are "dressed like a guy." Feminine attire worn by transgender women is pervasively cited by police as grounds

for suspicion that they are engaged in prostitution or "lewd conduct."
Vivianna Hernandez of the Los Angeles LGBT Center told me as I was
researching *Stonewalled*, "They used to arrest us for wearing women's
clothing. Now they arrest us for loitering with intent to solicit."[29] The
ease with which one charge is substituted for another should come as
no surprise: according to Clare Sears, "The emergence of cross-dressing
law was intimately bound up with the regulation of prostitution," as
both offenses were prohibited within a broader set of regulations governing what Sears terms "problem bodies."[30]

Enforced in the United States until as recently as the 1980s, sumptuary laws left a powerful legacy of presumptions that people whose appearance is deemed gender nonconforming are inherently fraudulent
and mentally unstable.[31] For instance, in the 1950s, a Native person was
convicted for "defrauding the government" for living life as a woman,
marrying a soldier, and collecting associated entitlements, and was ordered to undergo psychiatric treatment to "bring out . . . masculine
qualities."[32] Half a century later, Meagan Taylor, a Black trans woman,
checked into a hotel in Des Moines, Iowa, with a friend on their way
to a funeral. The hotelkeeper called the police when the gender marker
on Meagan's ID didn't match her gender expression, assuming on this
basis that she was engaged in prostitution. Once police arrived, Meagan says they "were very forceful and disrespectful. They tried to make it
seem like we were doing something other than we were. They made my
friend take out the stuffing in her bra." Finding no evidence of prostitution, the police nevertheless arrested Meagan and charged her with using
a "fraudulent" ID and for carrying medication without a prescription,
something many of us do on a regular basis, yet in her case it was seen
as another crime of "fraud." She and her friend spent eight days in jail
because they couldn't post bail—and missed the funeral they were traveling to attend. Meagan filed a complaint against the hotel before the
Iowa Civil Rights Commission, and the case was settled to her satisfaction. Meagan later wrote, "When this all happened, I knew exactly what
it was: the racial profiling, the transgender profiling, the harassment, the
solitary confinement. I knew why it was happening, and I knew it wasn't
right. I knew something had to change. To experience so many levels of

discrimination makes you feel like less of a person. I want to stand up for myself and other Black and transgender people. And so I did."[33]

A perception of fraud also led to criminal charges for seventeen-year-old Bianca Feliciano, a Latinx trans woman. She was with a Black trans friend in the town of Cicero, just outside of Chicago, when they were stopped for "walking while trans." According to police, they were in "an area known for a high concentration for prostitution." There was no evidence that they were there to trade sex. When Bianca produced identification reflecting her legal name and a female gender marker, the officer told her she was not female "because she had a dick in between her legs." When she protested, he threatened her with physical violence and a fraud charge for misrepresenting her gender on her state ID. The officers then searched Bianca's purse and found a pack of menthol cigarettes and a sock with a rock in it—not of crack, but a stone for self-defense, presumably against transphobic attacks. Bianca was charged with possession of tobacco as a minor and a phony weapons-related offense. At the precinct, officers referred to her as male both to her face and in reports, mocked her "titties," and forced her to reveal the male name she was given at birth. To top it off, the police refused to give Bianca back her state ID upon her release. Represented by my *Queer (In) Justice* coauthor Joey Mogul, Bianca successfully sued the City of Cicero and secured an agreement that they would adopt a policy on police interactions with trans people.

According to law professor Gabriel Arkles, cross-dressing continues to be used as evidence in criminal cases and commitment proceedings.[34] For instance, in 2006, NYPD officers stopped a person wearing a women's sweater, eyeliner, an earring, and a ponytail as the person was standing on the street with two friends from a homeless shelter and looking for something in a purse. Claiming the individual was a "man with a purse," the officers questioned and then arrested the person for theft of the purse. The trial court found no lawful basis for the stop, noting that the person in question was unquestionably of "transgender appearance," and concluded that under the circumstances merely carrying a purse was not enough to justify the stop. However, the appellate court reversed the decision, determining that the person could not possibly be transgender because when arrested the person's face had stubble and the person was wearing a dark jacket over a red shirt and jeans. Having, with a stroke of the pen, determined that transgender people do not wear jackets and/or allow facial hair to show (even if homeless and recently arrested), the court ruled police could stop someone they perceived to be "an unshaven male rifling through a woman's purse," thereby explicitly condoning police presumptions of criminality based on arbitrary and unwritten rules of appropriate gender presentation and expression.[35]

BATHROOM POLICING

Even in the absence of laws explicitly regulating their use, bathrooms and other sex-segregated facilities become intense sites of enforcement of the gender binary, with particularly severe consequences for transgender people of color and women of color perceived to defy gender norms.[36] For instance, Mandy Carter, a founder of Southerners on New Ground, reported that following Hurricane Katrina, Sharlie Arpollo Vicks, a Black trans woman from New Orleans, was arrested and held for six days for using the women's shower at a Texas evacuation center.[37] Such arrests regularly take place nationwide, even though, with the exception of recently adopted North Carolina Public Facilities Privacy and Security Act, known as House Bill 2, and copycat legislation in other jurisdictions, there are generally no laws requiring individuals to have any particular set of characteristics in order to use a bathroom labeled "men" or "women."[38] Nevertheless, police can make arrests on the basis of offenses such as "disorderly conduct," "indecent exposure," or trespassing laws if a property owner or manager complains.

Though transgender people bear the brunt of police abuse in connection with use of gender-segregated bathrooms, nontransgender women of color who do not conform to racialized notions of feminine appearance are also caught in the web of gender policing. For instance, in *Arab American Feminisms*, Huda Jaddallah, a gender-nonconforming Palestinian lesbian, describes being mistaken for a man and being perceived as "violent and dangerous" when she enters a women's restroom.[39] Similarly, when I was researching *Stonewalled*, an activist told me about a nontrans Black woman who plays on a women's football team and was violently arrested after using the women's bathroom in a restaurant in the Washington, DC, area.[40]

"CLASSIFICATION ANXIETY"

Beyond directly policing the lines of gender by enforcing compliance with norms of attire and bathroom use, police enforce racialized gender conformity in myriad ways on a daily basis, in virtually every interaction with women and gender-nonconforming people of color. This includes demanding identification as proof of gender authenticity and imposing genders on individuals taken into police custody, often based on violative and unlawful searches. When officers experience "classification anxiety" in routine daily police interactions, they treat transgender and gender-nonconforming people as threatening because they place in question "identities previously conceived as stable, unchallengeable, grounded and 'known,'" which serve as critical tools of heterosexist culture.[41] As a result, failure to meet individual police officers' subjective expectations of gender appropriate behavior is read as embodying "disorder," giving rise at a minimum to intensified scrutiny that often escalates to verbal and sexual harassment, detention, and citation or arrest.[42] Ultimately, law enforcement officers imagine and enforce highly racialized and deeply classed social constructions and relations of gender in daily interactions with women and gender-nonconforming people of color. They project narratives rooted in white supremacist heteropatriarchy onto our racially gendered bodies, then act on and enforce them through surveillance and suspicion, violence and violation.[43]

By providing officers with a plethora of both vague and specific laws and almost unlimited discretion in enforcing them, broken windows policing facilitates the process of racialized gender policing. Take the case of Allen Galbreath, a Black gender-nonconforming former ballet dancer who one day in July of 2010 went to a park in Oklahoma City to perform morning exercises wearing high heels, carrying a red purse and a cane, and wearing lipstick. After receiving a 911 call describing Allen, a police officer accosted, questioned, and arrested Allen for "disorderly conduct," despite the absence of any evidence that

Allen was disturbing anyone's peace. Allen vigorously protested the stop and arrest as motivated by race and by gender nonconformity.[44] The criminal charges were dismissed, and Allen filed a civil lawsuit challenging the officer's actions as unconstitutional. Unfortunately, Allen's claims were ultimately dismissed after a jury trial endorsing officers' use of vague "quality of life" offenses to police gender expression in public spaces.[45]

In the context of broken windows policing, responses to police demands for identification during stops motivated by racial and other forms of profiling become sites of gender policing, such as when officers demand to see individuals' "real" IDs or know their "real" names when the gender markers on ID don't match the gender individuals are expressing, or what an officer thinks they should be expressing. Trans people face significant barriers to accessing IDs that accurately reflect their gender, facing a web of complex and often conflicting rules that vary widely from jurisdiction to jurisdiction and agency to agency.[46] This is further complicated by increasingly restrictive rules for obtaining any identification, primarily motivated by anti-immigrant sentiment and post-9/11 fearmongering. Consequently, many trans people have IDs that inaccurately list their gender, or have different gender markers on different pieces of ID. As in Bianca's case, an officer's request for identification can quickly escalate to verbal abuse, physical violence, and arrest.[47] Additionally, failure to produce ID can, in and of itself, serve as a basis for arrest, regardless of whether an individual has committed a crime.[48] Even in states that do not require individuals to produce identification on demand, other offenses, such as "disorderly conduct," are deployed to the same end.

Trans people also face criminalization for carrying syringes to administer hormones, whether prescribed or obtained by other means.[49] This can lead to arrest on the presumption that the presence of syringes signals intravenous drug use, and to physical violence based on perceptions that syringes endanger officers during searches. Additionally, lack of coverage for gender-affirming health care in many states leaves many trans people without health-care options. As a result, some trans people have formed informal networks of support, which can include giving, taking, buying, selling, and sharing information about hormones, silicone, and other forms of treatment without the intervention of medical authorities. This renders them more vulnerable to criminalization.

HARASSMENT AND PHYSICAL AND SEXUAL VIOLENCE

Police often respond to gender nonconformity with "street justice," administered through verbal harassment and abuse, including slurs such as "faggot," "dyke," "tranny," "he/she," "freak," and "bitch," and often accompanied by physical violence.[50]

Black lesbians frequently report being punched in the chest by officers saying something like, "You want to act like a man, I'll treat you like a man."[51] One woman filed a complaint with the New York City Civilian Complaint Review Board because an officer grabbed her as she was arguing with her girlfriend. When she protested, the officer replied, "I don't give a fuck if you're female, you gay bitch. I will arrest you right now if you think you're a man."[52]

More than half of transgender participants in the 2015 US Transgender Survey who interacted with officers who knew the participants were transgender reported some form of violence or abuse by police. Native trans women were most likely to report police violence, followed by Black trans women and multiracial trans women.[53] Organizations around the country have documented high levels of harassment and violence against trans women by police.[54] In studies conducted in New York and Los Angeles, more than half to two-thirds of respondents reported verbal or physical abuse.[55] Studies consistently find that Black, Native, and Latinx trans people are at greatest risk of harassment, physical assault, and sexual violence.[56] The community-based organization Make the Road New York reports Elena's experience: "The cops stopped her and asked her what she was doing. She replied she was getting coffee. The cops proceeded to take the coffee from her, throw it on the ground and on her feet and told her to 'get on your knees, you fucking faggot.' She was kept on her knees for over thirty minutes until she was finally put in a police van and taken to the local precinct."[57]Another trans woman told Human Rights Watch, "They pat-frisk you, they ask if you have fake boobs, take them off right there, if you have a wig, take it off. It's humiliating."[58]

Such acts of violence are part of the daily policing of gender taking place in communities across the country. Often acts of police violence are informed by racialized and gendered narratives framing women of color and transgender people of color as inherently devious, mercurially violent, superhumanly strong, and, most of all, deserving of annihilation or disappearance, to be literally stamped out or locked away.

SEARCHES

Law enforcement agents frequently conduct "gender checks": searches aimed solely or primarily at determining an individual's physical characteristics for the purposes of assigning a gender, to punish and humiliate trans people, to satisfy their curiosity, or for sexual gratification. From police officers calling out to transgender women on the streets saying, "Show me your tits," to groping chests and groins during routine searches, police gender checks are a daily reality for gender-nonconforming women and transgender people of color nationwide.[59]

One trans client of mine was ordered to drop her pants and bend over to expose her genital area in a New York City precinct so that an officer could "determine" her gender. Once brought to a booking facility, although she had already been held with women without incident, an officer groped her genitals during a pat search and placed her with men. When she questioned the searching officer about why she was being subjected to a search no other women transported with her experienced, the officer told her that another officer said she was "a guy." Hers is just one in a series of cases I have litigated or become aware of over the past decade. While there are variations on this theme—from demands that people raise their shirts or drop their pants to often painful and assaultive groping, to invasive and completely unnecessary and unauthorized questioning about anatomical features, surgeries, and medical treatment, to strip searches and visual cavity searches and other forms of discriminatory treatment in police custody—experiences such as this are as common as they are unconstitutional.[60]

RESISTANCE

Resistance to gender policing takes many forms, both individual and collective. The Welfare Warriors Research Collaborative of Queers for Economic Justice emphasized in *A Fabulous Attitude: Low Income LGBTQGNC People Surviving and Thriving on Love and Shelter*:

> As we negotiate social spaces, government agencies and our identities on a daily basis, we witness how all people are gendered both institutionally and relationally. In particular, we experience and know how . . . [we] must navigate and resist criminalizing forms of gendering while we powerfully self-determine our own genders . . . gender is a sociopolitical site of both violence and resistance.[61]

One of the first cases of resistance to police violence against trans people framed in the context of broader struggles against police brutality that I became aware of involved JaLea Lamot. JaLea was a Puerto Rican trans woman whose case was brought to light by the ALP's Working Group on Police and State Violence (WGPV), formed in 1997 "in response to a rash of street violence, repressive state violence tactics, an increase of police harassment, and brutality, and the 'Quality of Life' policies of the Giuliani administration."[62] WGPV was a member of the Coalition Against Police Brutality in New York City.[63] When JaLea's mother couldn't awaken her after she had taken cold medication, she called the police for assistance. By the time they arrived JaLea was awake, and responding officers began to sexually harass her. Upon discovering that she was transgender, they referred to her using slurs such as "trans-testicle" and beat and pepper-sprayed her and her family. Then they took JaLea to hospital for involuntary psychiatric observation, where she was held for seventy-two hours on the pretense that she was suicidal. Officers also arrested her mother and brother for coming to her defense. JaLea firmly believed that the treatment she and her family received was informed by officers feeling "tricked" by her gender expression—and embarrassed by their sexual attraction to her.[64]

JaLea's case not only reflects the punishment meted out by officers enforcing the gender binary—and against women who resist their

sexual advances—it also illustrates the deep roots of collaboration between law enforcement and psychiatric authorities to police and punish
trans and gender-nonconforming individuals. As Clare Sears notes, "A
cross-dressing arrest could trigger an insanity hearing with devastating
results" including incarceration in asylums and, for immigrants, deportation.[65] In many instances, police violence against women and gender-
nonconforming people of color is premised on perceptions that gender
nonconformity is linked to mental illness, and that mentally ill people
are threats who must be punished, confined, and "cured." Consequently,
law enforcement agents have systematically channeled transgender and
gender-nonconforming individuals into psychiatric institutions.

The ALP worked with the National Congress of Puerto Rican Rights
Justice Committee and other members of the Coalition Against Police
Brutality to call attention to JaLea's case, successfully generating outrage among nonqueer communities. Together they organized to get the
charges against JaLea and her family dropped, holding protests, press
conferences, and strategy sessions while supporting family members in
their quest for accountability. Dayo Gore, a member of the WGPV, later
said of the organization's work on the case that "it has allowed us to
both go beyond the 'gay ghetto' in our understanding of police violence,
have homophobic violence taken seriously by mainstream police brutality activists, and also to raise the level of understanding and commitment to police violence issues within LGBTST [lesbian, gay, bisexual,
Two Spirit, and trans] communities at large in New York City."[66]

Organizers have also fought for systemic changes to how police
interact with trans and gender-nonconforming people. For instance,
transgender and allied activists in San Francisco, working in concert
with communities of color and police accountability groups, were
among the first to successfully organize for police policies that protect
the rights of trans people in police interactions.[67] Among other provisions, the standing orders require police officers to refer to trans people
by their preferred names, pronouns, and gendered titles and establishes
a right of trans people to public space, stating that neither a person's
gender identity nor expression, age, or "disheveled or impoverished"
appearance justifies requests for identification or detention.[68] Several

years later, in 2005, the Washington, DC, police department also yielded to community pressure by trans activists to create policies for interacting with trans people. In addition to provisions similar to San Francisco's, DC's policies mandated that officers should not assume that gender identity or expression is evidence of prostitution and strictly prohibited gender searches.[69] In 2014, a lawsuit filed by Patti Hammond Shaw, a Black trans woman, changed the way that individuals' gender would be recorded in police databases, and in January 2015, DC's policy was updated to address organizers' concerns about police response to intimate partner violence against trans people, policing of sex work, and criminalization of youth.[70]

In 2005, I filed my first lawsuit in New York City, on behalf of a white transgender woman I met while providing legal support to protesters during the 2004 Republican National Convention. When she told me about the violative search she endured while in police custody, we decided to initiate litigation to challenge the long-standing pattern of gender searches identified by local organizations such as SRLP, FIERCE!, and ALP for decades.[71] At least four other transgender women, several of whom I also represented, subsequently sued the NYPD on the same grounds. Ultimately, in the face of litigation and public pressure, the NYPD expressed a willingness to change its policies. A group of advocates researched policies in DC and San Francisco, consulted with trans community members, including incarcerated transgender people and organizers from other cities, and developed a comprehensive set of policy proposals. After eighteen months of negotiations we reached an agreement with the NYPD, and new policies were adopted and announced in June 2012. Despite being the most progressive policies in place at the time, they continue to be violated on a regular basis. As a result, many of the groups involved in securing the changes have continued to call for an independent audit of the policies' implementation.[72]

In 2010, the DOJ responded to long-standing community pressure, intensified after egregious police violence following Hurricane Katrina, to conduct an investigation of the New Orleans Police Department (NOPD). That fall, the New Orleans–based organization BreakOUT! organized hearings with other community organizations during which

LGBTQ youth, particularly Black transgender young women, reported pervasive profiling, verbal and sexual harassment by police officers, accusations of falsely identifying themselves when they presenting their IDs, and arrests of queer youth after they had called for help. LGBTQ youth reported that they had been called names and verbally harassed, approached for sex or sexually assaulted by NOPD officers, or had their rights abused in other ways. Ultimately, the DOJ specifically named discriminatory policing practices against LGBTQ youth and transgender women as an area of top concern.

Anchored by the Louisiana Justice Institute, community activists and organizations drafted a "People's Consent Decree" outlining changes that they wanted to see mandated by the DOJ, including policies related to the policing of LGBTQ people collectively developed by BreakOUT! members. In July 2012, thanks to these efforts, the DOJ and NOPD adopted a consent decree that included unprecedented language prohibiting police profiling and harassment based on sexual orientation and gender identity, and requiring the department to develop a policy governing interactions with LGBTQ people.

BreakOUT! members engaged in a collective process to develop a proposed policy, sifting through policies from San Francisco, Washington, DC, New York, and Portland, and relying on the experiences of its members as the experts on reforms that were needed. The organization mounted a campaign highlighting the common interests of LGBTQTS, youth, racial justice, and immigrant rights groups in fighting discriminatory policing and police profiling, culminating in a rally at the steps of the NOPD headquarters in support of the proposed policy. Ultimately, the NOPD adopted policies including many of the provisions proposed by BreakOUT! youth, although it has been slow to implement them. BreakOUT! continues to work toward ending criminalization of trans and queer youth of color, recognizing that policy change is not enough to protect its members from abusive policing.[73]

Indeed, the state's interest in establishing and maintaining clear and immutable racialized gender categorizations as a means of distributing and regulating power and access to social benefits persists, even as laws explicitly regulating public expressions of gender are struck down, justice is achieved in individual cases, and police policies evolve.[74] It is therefore essential that we attend to and challenge the ways in which police enforce the borders of the gender binary and regulate and criminalize racialized gender nonconformity in daily interactions within broader analyses of profiling and criminalization.

CHAPTER 7

POLICING SEX

Policing sex, often inextricably intertwined with the racialized policing of gender, is one of the cornerstones of policing of women of color.[1] As stated in *Queer (In)Justice*, "The role of policing in upholding systems of gendered power relations, conventional notions of morality, and sexual conformity cannot be overlooked. Gender and sex policing are not only important weapons of policing race and class, but also critical independent functions of law enforcement."[2] For women of color, policing of sex and sexuality takes place primarily through enforcement of laws against prostitution but also through police violence toward, and responses to, lesbian, bisexual, queer, and trans women.

Policing of prostitution[3] is a principal site of criminalization of women of color, fueled by controlling narratives deeply rooted in colonial logics and relations of power that frame Black, Indigenous, and Asian women as inherently and pathologically sexually deviant, prone to promiscuity, and ultimately interchangeable with the social category of "prostitute"—a term generally intended and experienced as a slur, reducing the person described to a profoundly stigmatized act and set of assumptions about people who engage in sexual exchange. As introduced in chapter 1, as a result of colonial land theft and genocide, Indigenous women were often forced, expected, chose or had no choice but to trade sex for their own survival and that of their families and communities. This reality, on which images of sexually degenerate Native peoples propagated by colonizers were superimposed, produced persistent perceptions of Indigenous women as inherently inclined to prostitution and therefore undeserving of protection from sexual and other forms of violence. Similarly, controlling narratives of the licentious "Jezebel" projected onto enslaved African women as cover and justification for systemic rape during chattel slavery engraved the intractable label of "prostitute" onto Black women's bodies.[4] Perceptions of Asian women as "prostitutes," and "vector[s] of disease" drove the introduction of the 1875 Page Act to exclude Chinese women from the United States.[5] Although not as enshrined in law, immigration enforcement and policing practices also cast similar aspersions on the morality of South Asian women.[6] Latinxs, historically stereotyped as "passionate" and "hot blooded," are also framed as prone to prostitution: for instance, in mid-nineteenth-century San Francisco, Latinx women who lived in the Little Chile neighborhood were described as "immodest and impure to a shocking degree. . . . By night . . . they were only prostitutes."[7] Finally, gender nonconformity in appearance or behavior across racial groups has historically been perceived as a sign of sexual deviance and depravity by police, leading to pervasive profiling and verbal and physical abuse of transgender and gender-nonconforming women as sex workers, and of gender-nonconforming lesbians as pimps, or "promoters," of their more feminine partners.[8]

Together, these narratives serve as the backdrop for policing of prostitution then and now. While the policing of prostitution has at times been justified as "protection" or rehabilitation of "wayward" (white) women, police have consistently perceived women of color's bodies as a sexualized threat in public spaces and have punished them through profiling, criminalization, and violence.

EVOLUTION OF ENFORCEMENT OF ANTIPROSTITUTION LAWS

As historian Clare Sears elaborates, in the second half of the nineteenth century, emerging urban police forces took on the regulation of gender and sexual mores through street policing and vice operations.[9] From its inception, the enforcement of prostitution laws evoked "spatial governmentality," requiring the removal from public spaces of individuals branded as signs of disorder—similar to today's broken windows policing. These "problem bodies," as Sears describes them, included "Chinese immigrants, prostitutes, and those deemed diseased or maimed," who were treated as "urban blight" and subject to "spatial control" through "exclusion, confinement, concealment and removal."[10] In addition to selective enforcement of prostitution laws against Chinese women, in 1865, the San Francisco government also issued an "order to remove Chinese women of ill-fame from certain limits of the city."[11] The following year, 137 women—virtually all Chinese—were arrested as "common prostitutes," and the chief of police "boasted that he had used the law to expel three hundred Chinese women."[12]

Enforcement of prostitution laws has also always been highly discretionary and selective. According to Sears, "Early attempts to police prostitution targeted Chinese and Mexican women, overlooking similar acts by European Americans." Sears points to an 1855 cartoon as evidence "depicting two policemen forcefully arresting fully clothed Chinese women while ignoring the blatant sexual display of a semi-naked European American woman who beckoned a man into a brothel."[13] Racial disparities in enforcement were justified by framing "Spanish and Chinese" women engaged in prostitution as "subhuman 'vile characters' who 'infested' the city and deserved to be 'treated with little mercy.'"[14]

In Chicago's Levee district, similar principles were applied to clear public spaces and neighborhoods of "black women of bad character," who were subjected to fines up to twenty times those imposed on white women.[15] Brothel raids were also a daily occurrence in which "portraits of unsafe and disorderly black women and their places of work were vividly juxtaposed against descriptions of gentility and the grandeur of the Levee's [white] parlor houses and their white employees." The presence of the sex trade in the Levee was attributed to the neighborhood's "unclean and reprobate immigrants and lodgers 'of African extraction.'" Racist tropes were projected onto the bodies of Black women who worked in the area, who were depicted as "dark forms lurking in alleyways and doors eager for prey," "dusky female characters of whom the police have a wholesome dread," and "of such marvelous strength that no officer on the force would undertake to arrest her single-handed." One Black woman, dubbed "the Bengal Tigress," was described as having "the explosive violence of a predatory animal," and "always was ready to battle with the police when her place was raided." According to Blair, "A composite sketch of the black prostitute . . . pulls together a strange bundle of excesses. Extraordinarily large in height and girth and possessing brutish strength and cunning, she was prone to violent rages and harbored an insatiable appetite for criminal activity . . . in sheer strength and violence of character, she was larger-than-life." Such imagery firmly removed Black women from the realm of femininity.

As a result, prostitution arrests in turn-of-the-century Chicago evidenced significant racial disparities—as they continue to do today. In 1922, Black women made up less than 5 percent of the city's population, yet

> Black women accounted for one third of all women arrested as inmates in houses of prostitution in Chicago. By 1924, black women consistently composed more than half. . . . At the outset of the Great Depression, black women's proportion of all such arrests had increased to an astounding 78 percent. The same pattern held for women arrested as keepers of houses of prostitution. In 1922, 28 percent were African American, but in 1930, 70 percent of all women arrested for running a house of prostitution were black.

Eventually, Chicago city officials seeking to expand business districts deployed police with orders to push the sex trade into the Black Belt of the city's South Side, which in turn became an increasingly criminalized neighborhood, leading to continuing police harassment and arrests of Black women in the sex trade. Similar forces resulted in the closure of San Francisco's Barbary Coast, pushing prostitution into Chinatown and the Tenderloin and Mission districts, all predominantly populated by people of color, who continued to make up a disproportionate number of arrests.

In 1919, the federal government promoted model legislation known as the Standard Vice Repression Act, which ultimately led every state, and most municipalities, to enact local laws that prohibited acts of sexual solicitation and negotiation; banned the performance of sexual acts for commercial gain; and created a stigmatized status called "common nightwalkers," which referred to individuals with a prior history of prostitution. While "common nightwalker" provisions have since been struck down on constitutional grounds, their legacy lives on in the daily policing of prostitution, where in many jurisdictions simply being or being perceived to be a "known prostitute" is an element or evidence of prostitution-related offenses.[16]

In the early twentieth century, vagrancy laws—now retooled into offenses like "loitering for the purposes of prostitution"—were used to target people believed to be engaged in prostitution, including transgender people.[17] In the 1940s and 1950s, police in San Francisco and other cities waged a "war on vice," which targeted "homosexuals," "prostitutes," and women in bars.[18] Raids of queer bars, although primarily framed as attacks on white gay men, also captured women of color, such as Ethel Whitaker, a butch Black woman arrested in the infamous 1961 raid of the Tay-Bush Inn.[19] Lesbians—often conflated with "prostitutes" in the public imagination and sometimes engaged in the sex trades—were targeted for arrest for vice-related offenses, including "frequenting a house of ill repute."[20]

PRESENT-DAY ENFORCEMENT OF ANTIPROSTITUTION LAWS

Policing of prostitution now takes place through a combination of street-based enforcement of "loitering for the purposes of prostitution" statutes in the context of broken windows policing, "buy-bust" operations in which undercover officers lure targets into making agreements to trade sex for money in person or online, vice raids of locations in which prostitution is believed to be taking place, federal anti-trafficking raids, and civil nuisance enforcement designed to shutter places of "ill repute."

The presumed association between sex work, the drug trade, and violent crime is frequently used to justify sweeps of areas where prostitution is believed to take place. Additionally, vague "quality of life" regulations such as "loitering for the purposes of prostitution" or disorderly conduct allow police officers considerable discretion when determining who is disorderly or what constitutes evidence of intent to prostitute. Both are clearly very much in the eye of the beholder, whose perceptions are deeply informed by the operation and reinforcement of controlling narratives framing women of color, including trans women of color, as inherently and always engaged in sexually deviant activity.[21]

Associations between gender nonconformity and involvement in the sex trade are so prevalent that pervasive profiling of trans women has been dubbed "walking while trans." GiGi Thomas, formerly an outreach worker with Helping Individual Prostitutes Survive (HIPS) in Washington, DC, reports that police "arrest all transgender women in certain areas on suspicion of their engagement in prostitution"[22] Thirty percent of Black trans women, 25 percent of Latinx trans women, 23 percent of Native trans women, and 20 percent of Asian trans women who participated in the 2015 National Transgender Survey and reported interactions with police who knew they were transgender described being profiled as being engaged in prostitution.[23] Bamby Salcedo, one of the founders of the TransLatina Coalition in Los Angeles, told Human Rights Watch, "We've done protests in front of the police department about the continuous harassment to the community members. . . . They have to go to the store, they have to take a bus, and just because they are walking they get stopped and harassed and sometimes arrested just because of where they are and how they are."[24] Sixty-three percent of young women and trans men who participated in a study of LGBTQ youth in the sex trades in New York City had been stopped by the police; over half believed racial, gender, and sexual-orientation-based profiling was the reason.[25] Kate Mogulescu, an attorney at New York City's Legal Aid Society who runs a program representing people charged with prostitution-related offenses in criminal cases, explained, "There is no other law that I can think of that gives the police that much power and discretion. . . . What you see is simply identity-based policing."[26]

Racially gendered profiling and a focus on street-based prostitution combine to produce continuing racial disparities in prostitution arrests.[27] According to one ACLU study, in the 1970s it was "seven times more likely that prostitution arrests will involve black women than women of other races."[28] A more recent study of prostitution arrests in three North Carolina cities between 1993 and 2000 found that "law enforcement's focus on outdoor prostitution appears to result in black females being arrested for prostitution at higher rates than their white counterparts and at rates disproportionate to their presence in online advertisements for indoor prostitution."[29] A 2016 lawsuit filed by the

Legal Aid Society of New York noted that 85 percent of people charged for loitering for purposes of prostitution in New York City between 2012 and 2015 were Black and Latinx, groups that together make up only 54 percent of the city's population. Half of Black transgender respondents to the 2015 US Transgender Survey who were or were perceived to be involved in the sex trades were arrested, reporting higher arrest rates than non-Black respondents.[30] Black women are also more likely to be charged with more serious prostitution-related offenses. For instance, Gloria Lockett, a Black woman who would later go on to codirect the sex workers' rights organization COYOTE (Call Off Your Old Tired Ethics), was once arrested for felony "pimping" because she was holding another woman's money for her. According to Lockett, "Racism . . . meant that she was accused of felony pimping while police charged the white women with simple misdemeanor prostitution."[31]

The Legal Aid Society litigation also highlights the ways in which antiprostitution enforcement facilitates racialized gender policing and punishes women of color for dressing "provocatively," thus reinforcing historic controlling narratives. Police complaints cited women's "tight black leggings," "mini dress with bra strap showing," "tight jeans and tank top showing cleavage" as evidence of intent to engage in prostitution.[32] Drive by the clubs on the city's Lower East Side on any given night and you'll see plenty of white women similarly attired, but arrest stats clearly demonstrate that they are not being policed in the same ways.

As Sylvia Rivera pointed out decades ago, feminine clothing on trans women is particularly likely to result in arrest. Where my client, a Black trans woman, was concerned, the officer simply told her, "We know what you trannies are doing out here," before issuing her a ticket for "loitering for the purposes of prostitution" as she stood outside a convenience store where she had just bought a snack with a group of friends. When she went into the local precinct to complain, she was violently tackled to the ground by four officers, arrested, handcuffed to a railing for eight hours, subjected to transphobic slurs, and taken for a psychiatric examination—to the bewilderment of the examining doctor, who told the police there was absolutely nothing wrong with Ryhanna that they themselves hadn't inflicted. As Tiffaney Grissom, a

Black trans woman and one of the plaintiffs in the Legal Aid lawsuit, put it, "Whether you are 'hoing or not 'hoing . . . even if you look like you might be trans, you are going to jail. . . . It is a stigma that comes with being trans. You are automatically a sexual object or a sex worker. You are no longer just a normal person."[33]

Another night, the same client was walking down the street when officers accosted her, claiming that she had nine condoms in her purse and that these were evidence of intent to engage in prostitution. In fact, she was walking to a McDonald's to grab a bite after a night at the club—as many of us have been known to do. In the context of prostitution enforcement, the presence or possession of condoms commonly serves as a tool of gendered racial profiling. Bianey Garcia, a leader at Make the Road New York, has frequently recounted similar treatment. One night in 2010 she was walking home hand-in-hand from a club with her boyfriend when eight undercover officers stopped them, threw them both up against a wall to frisk them, and emptied Bianey's purse onto the sidewalk. She was carrying three condoms, which the officers then cited as evidence to justify her arrest for engaging in prostitution.[34] Forty-four percent of respondents to the 2015 US Transgender Survey said the police considered condoms to be evidence of prostitution.[35] The study of LGBTQ youth in the sex trades in New York City found that 15 percent reported having condoms confiscated by police, leaving many confused and angry.[36]

Although many people I talk to about the use of condoms to criminalize react with shock, the practice has been going on for some time. As we were researching *Stonewalled* in 2003 and 2004, organizations across the country reported that police were seizing condoms found on or near women and citing them as evidence of prostitution. The practice was so pervasive that many believed that there was a "three condom rule"—anyone caught with three or more condoms would be charged with prostitution. A decade later, Human Rights Watch found similar perceptions.[37] In reality, there is no magic number—I have seen criminal complaints listing a single condom as evidence of intent to engage in prostitution-related offenses.[38] There is in fact no legal limit on the number of condoms anyone can carry, but the lived reality is that police officers, by exercising their discretion to confiscate and cite them as evidence of wrongdoing, enact and enforce an unwritten rule that places people's health and safety at risk.

In 2008, the Sex Workers' Project at the Urban Justice Center (SWP), which provides legal services to people involved in the sex trades, learned about a state bill that would ban the confiscation and citation of condoms as evidence, introduced by Senator Velmanette Montgomery, a Black woman representing sections of Queens, New York, where women and service providers reported this practice. In 2009, soon after I joined SWP as director, we began organizing a campaign for passage of the legislation, building a broad-based coalition of advocates for civil rights, police accountability, sex workers' rights, harm reduction, HIV prevention, immigrant rights, women's rights, reproductive rights, LGBT rights, and antitrafficking groups. These groups and others directly impacted by condom-based racial profiling called on the police commissioner, district attorneys, and legislators to put an end to the practice because it placed their health, safety, and reproductive rights at risk.

When policymakers demanded evidence of the practice's effects, we gathered copies of criminal complaints and surveyed our constituencies, publishing the findings in a 2012 report, *Public Health Crisis: The Impact of Using Condoms as Evidence of Prostitution in New York City.* Almost half the people we surveyed—the vast majority Black and Latinx women—reported that at some point they had not carried condoms for fear of police harassment or arrest.[39] Over half reported that their condoms been taken by police officers.[40] One Black Puerto Rican gender-nonconforming respondent asked, "Why do they take our condoms? Do they want us to die?" A Latinx reported an officer telling her as he took her condoms, "If you don't have this, you won't have sex."[41] The Red Umbrella Project commissioned artwork illustrating quotes gathered from people surveyed, and turned them into postcards to legislators. Survey results were also incorporated into *Criminalizing Condoms,* a report tracking the practice in seven countries including the United States and presented at the 2012 World AIDS Conference in Washington, DC.[42] Around the same time, Human Rights Watch partnered with community organizations in five cities, including New York City, to document the practice, and launched a year-long advocacy campaign to support and amplify local efforts to fight it.[43]

Ultimately our efforts over a three-year period secured partial policy and legislative changes by police, prosecutors, and, eventually, New York State lawmakers. Thanks to counterorganizing by a small minority of antitrafficking advocates who collaborated with prosecutors, condoms can still be used as evidence of trafficking, promoting, and other prostitution-related offenses. Trafficking survivors—and the vast majority of organizations who serve them—argued that continuing to use condoms as evidence of trafficking and promoting harms the very people that this group of misguided advocates purport to protect by creating strong disincentives to traffickers to make condoms fully and safely available to the people they exploit.[44] It also creates strong disincentives for businesses to have condoms available on the premises—and causes some to store them in ways that decrease their effectiveness.[45] This reduces access for the entire community, and for people who may in fact be trafficked. It also perpetuates the disincentive to carry and distribute condoms for fear of police harassment and prosecution. One trans Latinx testified to legislators that she was arrested with a friend while walking down the street; her friend was charged with loitering for the purposes of prostitution and she was charged with promoting her friend because she was carrying condoms. Finally, given that any prostitution involving a person under the age of eighteen is legally deemed human trafficking, young people distributing condoms to peers continue to bear the risk of prosecution for the serious offense of trafficking.

Activists in DC and San Francisco have similarly achieved partial policy changes and continue to advocate for a full ban on the use of condoms as evidence, as do New Yorkers: in 2016, the New York City Council Young Women's Initiative recommended a full ban on the confiscation or citation of condoms as evidence of intent to engage in any prostitution-related offense, in all circumstances, without exception.[46] Additionally, at the national level, the President's Task Force on 21st-Century Policing recommended that police departments follow the recommendation of the President's Advisory Council on HIV/AIDS and stop using condoms as evidence.[47]

Advocates have also used these campaigns to spotlight the racially discriminatory gender profiling inherent in the policing of prostitution, to argue for striking down statutes that facilitate it, such as "loitering for purposes of prostitution," and to deprioritize antiprostitution enforcement as part of a broader decriminalization agenda. In this way, campaigns to stop the use of condoms as evidence represent important examples of listening for the ways in which women and trans folks experience policing differently, and eliminating mechanisms police use to engage in racially gendered profiling.

In addition to racial profiling and discriminatory arrests, women of color who are or are perceived to be engaged in prostitution continue to be subjected to verbal harassment and abuse and police violence.[48] Nearly nine out of ten respondents to the 2015 US Transgender Survey who reported involvement in the sex trades also reported police harassment, assault, or mistreatment.[49] Analysis of data from three studies of street-based prostitution in a Midwestern city spanning the years 1998 to 2004 found that 26 percent of women had experienced some form of police violence—including slapping, kicking, choking, stalking, or robbery—in the past year.[50] In two New York City studies, 30 percent of street-based sex workers and 14 percent of indoor sex workers reported physical violence by police officers, including kicking and beating.[51]

Behind the numbers are individual stories of police violence. When I was researching *Stonewalled*, advocates on Chicago's West Side told us about a group of Black women officers who would beat Black women in the sex trade, then take their shoes from them, forcing them to walk in the snow in bare feet.[52] In *Queer (In)Justice*, my coauthors and I described in detail the case of Duanna Johnson, a Black trans woman living in Memphis who was profiled and arrested for prostitution in the absence of any evidence other than being Black, trans, and walking down the street late at night. She was then held down by one officer and beaten about the head and pepper-sprayed in the face by another one, who had methodically wrapped metal handcuffs around his knuckles. She later said, "My eyes were burning, my skin was burning. I was scared to death. . . . I didn't feel like I was a human being."[53] In 2012, I represented a Latinx immigrant trans woman whose head was repeatedly slammed to the ground by arresting officers during an indoor sting operation, breaking her tooth and bones in her face. When her skirt rode up during the assault, exposing her genitals, an officer grabbed them and sadistically twisted them while all the officers involved taunted her as a "faggot." These are but a few of myriad instances of daily physical abuse by police officers of women of color in the sex trades.

Police violence extends to people police believe to be trading sex, no matter how flimsy the evidence. One August 2008 evening in Galveston, Texas, the mother of Dymond Milburn, a twelve-year-old honor student, sent the girl outside around eight o'clock to flip a circuit breaker that had tripped as she was getting the children ready for school the next day. Soon after, three plainclothes police officers jumped out of a van and grabbed Dymond, saying "You're a prostitute; come with me." Dymond tried to get away, began screaming for her father, and grabbed on to a tree, reasonably fearing she was being abducted from her front yard by strangers. One of the officers covered her mouth while the other beat her about the face and throat. It turns out the officers were responding to a call about three *white* women believed to be engaged in prostitution in the area, but picked up the unmistakably Black girl on the grounds that she was wearing "tight shorts," although Dymond maintains she wasn't. Dymond was ultimately hospitalized with a bloody nose, black eyes, sprained wrist, and injuries to her ear and throat. She continues to suffer from nightmares that police will kidnap her, rape her, and cut off her fingers.

It would have been bad enough if the case had ended there, but several weeks later police showed up at Dymond's school to arrest her for assault on a police officer, an offense she was *twice* tried for. The first trial ended in a mistrial; the second, in a hung jury in which a single juror voted to convict her.[54] Piling injury upon injury, her civil suit against the officers was dismissed in 2010 on the grounds that, while they may not have had reason to stop her, the fact that Dymond ran away from three strangers she believed were trying to kidnap her gave rise to the requisite suspicion such that she was not entitled to resist the arrest.[55] In the end, the message is clear: Black women and girls, no matter how young or how innocuous their behavior, will be perniciously profiled as being involved in prostitution and then policed, violated, punished, and denied justice on the assumption that they are "prostitutes" who are so monstrous and imbued with superhuman physical strength that they must be subdued with tremendous force.

As detailed in chapter 4, the policing of prostitution is also a primary site of extortion of sex and sexual violence by police officers. According to a 2008 participatory research study conducted by the Chicago-based Young Women's Empowerment Project (YWEP), "Many girls said that police sexual misconduct happens frequently while they are being arrested or questioned."[56] One participant told researchers, "He told me he would let me go if I gave him some, but then he still took me down to the station." A subsequent study showed that police represent the largest slice of a pie chart depicting sources of violence reported by young women in the sex trades, while violence by individuals (clients, "pimps," and others) make up much smaller slivers. Eleven percent of all incidents of violence reported by young people in the sex trades involved police sexual violence, and police sexual violence made up 15 percent of all complaints of police violence.[57] LGBTQ youth in the sex trades in New York City similarly reported being propositioned or extorted for sex by police officers.[58] Rates of sexual assault increased for homeless transgender people. In Washington, DC, a survey by the community organization Different Avenues found that one in five sex workers approached by police had been asked for sex.[59] For instance, Toni Collins, cofounder of DC's Transgender Health Empowerment, reports that countless officers would tell her, "You do it with me, or I'm going to arrest you for prostitution."[60] A DC police sergeant admitted, "Everybody messes over the prostitutes."[61] Earlier studies by SWP found that up to 17 percent of indoor and outdoor sex workers reported sexual harassment or violence by police officers.[62] In the analysis of three studies of a Midwestern city, 15.4 percent of women reported being forced to have sex with a police officer, almost half (45.5 percent) had engaged in paid sex with police, and 18 percent reported being extorted for free sex.[63] Nationally, more than 25 percent of respondents to the 2015 US Transgender Survey who were or were perceived to be involved in the sex trades were sexually assaulted by police, and an additional 14 percent reported extortion of sex in order to avoid arrest.[64] Despite these realities, police are often where the greatest investment is made to reduce violence against women in the sex trades.

One of the many stories behind these numbers is one that has stayed with me for over a decade—that of a Navajo trans woman I met in 2003 at a street outreach van in Los Angeles when researching *Stonewalled*. She told me she had been raped by two police officers who initially said they were taking her to jail for prostitution, but instead took her to a secluded location to brutally violate her. They did not use condoms. The words yelled at her by police officers on this and other occasions made clear that the officers felt entitled to her body because she is Native, "a fucking whore," and "a fucking faggot." When she called for help, paramedics laughed at her, leading her to believe "nobody gives a shit about me."[65] When I asked about her on my next trip to Los Angeles, I was told she had returned home to Arizona in an effort to escape constant police and community violence.

Violence and criminalization of people in the sex trades also takes place in the context of antitrafficking enforcement. In *Kicking Down the Door: The Use of Raids to Fight Trafficking in Persons*, published in 2009, researcher Melissa Ditmore reports that Latinx, Asian, and European trafficking survivors were repeatedly arrested in police raids on brothels and other sex work venues—sometimes up to ten times—convicted of prostitution, and sent to jail without ever being identified as having been trafficked. Reflecting broader policing trends in the United States, Latinx and Asian women were more likely to have been arrested for prostitution than Eastern European women.[66] The study found that trafficking raids were also accompanied by physical and sexual violence. One Asian woman who had been trafficked reported that during a raid "a police officer struck me in the back of the head with the back of a gun and I fell to the floor and I passed out. . . . I was struck in the head really hard. . . . A female officer . . . opened up my skirt and revealed my undergarments in front of everyone to see if I was hiding anything on me. I was scared." She later reflected, "A better way to leave my situation would be anything that didn't involve the police." Another service provider said, "What ICE [Immigration and Customs Enforcement] calls a rescue is barging into someone's apartment at 6 a.m. and terrorizing them."

Social service providers also described sexual harassment and other police misconduct in the context of raids and their aftermath. One service provider working with people who have been trafficked said of the local vice squad, "The typical stuff that I hear is that they are having sex [with women who have been trafficked], they are getting blow jobs or hand jobs, *then* they turn around and arrest people. They are not letting them use the bathrooms afterward, and girls have pissed themselves. Then they steal from them. I have heard that from a lot of people."

Others described post-raid questioning of trafficking survivors without an attorney present in which women were subjected to intimidation and abusive interrogation tactics designed to "break them"—into admitting they are trafficking victims. I once heard an FBI officer describe with pride her approach to young women she "rescued" from the sex trade—"I tell them, if they run, I will hunt them down." It was hard to distinguish this statement from those I have heard countless times from abusers of all kinds.

In other words, unfortunately, antitrafficking raids—like antiprostitution raids (indeed, they are often one and the same)—are often accompanied by violations of the rights of the very people they are purported to protect.

POLICING OF SEXUALITY

Much of the discussion of sexuality-based policing of LGBTQ people has focused on gay men, rendering invisible queer women's experiences of policing—including in the context of prostitution enforcement. Yet, policing of sexuality takes place on a spectrum that includes lesbian, bisexual, and queer women of all gender identities, who are also punished for their "very deviance from heterosexual, monogamous norms [in order to] render the public sphere 'safe' from non-normative sexuality."[67]

In the 1980s Joan Nestle described police attacks on Black lesbians in New York City's Washington Square Park.[68] Sadly, such violence is not a relic of a distant past: in 2009, I filed suit on behalf of two women, Jeanette Grey and Tiffany Jimenez, who had been beaten outside a

Brooklyn club on "ladies' night" by police officers who called them "dyke-ass bitches." Jeanette is Black and gender nonconforming; Tiffany, a petite Latinx femme who was wearing a white party dress and heels. Both were described as aggressive—more a product of the fact that they were assumed to be queer than their behavior—and both were thrown to the ground by multiple officers, beaten, and arrested for "disorderly conduct." Jeanette's tooth was broken when an officer slammed her face against the hood of the police car.

The next morning, Jeanette sent out an e-mail calling for video footage and community support. The Audre Lorde Project (ALP) and Make the Road New York immediately mounted a campaign calling for charges against the two women to be dropped, held a rally opposite the police station where they had been taken, and organized a march from the station to the club where they had been violated. As we marched through the community, residents came out to chant familiar refrains like "No Justice, No Peace, No Racist Police!" Some onlookers were startled to see that the focus of the march was two young women, and to see rainbow flags. But then many picked up the chants again, demonstrating the power of organizing around common experiences to build bridges across gender and sexuality within communities of color.

Further examples of police violence against lesbians and gender nonconforming women of color, and of resistance to it, can be found throughout this book.

RESISTANCE

At times, resistance to police violence has explicitly focused on the experiences of women of color in the sex trades. In 1967, Reverend Cecil Williams in San Francisco, a leader in the fight against police brutality, organized around the case of "three Black prostitutes [who] were brutally beaten by police"; he formed an organizing committee, demanded investigations, and filed law suits. According to historian Mindy Chateauvert,

> Williams understood from this experience that decriminalizing prostitution was both a women's issue and a race issue. Police got away with brutalizing street-based sex workers because so many were women

of color. Race discrimination by "plush hotels" that refused entry to black prostitutes led to a racially skewed pattern of arrests and sentencing. . . . The biggest danger to women of color was the police, not the pimps, not the customers.[69]

This theme was picked up almost fifty years later by Atlanta's Solutions Not Punishment Coalition (SNaPCo), which in 2016 issued *The Most Dangerous Thing Out Here Is the Police*, a report based on surveys of trans people that concluded:

> Trans and gender nonconforming people and especially trans women of color are currently being profiled, sexually abused, and physically and emotionally endangered by the actions and attitudes of [Atlanta Police Department] officers. Instead of protecting the lives of trans people, our police department is actively contributing to making life unsafe for us and our families.[70]

Eighty-six percent of trans people surveyed had been approached by the Atlanta Police Department in the preceding year; almost half were targeted for prostitution-related offenses. Nearly one in twelve trans women surveyed had been forced to engage in sexual activity with, or had experienced unwanted sexual contact by, an Atlanta police officer within the previous year.

SNaPCo advocates for systemic changes to address the trends highlighted by the survey, calling for municipal authorities to thoroughly investigate police misconduct against trans people, to release and stop arresting trans people until policies are in place that will increase safety and dignity in police custody, and to address and repair harm to individuals and the community. Recognizing that police will use any law vague enough to police gender and punish gender nonconformity among low-income and homeless trans people of color, it is also calling for passage of an ordinance to decriminalize not just prostitution-related offenses but all so-called quality-of-life ordinances used to target, harass, and sexually assault trans people. These include "idling and loitering," "pedestrian walking in a roadway" or "obstructing traffic," "prohibited conduct in a park," "disorderly conduct," "obstructing a sidewalk," and "breach of the peace." SNaPCo also demands investment in job training and placement programs specific to trans and gender-nonconforming people; expanded funding to "community-based, gender-affirming services including harm reduction based drug treatment; safe and affirming housing, physical and mental health care, social services and education"; and accessibility and accountability of services, facilities, and programs for survivors of violence—including police violence—to trans survivors.

Police profiling and discriminatory enforcement of antiprostitution laws carry devastating consequences. Conviction of prostitution-related offenses renders immigrants immediately deportable, and in many jurisdictions operates as a complete bar to public housing and certain professions, regardless of immigration status. It can also interfere with access to private housing and child custody. After Hurricane Katrina, discriminatory enforcement of prostitution laws in Louisiana brought harsh collateral consequences of prostitution convictions into particularly sharp relief.

For two centuries, racialized policing of sexualities deemed deviant was facilitated by the existence of a "crime against nature" law that penalized nonprocreative sex acts such as sodomy.[71] In 1982, Louisiana added a "crime against nature by solicitation" (CANS) law that singled out solicitation of oral or anal sex for harsher punishment, including mandatory registration as a sex offender for fifteen years to life.[72] Predictably, a law rooted in condemnation of sexual acts traditionally associated with homosexuality, enforced in a context in which Black women's sexualities have historically and continue to be framed as deviant, was discriminatorily applied to low-income Black women, including transgender women. Consequently, until 2013, when the registration requirement was struck down, 97 percent of women in Orleans Parish on the sex-offender registry were there because of a CANS conviction; an overwhelming majority were Black.[73]

Police and prosecutors enjoyed unfettered discretion about when and who to charge with CANS, creating conditions ripe for rampant profiling and targeting of Black low-income women. That decision could literally change the entire course of a person's life by determining whether they could be convicted of a misdemeanor under the prostitution statute or a felony under the CANS law, which would result in mandatory registration as a sex offender.[74] Additionally, by increasing penalties and consequences, the threat of a CANS conviction also gave police greater leverage to extort sex.[75]

The CANS law first came to my attention in 2009. While working as the director of the Sex Workers Project, I was contacted by Laura McTighe, a board member at Women With a Vision in New Orleans. WWAV was founded by and for Black women in 1991 to respond to the spread of HIV/AIDS by engaging in harm reduction and policy advocacy that challenges the criminalization of women of color.[76] McTighe was working with WWAV's executive director, Deon Haywood, to raise national awareness of heightened enforcement of CANS following Hurricane Katrina. According to Haywood:

> This issue first came to our attention in 2007 when a woman came into our office and showed us her driver's license with a big orange sex offender [marking] on it. Since then we've heard dozens of stories from women who are on the registry because of this charge. . . . They are grandmothers and mothers. They have struggled with poverty and many have struggled with addiction. They did what they had to do to survive, to put food on the table. Not only are many of the women we are talking about . . . survivors of rape and domestic violence, they are also survivors of police violence, including sexual harassment, physical abuse, improper strip searches and rape by law enforcement officers. . . . Many of the [domestic violence] shelters here won't take them, the drug treatment programs won't take them, neither will the homeless shelters. . . . They have served their time, but now they have to serve an additional sentence, often a life sentence.[77]

After initial legal research into the viability of several constitutional claims, I approached the legendary Louisiana lawyer and law professor Bill Quigley, then the legal director of the Center for Constitutional Rights (CCR). In collaboration with WWAV, we convened a meeting of women's health and reproductive justice organizers, policy advocates working on criminal legal reform, and HIV/AIDS activists to map out a campaign to eliminate the CANS sex offender registration requirement. Litigation, in addition to legislative advocacy, would be one tool to advance the overall goals of the campaign.

We filed suit in February 2011.[78] The experiences of Hiroke Doe, one of the anonymous plaintiffs in the case, was representative of those of many transgender women of color whose gender identity and sexuality were routinely policed through the CANS law. As a teenager just coming out as transgender, Hiroke would meet men on the street who would express interest in her. Assuming she was soliciting them for money, police arrested and charged her with CANS. Like many transgender women, she elected to plead guilty in exchange for immediate release, rather than risk being jailed pretrial with men in the Orleans Parish Prison.[79] Hiroke's experiences differed from that of transgender women across the country only in that she was shocked to learn, upon meeting with her probation officer, that the offense she had pled to was a felony and required sex offender registration.[80]

Ongoing discrimination and marginalization faced by Black women was compounded by CANS registration requirements. As one woman said, "People won't hire you if you're black, gay, trans, and then now you got this on your license too?"[81] Already denied access to services, Black women forced to register as sex offenders faced insurmountable obstacles: think of all the places you have to show ID—at the bank, at the bar, enrolling your children in school. Now imagine doing that with "sex offender" on it. One woman described the registration requirement as a modern-day scarlet letter, saying, "I am trying to put that in my past—but it's not gonna be in my past because it's in my present, and it's going to be my future for the next thirteen years."[82]

One of the many strengths of the litigation, advocacy, and organizing campaign we mounted is that it linked all populations whose sexuality is framed as deviant and whose struggles to survive are criminalized. As one of our clients put it, "They only charge poor Black women, trans women and gay men with this charge—we're all queer out here."[83] Following this lead, we challenged the criminalization of all sexualities deemed "deviant" and the use of policing and punishment of sexual and gender nonconformity to further the gentrification and ethnic cleansing of New Orleans. In the end, these efforts not only resulted in the elimination of the CANS sex offender registration requirement in Louisiana in 2012 but eventually in the removal of more than eight hundred people who were on the sex-offender registry as a result of CANS.

Although the consequences of CANS charges in Louisiana lessened as result of our campaign, racially discriminatory enforcement of prostitution statutes continues. The moral of the story is that notwithstanding the success of short-term efforts to strike down unfair laws and eliminate the practices that facilitate profiling and punish women of color under the guise of prostitution enforcement, which are helpful harm-reduction strategies, the most frequent recommendation to end police violence from people in the sex trades is the decriminalization of prostitution. Some claim that decriminalizing prostitution would promote the violation and exploitation of women of color in the sex trades. But the reality is that for many, police, not pimps, are the primary source of violation and vulnerability to exploitation. Our task, then, is to address the root causes of violence against people in the sex trades by listening to and empowering them. The "demand" driving involvement in the sex trades is not one that can be policed and punished away—it is the need for housing, food, shelter, gender-affirming health care, and living wages. Moreover, both history and present-day enforcement clearly show us that decriminalizing prostitution is not enough if more general offenses are left in place that can and will be used to achieve the same ends.

CHAPTER 8

POLICING MOTHERHOOD

Malaika Brooks, thirty-three years old and seven months pregnant, was driving her eleven-year-old son to school in Seattle one November morning in 2004 when she was pulled over for speeding. She gave the officers her driver's license. They gave her a ticket. She refused to sign it, believing that doing so would amount to admitting guilt. The officers threatened to arrest her in front of her son and ordered her out of her car. When she refused, they tasered her pregnant body three times within a minute, hitting her in the thigh, arm, and neck, causing permanent burn marks. She fell out of the car. Officers then dragged her facedown on the street, handcuffed her, and charged her with refusing to sign the ticket and resisting arrest. She had told the officers she was pregnant when they first took out the Taser. Their only response was to avoid shocking her directly in the stomach.

I first learned about Malaika in 2006 while working with Tonya McClary of the American Friends Service Committee on *In the Shadows of the War on Terror: Persistent Police Brutality and Abuse in the United States*, a "shadow" report to the UN Committee Against Torture on the US government's failure to comply with the UN Convention Against Torture. As we were building the case that police use of Tasers—electroshock devices that deliver fifty thousand volts of electricity, causing what many describe as excruciating pain along with temporary immobilization—violated international law, I came across the story of Malaika's traffic stop, which had turned into torture. Although I had already read about many horrific instances of Taser use, Malaika's story and the officers' callous infliction of pain over a minor infraction, with complete indifference to the fact that she was pregnant, immediately reminded me of historic accounts of brutal "plantation justice" administered to pregnant enslaved women.

Today, I can't help but think of the parallels between Malaika's and Sandra Bland's traffic stops. Like Sandra, when Malaika asked legitimate questions about whether she was required to do what the officer told her to, she was immediately deemed "defiant" and was threatened with electric shock to secure immediate compliance. In Sandra's case, Officer Encinia threatened to "light her up" with a Taser if she didn't get out of the car; in Malaika's case, despite her visible pregnancy, the officers followed through on the threat. In both cases the officers later tried to argue that both Black women—both seated in their cars, unarmed— posed a threat to their safety. In both cases, Black women were punished for failure to engage in the level of obedience and obeisance expected of them, despite the minor nature of the offenses they were stopped for. In both cases, it is hard to imagine officers treating a white woman in the same way under the same circumstances.

At her trial, Malaika described the incident as "probably the worst thing that ever happened to me." She testified, "As police officers, they could have hurt me seriously. They could have hurt my unborn fetus. . . . All because of a traffic ticket. Is this what it's come down to?" Thankfully, her baby girl was born healthy several months later. Ultimately, Malaika was convicted of refusing to sign the ticket, a misdemeanor, but charges of resisting arrest were dismissed.[1] She sued the officers who shocked her, and in the end, the case settled in her favor.[2]

Malaika's story is a powerful illustration of the perils of Tasers. They are promoted as a life-saving alternative to deadly force, but in reality they are a "go-to" weapon employed by officers in wildly inappropriate circumstances—like breaking up children fighting in a school hallway and on an elderly woman who refused to let an officer in her home—all too often with deadly results. Their use against pregnant women, children, elderly people, and people in mental health crises or under the influence of alcohol or drugs[3] has prompted activists to call for complete bans, strict regulation limiting their use to situations in which the only alternative is lethal force, or, at minimum, limitations of their use against populations most likely to suffer harm, including pregnant women.[4]

At its core, Malaika's story also shows how police enact and enforce deep devaluation of Black motherhood. As Malaika so clearly articulated, a signature on a traffic ticket was deemed more important than her health and safety, and more important than the life and well-being of the future Black child she was carrying. A matrix of narratives rooted in slavery inform this reality: the stereotype of Black women as promiscuous, which defined them as bad mothers; the devaluation of Black motherhood used to justify ripping Black children from their mothers' arms to sell them away for profit; and the devaluation of Black children once they no longer represented property and members of an unpaid workforce.[5] As law professor Dorothy Roberts, who has written extensively on the criminalization of Black mothers, emphasizes, "From the moment they set foot in this country as slaves, Black women have fallen outside the American ideal of womanhood," including idealized motherhood.[6] Additionally, as described in chapter 1, pregnancy and motherhood served as a tool of punishment for Black women.[7] Unlike white pregnant women, perceived to exemplify the highest standard of womanhood, Black pregnant women were entitled to no protections except those required to protect slave owners' "property" in the form of future Black children. After the abolition of slavery, the value of Black women's future children vanished, as exemplified by the 1908 lynching of Mary Turner when she was eight months pregnant, during which the lynch mob cut her belly open and dashed the skull of the unborn child on the ground. Applying fifty thousand volts of electricity to the body of a pregnant woman who won't sign a paper charging her with a traffic infraction only becomes "understandable" within a framework informed by narratives like these.

In the 1980s the image of the "welfare queen" and "welfare mother" was added to the perceptions of Black women rooted in slavery, joining in a toxic combination in which Black motherhood and Black children represent a deviant and fraudulent burden on the state that must be punished through heightened surveillance, sterilization, regulation, and punishment by public officials.[8] The Black "welfare mother" is posited to give birth solely to increase the size of her check, only to neglect and abuse her children while spending money on extravagances for herself, all the while engaging in criminalized acts such as welfare fraud. Latinx, Indigenous, Asian, Arab, and Middle Eastern women's pregnancy and motherhood are similarly devalued under a variety of logics. Immigrant women, and particularly Latinxs, are posited to give birth for the sole purpose of creating "anchor babies" to establish immigration status, rendering their reproduction a threat. Simultaneously, the separation of immigrant women from their children through deportation and exclusion is justified and enacted by denying their value as mothers. Additionally, Asian women are demonized as uncaring mothers who would kill or abandon their own children under "barbaric" sex selection practices, while Arab and Middle Eastern women are framed as repro-ducing an army of suicide bombers and terrorists.[9] In the context of the war on drugs, immigration enforcement, and the "war on terror," these images have created an open season on mothers of color. It is within these larger contexts that Malaika's traffic stop, and the incidents that follow, unfolded.

POLICE BRUTALITY AGAINST PREGNANT WOMEN

Malaika's experience was far from unusual. Instead, it is representative of a gender-specific form of race-based police brutality. As author Vic-toria Law points out, "Both the criminalization of pregnancy and the arrests of pregnant women constitute their own forms of police vio-lence, but . . . are often overlooked by many of the larger organizing movements against police violence that have been sweeping the country since the deaths of Michael Brown, Eric Garner, and Tamir Rice. Yet they are no less torturous and brutal than the violence being protested on the streets nationwide."[10]

Amnesty International's 2008 report on Taser use in the United States catalogued several instances of Taser use on pregnant women, and pointed to the paucity of data on the risks.[11] A number of cases have come to light more recently demonstrating the persistence of the prob-lem. In June 2012, Tiffany Rent, a Black woman who was eight months pregnant, had just been issued a citation outside a pharmacy on Chi-cago's South Side for parking in a spot designated for people with dis-abilities. She tore up the citation and cursed at the officers before getting

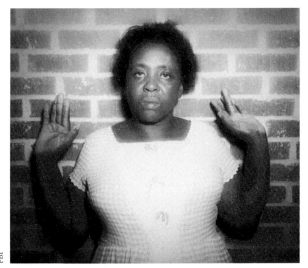

Following her 1963 arrest for desegregating a restaurant with other SNCC activists, civil rights leader Fannie Lou Hamer was beaten and sexually abused by police in Winona, Mississippi.

06/15/2015 12:33:08
X L

Austin Police Department

A still from the dash-cam video of Austin, Texas, police officers violently arresting elementary school teacher Breaion King following an alleged traffic violation.

A California Highway Patrol officer punches Marlene Pinnock ten times in the face and neck by the side of a highway in an incident captured on cell-phone video by a passing motorist.

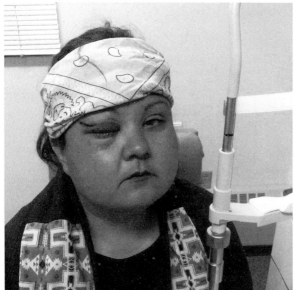

Water protector and Diné warrior woman Vanessa Dundon, also known as Sioux Z, was shot directly in the eye with tear gas by a Morton County, North Dakota, sheriff's officer as she tried to help a woman reporter leave the area of an action against the Dakota Access Pipeline. Vanessa later said police were targeting women that night. She is unlikely to regain full sight in her right eye.

Charles Meacham

Muslim Bangladeshi American attorney Chaumtoli Huq was violently arrested by New York City police officers for "blocking the sidewalk" in Times Square in September 2014 as she waited for her family to use a restaurant restroom.

Evy Mages/The Washingtonian

Roksana Mun of Desis Rising Up and Moving (DRUM) leads a January 2017 rally to shut down a proposed Muslim registry. For more information and to support DRUM's critical work, please visit www.drumnyc.org.

Members of OKC Artists for Justice protest former Oklahoma City police officer Daniel Holtzclaw's sexual assault of more than thirteen Black women and girls.

After a 2014 traffic stop, Juan Evans, a Black trans man, was threatened with a "genital search" to assign him a gender by an East Point, Georgia, police officer. Evans returned to the police station a week later with more than a hundred members of the Solutions Not Punishment Coalition to demand justice—and went on to win a new policy for police interactions with transgender people. For more information and to support the coalition's critical work, please visit www.rjactioncenter.org.

Family members of Black women killed by police, including Natasha Duncan, sister of Shantel Davis; Cynthia Howell, niece of Alberta Spruill and founder of Families United for Justice; Valarie Carey, sister of Miriam Carey; Martinez Sutton, brother of Rekia Boyd; Cassandra Johnson, mother of Tanisha Anderson; Sharon Wilkerson, mother of Shelly Frey; and Frances Garrett, mother of Michelle Cusseaux, on stage at the Say Her Name Vigil, organized by the African American Policy Forum, May 20, 2015.

JUSTICE FOR CÂU TRÀN
Stop Police Brutality

On July 13, 2003 Vietnamese immigrant Cau Thi Bich Tran, was shot dead in her kitchen by a San Jose policeman.

The police officer, Chad Marshall was responding to a 911 call from Ms. Tran's neighbor that an unsupervised toddler was roaming the street.

Within seconds, the 25-year-old mother of two pre-schoolers, was dead from a gunshot wound to the chest.

Officer Marshall claims that the four-inch vegetable peeler that Ms. Tran was holding was a ten-inch knife or cleaver that she could have used to attack him with.

Immediately following the incident and before launching an investigation, San Jose authorities claim the victim was a violently crazed attacker with a deadly weapon, an attempt to defend and even justify the killing.

Police are being allowed to kill with impunity, accept no responsibility, and have their crimes covered-up by the authorities.

We must not allow this to continue!
We must stand together to fight police brutality and hold authorities accountable for their actions!

Members of the community are urged to attend the open Grand Jury hearings beginning on October 21, at 9 a.m. at the Superior Court Hall of Justice Courtroom 31, 190 W. Hedding Street, San Jose. The hearings are scheduled for October 21, 22, 23, 24, 27, 28, 29, and 30. The court will provide a separate room with live Vietnamese translation.

For more information on the local organizing around the case of Cau Bich Tran, you can contact:

Richard Konda
Coalition for Justice and Accountability
c/o Asian Law Alliance

184 Jackson Street
San Jose, CA 95112
(408)287-9710
sccale@pacbell.net

For more information on the October 22nd Coalition, please call (415) 664-8193 or e-mail oct22sf@energy-net.org

Poster demanding justice for Bich-Cau Thi Tran, a Vietnamese mother of two shot to death in 2003 by San Jose, California, police responding to a call for assistance. Created by the Coalition for Justice And Accountability.

WE STAND WITH MONICA JONES
STOP PROFILING TRANS WOMEN OF COLOR

Monica Jones is a Black trans woman and an activist with the Sex Worker Organizing Project in Phoenix, Arizona. In May 2013, she was profiled and falsely arrested for "manifesting prostitution" while walking in her neighborhood.

Because Black trans women are often locked out of legal employment due to discrimination, many survive through sex work. The biggest danger faced by all sex workers is police violence, and Arizona has some of the most harmful anti sex worker laws in the US. Trans women of color are routinely profiled as sex workers by police, and then jailed with men and sexually assaulted.

Monica fought the conviction for two years, bringing international attention to racist and transmisogynist police violence. Her charges were eventually dropped, but Arizona's "manifesting prostitution" laws were upheld.

REST IN POWER

PROTECT OUR QUEER YOUTH OF COLOR — PUT A STOP TO POLICE BRUTALITY

JESSICA HERNANDEZ

Poster developed by movement artist Micah Bazant in partnership with Sex Workers' Outreach Project Phoenix as part of a campaign in support of Monica Jones, a Black trans woman falsely arrested for "manifestation of intent to commit or solicit an act of prostitution."

Poster by artist Rommy Torrico commemorating the life of Jessie Hernandez, a seventeen-year-old queer Latinx shot and killed by Denver police in January 2015.

Members of BYP100 shut down the Chicago Police Board month after month until they won a recommendation to fire Dante Servin, the officer who killed Rekia Boyd. For more information and to support BYP100's critical work, please visit www.byp100.org.

Altar for Korryn Gaines, Skye Mocabee, and all Black women killed by police and community created in the Bronx, New York, as part of a nationwide #DefendBlackWomanhood action called by Black Feminist Futures in August 2016.

Lisa Earl, mother of Jacqueline Salyers, a member of the Puyallup tribe killed by police in Tacoma, Washington, speaks at a March 2016 Justice for Jackie rally.

100 Black Women & Girls Killed by Police

Tomasa Africa,
Delicia Africa,
Netta Africa,
Carolyn Adams,
Rhonda Africa,
Shelley Amos,
Tanisha Anderson,
Anonymous,
Venus Renee Baird,
Carolyn Sue Botticher,
Anonymous,
Rekia Boyd,
Anna Brown,
Martina Brown,
Eleanor Bumpurs,
Cheryl Burton,
Marcella Byrd,
Miriam Carey,
Alexia Christian,
Derrinesha Clay,
Erica Collins,
Brenda Faye Cooper,
Jacqueline Robinson Culp,
Michelle Cusseaux,
Danette Daniels,
Shantel Davis,
Mattie Debardebelen,
Monique Deckard,
Emily Marie Delafield,
Sharmel Edwards,
Delores Epps,
Marie Fares,
Janisha Fonville,
Shereese Francis,
Shelly Frey,
Pamala Frowner,

Anita Gay,
Denise Gay,
Pearlie Golden,
LaToya Grier,
Kim Groves,
LaTanya Haggerty,
Mya Hall,
Darnisha Harris,
Denise Hawkins,
Teresa Henderson,
Yvette Henderson,
Meagan Hockaday,
Karen Day Jackson,
Laveta Jackson,
Kendra James,
Kathryn Johnston,
Aiyanna Jones,
Cora Jones,
Sophia King,
Andrena Kitt,
Summer Marie Lane,
Nuwnuh Laroche,
Eula Love,
Audrey Marshall,
Alicia McCuller,
Sharon McDowell,
Della McDuffie,
Natasha McKenna,
Yvonne McNeal,
Iquisha Middleton,
Adaisha Miller,
Rebecca Miller,
Tyisha Miller,
Margaret LaVerne Mitchell,
Mary Mitchell,
Kayla Moore,
Laura Nelson,

Gabriella Nevarez,
Jacqueline Nicholson,
Heather Parker,
Frankie Perkins,
Charmene Pickering,
Lillie Dell Power,
Jimmi Ruth Ratliffe,
Mackala Ross,
Aura Rosser,
Alma Shaw,
Quenyia Tykia Shelton,
Latricka Sloan,
Yvette Smith,
Ellosie Spellman,
Alberta Spruill,
Sonji Taylor,
Yolanda Thomas,
Alesia Thomas,
Patricia Thompson,
Virginia Verdee,
Laporsha Watson,
Shulena Weldon,
Desseria Whitman,
Brenda Williams,
Kesha Williams,
Malissa Williams,
Robin Taneisha Williams,
Tarika Wilson,
Vernicia Woodard,
and many other black trans and non-trans women & girls, counted and uncounted, whose lives were stolen at the hands of the police.

Antonia Clifford

Poster "100 Black Women & Girls Killed by Police" researched by Andrea Ritchie, Mariame Kaba, and Deana Lewis, and designed by Antonia Clifford, for the exhibit *Blood at the Root: Unearthing the Stories of State Violence Against Black Women*. For more information, please visit: https://bloodatrootchicago.wordpress.com/.

back in her car. Having already issued the citation, the officers could have just walked away. If she failed to appear in court or answer the citation, she would bear the consequences. Instead, the officers chose to write her another ticket, this time for littering. When she began to drive away, they claimed that she was attempting to escape. They proceeded to shock Tiffany with a Taser, drag her out of her car, force her to the ground, and handcuff her in front of her two young children. Her sister later said, "How could you be so cruel to a human being? A pregnant human being?" Chicago Police Superintendent Gerry McCarthy was unapologetic, defending the officers' use of force with an offhand "You can't always tell if someone is pregnant."[12] Rent gave birth to a baby boy the following month, and received a $55,000 settlement from the city the following year. "I don't think that it should have went this far," she said. "It just makes me afraid of the Chicago Police Department because there's other women that may have went through this or that's going through this."[13]

Some departments have developed policies regulating incidents such as these—although most have loopholes allowing use of Tasers against pregnant women under some circumstances.[14] However, my research revealed that a significant number—38 percent of thirty-six of the fifty largest police departments—have no policy whatsoever specifically governing use of force, including Tasers, against pregnant women.[15]

Yet police violence against pregnant women extends beyond the use of Tasers—and has been characterized as an "epidemic."[16] One blog cataloguing a series of brutal incidents of physical force against pregnant women concluded that if "pregnant Black women can be routinely attacked—something we can't even imagine happening to White women—and their growing babies treated as fair game, there is no sanctuary to be found."[17]

There was certainly no sanctuary to be found for Nicola Robinson. Her crime? Laughing at a Chicago police officer who had failed to catch a person he was chasing on a spring day in 2015. Her punishment? The officer punched her hard in the right side of her stomach as she stood in front of her own home, despite the fact that, at eight months, she was very visibly pregnant. The role of her race and gender in the officer's actions were plain as day when he shouted, "You black bitch, you better be glad I didn't hit you hard enough to make you lose your fucking baby."[18] Immediately following the incident Nicola went into premature labor and was hospitalized. She was later released and gave birth to a healthy child. While her case may seem like an outlier, fifteen years earlier another Chicago cop hit another pregnant Black woman while his partner told her "we don't like Black pregnant women."[19]

Each of these cases began as an interaction in the context of enforcement of a minor offense, or no offense whatsoever. All the women were either obviously pregnant, or told the officers they were. Yet, consistent with controlling narratives tolerating nothing but subservience from Black women and the devaluing of Black mothers and their fetuses, officers took swift and brutal action, causing harm to women who posed no threat to them.

Physical violence by police has produced miscarriages.[20] In Harvey, Illinois, in 2011, Kwamesha Sharp lost her pregnancy when a police officer, Richard M. Jones, slammed her to the ground and pressed his knee into her abdomen for an extended period of time, saying he didn't care that she was pregnant.[21] She later said, "It felt like I lost myself. Never knew what my child would have been." Four years later, the same officer extorted sex from another pregnant woman after a traffic stop. The officer was not held accountable for either incident, although the City of Harvey settled Kwamesha's civil claim for $500,000.[22]

Narratives devaluing Latinx mothers, framing them as drug users and sex workers, and their fetuses as immigration threats, produce similar outcomes. Destiny Rios was walking home one evening in July 2012 to her grandmother's in San Antonio, Texas, when an officer stopped her, telling her he had been instructed to stop anyone in the neighborhood. Rios provided her ID and allowed the officer to search her purse. Although the officer told her she was free to leave when no prior criminal history or illicit drugs were found, when she walked away the officer grabbed her by the back of the neck, threw her to the ground, placed his knee and then his foot in her back, handcuffed her, and arrested her, allegedly for an outstanding warrant for prostitution. Along with three other officers, he repeatedly struck the 126-pound woman in the head, face, and body as she lay handcuffed and pinned to the asphalt screaming that she was pregnant. The officers initially denied her pleas for medical help, taking her to the jail instead as she complained of cramping, pain, bleeding, and leakage of amniotic fluid. She was later taken to the hospital, where she suffered a miscarriage. A suit was brought against the San Antonio Police Department. The police chief vehemently defended the use of force, insinuating, in response to the suit, that it was not the beating but Rios's drug use the previous day that had caused the miscarriage.[23] His response is not uncommon: miscarriages resulting from police brutality are often treated with indifference at best, and at worst are framed as deserved, appropriate, or the mother's own fault.

Immigration enforcement has also led to loss of pregnancy. In one 2006 case, a Chinese woman miscarried her twins after she appeared for a routine interview with immigration officials that subsequently turned into a violent deportation attempt. According to the woman and her family, "the authorities decided to deport her when they learned she was pregnant, to prevent her from giving birth to another United States citizen."[24] In another case, a woman in Nogales, Arizona, miscarried in 1997 after an immigration raid of her house during which agents terrorized her and her children.[25]

Even when law enforcement officials do not use direct force against pregnant women, their actions, inaction, or denial of necessary medical attention often cause harm to pregnant women and their children. Officers of the Kansas City police stopped Sofia Salva, a Sudanese immigrant, for a traffic infraction in 2007. Sofia repeatedly told officers that she was trying to get to the hospital because she was three months pregnant, bleeding, and concerned that she might be miscarrying. The officers repeatedly ignored her requests for help, characterizing them as a "line of excuses." They later told her she could take care of her medical condition "when we get done with you," as they searched her car, purse, and groceries. They scolded her, saying that, while she may be bleeding, she had "a lot more problems" as a result of unpaid traffic tickets and outstanding city warrants. Sofia miscarried after being held overnight in jail.[26] The officers' clear disregard for Sofia's pregnancy, health, and well-being reflects the simultaneous devaluation of Black and immigrant motherhood.

In each of these cases, no officers were held accountable—while, as discussed in greater detail below, Black women and women of color are routinely held accountable for any adverse outcomes to their pregnancy, regardless of fault or intent.

THE WAR ON DRUGS AND THE CRIMINALIZATION OF BLACK MOTHERS AND MOTHERS OF COLOR

Just hours after giving birth in a public hospital serving a predominantly low-income Black community in Charleston, South Carolina, a Black mother is hauled away by police in handcuffs and shackles attached to a belt around her belly, still bleeding. She is charged with delivering drugs to a minor—the baby she just delivered—on the grounds that traces of drugs were found in the blood of the umbilical cord. She is held in the county jail without follow-up care, separated from her newborn until she goes to trial, and is convicted of child abuse for delivering drugs to a minor.[27]

This was a scene that played out multiple times in 1989 at the now infamous Charleston public hospital whose practice of testing of umbilical cord blood for drugs without maternal consent well into the 1990s was ultimately successfully challenged in the US Supreme Court. Nearly all pregnant women and new mothers arrested under circumstances like these were Black. The exception was a white woman listed on medical documents as living with a "Negro" boyfriend.[28]

Dorothy Roberts points out that these scenes strongly evoke images of the brutality and degradation Black mothers were subjected to under slavery, and they are informed by the slavery-era mythology conjured to justify this treatment: Black women as animalistic, promiscuous, uncaring, indulgent, incompetent, and infanticidal mothers.[29] Roberts further theorizes that, in this context: "Black reproduction . . . is treated as a form of *degeneracy*. . . . They damage their babies in the womb through their bad habits during pregnancy. Then they impart a deviant lifestyle to their children through their example."[30] Within this framework, the logics underlying singling out Black women for drug testing during pregnancy and delivery become clearer.

Delivery-room arrests represent a gender-specific front of the war on drugs that could easily be characterized as "giving birth while Black"—presumed to be a bad mother, giving birth in a public hospital, subject to the presumptions that you are entitled to no privacy the medical establishment or government is bound to respect, and being a familiar target for arresting officers. They were further fueled by now soundly debunked junk science raising monstrous specters of Black "crack mothers" and "crack babies" destined to become "superpredators." Much has been written about the impacts of prosecutions of pregnant Black women and new mothers, the contortions of child abuse and drug laws used to charge and convict them, and courts' and the public's distorted perceptions of Black mothers and their right to parent. However, the role played by police in the arrests of pregnant and new mothers accused of drug use has largely escaped scrutiny by broader police accountability movements.

Far from simply executing the wishes of misguided health-care officials or ambitious prosecutors, law enforcement played a leadership role in the South Carolina program. The police department was involved in developing procedures to preserve chain of custody for specimens taken without mothers' consent and protocols for arresting women who tested positive, and in the day-to-day administration of the policy.[31] Police officers executed orders to take women from recovery rooms in shackles and toss them into cells. In other cases, a police team, using information obtained from health-care providers, "tracked down expectant mothers in the city's poorest neighborhoods."[32] In one case, an officer placed a woman in a choke hold to detain her. Another woman, arrested before giving birth, was transported to and from the hospital in handcuffs and shackles for prenatal appointments, and was forced to give birth chained to a hospital bed.[33]

Ultimately, the US Supreme Court declared the South Carolina program unconstitutional precisely because of the inextricable involvement of law enforcement.[34] Such police–service provider collaborations disproportionately affect low-income Black women and women of color, who have no choice but to use public health facilities and are therefore denied the privacy afforded those who can afford private health care. Simply put, increased scrutiny in public health-care settings increases the likelihood that low-income mothers of color will be criminalized.[35] The result? Despite similar rates of drug use among pregnant Black and white women, Black women are more likely to be reported to police than white women. In Florida, ten times as likely.[36]

Anannya Bhattacharjee argues that treatment of pregnant women and mothers of color reveals an important fissure in the facade of police protection, making it a site of obvious dissonance in the ways the state relates to Black women and their children. Police do not hesitate to punish Black women for alleged harm to their fetus or child, and simultaneously routinely subject pregnant women to violence that places mother and child at risk.[37] Historian Sarah Haley describes the same phenomenon in the Jim Crow South:

> Black life (the life of the child) becomes legible when it is deployed by white authorities in order to enact violence (imprisonment), but is illegible when deployed by black subjects to defend against violence (motherhood as a ground for pardon). Georgia's legal system disproportionately imprisoned black women thereby destroying their ability to care for their children, but also arrested them when they allegedly caused the deaths of their children.[38]

In other words, the safety of Black children is only of concern to the state when it serves larger interests of criminalization and control over Black women, much as Black women's childbearing was only valued because it increased the pool of enslaved labor.[39] In the end, as in slavery, Black motherhood and children are simply deployed as another tool of punishment and control, wielded with impunity, in whichever way will bolster further criminalization.

As Roberts puts it, "When a nation has always closed its eyes to the circumstances of pregnant Black women, its current interest in the health of unborn Black children must be viewed with distrust."[40] She concludes that there is in fact no contradiction in police practices toward Black women because Black women are not being punished for harming their fetuses, *they are being punished for having babies.*[41] The state criminalizes Black women to punish them for reproducing in the first place, by placing them and their babies at risk via physical attacks, denial of medical attention, or post-delivery arrests and harassment. The state, Roberts emphasizes, is saying "not so much 'I care about your baby' as 'You don't deserve to be a mother'" if you are a Black woman, and especially if you use drugs.[42]

The state has the same message for Indigenous women, albeit under different logics. The disappearance of Native peoples is a precondition to taking their land and resources, rendering continued existence and reproduction by Native women a site of continued policing and punishment. Martina Greywind, a Native woman, was arrested in Fargo, North Dakota, in 1992 when twelve weeks pregnant and was held for two weeks in jail on a charge of reckless endangerment, premised on the notion that inhaling paint fumes was a danger to the fetus she was carrying.[43] On the Pine Ridge Reservation, "pregnant [Native American] women with drinking problems are put in jail."[44] Arresting pregnant women exposes the state's concern for the children of Indigenous women and women of color as an empty pretext, as incarceration of pregnant women increases rather than decreases the likelihood of adverse outcomes. For example, one-third of pregnant women in prison miscarry, in large part due to inadequate health and prenatal care.[45]

Law enforcement often subjects pregnant women, particularly women of color, to punishments that contradict the state's expressed intent to protect women and children, reflecting the actual underlying devaluation of both their motherhood and children. In Wisconsin, Alicia Beltran was arrested in 2014 under what became known as the "Cocaine Mom Law." Since its passage in 1998, the state has been permitted to arrest and incarcerate pregnant women if they are merely accused of using alcohol or drugs and to force them into treatment. In Alicia's case, the contradictions are painfully apparent. Arresting Alicia for alleged and potential harm to her fetus, officers placed her at risk of actual harm by forcing her to kneel on the floor as they cuffed and shackled her, holding her without food or water, and then ordering her into treatment for seventy-five days where no prenatal care was provided. Victoria Law points out, "Had anyone other than a government official inflicted these kinds of scenarios—including physically restraining, denying medical care and failing to provide food or water . . . they would risk criminal charges. In 38 states, violence against women that results in pregnancy loss is called fetal homicide." But, as Sara Ainsworth, NAPW director of legal advocacy, notes, some pregnant women "are viewed as deserving of this kind of violence . . . whether you want to call it police violence or medical violence or both."[46]

A study of more than four hundred US arrests of pregnant and parenting women between 1973 and 2005 concluded that law enforcement overwhelmingly targeted low-income women, and disproportionately targeted women of color. In two-thirds of the cases, there was no evidence whatsoever of harm to the fetus or child. In addition to alleged drug use during pregnancy and allegations relating to mental health issues, arrests were also made on the basis of a woman and her doctor electing a caesarian section instead of a vaginal birth, and for failure to seek prenatal care—further evidence of the extreme extent of reproductive control in the lives of women of color.[47] In many cases, mothers were subjected to bedside interrogations shortly after giving birth to or losing a child. The study's authors conclude that "harsh treatment imposed on the pregnant women in our study, including being taken straight from their hospital beds and arrested shortly after delivery, being taken in handcuffs, sometimes shackled around the waist, and at least one woman being shackled during labor, is consistent with a long and disturbing history of devaluing African American mothers."[48]

ENFORCEMENT OF CHILD-WELFARE LAWS

Another contradiction evident in the policing of mothers of color is the reality that "women of color, both immigrant and US-born, are prevented from caring adequately for their children while they are simultaneously accused of child abuse and neglect."[49] In the majority of child-welfare cases, Roberts argues, what is labeled as neglect is really defined by poverty.[50] Additionally, when Black mothers and mothers of color turn to public institutions for support for themselves and their families, their parenting is subject to additional scrutiny by agency staff who are likely to report perceived deviations from white middle-class parenting standards to child-welfare authorities or police.[51] This lack of privacy for low-income women and mothers of color operates in dangerous combination with stereotypes of Black mothers and mothers of color.[52] As David Love theorizes, "Women of color are more likely than [w]hite women to be monitored and supervised by the state, and more likely to experience state control over their bodies and their children. Call it a holdover from slavery, when Black women had no right to privacy, were violated at will, and could not make decisions regarding themselves, their bodies or their families."[53]

How a mother's actions are perceived is very much linked to how good a mother she is perceived to be; as Roberts puts it, "Black women are burdened with myths about their unfitness as mothers, which distort the public's view of their maternal failures."[54] The myths in question are variations on now-familiar themes. Black women were framed as unable to care for their own children on the basis of high infant-mortality rates during slavery, which in fact are easily attributable to the hard physical labor, punishment, and deprivation suffered by mothers during pregnancy and forced separation of children from their mothers at an early age. Separation from their own children to serve as Mammy to white children was turned into a stereotype of Black mothers as being more interested in pursuing their own interests—whether drugs, material goods, or sex—than in caring for their own children.[55] Against this backdrop, argues Dorothy Roberts, authorities "often seem less concerned with protecting children from abuse than with imposing an idealized and racialized standard of selfless motherhood."[56]

Police officers play a largely invisible role in the enforcement of child welfare, yet this serves as another site of enforcement of racialized gender norms. The police are often called to respond to complaints or to enforce caseworkers' orders to remove children, yet the way they do so is indicative of the way they perceive the mothers and the children involved. For instance, in 2012 in Los Angeles, a white female officer brutalized and beat Alesia Thomas after she was dispatched to Alesia's home to arrest her for abandoning her children at a police station because she could no longer care for them. The officer repeatedly kicked Alesia in the groin, abdomen, and thigh, and jabbed her in the throat while she was handcuffed and shackled in the backseat of a police patrol car. Alesia can be heard on the car's dash-cam video telling the officer she can't breathe and can be seen struggling to stay conscious before passing out. In complete disregard for Alesia's well-being, the officer smoked a cigarette and waited thirty minutes before calling for help. Alesia was later pronounced dead at the hospital.[57] Following a rare criminal prosecution—for assault, not murder—the officer was sentenced to thirty-six months in jail, with the last twenty suspended.[58] The family was awarded $2.5 million in a settlement.

In July 2014, Denise Stewart, an asthmatic forty-seven-year-old grandmother in New York City, answered her door when police knocked. Responding to a complaint that a child was being harmed, they had come to the wrong apartment. Denise informed them that they had the wrong location and that she had just come out of the shower. Refusing to believe her, police officers dragged Denise, half naked, out of her towel and into a hallway as she begged for her inhaler and later collapsed. Her neighbors protested and videotaped the officers, to no avail. Minutes passed as an officer held Stewart naked in the hallway of her apartment building in utter disregard for her rights and dignity while a group of officers ultimately proceeded to the correct apartment. Police also dragged her four children into the hall and handcuffed them. Eventually, an officer threw a towel over Denise. Mariame Kaba, founder of Project NIA, pointed out in a blog post about the incident that Denise "is ungendered to the cops and as a black person she is unhuman to them."

Later that year, Michelle Siguenza Anderson was subject to a violent arrest in her driveway in Salt Lake City, Utah, by officers responding to a child-welfare call. After Michelle cursed and spat at one of the officers, he responded by punching her and taking her to the ground while calling her a "bitch" and telling her she deserved to have her "ass kicked," as her nine-year-old daughter cried, witnessing the assault on her mother. Prosecuting attorneys were shocked to see the incident on dash-cam video and later called for an investigation.[59]

Beyond responding to calls, police are now also independently taking up child-welfare enforcement, including in minor cases that would previously have been handled administratively. For instance, according to Roberts, misdemeanor child-welfare arrests tripled in New York City in the 1990s as part of "quality of life" policing under Mayor Giuliani, under the theory that "arresting mothers on minor neglect charges . . . will prevent more serious cases of abuse." Officers were charged with making arrests to protect children in "dangerous situations," defined, as always, more by officers' racialized perceptions than objective realities, which in turn are more often a result of poverty and a lack of child-care options than instances of actual harm. These realities are addressed through arrest rather than support to the mother to address conditions of concern. Roberts reports that, in one case, "Laura Venegas was arrested when police found her two sons playing alone outside their aunt's East Harlem apartment."[60] In another, police arrested thirty-four-year-old Sourette Alwysh, a Haitian immigrant "who was led away in handcuffs when police found her living with her five-year-old son in a foreclosed building without electricity or running water," rather than working to find housing for the mother and child. In a third, "Sidelina Zuniga, a 39-year-old Mexican immigrant, came home from grocery shopping to discover the police had taken her boys, ages ten and four, because she left them alone for an hour and half." No child-care options were explored for her and her children. Many parents leave their children in the care of babysitters not much older than Sidelina's oldest son. Certainly no one came to take away the parents of the white suburban children I babysat for at the age of eleven or twelve. Yet handcuffs appear to be the default response where Black mothers and mothers of color are concerned. The situation was even more preposterous for Geraldine Jeffers. She was arrested and later convicted for child endangerment for leaving her four younger children in the care of their fifteen-year-old sister when she had to go to the hospital due to complications with her pregnancy and wound up being admitted overnight.[61]

Roberts points out, "When a mother leaves her child locked in the house, playing in the park or sitting in the car while she goes to work, she alone is arrested and vilified in the media."[62] Shanesha Taylor, a homeless Black mother, was arrested for leaving her two sons in an SUV while she attended a job interview in an effort to better support them financially. Her child care had fallen through that day, and Shanesha had to make an impossible choice in the name of breaking out of the cycle she found herself in—as low-income mothers are repeatedly told to do by public officials. Shanesha was sentenced to eighteen years of supervised probation; meanwhile, a man who left his child in a parked car at a train station for thirty minutes just days before Shanesha's court appearance faced no charges whatsoever.[63] Laura Brouder had just gotten a call for a last-minute job interview after moving to Houston; having no child care, she brought her children with her and asked them to wait in the food court while she attended the interview. She was arrested after accepting the job. After the arrest, she said, "I had an interview with a very great company with lots of career growth. I am a college student and mother of two. . . . My children weren't even thirty yards away from me. I fed them and sat there with them until it was time to meet with my interviewer." Both Laura and Shanesha were eventually reunited with their children, but they carry the scars of the arrests and punishment they suffered for making tough choices under difficult circumstances.[64] Meanwhile, in her book *Shattered Bonds: The Color of Child Welfare*, Roberts describes a white woman who dropped her child off thirty minutes early every morning at a school across from Roberts's house in an affluent neighborhood where she left him to play alone in the school playground until staff and other children began to arrive. She escaped police attention altogether.[65]

As Anannya Bhattacharjee put it, the state "disrupts caregivers' ability to fulfill their responsibilities, while at the same time, the legal apparatus of the state is used to accuse women of irresponsibility and abuse—with charges sometimes directly stemming from the harm caused by law enforcement or public agencies."[66] A series of cases in which Black mothers have been arrested for taking steps to improve their children's education also highlights the no-win situation Black mothers often find themselves in.[67]

How might the experiences of Black mothers and mothers of color targeted for police violence and arrest change our organizing strategies and demands? It might be as simple as organizing around cases involving pregnant women, as Newark residents did for Danette Daniels in 1997. In violation of police policy, officers shot the thirty-one-year-old Black pregnant woman in the head after arresting her for what they believed was a drug transaction, as she tried to drive a police car away. The community rose up in protest, holding weekly demonstrations in which they called for indictment of the officer responsible for shooting Danette. In the end, no criminal charges were brought, but the officer was suspended without pay for ninety-two days for not taking measures required by policy to prevent Danette's death, and some changes were made to departmental policies.[68]

Beyond organizing on behalf of Black mothers and mothers of color, if we center their experiences, we begin to ask new questions, including how use-of-force policies should address experiences of pregnant women. One approach might be to advocate for policies that effectively prevent and address police violence against pregnant women, including the use of Tasers and chemical weapons, front and rear handcuffing, takedowns and use of physical force to the abdomen. Another strategy might be developing and enforcing protocols to govern the provision of medical care to pregnant women in police and immigration custody—or, better yet, advocating that they not be locked up at all. Ultimately, mothers' experiences of policing require us to look beyond traffic and pedestrian stops and police encounters visible in the streets, and pull back the curtain on hidden experiences of racial profiling and violent arrests in homes, hospitals, and other private spaces. They also require us to expose collusion and collaboration between police and "helping" institutions, such as hospitals and child-welfare enforcement agencies; to end the war on drugs; and to adopt a public health rather than a punitive approach to drug use by pregnant and parenting women. They require us to re-envision our approach to child welfare from a punitive one to a community-based support network.[69] Most of all, they require a commitment to shifting perceptions of Black mothers and mothers of color, and of their right to become parents and care for their children.

It also requires changing the conditions under which Black women and women of color often parent, including prioritizing meaningful access to housing, education, and living-wage employment.

Police violence against and the criminalization of pregnant women and mothers of color brings policing squarely within the frame of movements for reproductive justice. One of the first marches I ever attended was the 1989 March for Women's Lives on the Washington Mall. Throughout college I was active in the movement for reproductive rights, circulating petitions arguing for state coverage of abortions and the repeal of the Hyde Amendment, and learning to perform abortions in the event that they were once again banned—a skill I hope I am never called on to use. Never once did it occur to me, then or later, to link struggles for the right to choose when and how to parent to movements against police violence. Not until I read Bhattacharjee's paper "Whose Safety? Women of Color and the Violence of Law Enforcement," in which she squarely places multiple forms of violence, neglect, manipulation, and punishment of mothers of color within a conversation about law enforcement violence, did I understand that, for women of color, pregnancy and motherhood are additional sites and weapons of police violence that demand a response from both police accountability movements and movements for reproductive justice. [70]

Beyond demanding that all women be given the chance to raise their children and benefit from their love, companionship, and care through old age without fear that they will be gunned down in the street or left to die in a cell, movements for reproductive justice can take up the ways in which the state directly interferes with our right to parent through police fists and Tasers, deliberate indifference to the welfare of pregnant women and their children, ripping mothers from children at the moment of birth, arresting us for decisions we make about our bodies, and criminalizing us for making impossible decisions under impossible conditions.

CHAPTER 9

POLICE RESPONSES
TO VIOLENCE*

I was sitting in the audience at the Black Feminism 2000 conference in March 2000, when UCLA professor Robin D. G. Kelly, a Black man, told a story about woman named Cherae Williams. Cherae was thirty-seven, Black, and living in the Bronx when she was beaten by her boyfriend. When she called the police for help she was then beaten within an inch of her life by NYPD officers. Though 1999 had been a year of protesting police brutality after NYPD officers shot Amadou Diallo forty-one times in the doorway of his own home, Kelly noted the lack of national attention to Cherae's case, as well as to police killings of Tyisha Miller in Riverside, California, and LaTanya Haggerty in Chicago that same year. Citing this invisibility as evidence of an absence of gender analysis in the anti–police brutality movement, Kelly emphasized that Black feminism demands action around Black women's experiences of police violence. On the same panel, Black feminist foremother Barbara Smith, who had been actively organizing around Diallo's murder, echoed Kelly's points and expanded on his call to action to include police violence against Black LGBTQ people.[1]

I immediately set out to learn everything I could about Cherae's experience. On September 28, 1999, she called 911 during a domestic violence incident.[2] When the police arrived, the two white police officers refused even to get out of their patrol car to take her complaint. When Cherae asked for their names and badge numbers, they responded by putting her in handcuffs, shoving her into their patrol car, and driving

---

* This chapter is based in part on a draft chapter written with Beth E. Richie in 2010.

her to a deserted parking lot.³ Terrified, she managed to get one hand out of the cuffs while in the car, only to be pepper-sprayed in the face by the officers. When they arrived at the lot, the officers pulled her out of the car by her hair, repeatedly shook her, and struck her head against the car. They then beat her so badly they broke her nose, burst her spleen, and fractured her jaw, which later had to be wired shut.⁴ Cherae testified shortly after the incident before a New York City Council hearing on police responses to domestic violence: "They beat me until I was bloody. . . . They left me there dazed and with a warning. They told me if they saw me on the street, that they would kill me. . . . I called the police to prevent a serious incident, and they brutalized me."⁵ For a long time, I opened every presentation with Cherae's story—consistently drawing gasps of horror—to amplify the voice she raised in protest at that City Council hearing and to point to her experience as a quintessential example of Black women's vulnerability to both interpersonal and state violence.

A month after the Black Feminism panel, Angela Y. Davis, who has consistently spoken out about her own and other women's experiences of police violence throughout her activist life, opened the historic founding conference of INCITE! at the University of California, Santa Cruz, with the following story:

> Many years ago, when I was a student in San Diego, I was driving down the freeway with a friend when we encountered a black woman wandering along the shoulder. Her story was extremely disturbing. Despite her uncontrollable weeping, we could surmise that she had been raped and dumped along the side of the road. After a while, she was able to wave down a police car, thinking that they would help her. However, when the white policeman picked her up, he did not comfort her, but rather seized upon the opportunity to rape her once more.
>
> I relate this story not for its sensational value, but for its metaphorical power.
>
> Given the racist and patriarchal patterns of the state, it is difficult to envision the state as the holder of solutions to the problem of violence against women of color. However, as the anti-violence movement has

been institutionalized and professionalized, the state plays an increasingly dominant role in how we conceptualize and create strategies to minimize violence against women. One of the major tasks of this conference, and of the anti-violence movement as a whole, is to address this contradiction, especially as it presents itself to poor communities of color.[6]

For me, these two stories—posed as challenges to both the anti–police brutality movement and the antiviolence movement—were foundational. They resonated with my own experiences of police violence when I sought protection, as well as the consistent findings of my research over the past twenty-five years: police violence against women of color takes place disproportionately, and with alarming frequency, in the context of responses to domestic and sexual violence. Similarly, our research for Amnesty International's 2005 report *Stonewalled: Police Abuse and Misconduct Against LGBT People in the United States* and for the book *Queer (In)Justice* made it clear that responses to family, interpersonal, and homophobic and transphobic violence are frequent sites of police violence against LGBTQ people.

At a keynote presentation at the 2006 National Coalition Against Domestic Violence (NCADV) conference, I told Cherae's story as a cautionary tale about the consequences of relying on police as the primary, if not exclusive, response to violence against women, notwithstanding challenges raised for decades by women of color to this approach. I concluded a litany of stories and studies by saying, "As a general rule, law and order agendas have never been about protecting us, and, in fact, have led to increased violence against women of color in the home, in the community, and at the hands of law enforcement." I talked about the call issued by the 2002 "INCITE!—Critical Resistance Statement on Gender Violence and the Prison Industrial Complex" and urged the audience to take up its challenge to envision, develop, and pursue responses to violence that do not rely on or produce police violence.

My copresenter, representing Manavi, an organization working with South Asian survivors of violence, issued a similar call for non–law enforcement, community-based responses to violence. She drew attention to the fact that for Manavi's constituency, law enforcement responses were potentially dangerous on many levels, ranging from potential immigration consequences and failure to protect based on assumptions about South Asian "culture" to arrest of or additional violence against survivors. After our presentation, the room slowly began to empty, a trickle becoming a flood. No one thanked us for our presentation or approached us to engage with us or the content of our talks. We instinctively moved closer and closer together until we were hugging, alone in a conference room full of people who had no desire to hear the message we were delivering. Since then, there has been some progress: dozens of antiviolence coalitions and activists signed on to a submission to the President's Task Force on 21st-Century Policing focused on women of color's experiences of policing, and there is growing recognition among antiviolence advocates that police responses to violence—including "mandatory arrest" policies—need to be revisited.[7] Nevertheless, much of the mainstream antiviolence movement remains conspicuously silent on the issue of police violence against women of color.

Pulling back the veil reveals that police violence in the context of responses to domestic, sexual, family, homophobic, and transphobic violence takes many forms: verbal abuse, physical violence, and refusal to respond, as in Cherae's case. Respondents to a 2015 survey of more than nine hundred antiviolence advocates, survivors, and other stakeholders from almost all fifty states undertaken by law professor Julie Goldscheid and her colleagues found that police were sometimes or often demeaning or disrespectful to survivors, did not believe them, or did not take domestic violence or sexual assault seriously.[8] Almost a third of respondents said that police sometimes or often used inappropriate force against survivors. They also reported that officers threatened to arrest survivors, particularly if they were called multiple times. Police violence in the context of responses to violence can also include sexual harassment, assault, and abuse, profiling of survivors as perpetrators of violence, arrest or referral to immigration authorities, "outing" of LGBTQ survivors, and loss of housing and children.

In all too many cases, police responses to violence prove deadly to survivors, including many whose stories we don't yet know.[9] For instance, Melissa Ventura, a Latinx mother of three described by her sister as the "heart and soul of her family" and by a neighbor as happy about the recent arrival of her two-month old baby, was killed by police officers responding to a domestic violence call at her home in Yuma, Arizona, in July 2016. Police officers were the only witnesses to the killing, and none have been held accountable.[10] On February 18, 2015, Janisha Fonville and her girlfriend, Korneisha Banks, both Black women living in a Charlotte, North Carolina, housing project, had been fighting. Eventually, Banks asked her sister to call the police and left the house. When police responded, she went back to the house with them, where they found Janisha lying on the couch. As Janisha rose from the couch in protest of the police officers' arrival, one of the officers shot her in the chest, claiming she was lunging at them with a knife. Korneisha says Janisha was empty-handed, and that there was no threat to the officers from the one-hundred-pound woman. Family and friends described Janisha as loving and funny, and as someone who struggled with mental health issues and was trying to manage them.[11] They can also prove to be deadly to bystanders such as Yvette Smith or Bettie Jones, women who were killed by officers responding to calls involving other members of their households or neighbors.[12] Once brought out of the shadows, these stories require us to shift and expand our responses to violence in all its forms—including police violence.

Police violence against survivors of violence often takes place away from public view, cameras, and cop watchers. Survivors of violence are less likely to be able to speak out, because they need the police to remain willing to respond to future calls for assistance or because of shame, silence, and fear of retaliation. As a result, racial profiling and police brutality in the context of responses to violence remains, quite literally, invisible.

Even when women do come forward, their stories too often go unnoticed by antiviolence and police accountability groups alike. Cases like Cherae's are often hidden in plain sight, the subject of public testimony or news coverage that meets with little response from anti–police brutality activists because it is perceived as a domestic violence–related problem and thus a women's issue, not a problem of racial profiling or police violence—a men's issue. The same year Cherae testified before the New York City Council, a Black woman testified at an Amnesty International hearing on police brutality in Los Angeles to tell her story that officers responding to a "family quarrel" had beaten her in her home until she fainted, while her children were locked outside, powerless to answer their mother's cries for help. The officers then gagged her and dragged her across her yard to their police car.[13] It is telling that neither case became a rallying cry for either antiviolence or anti–police brutality movements.

In addition to engaging in physical violence against survivors, as detailed in chapter 5, officers like Daniel Holtzclaw and Roger Magaña take advantage of their position to prey on survivors when responding to calls for help or when entering private premises without a warrant on the pretense that they believe someone is in danger.[14] In a 2006 series on police sexual violence, the *Philadelphia Inquirer* reported: "A Glenolden, Delaware County, officer was convicted of raping a woman in 2002 after he answered a domestic-dispute call. 'He had his police uniform on, his gun, his nightstick,' the woman said. 'I did exactly what he asked me to do.'"[15] A Pennsylvania state trooper who had been convicted of multiple sexual assaults in 2000 explained the underlying dynamics: "I would see women that were vulnerable where I could appear as a knight in shining armor. . . . I'm going to help this woman who's being abused by her boyfriend, and then I'll ask for sexual favors."[16]

In one particularly infuriating case in Chicago in 2010, Tiawanda Moore called police during a dispute with her boyfriend. As he was trained to do, an officer took her into a private room to take her statement. But instead of doing so, he fondled her breasts, groped her buttocks, and left his number with the suggestion that they "hook up." She called his supervisor to report him, and met with a lieutenant and internal affairs officer. According to her attorney, Robert Johnson, when she tried to report the assault, internal affairs "gave her the run-around."[17] She demanded that the officer be fired. They prevented her from leaving the room while discouraging her from filing a complaint, among other things referring to the fact that she was a "stripper." She began recording the conversation on her Blackberry. They charged her with two counts of felony wiretapping, under an Illinois law that says you need the consent of both parties to record a conversation. She spent two weeks in jail and over a year fighting the charges, until she was finally acquitted in 2012.[18] The officer who assaulted her was never charged or disciplined. Her experience confirmed the reality for so many survivors of police sexual violence: if you come forward, you are the one who will be put on trial, not the officer responsible. That same year, Tiawanda filed a civil suit against the officer who assaulted her and the city and county officials who let him get away with it.

As in other contexts, sexual violence during domestic-violence calls may take the form of strip searches. For instance, in 2005, a police officer working in a Chicago suburb was charged with official misconduct for making women strip naked when he responded to domestic-violence calls. For trans women, such searches may be the pernicious "gender check." While litigating *Tikkun v. City of New York* in the 2000s, a case alleging a pattern and practice within the NYPD of conducting unconstitutional searches to assign gender based on anatomy, a fellow attorney sent me a notice of claim filed against the City of New York in 1999 by Anothai Hansen-Singthong, a Thai transgender woman who called police for protection from her abusive partner. Instead of being protected, she was arrested and strip-searched at the precinct after her abuser told officers she was trans. While I was never able to locate additional information about her case, it always struck me as yet another invisible instance of police violence against a woman of color that came to my attention only by happenstance and never would otherwise have seen the light of day.

Denial of protection is also a form of police violence, and increases vulnerability to other forms of violence by signaling to abusers and bystanders that violence against women of color is acceptable. Explicit or implicit punishment for deviation from, or the inability to meet, racialized gender norms often underlies the denial of police protection. Racial profiling informs not only officers' perceptions of who is committing violence but also of who is a victim. Black women, Indigenous women, and other women of color are defined as inherently existing outside the bounds of womanhood—rendering the status of "good victim" unattainable. This reality is exacerbated and compounded for women of color who are perceived to further deviate from racialized gender norms, transgender and gender-nonconforming women of color; women who use alcohol or controlled substances, and women who are criminalized, such as sex workers. These deviations mark them as unworthy of protection and deserving of arrest in the eyes of law enforcement officers responding to violence.[19]

More than half the respondents in the service-provider study cited earlier reported anti-immigrant, anti-Muslim, and anti-LGBTQ perceptions among police officers. They also noted police failure to take seriously violence against young survivors, survivors with mental health issues, drug users, and homeless and low-income survivors, an attitude rooted in perceptions that violence is simply part of an "impoverished or 'ghetto' lifestyle."[20] Again and again, study participants noted the ways in which controlling narratives informed police responses to women of color:

> Police are much more interested in helping light skinned victims. I think this ties in to their inherent racial bias and ideas about who is a good, deserving victim and who is a troublemaker who brought this violence on. I think that there are especially dangerous stereotypes about assertive black women that the police buy into and keep them from helping black women who are victims of abuse.
>
> My African-American clients seem to be treated worse by police. Police are more likely to suspect them of contributing to the violence or in some other way being at fault for what has happened. They also seem to take claims of black victims less seriously.
>
> The police often assume that if the victim is Native American that she/he has been drinking, thus causing the problem.
>
> Victims of Hispanic/Latina descent are assumed to be lying about the crime to qualify for immigration remedies, even if the victim is a US citizen. . . .
>
> The assumption is [that] Muslim women, South Asian/Arab/ Middle Eastern women, aren't deserving of responses because of the

problematic assumptions that equate Muslim women with being op-pressed due to their inherent religious identity. . . .

People who don't speak English are discriminated against. Because they are hard to communicate with, police don't investigate their cases as thoroughly. They also ignore important protocols (such as separat-ing family members to interview them) because it's less convenient. Police are also less likely to inform undocumented immigrants of their legal rights.[21]

Transgender people of color are relentlessly and ruthlessly denied protection by police and often blamed for violence they experience. When researching *Stonewalled*, we learned of an instance when Los An-geles police responded to a violent assault on an undocumented Latinx transgender street vendor by saying, "If they kill her, call us."[22] We also heard about an incident in which an Asian Pacific transgender woman reported a hate crime to police, who refused to photograph her inju-ries, telling her, "You're not a victim of violence. If you didn't tell people you're a transsexual, people would leave you alone."[23] Advocates also told us that, where domestic violence against transgender women is con-cerned, officers often laugh, or say, "You're a man, too. You can handle yourself," or "Oh, guys, forget it; this is a man."[24] One young Black trans woman living in Los Angeles repeatedly called police for assistance when her boyfriend was abusive. Each time, despite the visible bruises on her body, officers said that there was nothing they could do. Instead, two undercover officers knocked on her door one morning and told her she was under arrest on an old warrant for a solicitation charge.[25]

Indeed, trans people are often criminalized rather than protected by police. In one case that prompted a national organizing campaign, CeCe McDonald, a Black transgender woman, was arrested and impris-oned for defending herself against a neo-Nazi who pursued her as she tried to leave after his friend smashed a broken glass into CeCe's face, lacerating her cheek and a salivary gland. Instead of celebrating her sur-vival, police and prosecutors punished her for it. The moral of the story is that transgender women are treated by police as if they have the right to neither protection nor self-defense.

Lesbians, deemed gender nonconforming by virtue of their existence outside the heteropatriarchy, are also ignored and punished. One
survivor interviewed by the Family Violence Project in New York City
said that the police "show up and . . . are like . . . dykes, damn it . . . God,
they deserve this."

In 2015, the National Coalition of Anti-Violence Programs (NCAVP)
reported that 12 percent of the 33 percent of LGBTQ survivors who reported intimate-partner violence to law enforcement said that the police were hostile.[26] Among survivors of homophobic or transphobic
violence who reported to the police, 39 percent said police were hostile,
33 percent experienced verbal abuse, and 16 percent experienced physical abuse.[27] In 2013, 5 percent of LGBTQ survivors of intimate partner
violence reported physical violence by police.[28] Often, such violence is a
manifestation of racialized gender policing. For instance, advocates and
survivors alike report that once a transgender woman's gender identity
is discovered by officers responding to a domestic-violence call or is
disclosed to them by an abuser, she is treated as if she has deceived the
police and punished with violence.

Gender nonconformity in behavior also produces both police violence and exclusion from protection. In one study, survivors of violence
who were arrested tended to be using drugs or alcohol, "thus deviating from gender-role prescriptions of appropriate female behavior."[29]
Women survivors of violence arrested in Boulder, Colorado, also reported that they believed that use of alcohol was among the top three
reasons they had been arrested.[30] Similarly, women who are or are perceived to be involved in the sex trades are denied protection: Cyndee
Clay, executive director of HIPS, a sex workers' organization in Washington, DC, has stated that women perceived to be departing from gendered norms of acceptable behavior by engaging in sex work are almost
universally subject to dual arrest—in which both parties to a dispute
are arrested—when police respond to domestic violence against them.
Similar perceptions govern police response to sexual assault, particularly for Black women who are believed to be engaged in the sex trade.[31]

Despite the constant pathologizing of women who don't "fight
back" against rape and other forms of violence, women who defend

themselves are also denied protection by police because their behavior is perceived as a deviation from a gender-normative, defenseless response. In Florida, Marissa Alexander was arrested for firing a warning shot in the air to stop an assault by her abusive husband. As a Black woman, she was already at a disadvantage, more likely to be perceived as violent than as victimized. When, instead of performing victimhood in expected ways—cowering, crying in a corner—she "stood her ground," Marissa was punished with arrest and was charged with a felony offense carrying a twenty-year prison sentence, even though no one was harmed or even in danger of being harmed by her actions.

Black women who are queer are also more likely to be framed by police as perpetrators rather than victims when they defend themselves. This was glaringly apparent in one case that gained national attention through local organizing, depicted in the award-winning documentary *Out in the Night* and described in Beth Richie's *Arrested Justice* and in *Queer (In)Justice*. Seven Black lesbians who became known as the New Jersey 7 were out in New York City one hot summer's night when a man made a lewd comment to one of them. When they responded that they weren't interested because they were gay, his tone quickly turned violent as he followed them down the street, shouting, "Dyke bitches, lesbian bitches, I'll fuck you straight, sweetheart!" Then he spat on one of the women, threw a lit cigarette at the group, and climbed on top of another, pulling her hair out at the roots. One of the women, Renata Hill, said that, "With him approaching me in the manner that he was approaching, and saying the things he was saying, basically you're saying that you're going to rape me." The women defended themselves and were walking away when police stopped and arrested them, guns drawn. Initial police radio reports described the incident as minor, involving minimal injuries, "not gang activity." Yet eventually, based largely on perceptions rooted in the women's sexual orientation, gender identity, and expression, things changed.[32] As INCITE! and FIERCE! later wrote about the incident,

> Police characterized the incident as one of "gang violence" by a group
> of Black lesbians, rather than as one of homophobic and misogynist

sexual and physical violence by a straight man against a group of women. Based in large part on the police version of the events, the media constructed and reinforced identities of "killer lesbians" forming "a seething Sapphic septet," and a "lesbian wolf pack," before the courts and prison industrial complex took over their enforcement and punishment. How police responded to and investigated this case drove its ultimate outcome.[33]

The women were tried, charged, pled guilty or were convicted, and sentenced to periods of up to eleven years in prison. Though eventually all were released on appeal, with the support of a bicoastal campaign to win their freedom, their lives were forever changed. Each had lost years of their freedom, missed the funeral of a loved one, and time with their children and families.

These are only a few instances in which Black women—perceived as gender nonconforming on the basis of race, sexual orientation, gender identity, behavior, or appearance, or some combination thereof—were denied victim status and were criminalized for defending themselves. *No Selves to Defend*, an exhibit mounted by Mariame Kaba and Rachel Caïdor, catalogues many more,[34] and the national coalition #SurvivedandPunished organizes around active cases of survivors of violence penalized for self-defense.[35]

For these reasons and more, for many women of color, calling on law enforcement for protection is simply not an option. Historical and current realities fuel perceptions of law enforcement agents and the criminal legal system as further threats to women of color's own safety and that of their families and communities, rather than as sources of protection from violence in the home. More than 80 percent of respondents to the 2015 service-provider survey believed that police relations with communities of color influenced their clients' willingness to call the police for help.[36] Criminalized survivors are particularly reluctant to contact police. Service providers report, "Many of our clients were committing crimes (using illegal substances, participating in sex work, had a taser in their possession, etc.) while they were being abused. Clients are afraid of being prosecuted for those crimes while their abusers go free."[37]

Historic and current state violence against Native women renders many Native women reluctant to call on law enforcement for assistance when facing violence in their communities. Even when Native women do seek assistance from police, they are often disbelieved based on stereotypes focused on actual or perceived alcohol use. Vulnerability to violence is further compounded for Native women living on reservations who remain almost completely unprotected due to restrictions that prevent tribal law enforcement from exercising jurisdiction over felony cases or cases involving non-Natives. This leaves pursuit of abusers to federal law enforcement agencies, who frequently fail to adequately investigate and prosecute crimes against Native women.[38]

For undocumented women, reliance on the state for protection can have devastating consequences. This is especially true in border states such as California, Texas, and Arizona, where Border Patrol agents often ride with local law enforcement agents, as well as in the increasing number of jurisdictions where local law enforcement agents have been deputized to enforce federal immigration laws. According to one 2003 study of Vietnamese immigrants living in Houston, survivors of violence call the police at one-fifth the rate of other ethnic groups, regardless of immigration status, due to fear of problems with immigration authorities and racial or ethnic discrimination by law enforcement.[39]

And given high levels of police violence and denial of protection to transgender people, it is not surprising that more than half of respondents to the 2015 US Transgender Survey said they would feel uncomfortable asking the police for help if they needed it. Middle Eastern, Black, and multiracial respondents, as well as people living with disabilities and people living in poverty, were most likely to feel uncomfortable seeking assistance from police.[40]

MANDATORY AND PRO-ARREST POLICIES

"Mandatory" and "pro-arrest" policies all too often contribute to the criminalization of women's efforts to prevent and avoid violence, and to defend themselves and their children and families. Far from eliminating the effects of police discretion in responding to domestic violence, such policies simply mandate an arrest, leaving police with the discretion to determine who to arrest, with predictable results.[41] Of particular concern has been the growing numbers of arrests of survivors of violence under such policies.[42] Joan Zorza, a longtime advocate for survivors of violence, concludes that, at their worst, mandatory arrest policies "may be utilized as a weapon to exploit and further victimize battered women."[43]

In 1995, following the adoption of mandatory arrest policies, 14.3 percent of domestic-violence arrests in Los Angeles were of women, double the rate of the previous five years. Overall arrests for domestic violence increased under mandatory arrest policies between 1987 and 1995, but three times as many women were arrested in 1995 as in 1987, compared to less than twice as many men.[44] In Maryland, the number of women arrested for domestic violence tripled between 1992 and 1996, and in Sacramento the number of women arrested for domestic violence increased 91 percent between 1991 and 1996.[45] In 2001, feminist researcher Susan Miller reported that in some cities, over 20 percent of those arrested following domestic-violence complaints were women. She concluded: "An arrest policy intended to protect battered women as victims is being misapplied and used against them. Battered women have become female offenders."[46] In 2000, a study of domestic-violence survivors under New York State's mandatory arrest policies found that, over a two-and-a-half year period, survivors of domestic violence had been arrested in 27 percent of cases received through a domestic-violence hotline.[47] Eighty-five percent of survivors who were arrested had a prior documented record of being subjected to domestic violence, and 85 percent were injured during the incident that led to their arrest.[48] Arrests of survivors are particularly common in police responses to incidents of violence involving two people perceived to be of the same gender. According to a 2010 NCAVP report, incidents of "misarrest" of LGBTQ people increased 144 percent from 2008 to 2009.[49] In 2015, misarrests of survivors increased to 31 percent, from the 17 percent reported in 2014.[50]

There are several scenarios in which survivors are revictimized by mandatory arrest policies. Sometimes, responding officers are unable to or don't try to (or simply can't be bothered to) discern which party is the primary aggressor and opt to arrest both parties to a domestic dispute. Other times, notwithstanding often lengthy histories of being subjected to violence, survivors are deemed by arresting officers to be the aggressor because they acted in self-defense. And still other times, the survivor ends up in handcuffs because the abuser, familiar with and able to manipulate the legal system, called the police first. One Los Angeles case is typical: a Middle Eastern woman who endured her husband's abuse for over a decade and finally bit him during a struggle was arrested by officers called by neighbors.[51] In another, Dariela, a Honduran immigrant, was arrested when her abusive partner, Maria, called the police. Dariela later said, "But that is how the law is. . . . She is American, and I did not speak English, and I am an immigrant; things went bad for me." Chicana studies professor Martha Escobar concluded that for Dariela, "her undocumented status, inability to speak English, and sexuality [were] all factors constructed as deviant."[52]

Thus, profiling doesn't stop when the police shift from enforcers to "protectors": who is perceived as a legitimate victim and who is perceived as violent is deeply racially gendered. Police officers' responses to calls for help are informed by controlling narratives of women and gender-nonconforming people of color as violent, threatening, and incapable of being raped or abused and complicit in the violence perpetrated against them. Officers implementing mandatory arrest policies thus engage in racialized gender profiling by arresting the person who is of color, is more gender nonconforming, is an immigrant, or speaks limited English. Consequently, it is not surprising that the impacts of survivor arrests appear to fall disproportionately on low-income women of color. A significant majority (66 percent) of survivors of violence in the New York City study who had been arrested along with their abusers (dual arrest) or arrested as a result of a complaint lodged by their abuser (retaliatory arrest) were African American or Latinx.[53] Forty-three percent were living below the poverty line, and 19 percent were receiving public assistance at the time.[54] As noted earlier, studies have also found that survivors of violence are also more likely to be arrested if they were under the influence of alcohol or controlled substances at the time of police response, fought back against their abuse, were engaged or perceived to be engaged in sex work, or are transgender or gender nonconforming in appearance.

Arrest of survivors under mandatory arrest policies subjects people who have already been targets of violence in their families, homes, and communities to further violence, this time at the hands of the state. The retraumatization experienced when survivors of violence are arrested when police respond to a domestic-violence call is predictable. One survivor who was subject to a mandatory arrest said she "got arrested like *two* times. . . . That's traumatizing. . . . The police officer . . . he *pushed me* inside the car! He *pushed* me inside, 'Tell that to the judge!' He sees me *crying* and *trembling* and stuff. He just *pushed* me . . . '*Shut up back there!!*' And I was crying. I said, 'It's not fair' . . . 'Shut up!!' . . . He pulled me out of the car. . . . He pushed me against [a desk]."[55]

Such arrests also have devastating collateral consequences in terms of immigration status, losing children, access to employment, denial of benefits, being pushed further into criminalized survival economies, and increased vulnerability to violence. For immigrant women, the consequences of mandatory arrest policies can be doubly devastating in the context of ever-increasing collaboration between immigration enforcement and local law enforcement authorities, described in chapter 2. Many undocumented women have reported cases of sexual and domestic violence only to find themselves deported after being arrested under mandatory arrest policies or subject to inquiries into their immigration status by law enforcement officers.[56]

CHANGING THE NARRATIVE, CHANGING THE VISION

The Ann Arbor Alliance for Black Lives initially arose out of a solidarity march with Ferguson in the wake of the murder of Mike Brown in August 2014. Since then it has largely focused on demanding accountability for the killing of Aura Rain Rosser, an artist and mother of three killed by Ann Arbor police three months later. Officers David Ried and Mark Raab responded to a domestic violence call at Aura's house.[57] Claiming that Aura caused them to fear for their safety as she walked toward them from fifteen feet away holding a four-inch knife, officers made no effort to deescalate the situation or give her an opportunity to drop the knife. Instead, five to ten seconds after arriving, they shot her. The officers and city officials retroactively justified the shooting by saying that Aura "opened her eyes very wide," "appeared to be in a deranged state," and had "a blank stare," echoing the justifications offered by the officers who killed Michelle Cusseaux months earlier, and drawing on historic depictions of Black women as congenitally deranged, superhuman, and posing an inherent threat.

"A People's Retort" to the prosecutor's report in the case draws parallels between justifications offered for Aura's shooting with Darren Wilson's characterization of Mike Brown as a "demon," using racist tropes to transform Aura into a mortal threat rather than a woman in the midst of "an angry dispute with her ex-boyfriend."[58] Local organizer and scholar-activist Austin McCoy notes the multiple dynamics at play in both Aura's death and the state's response: "The crucial difference is that Rosser is black and female. Being black and female in America today means that black women not only die at the hands of the state like men, their suffering is obscured while making their physicality and their psychological state hypervisible. Black women's suffering is unseen by authorities, but the state tries to highlight how they are 'aggressive' and 'hysterical.'"[59]

The organizing around Aura's case highlights a welcome expansion in the movement for police accountability compared to the relative silence around Cherae Williams's case fifteen years earlier. Rosser's image is one of many circulating in cyberspace under the Black Lives Matter hashtag, her death is the motivation for marches drawing thousands, her name is invoked alongside Brown's at rallies, demonstrations, and vigils across the country.

When longtime antiviolence activist Mariame Kaba first read a *New York Times* article about Tiawanda Moore, she was shocked that she hadn't known earlier about her case, which took place in Chicago, where Kaba was living. Kaba immediately mobilized the Chicago Task Force on Women and Girls to raise awareness about Tiawanda on social media, to campaign for since-deposed prosecutor Anita Alvarez to drop the charges, and to pack the courtroom with supporters throughout Tiawanda's trial. Kaba never forgot the case, later playing a leadership role in the campaign to remove Alvarez as district attorney during the 2016 election under the hashtag #ByeAnita. Kaba's organizing around Tiawanda's case was consistent with Angela Davis's call fifteen years earlier at the 2000 INCITE! conference: to recognize and organize from a place that makes visible survivors' vulnerability to both state and interpersonal violence.

Survived and Punished, cofounded by Kaba, is among the organizations that have taken up the case of Ky Peterson, a Black trans man raped as he walked home from a convenience store in Americus, Georgia, in 2011. Ky defended himself, killing his attacker. Based on prior experiences, he didn't think he would be believed by police, so he concealed the body and hoped for the best. His instincts were right—when police eventually did get involved, they didn't see Ky as a victim, despite evidence from a rape kit that supported his version of events. Instead police pursued theories involving consensual sex and robbery that ultimately forced Ky to enter a guilty plea in an effort to avoid a lifetime of imprisonment. He was sentenced to twenty years. Chase Strangio of the ACLU concludes, "What this case highlights is how difficult it is for trans people of color to claim the status of victim."[60]

Beyond organizing around individual cases, these realities require us to acknowledge that racial profiling and police violence take place not just in street and traffic stops, but also when police respond to complaints of violence. Community efforts by anti–police brutality and antiviolence groups to document and redress violence should therefore explicitly include police violence that takes place in the context of responses to violence. Additionally, cop-watch groups need to support domestic-violence survivors in safely documenting their own experiences of policing and exposing police violence in these contexts.

Perhaps most importantly, Black women's and women of color's experiences of police responses to violence demand that we radically rethink our visions of safety, including by ending mandatory arrest policies and developing responses to violence that don't involve the police. Some in the mainstream antiviolence movement have already started down this road. In March 2016, I found myself, to my great surprise, at a gathering convened by the federal Office of Juvenile Justice,

Detention, and Prevention to discuss ending mandatory arrest policies in the context of responses to family violence involving girls, which are among the primary drivers of girls' arrest and incarceration.[61] Perhaps if this had been achieved in Kentucky, Gynnya McMillen, who died in custody after being arrested following a dispute with her mother, would still be with us today. In June 2016, the New York City Council Young Women's Initiative recommended the establishment of a task force to consider the repeal of mandatory arrest policies in one of the first cities that adopted them. The initiative also advocated for programs that would empower women to prevent, avoid, and leave violence, including increased access to housing, employment, and health care, and legalizing their immigration status. By investing in the needs of communities and survivors, the goal is to reduce police responses to violence and support alternative approaches to advancing safety of young women and girls.[62]

Some organizations have been laying the groundwork for community-based responses to violence: Communities Against Rape and Abuse and Sista II Sista both wrote powerful pieces in *Color of Violence: The INCITE! Anthology* detailing their experiments. Creative Interventions, Gen 5, Harm Free Zones, and the Audre Lorde Project Safe Outside the System Project have all piloted, practiced, and reflected on how we respond to violence without police. Many of the lessons learned are highlighted in the *Creative Interventions' Toolkit: A Practical Guide to Stop Interpersonal Violence*, inspiring newer formations, like the Dream Defenders, and others to follow in their footsteps.[63] Ultimately, the experiences described in this chapter, along with countless others, counsel strongly in favor of a critical examination of current approaches to violence against women, and the development and support of alternative, community-based accountability strategies that prioritize safety for survivors; community responsibility for creating, enabling, and eliminating the climates that allow violence to happen; and the transformation of private and public relations of power.

The Critical Resistance–INCITE! statement calls on movements concerned with ending police violence and violence against women to "develop community based responses to violence that do not rely on the criminal legal system AND which have mechanisms that ensure safety and accountability for survivors of domestic and sexual violence."[64] Such responses are essential if we are to move away from reliance on law enforcement–based approaches to violence; achieve true safety for survivors of domestic violence; and, ultimately, end violence against women of color in all its forms.

CHAPTER 10

RESISTANCE

"We do this for Marissa! We do this for Rekia! We do this for Tanisha! We do this for Islan! We do this for Aiyanna! We do this for Mya! We do this for Malissa! We do this till we free us!" These words—a riff on the famous Ferguson chant "Turn up! Don't turn down! We do this for Mike Brown!"—were our chant as we marched through the streets of New York City on May 21, 2015. We were marking the first National Day of Action to End State Violence Against Black Women and Girls, called by Black Youth Project 100 (BYP100), Black Lives Matter (BLM), and Ferguson Action. We had just left a beautiful and moving ceremony led by members of Harriet's Apothecary, a collective of Black women and queer and trans healers, and organized by the New York City chapters of BYP100 and BLM at the African Burial Ground monument in lower Manhattan. There we had commemorated the lives of Black women lost to state violence. Now we were marching toward city hall to join a rally to protest the addition of one thousand police officers to the nation's biggest police force—and one of its deadliest.

At the ceremony preceding the march, one participant told the story of Shereese Francis, a former day-care worker who was warm, outgoing, and beloved by her community and church. On March 15, 2012, concerned family members called for an ambulance when Shereese went into an emotional crisis after she stopped taking medication prescribed for schizophrenia. The police responded first. Four NYPD officers chased Shereese through her home and piled on top of her, one of them punching her. They handcuffed her as she lay facedown on a bed and suffocated her—much like police across the country would do to Kayla Moore a year later.[1]

Another participant told the story of Islan Nettles, a twenty-one-year-old Black trans woman who worked at a fashion company, who was beaten to death across the street from a Harlem police station. Islan had been walking with a group of friends when a man tried to flirt with her. When his friends made fun of him, he took his rage out on Islan, killing her.[2] Islan's murder sparked protests by trans community members and allies, who called attention to her death as emblematic of endemic and often fatal community violence against trans people, and of pervasive police indifference to Black trans lives.[3]

After the ceremony, we marched out the other side of the monument, through a representation of the "door of no return," carrying a coffin bearing the name of Shantel Davis, a twenty-three-year-old Black woman—a loving sister, niece, daughter, auntie, and friend, with a warm and contagious smile, strength of character, and generosity. Shantel was killed by New York police detective Philip Aikins in June 2012 as she sat in a car, unarmed, in Brooklyn.[4]

We made our way, chanting, solemn, and determined, to city hall. There, activist Carmen Dixon had just testified on behalf of BLM, in the name of Black women targeted for police violence and Black mothers who have lost children to police violence, against the proposal to add a thousand more officers to the force. She concluded by saying:

> When I close my eyes, and think about what makes me feel safest, I think of all my needs being met and the presence of people I love and respect. I do not think of one thousand additional police officers. . . . That is why Black Lives Matter NYC and the Safety Beyond Policing Coalition call on the NYC Council to redirect more than two hundred million dollars that would be spent over the next three years on additional police instead to adequately fund NYCHA [the New York City Housing Authority], jobs for youth, transportation, and mental health services, preventive services to keep children out of foster care, doula programs, food cooperatives, a fund for victims of police violence, and other urgent community needs.[5]

That afternoon, BYP100 and BLM members fanned out through Flatbush, a predominantly Black, immigrant, working-class neighborhood, to talk about state violence against Black women and girls. We ended the day at a monthly rally organized by Anita Neal, mother of Kyam Livingston, a thirty-seven-year-old, loving Black mother who worked as a security guard and died in a Brooklyn police lockup after being denied medical attention.[6] Throughout the day, I watched as news of events held in more than twenty cities across the country marking the national day of action unfolded—marches, rallies, vigils, and direct actions, from Chicago to Charlotte, New York to New Orleans, Ann Arbor to Austin, Seattle to San Francisco.[7]

The night before, I had attended a vigil in Union Square honoring families of Black women killed by police—the first of its kind—organized by the African American Policy Forum (AAPF) (see insert for vigil photo). I stood next to Kayla Moore's sister Maria, along with family members of Tanisha Anderson, Rekia Boyd, Miriam Carey, Michelle Cusseaux, Shantel Davis, Shelly Frye, and Alberta Spruill, as we remembered not only how their daughters, sisters, or aunts had been killed but also who they were. And we envisioned what justice for them would look like. It was the first anti–police brutality event I had ever been to where I hadn't left feeling frustrated, angry, or saddened at the erasure of Black women's experiences and voices as targets of police violence and leaders in struggles against it. Instead, I felt whole in resistance.

One year later, at an event marking the second National Day of Action to End State Violence Against Black Women, Girls and Femmes, I stood behind a person wearing a BYP100 hoodie proudly proclaiming "Through a Black Queer Feminist Lens." Tears came to my eyes—I never imagined I would be able to be a part of a broad-based movement that embraces a politic that has, until now, been limited to much smaller formations, relegated to the margins of feminist movements and movements for racial justice, never in the leadership of a national movement fighting police violence. After two decades of meetings, rallies, marches, conferences, and conversations on racial profiling and police brutality exclusively focused on Black and Brown men (and never Indigenous men) where I was a lone voice—never the only one, but often the only one in the room—calling for attention to Black women and women of color's experiences of policing, asking people to at least say "Black and

Brown men *and women*," feeling like I was constantly talking under water, I suddenly felt like I had popped above the surface.

The tears returned many times that day, as once again I watched actions unfold across the country—from a banner drop at a Chicago White Sox game, to an MTV News video, to Black Lives Matter's tribute to women lost to state and interpersonal violence and to women whose leadership inspires (which originated as a high school art project), to a projection of the names of Black women killed by police onto the walls of the US Department of Justice.[8] Later came tears of rage and sorrow as I learned that on that very day, San Francisco Police had shot Jessica Nelson Williams, a mother of five, described by her family as a loving, caring, strong, and talented woman.[9] While Jessica's killing prompted the resignation of the San Francisco police chief, it rammed home the reality that even on a National Day of Action to End State Violence Against Black Women, Girls, and Femmes, no Black woman is safe from police violence.

There is no question that the shroud of invisibility around Black women's and women of color's experiences of police violence has been irrevocably lifted in the post-Ferguson moment and movement. It has been forcefully pushed aside by young women on the front lines in Ferguson and by bloggers and organizers across the country who were speaking out in the days and months following Mike Brown's killing, who were outraged at Dajerria Becton's assault in McKinney, who rose up in widespread protest following Sandra Bland's death in police custody, and who unapologetically demanded attention and action around #AssaultatSpringValleyHigh and the rape of thirteen Black women by Oklahoma City police officer Daniel Holtzclaw, and who demanded justice for Rekia Boyd.

In the past I had to hunt down and unearth women's experiences of policing from archives, reports, transcripts of testimony, listservs, interviews, and one-on-one conversations. Now social media makes it possible to share these stories in unprecedented and unfiltered ways, coupled with insistence that we organize around them with as much fervor and indignation as we do for cases involving men. Now I have access to so many women's stories that I can't keep track of them all, and struggled with decisions about which to include in this book. Now it is much rarer to see an event, rally, or public statement around police brutality that doesn't mention at least one woman. It seems that we will never go back to the time when Black women and women of color were expected to organize and lead marches protesting police violence against men but to remain silent about our own experiences and those of our sisters and trans and Two Spirit siblings. Our experiences and realities can no longer be ignored.

But we still have a long way to go. Organizers of events for the National Day of Action described resistance to placards featuring women's names, with men insisting that *all* victims of police violence be represented—which was ironic, given that women's identical demands were so consistently ignored in the past. Some have hurled homophobic and transphobic abuse at Black queer women leading or speaking at rallies, marches, and direct actions—sometimes while these very same women made sure that the men attacking them wouldn't be attacked by the police. An early 2015 New York City rally for Rekia Boyd, a young Black woman killed by an off-duty Chicago police officer, drew fewer than one hundred people, while rallies for Mike Brown and Eric Garner had drawn thousands night after night just a few months before.

In many arenas, women of color's experiences of policing continue to be shrouded in invisibility, or token visibility, in conversations around racial profiling, police violence, and mass incarceration. Sandra Bland's mother is often the only mother of a woman killed by police invited to speak on police brutality, and no family members, chosen or original, of trans people killed by police are ever lifted up by mainstream civil rights leaders or in mainstream media to speak out on the issue. Numerous books and studies focused exclusively on Black men's experiences of policing continue to be published; analyses of the issues continue to presume men of color as the primary and sole targets of racial profiling and police brutality.

Nevertheless, we are at an unprecedented moment of awareness of Black women and women of color as subjects of police violence. This represents a culmination of decades of labor and resistance within movements against violence and for police accountability, LGBTQ liberation, and reproductive justice, which has produced an analysis of policing that inextricably incorporates race, gender, gender identity, and sexuality.

As Angela Y. Davis points out in *Freedom Is a Constant Struggle*, the evolution of this intersectional analysis has been a long and collective process, grounded not in the halls of academia but in movement formations and lived realities of activists on the ground.[10] Throughout the 1970s, '80s, and '90s, Davis herself led the way in articulating a gendered analysis of police violence and criminalization of women of color which profoundly inspired and shaped my, and many others', evolving understanding.[11] In *Resisting State Violence*, published in 1996, Joy James calls out the lack of such an analysis among advocates for women's rights and racial justice. She also points readers to *Black Women Under Siege by New York City Police*, a 1987 report compiled by the Center for Law and Social Justice at Medgar Evers College decrying the framing of police attacks on Black women like Eleanor Bumpurs as isolated incidents, instead naming them as "part of an historical and recently increased trend."[12] The Audre Lorde Project's long history of fighting police violence against women and queer and trans people of color and producing razor-sharp intersectional analysis has also deeply informed this work. In 2000, ALP wrote of broken windows policing in New York City, "The presence and actions of women and trans people of color, and particularly youth, sex workers, and homeless people, are always likely to be deemed 'disorderly,' causing 'quality of life policing' to curb our freedom of movement and legitimize and even facilitate police violence towards us."[13] Beth Richie, one of the founders INCITE!, in the early 2000s urged us to "take as a starting point the need to interrogate the ways that gender, sexuality, race, and class collide with harsh penal policy and aggressive law enforcement."[14] The "INCITE! Critical Resistance Statement: Gender Violence and the Prison Industrial Complex," drafted in 2001 by women of color working within movements challenging violence against women and prison and police violence, highlighted the invisibility of women of color targeted for police violence. The statement called on movements to develop strategies to address "how entire communities of all genders are affected in multiple ways by both state violence and interpersonal gender violence," and to "center stories of state violence committed against women of color in our organizing efforts."[15] In 2002, Anannya Bhattacharjee answered the call in "Whose Safety? Women of Color and the Violence of Law Enforcement," a publication of the Committee on Women, Population and the Environment and the American Friends Service Committee, which documented stories and patterns and provided an analysis of police violence against women of color that still resonates more than a decade later.[16]

This analysis extended beyond local policing. In the wake of 9/11, ALP partnered with the American Friends Service Committee to convene grassroots LGBTQ organizations from across the United States for discussions about the impacts of the "war on terror" on LGBTQ people of color and on our communities. In 2003, we drafted a statement describing the increased violence against all marginalized communities fostered by a climate of white supremacy, militarization, and rampant racial profiling.[17] In 2006, as enforcement of immigration laws intensified, ALP issued another statement that emphasized, "When it comes to enforcement, visibly LGBTSTGNC [lesbian, gay, bisexual, Two Spirit, trans, and gender-nonconforming] immigrants of color, undocumented folks, low wage workers, women, youth and elders who are LGBTSTGNC POC [people of color] are exceptionally vulnerable to all facets of the detention and the prison industrial complex." ALP opposed "all provisions to build more walls, fund more border enforcement units."[18] These statements, too, carry similar resonance today.

This intersectional analysis of law enforcement violence, collectively elaborated by Black feminists, feminists of color, and grassroots organizations led by women and LGBTQ people of color over decades, remained largely invisible within larger movements for racial justice and police accountability. Thankfully, Black queer feminists who founded Black Lives Matter and BYP100, along with the organizations that came together to articulate A Vision for Black Lives, as well as groups like AAPF and the Transforming Justice Coalition, have seized upon the post-Ferguson moment to advance a more comprehensive understanding of police violence, one that uncompromisingly centers the experiences of women and queer and trans people of color.

While the current level of discourse around women's experiences of policing is unprecedented in volume, it is not unprecedented in fact. Even more invisible than police violence and criminalization of women of color has been resistance to these phenomena throughout history. The names of Black women, Indigenous women, and women of color harmed by police may not have not rolled off the president's tongue or popped up in the pages of *People* magazine. But we have said them, repeated them to each other, blogged about them, testified about them, insisted their names be read at rallies, and demanded that their stories, and countless others like them, be at the center of our movements. And in so doing, we have followed in the footsteps of a long line of women who have pushed back against the notion that state violence and racial justice are exclusively the purview of Black men and men of color, with "race women" typecast in the role of supporting actors and sorrowing family members.

Here, I endeavor to render visible our long-standing resistance to state violence against women. Though I am most familiar with specific acts of resistance within the Black community, I recognize and honor that Indigenous, Latinx, and Asian women, throughout history, have also vigorously resisted police and state violence. Indigenous women and gender-nonconforming people resisted and continue to resist colonialism at every stage. As Angela Davis points out, "Women resisted and advocated challenges to slavery at every turn," in ways "often more subtle than revolts, escapes, and sabotage."[19] Likewise, immigrant women consistently challenged violence and exclusion at the nation's borders. A few of their names have come down through the historical record—Pine Leaf Woman, Lozen, Buffalo Calf Road Woman, Moving Robe, Harriet Tubman, Sojourner Truth—but countless others, and their means of resistance, remain buried in history.

According to Danielle McGuire, during the civil rights movement, "in order to reclaim their bodies and their humanity, African-American women called on a tradition of testimony and truth-telling that stretched back to slavery," a tradition kept alive by Ida B. Wells-Barnett's documentation of women's experiences of lynching, alongside those of men, in *The Red Record*.[20] We also know, thanks to McGuire, that much of the organizing preceding struggles around school segregation in Little Rock and the Montgomery bus boycott focused on police violence against Black women. For instance, in the 1940s, Daisy Bates, an NAACP leader and advisor to the Little Rock 9, a group of students who integrated a high school in Little Rock, Arkansas, in the face of violent state and community resistance, called on white and Black leaders to address police brutality and abuse of Black women. In 1942, the newspaper Bates ran, the *State Press*, published photographs of two officers who raped Rosa Lee Cherry, a nineteen-year-old student at Little Rock's Dunbar High School, prompting the officers' indictment.[21] In 1946, the inaugural meeting of the Montgomery Women's Political Council, called by Mary Fair Burks, started with her own testimony about being beaten by a white police officer, and "nearly every woman at the meeting chimed in with similar stories of brutalization." Later, led by Jo Ann Robinson, an unsung leader of the boycott, the organization "repeatedly confronted the city commissioners with complaints about police brutality." In 1949, a group of organizations including the NAACP and the Negro Improvement League came together to form the Citizens' Committee for Gertrude Perkins, a twenty-five-year-old Black woman raped by two Montgomery police officers as she walked home late one night. The group resisted efforts to frame Gertrude as a "common street woman" or to justify the assault on her on that basis.

McGuire's research also reveals that at the height of the civil rights movement, in 1963, Dorothy Height, president of the National Council of Negro Women, and Jeanne Noble, president of the Black sorority Delta Sigma Theta, published a report documenting an investigation, conducted by twenty-four women's groups, of the treatment of women civil rights activists by police and jailers in the South. The report documented instances of rape, sexual assault, strip searches in front of male prisoners and officers, and violent, degrading, and unsanitary cavity searches. Height followed up by convening a meeting of women's organizations in Atlanta in 1964 at which an interracial coalition was formed to address the issue. Yet, writes McGuire, stories of sexual violence against women civil rights activists "garnered neither the media coverage nor the organizational support necessary to stop them from happening."

A decade later, women's and racial justice groups once again came together in a campaign focused on sexual violence in Southern jails when Joan Little was charged with the murder of a police officer, Clarence Alligood, who attempted to rape her in a Beaufort County, North Carolina, jail. According to McGuire,

> In 1974 Joan Little became the symbol of a campaign to defend black womanhood and to call attention to the sexualized racial violence that still existed ten years after Congress passed the 1965 Voting Rights Act.
>
> The Free Joan Little campaign brought disparate activists and organizations, each with their own resources and agendas, into a loose but powerful coalition. Feminists and women's liberation organizations spoke out against sexual violence and advocated a woman's right to self-defense; civil rights and Black Power groups saw the Little case as another example of police brutality and Southern injustice; opponents of the death penalty and prison reformers hoped the case would draw attention to their emerging campaigns.

Predictably, Joan's prosecution focused on old familiar tropes, framing her alternately as "a prostitute," "a madam," diseased, and lesbian, and always as a conniving seductress who had lured Alligood into her cell to kill him and escape, rather than recognizing him as a sexual predator supported by the full weight of white supremacist patriarchy and unfettered access to Black women's bodies.

Local grassroots groups rallied around the case as Concerned Women for Justice, joined by regional and national organizations including the National Organization of Women, the Women's Legal Defense Fund, the National Black Feminist Organization, the Black Panther Party, the Southern Christian Leadership Conference, and the Southern Poverty Law Center. Angela Y. Davis published an article in *Ms.* magazine that placed Joan's case in historical context. Rosa Parks helped found a Detroit chapter of the Joan Little Legal Defense Committee. Bernice Johnson Reagon, founder of freedom singers Sweet Honey in the Rock, wrote a song that became the anthem for the Free Joan Little movement. At her July 1975 trial in Wake County, North Carolina, Joan's defense raised the long history of sexual violence against Black women, and Alligood's long history of sexual violence against Black women in the Beaufort County jail. Joan testified in her own defense, recounting how Alligood told her no one would believe her over a police officer if she reported his assault, much as Daniel Holtzclaw told his victims four decades later. Ultimately, the jury acquitted Joan of Alligood's murder.[22]

Five years later, women's groups and racial justice organizations would come together again around police and sexual violence—this time, the failure to investigate it. In 1979, members of the Combahee River Collective, founded in 1974, organized with white feminists and Black organizers to demand police accountability in the investigation, or lack thereof, of the murders of twelve Black women in Boston. The group published a pamphlet highlighting the fact that "the police . . . handled the situation as if there was no reason for concern," telling one mother who reported her fifteen-year-old daughter missing that she had "probably gone off with a pimp."[23]

Since then, however, for the most part the mainstream women's movement's has largely failed, beyond isolated moments of engagement, to take up Angela Y. Davis's 1985 call to become fearless fighters against police violence and to stand in "passionate solidarity with the racially and nationally oppressed people who are its main targets," including and especially Black women, Indigenous women, and women of color.[24] This glaring and frustrating abandonment of women targeted for police violence has mirrored and is the product of the antiviolence movement's growing investment in law enforcement–based approaches to domestic violence and sexual assault, as brilliantly documented in Beth Richie's *Arrested Justice*, Mimi Kim's *Dancing the Carceral Creep*, and *Color of Violence: The INCITE! Anthology*, among others.[25]

The same has been true, until recently, of the mainstream LGBT movement, even though it is commonly understood to have its roots in resistance to policing of queer and trans communities. Decades before the 1969 Stonewall Uprising, during a 1943 raid of a gay bar in San Francisco's Chinatown, two lesbians fought back, leading to a "small riot" during which dozens were arrested.[26] In May 1959, fed up with daily demands for identification and arrests for prostitution, vagrancy, and loi-

tering, and sparked by another nightly round-up of patrons, Black and
Latinx transgender women, street youth, and gay men rose up against
police harassment at Cooper's Donuts, a popular gathering place in Los
Angeles.[27] Between 1965 and 1970, a group of homeless gay and trans
youth in San Francisco, many of whom traded sex, came together as
Vanguard, "an organization of, by, and for the kids on the streets," to
fight police harassment and abuse through organizing, publications,
and direct action.[28] Vanguard played an instrumental role in sparking
the 1966 Compton's Cafeteria riot, where "drag queens" fought back
when police tried to arrest them for doing nothing more than being out.
Three years later, on a hot June evening in 1969 at the Stonewall Inn in
New York City, police attempted to arrest trans women and butch lesbians under anti–cross-dressing laws. Trans women of color and street
youth led the revolt against police harassment and abuse. The following
year, as documented by Regina Kunzel and publicized by transgender
activist and filmmaker Reina Gossett,[29] a march held to commemorate
the first anniversary of the Stonewall Uprising ended at the Women's
House of Detention, where members of the Black Panther Party were
being held, with chants of "Free Our Sisters! Free Ourselves!"[30] Stonewall leaders Sylvia Rivera and Marsha P. Johnson later organized as
STAR (Street Transvestite Action Revolutionaries) to fight the criminalization of and support the survival of transgender street-based
youth. A decade later, a violent and homophobic 1982 raid on Blue's,
a Black working-class gay and lesbian bar in New York City, coming
at a time of increased police attacks on Black lesbians in Washington
Square Park and renewed arrests of "men wearing women's clothing"
on Long Island, prompted activists to organize once again. They framed
police violence against LGBTQ people as "part of increasing right-wing
violence and police abuse directed at Black, Latin, Asian and Native
peoples, women, unionists, undocumented workers and political activists," emphasizing that "your race, class, sex and sexual identification all affect how police treat you."[31] Yet in the four decades following
Stonewall, mainstream LGBTQ organizations increasingly focused on
securing the right to marry and on collaborating with law enforcement
to increase penalties for homophobic and transphobic violence ("hate

crimes") but remained largely silent about ongoing policing and crimi-nalization of LGBTQ people, primarily LGBTQ people of color. This left under-resourced grassroots organizations—led largely by people of color and low-income LGBTQ people—to continue to document on-going police violence against LGBTQ people of color and advocate for systemic change.[32]

Nevertheless, protest occasionally erupted around individual cases of police violence against women of color. In the 1970s, police harass-ment and violence against women in Black liberation movements often prompted public outcry. The campaign in support of Assata Shakur highlighted the fact that she had been shot by a New Jersey state trooper while she held her hands raised in the air in surrender, and that she was further brutalized by New Jersey police officers as she lay shackled and partially paralyzed in a hospital bed. In 1979, the fatal shooting of Eulia Love by Los Angeles police officers summoned to resolve a dis-pute about her gas bill led to widespread criticism. Similarly, New York-ers vociferously protested the 1984 killing of Eleanor Bumpurs during an eviction.

In 1994, New Orleans exploded in outrage when police officer Len Davis put a hit out on Kim Groves, a Black mother of three, and had her killed after she filed a complaint against him for pistol-whipping a young man in her neighborhood. Chicagoans took to the streets of the city's South Side in 1999, chanting, "It's a cell phone, not a gun! Police training 101!" after LaTanya Haggerty was shot in 1999—the same year Amadou Diallo was killed. In LaTanya's case, officers claimed to have mistaken her cell phone for a gun, whereas in Diallo's, they claimed to have mistaken his wallet for a gun. Also in 1999, residents of Riverside, California, held weekly protests at city hall and the district attorney's office after Tyisha Miller, a nineteen-year-old Black woman, was shot twenty-two times by officers who had been called for help because she was found unconscious and having a seizure.

In 2003, New Yorkers once again protested when Alberta Spruill, a fifty-seven-year old Black woman described as a devout churchgoer and hardworking city employee, died of a heart attack after police threw a concussion grenade into her apartment during a drug raid conducted at the wrong address.³³ The same year, hundreds of members of the Vietnamese community and immigrant rights activists held protests and vigils after Bich-Cau Thi Tran, a Vietnamese mother of two who had been diagnosed with schizophrenia, was shot and killed by San Jose, California, police as she was pointing a vegetable peeler at the door to a locked bedroom (see photo insert for image of poster demanding justice). They formed the Coalition for Justice and Accountability, which originally advocated for less lethal responses such as Tasers, but reevaluated its position after Taser use was shown not to decrease the number of fatal shootings but in fact increased the number of incidents in which people were tasered in nonlethal situations.³⁴

As time went on, more general campaigns were launched beyond individual cases. Throughout the 2000s, Muslim advocacy groups challenged religious profiling and inappropriate searches of Muslim women wearing hijab, particularly at airports, while immigrant rights groups such as the National Network of Immigrant and Refugee Rights; Coalición de Derechos Humanos in Tucson, Arizona; and Human Rights Watch documented sexual violence against immigrant women at the Mexican border and during raids in the US interior. In 2002, grassroots organization Sista II Sista began documenting police sexual harassment of young Black and Latinx women in a Brooklyn neighborhood, screening a video and performing skits on the subject at a street fair across from the local precinct. At the same time, groups like the Audre Lorde Project, FIERCE, Community United Against Violence and more were documenting police violence against queer and trans women of color.

In 2005, INCITE! launched a national campaign to fight law enforcement violence against women of color at its third Color of Violence conference, held in the Treme quarter of New Orleans. The campaign culminated in the creation of the INCITE! *Organizer's Tool Kit on Law Enforcement Violence.* The first of its kind, the 120-page booklet features fact sheets on different forms and contexts of police violence against women and trans people of color, tools for documentation, and ideas for resistance centering women and trans people of color's experiences drawn from organizations across the country. It was launched in 2008 at a daylong preconference institute at the Critical Resistance ten-year-anniversary conference, and since then has been widely distributed at activist gatherings across the country.

In 2006, Washington, DC, passed legislation allowing for the declaration of Prostitution Free Zones (PFZ), areas in which people whom police ordered to "move along" were subject to arrest if they failed to do so, as were any group of two or more people congregating "for the purpose of prostitution." As activists pointed out, the legislation merely codified existing policing practices but placed greater numbers of women of color, trans and not trans, profiled as or engaged in prostitution at risk of arrest and police abuse. Different Avenues, a DC-based harm-reduction organization, conducted a participatory action research project documenting the impacts of PFZs as part of a broader campaign to strike down the legislation, led by the Alliance for a Safe and Diverse DC. Activists including Sharmus Outlaw, a Black trans woman and outreach worker for Different Avenues, testified to the harmful impacts of PFZs during DC council hearings on the legislation, describing profiling and targeting of queer and trans people of color in public spaces and removal of the sex trade to more isolated and dangerous parts of the city where transgender sex workers in particular were exposed to greater violence. Activist Che Gossett describes how, as part of the campaign, members of the alliance sought to address residents' concerns about condoms, lubricants, and other litter in neighborhoods designated as PFZs through cleanup days conducted under the slogan "Throw out litter, not people." Eventually, efforts of DC organizers and threats of legal challenges to the legislation led to the repeal of PFZ legislation in 2014.[35]

A year before, in May 2013, an Arizona State University social work student named Monica Jones, a Black trans woman, was walking down the street when she was arrested for "manifesting an intent to prostitute." Members of the Sex Workers Organizing Project in Phoenix packed the courtroom the day her case was heard to support her challenge to the constitutionality of the statute she was arrested under (see the photo insert for image of "We Stand with Monica Jones" poster). When the challenge was rejected, Monica vowed to fight on. She proclaimed, "It's time that we end the stigma and the criminalization of sex work, the profiling of trans women of color, and the racist policing system that harms so many of us." She appealed her conviction and led a national and international campaign to call attention to the discriminatory impact of laws like "manifesting an intent to prostitute" on women of color, and trans women of color in particular. Ultimately, Monica's appeal was successful, because the word of the arresting officer had been given undue weight in the trial, and the case against her was dismissed.[36] Monica continues to organize for sex workers' rights and to highlight police violence against Black women of all gender identities.

Despite these efforts, women's experiences, as well as a gendered analysis of racial profiling and mass incarceration, continued to prove elusive in the growing discussion of the impacts of racialized criminalization prompted by the 2010 release of Michelle Alexander's groundbreaking book *The New Jim Crow*. On a plenary on the subject at the July 2010 NAACP Convention, I argued that it was no longer tenable to approach issues of racial profiling, police violence, and mass incarceration without taking gender into account. I asserted that in order to effectively tackle these issues, we need to have a complete picture, one that reflects the full extent of the problem as it affects all members of our communities and that reflects how policing of gender and sexuality are used as tools in policing of race and class. The NAACP took up this charge with the release of the 2014 report *Born Suspect: Stop and Frisk Abuses and the Continuing Fight to End Racial Profiling in America*, which documents young women's and LGBTQ people's experiences of policing, and calls for comprehensive profiling bans that would provide protection on as many fronts as communities of color are policed.

Meanwhile, individual cases of police violence continued. In October 2011, I joined a group gathered in a park near the New Providence shelter in New York City for a vigil, organized by Queers for Economic Justice, to commemorate and protest the police shooting right outside the shelter of Yvonne McNeal, a Black lesbian in her mid-fifties, and member of a QEJ support group. The year before, QEJ had released a groundbreaking research report documenting police violence against low-income LGBTQ New Yorkers, including significant rates of sexual harassment against low-income queer and trans women, and high levels of ticketing, arrest, and physical violence.[37]

That same year, after two NYPD officers were acquitted of raping a woman they had picked up for being intoxicated, I wrote an op-ed to the *New York Times* calling for increased attention to systemic police sexual violence, as I had on several other occasions when stories of police rape surfaced. As usual, the *Times* didn't publish it. However, People's Justice for Community Control and Police Accountability (a citywide coalition that grew out of the 1990s Coalition Against Police Brutality, rekindled following the 2006 killing of Sean Bell) and Black Women's Blueprint (an organization formed in 2008 to create a blueprint for change centering Black women's experiences of state and interpersonal violence) joined forces to circulate my op-ed as a call to action on police sexual violence. In so doing, they emphasized "the need to incorporate women's experiences into discussions of police violence and develop systemic approaches to sexual abuse by the police."

Unfortunately, none of these grassroots efforts was successful in permanently integrating women of color's experiences into the national conversation around racial profiling and police violence.

Until now.

In the days and months after Eric Garner and Michael Brown were killed in 2014, as the conversation turned once again to the ways in which police violence targets Black *men*, I struggled to find time to once again write a piece highlighting the fact that it's not *just* Black men who are targeted. I quickly found I didn't need to; almost immediately, blog posts began to appear with increasing frequency calling for attention to Black women killed by police: Tanisha Anderson, killed by Cleveland police just months after Mike Brown was killed by Darren Wilson; Miriam Carey, a thirty-seven-year-old dental hygienist whose family had been calling for truth and justice in her case since she was shot in October of 2013 by Secret Service and Capitol Hill police with her thirteen-month old child in the backseat of her car; Yvette Smith, a forty-seven-year-old caretaker killed by police responding to her 911 call about a disturbance in her home in February 2014; Tarika Wilson, mother of five, shot with her infant child in her arms during a SWAT drug raid, prompting weekly marches in her hometown of Lima, Ohio; Aiyana Stanley-Jones, a seven-year-old Black girl killed by

Detroit police as she slept during a drug raid, to name just a few of the most frequently raised cases.[38]

In November 2014, AAPF held a day-long forum entitled "In Plain Sight: Toward Engendering the Fight for Racial Justice in the 21st Century," during which I had the honor of speaking on a panel on police violence with activists Ashley Yates and Johnetta Elzie, fresh from the frontlines of Ferguson. We were two generations of Black women meeting in a conversation affirming that we could not be a part of a struggle to end police violence as anything less than our full selves—Black women, some of us queer, and insisting on a voice and recognition that we were not only in the streets for Black men but also for ourselves. I left inspired. Several months later, at a "Reclaim MLK" march in New York City, Rachel Gilmer, then associate director of the AAPF, and I talked about reports we were both planning around Black women's experiences of policing and decided to join forces. That winter, AAPF founder Kimberlé Crenshaw, Gilmer, and current AAPF Associate Director Julia Sharpe-Levine coined #SayHerName in response to the absence of Black women's names and stories of police violence in protests and on social media. In May 2015, AAPF released a report I coauthored with Kimberlé Crenshaw, entitled *Say Her Name: Resisting Police Brutality Against Black Women*, updating it in July 2015 to include Sandra Bland's story. Since then, AAPF has hosted town halls, webinars, and activist camps aimed at lifting up the experiences of Black women in conversations around police brutality and for racial justice.

Meanwhile, organizing around cases involving Black women and trans and gender-nonconforming people gained traction. In October 2014, Juan Evans, a Black trans man, was arrested by the East Point, Georgia, Police Department during a routine traffic stop. Because he had left his wallet at the office, he provided his birth name and social security number. The officer accused him of lying about his identity. When Juan explained that he was transgender, the officer said he would force him to submit to a gender search on the side of the road. Juan refused, saying, "You don't have the right to search my genitals." Laughing in Juan's face, the officer responded, "I have the right to search your mother's genitals to find out who you are." He handcuffed Juan and

took him to the precinct, where he was once again threatened a forcible gender search. Throughout the encounter, police officers referred
to Juan as an "it" and "thing," and repeatedly asked him about his genitals. Like so many trans and gender-nonconforming people, this was
not the first time Juan experienced disrespect, ignorance, and abuse at
the hands of the police. Juan turned his violation into victory. In a video
about the incident, he fiercely said, "East Point Police Department, I
will not give you my courage, I will not give you my dignity, I will not
live in fear of you. And I will not let you shame and humiliate me into
submission. . . . I will unapologetically tell you who I am . . . and you
don't have the right to arrest me for being trans. . . . All that was said,
and all that was done, I still stand with my dignity intact."[39]

A week after the incident, Juan returned to the police precinct with
one hundred community residents and members of the Atlanta-based
Solutions Not Punishment Coalition (SNaPCo), a trans-led coalition
that works to build the power of people most likely to be victims of
violence and most likely to be arrested and harassed by police, including
trans and gender-nonconforming people of color, current and former
street-level sex workers, and formerly incarcerated people (see Stop Police Profiling in photo insert). They supported Juan's demand for an
investigation, an apology, and, most importantly, a change in East Point
police policies and practices. Later, Juan asked reporters, "I just wonder
how many other people have been humiliated like this at the hands of
the East Point police. How many others were outed in their jail cell in
front of other inmates?"[40] The action won immediate and public apolo-
gies from the mayor, city council, and chief of police. But the coalition
demanded more: new policies and in-depth training for all officers. Six
months later, in April 2015, SNaPCo secured what they had demanded:
the most progressive policies for police interactions with transgender
people to be enacted by a US police department. Juan, sitting at the
head of the table throughout the final negotiations, described the outcome as "a huge victory for everyone in my community." The coalition
also worked with the City of Atlanta to urge its administration to adopt
similarly comprehensive and progressive policies. Dee Dee Chamblee of
LaGender, Inc., an anchoring organization of SNaPCo, declared, "Trans

and gender-nonconforming people suffer at the hands of law enforcement every day and the community has finally said 'enough.'"[41] Tragically, Juan Evans passed away July 14, 2015, leaving behind a community in mourning and committed to continuing to fight on in his name.

October 2014 also marked the time when OKC Artists for Justice, founded by Grace Franklin and Candace Liger, began tirelessly organizing around Daniel Holtzclaw's sexual assaults of thirteen Black women and girls, calling attention to the case, holding protests in the courtroom, and supporting survivors, as described in greater detail in chapter 5. Although the group met with resistance from both white feminists and Black men to their message that "Black women matter," they were nevertheless successful in piercing the bubble of silence around the case and challenging antiviolence and Black Lives Matter advocates to speak out and take action. Most importantly, as Liger put it in a Facebook video, "we do it to make sure these victims know that they're not alone, and quite frankly, they hear us."

In January 2015, Jessie Hernandez, a seventeen-year-old Latinx queer person, was shot by Denver police as she sat in a car with friends in an alley. Police dragged her out of the car, slammed her to the ground, handcuffed her while unconscious, and searched her as she lay limp and motionless. Buried Seedz of Resistance (BSeedz), a local group organizing with queer and trans youth of color, immediately went into action, reaching out to the family to offer support. They silk-screened hundreds of T-shirts and bandanas with images of Jessie for the funeral, set up a memorial in the alley where Jessie was killed, and held healing circles for youth and members of her community. BSeedz and Jessie's family challenged the criminalization of her memory under the slogan Jessie Vive, ensuring that Jessie was remembered as a friend, an older sister, a lover, and a pillar of her community.[42] Six months later, in June 2015, in Jessie's name the organization shut down the Denver Pride march after local prosecutors announced that no charges would be brought against the officers responsible for her death. BSeedz has continued to call for accountability, as the BSeedz organizer Mimi Madrid evoked the original spirit of Pride: "Pride began as a revolutionary uprising to defend our bodies, to defend our identities and to defend our spirits. . . .

We're tired of the police just taking us out, picking us off. . . . So this is about bringing back that sacredness, [those] roots of uprising back into Pride."[43] Meanwhile, Jessie's family continues to mourn her loss: her sister Jo Hernandez said after the killing, "It was cruel how they ended you; they took half my heart and it will never be repaired. I see you watching me from up above. You'll never be forgotten my angel." (See insert for image of "Rest in Power Jessica Hernandez" poster.)

On April 9, 2015, the City of Chicago was preparing for the criminal trial of Dante Servin, a police officer who killed a young Black woman named Rekia Boyd in March 2012. Rekia had been standing with friends in a park, doing what young people do: talking loud, laughing, enjoying life, full of Black girl magic. Servin, an off-duty officer, approached the group and told them to quiet down. They had some words and turned to leave. As they did, one of the group pulled out a cell phone. Servin claims he thought it was a gun, and shot at the group, using his service weapon. He hit Rekia in the back of the head, killing her instantly. Servin's trial on charges of involuntary manslaughter finally began after a three-year struggle by Rekia's family, supported by Women's All-Points Bulletin (WAPB). Three weeks later, on April 20, all charges against Servin were dismissed. The judge ruled that Servin could not be convicted of involuntary manslaughter because his actions had clearly been intentional, a failure of what had already been a half-hearted prosecution. Family members, including Rekia's brother Martinez Sutton, who has been a tireless voice demanding accountability for her death, and activists, although demoralized, came together to plan the next steps in the campaign to get justice for Rekia. BYP100 began to work alongside Black Lives Matter and Ferguson Action toward a National Day of Action to End State Violence Against Black Women, Girls, and Femmes on May 21, 2015, timed to coincide with a Chicago Police Board hearing on Rekia's case. The Chicago chapters of BYP100, Black Lives Matter, WAPB, and We Charge Genocide mobilized for the hearing. The campaign to fire Servin was on.

As documented by Project Nia's powerful video *We Are Rekia's Haven*, Rekia's family, members of BYP100, and allied organizations powerfully took over and shut down Chicago Police Board meetings month after month, demanding justice for Rekia and calling for Servin's termination (see insert for photo of BYP100 members).[44] In November 2015, the Board finally recommended that Servin be fired. The recommendation was adopted by Chicago police superintendent Gerry McCarthy—days before he himself was fired in connection with the cover-up of the October 2014 shooting of Laquan McDonald. While focused on a single officer, Chicago-based organizing under the #SayHerName banner inspired grassroots organizing across the country. Project Nia director Mariame Kaba blogged: "The #FireServin campaign has not simply been about holding one officer accountable. It's also been about making visible the neglected forms of violence experienced by Black women and girls across this country and beyond. By calling for CPD to #FireServin, organizers in Chicago have centered the state violence experienced by all Black women and girls."[45]

Almost a year after the campaign began, just days before the second National Day of Action on May 19, 2016, which was timed to coincide with the Chicago Police Board hearing that would act on the recommendation to fire Servin, he resigned so that he could keep his city pension. Not missing a beat, local activists turned up the heat on a #DontPayDante campaign, launched the month before by groups including Black Lives Matter Chicago, Assata's Daughters, and Fearless Leading by the Youth. They demanded that Servin's pension be cut and funds redirected to Chicago State University, the only predominantly Black university in Illinois, and Rekia's brother's alma mater, where budget cuts threatened to close the doors.[46]

Meanwhile, the second National Day of Action unfolded in response to a call to

> acknowledge the forms of violence experienced by our women, girls, and femmes. We must fight against the criminalization of Black victims of sexual violence, intimate partner violence, and abuse. We must resist the policing of Black gender expression, sexuality, and bodies. We must condemn the passage and defense of gender discriminatory legislation. We must break down the narrow standards of respectable Black womanhood and femininity deemed acceptable. We must #SayHerName.[47]

Among the organizing efforts that took root in response to the call was a campaign to demand justice for Alexia Christian, a Black woman shot to death while handcuffed in the back of an Atlanta Police Department patrol car. Alexia's family, as well as activists from Women on the Rise and the Racial Justice Action Center, demanded an investigation and release of videotape documenting exactly what led up to the moment when Alexia was shot ten times by the officers who arrested her, dogging Atlanta's police chief and testifying before the Atlanta Citizen's Review Board.[48] Another, led by the Dream Defenders, a group that came together in the wake of the acquittal of Trayvon Martin's killer, focused on the deaths of Ashaunti Butler, Dominique Battle, and Laniya Miller, three young Black girls who drowned as officers stood by after the car they were driving went into a pond following a police chase.[49] Still another, led by Cat Brooks and the Anti-Police Terror Project in Oakland, demanded justice for Yuvette Henderson, a woman shot by a security guard after being accused of shoplifting at a Home Depot.[50]

In June 2016, activists across the country organized around the case of Jasmine Abdullah, the founder of Black Lives Matter Pasadena, a twenty-nine-year-old Black lesbian organizer who had been arrested, charged, and convicted by an all-white jury of "felony lynching," an offense involving taking a person out of police custody—generally speaking, with a mob—with the intention of killing them. The law had been enacted, ironically, to *protect* members of the Black community. Before her arrest, Jasmine was one of many who traveled to Ferguson in outrage and solidarity after seeing police tear-gas Black girls as young as seven and describes herself as "activist, freedom fighter, organizer." In an infuriating move believed by many to be retaliation for her activism, Jasmine was charged with felony lynching after police accused her of trying to "unarrest" a Black woman whom police were pursuing after a dispute with a restaurant owner. Jasmine and other activists had just come from an August 2015 peace march commemorating the police shooting of a nineteen-year-old unarmed Black youth by Pasadena police. Jasmine was the first Black woman to be convicted under the statute, which had also been used to charge a Black woman member of Black Lives Matter Sacramento. Although sentenced to ninety days in prison, Jasmine was released after three weeks under the tremendous public pressure of a nationwide #FreeJasmine campaign.[51]

The following month, in July 2016, BLM Los Angeles began an occupation of city hall that would last over fifty days when the Los Angeles Police Commission ruled that the August 2015 shooting of Redel Jones did not violate the department's use-of-force policy. Jones, described by her husband as kind and caring, a self-taught computer whiz and student of holistic health care, was killed by police who were looking for a woman suspected of robbing a pharmacy. They claimed that Redel ran away from them and then charged at them with a knife when they approached her. Eyewitnesses say that she was not approaching the officers but moving away from them when she was shot. Activists chanted her name monthly at police commission hearings in the year between her shooting and the decision not to hold her killers accountable.[52]

Nationally coordinated actions continued. After police killed Korryn Gaines, on August 1, 2016, and after the murder of Skye Mocabee—the seventeenth trans woman to be killed in 2016—Black Feminist Futures issued a national call to join the Defend Black Womanhood campaign by building community altars to express outrage at police killings of Black women by the state and indifference to the loss of Black women's lives, to "mourn and grieve collectively and publicly, to amplify the names of who we have lost."[53] Groups in more than twenty cities responded by creating living memorials (see photo insert for image of one altar).[54]

Though the most visible organizing around women's experiences of policing since 2014 has focused on Black women and girls, Indigenous communities in Arizona and Washington have come together to protest the police killings of Loreal Tsingine (discussed in chapter 4); Jacqueline Salyers, a member of the Puyallup tribe and mother of three shot by Takoma, Washington, police; and Renee Davis, a mother of three shot by King County, Washington, sheriffs on the Muckleshoot reservation. In Washington State, Puyallup tribe members' Justice for Jackie campaign has contributed to efforts to change the law concerning police accountability in use-of-force cases (see the insert for a photo of a Justice for Jackie rally).[55]

Groups like the National Queer Asian Pacific Islander Alliance have challenged multiple forms of police profiling while seeking to redefine security. As organizer Sasha Wijeyeratne put it, "Our communities will redefine security for themselves, without law enforcement agencies that routinely profile and harass South Asians and Muslims as terrorists, Southeast Asians as gang members, and LGBTQ API people as targets for harassment. . . . As LGBTQ APIs, we are in solidarity with all Black and brown people experiencing profiling from police, from ICE, and from all state agencies."[56] Asians for Black Lives have consistently staged actions in solidarity with Black Lives Matter, and Black Lives Matter activists came out in support of Theresa Sheehan, a Japanese woman shot by police seeking to remove her from her room on the grounds that she required assistance due to mental health issues.[57]

At the same time, groups like Southerners on New Ground (SONG) and Mijente have steadily been organizing campaigns focused on violations of the rights of immigrant women, both at the border and in the interior of the country. Immigrant women–led organizations such as Mujeres Unidas y Activas have played a key role in coalitions such as the San Francisco Immigrants Rights Coalition, which has successfully challenged police-immigration collaboration since 2011. And, beginning in January 2015, communities across the South came together through SONG to ask "What would it look like if LGBTQ people, Black folks, Brown folks, immigrants, women, working class and poor people could live Free From Fear in the variety of places we call home?" In response, the multiracial organization has mounted a series of campaigns in cities across the South to win protections from profiling, immigration enforcement, and police violence.[58] Cross-community collaborations in challenging police violence are growing across the country, whether in the form of solidarity between Black and Indigenous communities[59] or between Black and immigrant communities.[60]

———

It is not as though women of color have been completely absent from the narrative of police brutality until now. But more often than not, up until recently, they have been typecast solely as grieving mothers and family members. The power of women of color who have all too often been thrust into that role cannot be overstated. Mothers of children whose lives were stolen by law enforcement—including Iris Baez, Katadou Diallo, Mesha Irrizary, Harriet Walden, Margarita Rosario, Hawa Bah, and, more recently, Gwen Carr, Lesley McSpadden, and countless others— have moved mountains and led movements in the name of justice for their children and family members. In Chicago, mothers came together to demand attention and organize around the plight of survivors of torture at the hands of Chicago police commander Jon Burge, contributing to a successful movement for his prosecution and for reparations to his victims. Over fifty family members came together as Families United for Justice, successfully organizing for the appointment of a special prosecutor in cases of police killings in New York State. [61] Mothers Against Police Brutality groups exist across the country. Siblings and other relatives too have organized to obtain justice—sisters, such as Maria Moore, who has ensured that Kayla Moore's dignity and the full complexity of who she was is respected in the struggle for justice in her case; brothers, such as Martinez Sutton, Rekia Boyd's brother, who is one of the few Black men who has tirelessly organized around a case involving a Black woman; the powerhouse Cynthia Howell, the niece of Alberta Spruill and founder of Families United for Justice; and daughters, such as Erica Garner, who has consistently spoken truth to power in her father's name, have been fierce and dedicated leaders in movements for police accountability. Chosen family, too, have come together to honor the memories of trans community members like Mya Hall.

Women who have lost partners to police violence—such as Nicole Paultre Bell, whose fiancé, Sean Bell, was killed in a hail of fifty bullets by the NYPD on their wedding day—have also been powerful advocates. As I was finishing this book, I was haunted by the story of Diamond Lavish Reynolds and her four-year-old daughter, who were in the car when an officer killed Philando Castile during a traffic stop as Diamond recorded the interaction on video. Mother and daughter had both so deeply internalized the need to remain preternaturally calm—even the child, at four years old—to survive the incident. Diamond, like so many others before her, went straight from the precinct where she was held for hours after the killing to a protest demanding justice for Philando. And, like so many others before her, she had to pick up the pieces after her loved one's death without many resources or support.[62]

I am constantly reminded of the strength and fierceness of family members who fight for justice and for the memories of their loved ones in the face of criminalizing and dehumanizing narratives deployed to cover up the killing. The words of Cassandra Johnson, Tanisha Anderson's mother, echo those of many: "I will not stop, as all of the rest of the mothers have said, until I get some answers."[63]

Yet we often overlook the violence that family members face as they struggle for answers and accountability. For instance, many of the Black women who were lynched—such as Laura Nelson—were tortured and killed for challenging the unjust treatment of family members. Few may recall that the incident that sparked the 1965 Watts Uprising in Los Angeles involved not only the beating and arrest of a Black man, Marquette Frye, following a traffic stop, but also the police assault and arrest of his mother, Rena Price, who came to his defense and long suffered the consequences of that experience.[64] New York City's Justice Committee, which has worked tirelessly on behalf of families who have lost loved ones to police violence for more than two decades, continues to highlight police abuse of Ramarley Graham's mother and grandmother. In 2012, Graham's grandmother, Patricia Hartley, witnessed police officers kill her grandson in front of her in their home. When she cried out, Officer Richard Haste pushed her into a vase, telling her to "Get the f**k away before I have to shoot you, too."[65] Patricia was immediately taken to the police station and interrogated there for seven hours without an attorney present. When Ramarley's mother, Constance Malcolm, went to the station to demand answers and secure her mother's release, she was tackled to the floor and assaulted by police officers. She later said, "There's nobody standing up for us mothers. We standing here, we have to fight for justice."

Sometimes, women who seek to simply bear witness to police abuse of members of their communities are targeted. For instance, in 2013, protests erupted in my Brooklyn neighborhood in the wake of the police killing of sixteen-year-old Kimani Grey. Late one night, I found myself in the local precinct trying to negotiate the release of several Cop Watchers who had been arrested while trying to document and deter police violence at the demonstrations. One of them was Thenjiwe McHarris, now of the organization Blackbird, who was violently thrown to the ground by police as she tried to document an arrest. A year earlier, in 2012, Makia Smith was stuck in traffic when she saw cops surrounding a boy on the ground and began filming. She later said, "I was hoping that if they saw me, then maybe they would stop doing what they were doing." An officer ran toward her screaming, "You want to film something, bitch? Film this!" Makia tried to get back into her car, but the officer grabbed her phone, threw it to the ground, dragged her by her hair, and threw her on the hood of her car as her two-year-old screamed in the backseat. As they arrested her, police threatened to turn Makia's child over to child protective services, prompting her to ask a young woman by the side of the road, a complete stranger, to take her until the child's grandmother could pick her up.[66]

Yet even these experiences have historically been relegated to the margins, and mothers' and family members' leadership taken for granted.

How did the experiences of Black women and women of color become more visible in the wake of Ferguson? What made this historical moment different? Though similar challenges to the erasure of women's experiences of state violence had been made before, in many cases they were made by women whose leadership in civil rights movements had been all but erased. Later, individual woman of color activists, academics, and small groups of grassroots organizers worked to interject women's experiences of police violence into the discourse around racial profiling, police brutality, and violence against women. Yet we faced an uphill battle, pushing back against the overwhelming weight of a narrative centered around straight, cisgender Black and Brown men, attempting to raise women's experiences with virtually no resources or air time. This time, no doubt a combination of factors played a role in increasing visibility, foremost among them the emergence of a new generation of Black women leaders on the front lines and in the leadership of the post-Ferguson movement who forcefully pushed back against male-dominated groups and narratives, proudly proclaiming, in the words of Ferguson activist Tef Poe, "This ain't your grandparent's civil rights movement."[67] For these young women, intersectionality is a given in organizing in ways it was not in the 1990s or even in 2009, when Oscar Grant was killed. The advent of social media played a key role: Previously when women came forward and spoke at rallies, public hearings, investigations, and community meetings, their stories went unheard, filtered out of the conversation by mainstream media and racial justice organizations. Now we can post our stories and organizing messages directly, no longer dependent on intermediaries to lift them up. Whatever the factors contributing to the opening, now that we have seized the moment, the challenge is to continue to push past resistance, continuing invisibility, and silences to firmly seat gendered experiences of racial profiling and police violence at the center of our analysis.

It is also time to push past the challenge of visibility to analysis and action. How does centering the experiences of Black and Indigenous women, women of color, immigrant women, and Muslim women change the conversation? What does a holistic resistance to police violence look like? How do our experiences shape our organizing strategies, our policy demands, our litigation and legislative advocacy? I penned an article in *Colorlines* in honor of the second National Day of Action to End State Violence Against Black Women, Girls, and Femmes, in which I outlined seven starting points for shifting and expanding policy agendas to incorporate the realities of women's experiences of policing. These include focusing on racially gendered sites of profiling, such as antiprostitution enforcement, as well as on gendered forms of police brutality such as police sexual violence and the use of force against pregnant women. However, I concluded with a caution: "Of course, changing police policies is not a panacea to police violence against Black girls, women and gender nonconforming people. To strike at the root of the issue, we need to transform our responses to poverty, violence and mental health crises in ways that center the safety and humanity of Black women and our communities."[68]

That is what the Vision for Black Lives, the policy platform collectively developed in 2015 and 2016 by dozens of organizations that
make up the Movement for Black Lives begins to do. It calls for an end
to racialized gender policing and police abuses of trans and gender-
nonconforming people, accountability for and prevention of police
sexual violence, and an end to the fees, fines, and bail that keep women
in police custody, there to be assaulted or die of racially motivated neglect. It urges decriminalization of drug and prostitution offenses—two
of the top pathways to policing, criminalization, and prison for Black
women and women of color—and demands reparations for those who
have been targets of the war on drugs and the enforcement of antiprostitution laws.[69] Perhaps most importantly, the platform calls for "in-
vestments in Black communities, determined by Black communities,
and divestment from exploitative forces including prisons, fossil fuels,
police, surveillance and exploitative corporations." It sets forth a bold
vision for Black liberation and the liberation of all peoples that can be
further developed and guide us as we step into treacherous times ahead.

CONCLUSION

We know police brutality is scarring and killing people of color.
We know mass incarceration is hurting us. But I want to know
how oppression happens. Show me how. Then maybe I will
know how to disrupt it in the most effective ways.

—ANA MUÑIZ, *Police, Power and
the Production of Racial Boundaries*

I read this passage as I sat on the dock at the Blue Mountain Center in Upstate New York, having returned to this book some five years after I had put it aside when South End Press, its original home, closed its doors. As I finished the manuscript, I repeatedly returned to Muñiz's question, because it pressed me to do more than simply catalogue police violence against Black women, Indigenous women, and women of color and demand that it be given the attention it is due. It pushes us to try to *understand* it, to examine it from all angles, look where we haven't before, and mobilize what we learn to deepen our analyses of racial profiling, police brutality, and mass incarceration, and expand them along the axes of gender, gender identity, and sexuality alongside race, ethnicity, religion, class, nation, immigration status, and disability. Muñiz's question prompts us to ask more: What do the stories and statistics in these pages tell us about anti-Black racism, colonialism, white supremacy, and the ways they manifest? What do they show us about gender and gender-based violence? What gaps do they expose in our thinking and actions? And, most importantly, what can they teach us about how to disrupt police violence? What do they reveal to us about the world we want to build? While *Invisible No More* cannot offer answers to all these questions, I am hopeful that it will push new conversations forward.

For a long time, I would struggle with people—including friends, comrades, and colleagues—who would say, "But the numbers of women killed/stopped/arrested/incarcerated/deported are just objectively much smaller, a fraction of the numbers of men. So it's natural to focus the conversation on where there is the greatest volume, to say that stop-and-frisk, or police violence, or mass incarceration target Black and Brown men, because it is, in fact, true."

While it is in fact the case that fewer women are killed, brutalized by police, or incarcerated, a focus on police killings and more egregious uses of physical force elides women's more frequent experiences of less lethal violations, like sexual harassment and assault, which go undocumented. Additionally, "stops" of women are likely underreported because police make contacts with women in contexts where there is no record if no arrest is made, or at least not one that is reported in stop data, such as prostitution enforcement; welfare checks; responses to calls about domestic violence, sexual assault, or "hate crimes"; mental health crises; or child-welfare enforcement. Having also internalized narratives of what a "stop" and its target look like, police likely underreport stops of women because they may not think of encounters with women as "stops" in the same way as they do stops of men. Police may also have disincentives to record stops where they are sexually harassing, assaulting, or extorting women. Police contact with women also tends to take place in locations away from public view—and cameras—such as homes, clinics and public hospitals, welfare offices, public housing. The combination of these factors and more makes police interactions with women less visible, not only in the numbers but also in the public eye.

These realities require, at a minimum, that we collect and analyze data in ways that will make women's experiences more visible. Forms of police violence uniquely or disproportionately experienced by women, and contexts in which women come into contact with police more frequently, need to be subject to greater scrutiny. We also need to change the way information about police interactions is reported. Research on policing and mass incarceration continues to focus on racial disparities for men, to the exclusion of women. At best, data analysis compares the experiences of "Blacks" to "whites," without further disaggregating by gender *and* race, much less by immigration status, disability, among other races and ethnicities, or in ways that render Indigenous experiences—and dramatic disparities in rates of police killings and incarceration of Native women—visible. We need to find ways to make visible and understand police interactions with women of color, and to challenge what Angela Y. Davis terms the "tyranny of the universal," in which, in the words of Barbara Smith, "all the women are white, all the Blacks are men, and some of us are brave."[1]

In the end, beyond the numbers, the stories and patterns described in this book matter because the lives and experiences of Black women, Native women, and women of color matter. It is not a distraction to raise them. They merit equal time and have much to teach us about gendered manifestations of racism. In 1998, Davis wrote, "The relatively small number of African-American women drawn into the system should not relieve us of the responsibility of understanding the encounter of gender and race in arrest and incarceration practices."[2] Since then the numbers have only grown, as have the numbers of Latinx and Native women in prison. Today, women of color represent the fastest-growing jail and prison populations. This reality only increases our responsibility to better understand the processes that contribute to it, because, as Davis wrote in 2013, when we look at the experiences of women, including trans women, in the prison-industrial complex, despite the relatively small numbers, "we learn so much more about the system as a whole than we would learn if we look exclusively at men . . . about the nature of punishment writ large."[3]

When we focus on women's experiences in the places we are already looking and expand our frames to incorporate different forms and contexts of police contact, more women come into view, as do more forms of violence and more impacts on communities of color. For instance, expanding our focus to police sexual violence enables us to see greater numbers of women of color affected by police violence *and* to recognize the use of sexual violence by police against women, gender-nonconforming people, and men of color to establish and enforce relations of power. Attending to police violence against women of color, in all its forms, thus opens possibilities for genuine and deeper solidarity among men and women, among cisgender and transgender and gender-nonconforming people, among women of color, among movements against police and gender-based violence, and for reproductive justice and immigrant rights. It also offers fertile ground for building alliances between Global North and South by framing human rights violations against women not as "horribles" that happen elsewhere, fueling anti-Muslim/anti-Black/Orientalist logics justifying a never-ending machinery of war, but as tools of subjugation used against communities of color within the United States and around the world.

Additionally, as Davis also pointed out, the criminalization of women takes place in ways that are more complicated than for men, and "has had more to do with marking certain groups of women as undomesticated and hypersexual," beyond the bounds of womanhood.[4] This gendered process of dehumanization drives police violence against unarmed women and girls who simply question police actions, express frustration with their treatment by police, or engage in a dispute with a white person. In these interactions, criminalizing narratives eliminate the possibility that a Black woman, Indigenous woman, or woman of color can be entitled to protection, demand to be treated with dignity, stand up for a family member, or just be angry or have a bad day. Instead, controlling narratives developed in service of colonialism and white supremacy transform women of color into a caricature, an implicit threat justifying violent responses. If our behavior does not line up with that of a compliant Mammy, a noble (and submissive) Indian princess, or a "China doll"; if we are instead read as Sapphire, a "savage squaw," a "dragon lady," a "hot-tempered" and volatile Latinx, or a "terrorist," then we must be subjugated with brutal force, regardless of what we are actually doing. As Alexis Pegues, who served as a research assistant for this book, pointed out during one of our discussions, white supremacy demands such complete control of Black women and women of color that it takes very little to perceive us as out of control—particularly in combination with gendered perceptions that women are always out of control. Consequently, the minute a Black woman or woman of color questions or doesn't obey commands, police respond as if they have been physically threatened. These narratives also inform the sexualized profiling of women of color as "prostitutes," presumed subjects of sexual access and violence, arrest, and punishment. Given these realities, no matter how much "implicit bias" training police receive or how many police reforms we achieve, these perceptions will continue to inform police interactions with women of color because they are proliferated and reinforced daily to perpetuate existing systemic relations of power. We therefore have a responsibility to understand and challenge them in order to dismantle the systems of power that produce them.

Expanding our focus to center women of color also forces us to move beyond false dichotomies of "good" and "bad" victims of police violence, "armed" and "unarmed." The uncomfortable reality is that, in many cases, women killed by the police were armed—rarely with a gun but often with a knife, scissors, or household objects like a hammer. A focus on police killings of unarmed people therefore excludes many women and the racialized narratives that led to their deaths. Even when armed, even when resisting police, controlling narratives frame women of color as a much greater threat than white women under identical circumstances, and place a much lower value on Black, Native, Muslim, Latinx, and immigrant women's lives, thus giving officers license to use much greater and more brutal and lethal force. In a welcome departure from previous movements for police accountability, the Movement for Black Lives has challenged us to resist the instinct to organize only around those who are "innocent" and to move away from a politics of respectability. It has pushed us to ask ourselves what forces brought police into contact with women in the first place, what drives differential responses to both armed and unarmed individuals, and what visions and demands are necessary to truly value all Black lives. This expanded frame allows us to ask what brought Baltimore police to Korryn Gaines's door to serve a warrant for her arrest for failure to pay a traffic ticket, and what alternative approaches would have preserved Korryn's life and not left her child motherless.[5] It also pushes us to ask why we rely on police to respond to people in mental health crisis—situations in which people are not at their best and may be armed, or at least disoriented or frightened.

Centering the experiences of women of color also challenges us to ask how and why police—whose default response seems to be violence—continue to represent our primary response to interpersonal violence. Police responses to calls for help illustrate how narrowly conceptions of "womanhood," "motherhood," "childhood," "(dis)ability," and "victim" are drawn, and how many of us are excluded from the "protection" of the state. Much of the growth of law enforcement over the past four decades has been predicated, at least pretextually, on protecting women, LGBTQ people, and children as victims of violence. These pages make it clear what this reality has looked like for many women, LGBTQ people, and children of color, exposing the flaws of strategies that call for more law enforcement, policing, and punishment. What does it tell us when a Black woman can be charged with lynching, a mother charged with child endangerment because a police officer or her partner beat her, or a domestic-violence survivor can be beaten or killed by police after calling for help? Among other things, it exposes the fallacies of police serving as protectors for women, girls, and gender-nonconforming people of color.

Centering the experiences of women of color also requires that we expand our definition of police violence to include failure to respond to violence as a form of violence. Such failures not only operate as a figurative slap in the face but also make survivors more vulnerable to violation on all fronts in a society that offers no alternatives to police as protection, and they send a clear message that violence against certain bodies continues to be acceptable. The violence of failure to protect also cannot be solved by advocating for greater, more "responsive" police intervention, given the considerable violation and criminalization of women of color that accompanies heightened police responses to violence. Instead, it requires us to do the incredibly hard work of envisioning and enacting alternatives to the police that will genuinely produce safety for survivors and targets of interpersonal and community violence.

The high levels of violence faced by trans women of color place these mandates into sharp focus. Much of the recent organizing by Black trans women under the banner of #BlackTransLivesMatter has focused less on police violence and more on the ever-mounting death toll among Black trans women, as well as Indigenous trans women and Two Spirit people, and trans women of color killed by community members. These deaths must be laid not only at the door of the police, who make it clear that they will not protect trans women, but at all our doors. We have failed Black trans women by failing to take up with urgency the charge to create the conditions under which they can live without fear of becoming one of the dozens of trans women killed every year, and instead thrive and flourish. And we have failed all our sisters who are unable to call police or who do so only to be denied help, protection, safety, and freedom. In the end, the real challenge posed by women of color's experiences of police profiling and violence is to our collective conceptions of violence and safety, the role of police in our society, and to our ability and willingness to make building and nurturing values, visions, and practices that will produce genuine safety and security for all members of our communities a central task of movements against police violence.

Attending to women of color's experiences of police violence also opens the way to more comprehensive and effective resistance. If we fail to take women's experiences into account, we cannot confront the full measure of police violence, or articulate visions of justice that fully reflect the needs and experiences of all members of our communities. Police violence doesn't always look the same for women as for men, and therefore the solutions we pursue with only heterosexual cisgender men of color in mind are necessarily incomplete, and may even be potentially harmful when examined from a different perspective. For instance, what opportunities for action do we miss when the standard of police violence is a fatal shooting of a man of color? Do body cameras do more harm than good when worn by officers responding to domestic violence calls or conducting vice raids? Does unrestricted availability of police data and complaint files place at risk survivors of domestic violence, sexual violence, and stalking; LGBTQ people; or people who are or are perceived to be involved in the sex trades? Do complaint-based mechanisms such as civilian oversight create conditions that make it possible for women of color survivors of police violence to come forward and obtain justice?

Ultimately, the stories and statistics in *Invisible No More* tell us that police violence against Black women, Indigenous women, and women of color is systemic, not isolated, inherent to policing as an institution. As Keeanga-Yamahtta Taylor puts it, in *From #BlackLivesMatter To Black Liberation*, "The police reflect and reinforce the dominant ideology of the state that employs them, which explains why they are . . . resistant to substantive reform."[6] Given this reality, even reforms are, at best, harm reduction. Our goal, as Rachel Herzing so compellingly argues in her essay "Big Dreams and Bold Steps Toward a Police-Free Future," "should not be to improve how policing functions but to reduce its role in our lives."[7]

That said, as we pursue "incremental changes that lead toward the erosion of policing power rather than reinforcing it," we need to ensure that such changes are gender-specific and inclusive, and address the contexts in which Black women, Indigenous women, and women of color encounter police. Their experiences can also begin to inform our responses to the question of what is necessary to achieve genuine and sustainable safety for women of color as we resist increased policing, surveillance, militarization, criminalization, detention, deportation and incarceration. For instance, beyond eliminating all collaboration between immigration enforcement and local law enforcement, without exception, and establishing safe spaces for undocumented immigrants, these stories tell us that true safety for women of color requires an end to the "war on drugs," broken windows policing, and the "war on terror"; the elimination of gender as a marker of access to public space, public benefits, and protections; the removal of police from schools, hospitals, public housing, and health-care settings; and the repeal of "mandatory arrest" and other policies that facilitate the criminalization of survivors of violence; and support rather than violence and criminalization for pregnant people and mothers of color.

Ultimately, the stats and stories in this book expose the reality of policing in America, and the interests in racially gendered and classed power relations it is structured to protect. These truths are especially relevant as the nation's political climate swings toward increased fearmongering and even more blatant and virulent racism, which will in turn lead to greater surveillance, control, criminalization, exclusion, and mass incarceration of women of color. We can no longer be complicit in the notion that we can achieve safety through policing, particularly in this climate. Thus, instead of asking, "How can we reform policing to keep women safe?" we should ask, "What do women need to be safe?" How can the billions spent on policing go instead to resources such as safe and affordable housing, health care, education, living-wage employment, child care, and mental health treatment?

Our charge is to envision and build a world without police, and without the values that produce policing and punishment.[8] It is a world premised on what Angela Y. Davis terms "abolition feminism," a world "based on radical freedom, mutual accountability, and passionate reciprocity. In this society, safety and security will not be premised on violence or the threat of violence; it will be based on a collective commitment to guaranteeing the survival and care of all peoples."[9] Unfortunately, there is no ten-point plan to get there, but each of us can contribute to the conversation, dreams, and visions we need to find the way.

Let's get free.

AFTERWORD

Like the author, my understanding of the conditions of Black women and girls in society is an evolving story. My story begins in the Chicago Osteopathic Hospital, where I was born in 1985 to two young parents who could only afford a home in the Back of the Yards neighborhood on Chicago's South Side. Beyond the constant smell of the infamous stockyards that once existed there, I had no understanding of the historical significance of the neighborhood I lived in and the role it played in the evolution of community organizing. Organizer and movement theorist Saul Alinsky, and the institutions he organized with and built in the Back of the Yards in the 1930s, had long moved on. What I knew was that my family was the only Black family on my block and that my safety was not guaranteed.

My visibility in the classroom as a student labeled "gifted" and in the home as the oldest of three signaled various possibilities in a sea of people with limited options. However, that label meant nothing outside of my home, and only went so far to my advantage in the classroom. That label meant nothing to the police. I did not have the words to explain why I feared the police and security guards until I became an activist and organizer in Black liberation spaces. I did not have the words to explain the enduring angst I held about the survival and well-being of the socially and economically depressed communities I moved in between as a child and now an adult.

I told myself early on that I was no different from my family members who did not graduate from high school or had spent time in jails or prisons. I was only one in-school suspension for "sass" or having "attitude," or one ringing metal detector away from going down the same pipeline. I drilled the saying that "I was no special snowflake" into my head. Despite an exterior air of confidence and certainty, I held on to a sense of insecurity beneath my armor as if it were the only way to stay alive in a city where my girlhood wasn't valued or guaranteed. The high school security guards, administrative disciplinarians, metal detectors, and police surveillance reminded me of this reality every day.

Unlike the boys and young men around me, my parents didn't have "the talk" about police with me. And yet, my earliest experiences with policing told me that while their motto was to "serve and protect," they and their intermediaries had the power to dictate my daily existence (or nonexistence). I work to solve the puzzle of my constant anxiety and fear about the world around me through organizing on the ground in communities across the United States and in places around the globe. *Invisible No More* does the critical work needed to help explain just where that anxiety comes from for countless Black women and girls in this country. And it has done so in a more holistic way than most texts focusing on the impact of policing in the United States.

Today, I understand policing as inherently violent and beyond any state of repair. The reality of policing in the United States is much bigger than a few rotten apples. Just as the historical roots of the institution are rotten, so is the fruit that it bears in the United States and across the globe. Police are, and always have been, intermediaries and tools for wealthy elites, serving the interests of property owners over those of marginalized people. These realities are what produce images of our brutalized bodies and traumatized spirits on the Internet and stories of police violence from rape to murder splattered across social media and in the press. We have become hypervisible, and yet remain invisible at the same time.

Even in this invisibility, there are those who see us. I bristle at suggestions that "no one cares" in the aftermath of a killing, rape, or other form of violence. In reality, someone does care. It is often likely the person is not someone in power or seen as a valued source. For example, the Black trans and gender-nonconforming community (including some LGBQ folks, but not nearly enough) expresses outrage each time a

Black trans woman is murdered. One crucial part of the problem is that they, and the stories they amplify, are not heard or valued as much as they should be valued. They are rendered invisible.

Our stories are powerful fuel for our collective resistance. There is simply not enough political will to build the power we need to end the state-sanctioned violence that Black women and girls experience via the police or other sites of violent power. *Invisible No More* does the important work our movement needs by telling more complete stories and valuing the resistance of those most directly impacted. These stories should make us all uncomfortable. We should shift in our seats. We should cry. And we must organize. We must all commit to taking action to build the necessary political will to create a society where freedom isn't a constant struggle. Ella Baker teaches us that through collective organizing, we can develop the strong people, not just single leaders.

To the Black women, girls, and trans and gender-nonconforming folks who read this book, I know that you have stories that are untold. These are stories that must be heard, valued, and centered throughout our movements. Without them, our collective story is incomplete. I want to hear and learn more. The charge of *Invisible No More* is to not only shed light or increase awareness; it is to agitate us all into deeper political commitments to ending policing and abolishing all punitive in-stitutions in the United States, while developing alternatives to dealing with conflict and harm based in restorative and transformative justice models. None of this has been or will be easy. Taking up a political com-mitment to abolish punitive institutions tests the core of our humanity.

Frederick Douglass is known for saying that "power concedes noth-ing without a demand." I further that argument and say that *power con-cedes nothing without an organized demand*. The powers working against ending all forms of oppression are as old as efforts to resist them. Our people have always organized and imagined different possibilities. From the slave rebellions and lunch-counter sit-ins, to the Compton's Cafete-ria Riot and the Combahee River Collective—there is much to learn from our legacies of collective resistance and imagination. Yes, our movement today has escalated the call to #SayHerName. But our work cannot stop there. BYP100 is digging into deeper inquiry, outreach, and agitation to advance this work. These tumultuous times call for us to go big and ignite our collective imaginations. Our ancestors want more for and from us. Now is the time to build on the traditions of Black radical and revolutionary imaginations that beg the arguments for self-determination and self-love for the sake of our collective liberation. In doing so we will move closer toward the edge where our struggles and triumph will be *Invisible No More* in this lifetime.

—Charlene A. Carruthers, national director,
Black Youth Project 100 (BYP100)

ACKNOWLEDGMENTS

This book is the product of shared learning and struggle with literally hundreds of individuals, of countless conversations, meetings, workshops, gatherings, interviews, and readings, as well as feedback from audience members and students. Many people whose names are not listed here have contributed to these pages, and I am deeply grateful for their insights and teachings.

I owe a tremendous debt of gratitude to Beverly Bain, Punam Khosla, Datejie, Beth Jordan, Mary Pritchard, Sarita Srivastava, and the women of INCITE!, all of whom were foundational in shaping my identity, analysis, and understanding of these issues and in setting me on the path that has culminated in this book. Thanks to Andrea Smith for cocreating INCITE! and inviting me into what became my political home. Beth Richie, Joo-Hyun Kang, Paula Rojas, Trishala Deb, Remy Kharbanda, Patricia Allard, and *Queer (In)Justice* coauthors Joey Mogul and Kay Whitlock also all played critical roles in my evolving analysis. I am also deeply grateful to the members of INCITE!'s national campaign on law enforcement violence and to my collaborators on the INCITE! *Organizer's Tool Kit*: Alisa Bierria, Nada Elia, Shana griffin, and Xandra Ibarra; and to fellow organizers and participants of the COV4 and Critical Resistance 10 Law Enforcement Violence preconference institutes and the Allied Media Conference Say Her Name/Black Trans Lives Matter Network Gathering.

I finished this book during a period of tremendous personal, professional, and political turmoil. Throughout the last year of writing, death, loss, grief, critique, and self-reflection, both private and public, served as a constant backdrop. I am deeply grateful to the powerful Black women in my life who kept me grounded and focused, and served as doulas in the final stages of labor and self-doubt that preceded the book's completion. Brilliant Beacon Press editor Jill Petty was literally the very first person to encourage me to write this book after reading my piece in the *Color of Violence* anthology and has been a consistent champion, cheerleader, and comrade, providing insightful and incisive comments throughout, talking me off the ledge more times than I can count, and going above and beyond time and time again. Visionary, author, and coach adrienne maree brown; co-struggler, scholar, and organizer extraordinaire Mariame Kaba, who graciously penned a beautiful and moving foreword; my sister in struggle, Cara Page; and shero and mentor Beth Richie all offered much-needed advice, critical questions, and essential encouragement to put this work out into the world. This book would not be in your hands if it weren't for them, and for the many friends and strangers who reached out to offer words of encouragement and support over the past year. Endless appreciation also to Victoria Law, whose editorial insights were invaluable, and to Joey Mogul, Mia Mingus, Dani McClean, Monique Morris, Dean Spade, Gabriel Arkles, and David Perry for reading drafts. Heartfelt thanks to Alexis Pegues and Levi Craske, research assistants extraordinaire, for their critical commentary and dogged determination and skill tracking down information.

And, of course, deep appreciation to Gayatri Patnaik and all of the amazing staff at Beacon Press, who gave the book a new home and worked feverishly and thoughtfully to help make it the best and most beautiful it could be. Special thanks to Beth Collins, Nicholas DiSabatino, Ayla Zuraw-Friedland, Alyssa Hassan, Susan Lumenello, and Louis Roe, who truly went above and beyond, and to laurie prendergast, freelance indexer extraordinaire.

There is simply no question that I would never have completed this manuscript without the support of my brilliant, righteous, and fierce partner in love and struggle, Joey Mogul, who provided countless invaluable insights, endless encouragement, critical suggestions and edits, life-saving space and support, much-needed joy and laughter, and the best writing view ever.

My deepest gratitude to Emi Kane, Jenny Lee, Karla Mejia, Dean Spade, Marie Tatro, Urvashi Vaid, and Kyona Watts for their invaluable friendship and support over the years in so many ways; to Richard Brouillette, for keeping me in one piece and helping me become a better human; and to Clarence Patton, for starting the Pipeline Project, which saved my life. Deep gratitude also to my beautiful and beloved Allied Media Conference family, which every year for the past decade has re-grounded and reinspired me, creating spaces for all of us to envision and practice the world we want to see.

I am also deeply indebted to the Windcall program and the Blue Mountain Center for reconnecting me to myself, the world between work and rest, art as resistance, and to my calling as a writer, and for providing a refuge, a space to write, and a new home. Sincere apprecia-tion also to the Hambidge Center for offering space where significant work on this book took place, and to Stone House for creating and of-fering me Soul Sanctuary, and starting me on a road to healing.

Heartfelt appreciation to Brook Kelly-Green, Margaret Hempel, and the Gender, Race and Ethnic Justice Program of the Ford Foundation, and to Adam Culbreath, Christina Voight, and the Soros Justice Fel-lowship Program of the Open Society Foundations for believing in and supporting me and this project. Endless gratitude to Tina Campt, Janet Jakobsen, and the Barnard Center for Research on Women for hosting me as a Researcher-in-Residence, and to BCRW, the People's Law Of-fice, and the DePaul Law Civil Rights Clinic for research support.

I am profoundly grateful to my family of origin—to my father, for always believing in and standing with me, teaching me to fight for jus-tice, to stand for what I believe in, to cheer for the underdog, to never give up, to pursue my dreams, to take risks, to jump fearlessly, to make the best of every moment, and to enjoy the view and the flowers along the way; to my mother, for modeling determination, a taste for ad-venture and a refusal to accept a lesser life; to my brother Robert for shaping me politically and being one of the most consistent sources of support, laughter, and home in my life. Thanks also to Robert and my brother Greg; my sister, Cindy; and my sisters-in-law Diona and Maria Cristina for making it possible for me to write over the past year and for all each of them has given and taught me; and to my twin-in-love Alyssa

Mogul and to Honor Mogul. And, of course, to Che and Kente, who purred along as I wrote.

I am incredibly blessed to have had the opportunity to be in community and struggle with many whose brilliance, vision, dedication to justice, and joy have provided endless inspiration, including Ujju Aggarwal, Gabriel Arkles, Morgan Bassichis, Marbre Stahly-Butts, Flor Bermudez, Xochitl Bervera, Alisa Bierria, Caitlin Breedlove, Rachel Caïdor, Tara Cameron, Collette Carter, Shelby Chestnut, Eunice Cho, Loyda Colon, Gail Cooper, Jessica Danforth, Lisa Davis, Ejeris Dixon, Nada Elia, Monica Enríquez, Jordan Flaherty, Rebecca Fox, Veronica Bayetti-Flores, Elliot Fukui, Lisa Garrett, Pooja Gehi, Simmi Ghandi, Shana griffin, Miss Major Griffin-Gracy, Reina Gossett, Debbie Gould, Shira Hassan, Paris Hatcher, Kris Hayashi, Deon Haywood, Paulina Helm-Hernandez, Rachel Herzing, Darby Hickey, Amber Hollibaugh, Mary Hooks, Margaret Huang, Gaurav Jashnani, Xandra Ibarra, Myriam Jaïdi, Monica Jones, Naimah Johnson, Shaena Johnson, Che Johnson-Long, Alice Kim, Mimi Kim, J. Kirby, Erin Konsmo, Emi Koyama, Sarita Khurana, Alex Lee, Nakisha Lewis, Luce Lincoln, Deana Lewis, Jason Lydon, Rekha Malhotra, Rickke Mananzala, Meghan Maury, Rachel Mattson, Kate Mogulescu, Mandisa Moore, Addrana Montgomery, Maryse Mitchell-Brody, Anya Mukarji-Connolly, Soniya Munshi, Nadine Naber, Bhavana Nancherla, Isa Noyola, Julia Chinyere Oparah, laurie prendergast, Chanravy Proeung, Kyung-Ji Rhee, Clarissa Rojas, Penny Saunders, Edith Sargon, Joanne Smith, Brett Stockdill, Jay Toole, Ije Ude, Adaku Utah, Wes Ware, Joe Westmacott, Krista Williams, Toni-Michelle Williams, and so many more people I have been blessed to know and struggle alongside whose names I will kick myself for not remembering to include as soon as this book comes off the press.

Thanks to all my fellow steering committee members of Communities United for Police Reform, who model what principled, collaborative, fierce, and joyful intersectional organizing around policing issues can look like—including Yul-san Liem, Jose Lopez, Lynn Lewis, Monifah Bandele, Candis Tolliver, Kate Rubin, Brett Stoudt, Nahal Zamani, Delores Jones-Brown, and yes, Udi Ofer. Deep appreciation as well to the leadership of the No Condoms as Evidence/Access to Condoms Coalition for principled and relentless advocacy, and to the Federal LGBT Criminal Justice Working Group, which has achieved nothing less than a sea of change in how LGBTQ issues are understood at the federal level.

I am profoundly grateful for the intellectual and political labor and inspiration of Angela Y. Davis, whose writings on gender, race, class, and the prison industrial complex literally set me on the path of this work and who kindly and powerfully introduces readers to this book; and of Anannya Bhattacharjee, Devon Carbado, Cathy Cohen, Patricia Hill Collins, Kimberlé Crenshaw, Angela Y. Davis, Katherine Franke, Joy James, Monique Morris, Priscilla Ocen, Barbara Ransby, Beth Richie, Dorothy Roberts, Barbara Smith, and of Assata's Daughters, the Audre Lorde Project, Black Lives Matter, Black Women's Blueprint, Break-OUT!, Black Youth Project 100, Community United Against Violence, Critical Resistance, DRUM, FIERCE!, the Movement for Black Lives, Native Youth Sexual Health Network, Northwest Network of GLBT Survivors of Violence, Providence Youth Student Movement (PRYSM), the Racial Justice Action Center, SNaPCo, Southerners on New Ground, Streetwise and Safe, the Sylvia Rivera Law Project, Women With a Vision, and Young Women's Empowerment Project. Thanks also to Rachel Gilmer, Rachel Anspaugh, Julia Sharpe-Levine, and the staff and board of the African American Policy Forum. I am also deeply grateful for the opportunity to know, support, and be inspired by family members of women killed by police including Maria Moore, Frances Garrett, Martinez Sutton, Valarie Carey, Natasha Duncan, and Cynthia Howell.

Thanks to Lynn Lu, Asha Tall, and all the members of the South End Press editorial collective for their labor over the years to build and maintain a progressive press and for being the first to believe in this book. Asha Tall's editorial comments on an early draft of the chapter on sexual violence were as insightful ten years later and greatly improved the final result. Honor and appreciation to the following people who worked with me on early drafts of chapters: Gabriel Arkles ("Policing Gender Lines"; research on "Policing (Dis)Ability"), Xandra Ibarra ("Policing Sex"), Sheba Remy Kharbanda ("Policing Paradigms and Criminalizing

Webs"), and Beth Richie ("Police Responses to Violence"). Deep gratitude as well to professor and friend Michelle Scott Jacobs, for all of her support as advisor to my 2002 unpublished law review article, which presented many of the ideas in this book in embryonic form and was the basis for portions of chapter 1.

Thanks also to Alessandra Bastagli at Nation Books, who encouraged me to write in my own voice, and Diane Wachtell of the New Press, who offered early encouragement and advice on structure.

Portions of the manuscript are based on articles written for *TruthOut, The Public Eye, Colorlines,* the *New York Law Review for Social Justice, Loyola Law Review,* and *The Routledge History of Queer America.* Heartfelt thanks to editors Akiba Solomon, Kathryn Johnson, Alana Yu-Price, and Don Romesburg, and to the students at NYU and Loyola Law School, for making these portions of the book infinitely better than they otherwise would have been.

This book is an honor, a responsibility, and a gift to the fierce young Black women, Native women, and women of color on the frontlines of Ferguson, BYP100, Black Lives Matter, the Movement for Black Lives, #NoDAPL (No Dakota Access Pipeline) and Indigenous resistance throughout Turtle Island, #NotOneMore and movements for migrant justice, and countless other struggles for liberation. I am humbled, inspired, and deeply grateful for the fierce, principled, unapologetic, and visionary leadership of Charlene Carruthers, national director of BYP100, whose words of fire close the book, the BYP100 Chicago chapter whose struggle for justice for Rekia Boyd was an inspiration to many, and for BYP100 chapters across the country in leading grassroots organizing centering Black women, girls, and fem(me) targets of police violence. My thanks, too, to Janaé Bonsu, BYP100 policy director, whose image graces the book's cover, for her leadership, and to L'lerrét Ailith, BYP100 communications director, for always pushing us to center this conversation around those at the margins of the margins, to disrupt gender and make space for folk who live outside gender binaries, and for reminding me at a critical moment in the writing of this book of how my privilege intersects with my work. Thanks also to Sarah Jane

Rhee, for taking the gorgeous cover photo and for documenting our resistance so beautifully.

Finally, Cissy Dyke/Mama, Jean(ne) Knight, and all of my Black women ancestors whose names I will never know, and Chloe, Ellie Mac, Isabel, Layla, Meilu, Melody, Nikki, and all the girls and gender-nonconforming youth of color in my life, past, present, and future, this is for you.

NOTES

INTRODUCTION

1. All of these cases are described in Kimberlé Williams Crenshaw and Andrea J. Ritchie, *Say Her Name: Resisting Police Brutality Against Black Women* (New York: African American Policy Forum, July 2015). "Transgender," or "trans," refers to people whose gender identity or gender expression is different from the one typically associated with the sex assigned at birth. "Cisgender," or "cis," is used to describe people whose gender identity is consistent with that typically associated with the sex they were identified with at birth. "Gender nonconforming" is an umbrella term used to describe people who may not identify as transgender, or with any gender whatsoever, but whose appearance or gender expression is read as inconsistent with the gender they were assigned at birth or with normative understandings of gender. "Fem(me)" is a term used by people who manifest or identify with appearance, characteristics, or behavior generally understood to be feminine, and who experience gender-based violence because of it. Because gender-nonconforming people may not identify as women, the term "women and gender-nonconforming people" is sometimes used to honor gender self-determination of individuals who may not identify as women but are policed as such.

2. Alicia Garza, "A Herstory of the Black Lives Matter Movement," *Feminist Wire*, October 7, 2014, http://www.thefeministwire.com/2014/10/blacklivesmatter-2.

3. See Sylvia Rivera Law Project, *It's War in Here: A Report on the Treatment of Transgender and Intersex People in New York State Men's Prisons* (New York, 2007), 23, http://srlp.org/resources/pubs/warinhere.

4. The concept of controlling narratives has been elaborated by Black feminists to describe the powerful and enduring stories and images about Black women and women of color proliferated to establish and maintain structures of anti-Blackness, colonialism, and white supremacy. See Patricia Hill Collins, *Black Feminist Thought: Knowledge, Consciousness, and the Politics of Empowerment*, 2nd ed. (New York: Routledge, 2000).

5. The terms "Global North" and "Global South" have been used to describe countries in terms of industrial development, wealth, and standard of living, with countries of the Global North enjoying privileges at the expense of those of the Global South.

6. Andrea Smith, *Conquest: Sexual Violence and American Indian Genocide* (Cambridge, MA: South End Press, 2005), 28.

7. See Jihan Hafiz, "Video: Police Viciously Attacked Peaceful Protestors at the Dakota Access Pipeline," *The Intercept*, October 25, 2016, https://theintercept.com /2016/10/25/video-police-viciously-attacked-peaceful-protestors-at-the-dakota -access-pipeline/; Sam Levin, Nicky Woolf, and Damian Carrington, "North Dakota Pipeline: 141 Arrests as Protestors Pushed Back from Site," *Guardian*, October 28, 2016, https://www.theguardian.com/us-news/2016/oct/27/north-dakota-access -pipeline-protest-arrests-pepper-spray; Justin Worland, "What to Know About the Dakota Access Pipeline Protests," *Time*, October 28, 2016, http://time.com/4548566 /dakota-access-pipeline-standing-rock-sioux/; Amy Goodman, "Full Exclusive Report: Dakota Access Pipeline Co. Attacks Native Americans with Dogs & Pepper Spray," *Democracy Now*, September 6, 2016, http://www.democracynow.org/2016 /9/6/full_exclusive_report_dakota_access_pipeline.

8. Clare Bernish, "Water Protector's Retina Severed After Cops Fire Tear Gas Canister Into Her Face," TheFreeThoughtProject.com, November 26, 2016, http://thefree thoughtproject.com/water-protector-severed-retina-eye/#YAVPBQ3UUG0e3gcr.99.

9. Jane Doe, *The Story of Jane Doe: A Book About Rape* (Toronto: Random House Canada, 2003).

10. R. Lundman and R. Kaufman, "Driving While Black: Effects of Race, Ethnicity and Gender on Citizen Reports of Traffic Stops and Police Action," *Criminology* 41, no. 1 (2003): 215.

11. Crenshaw and Ritchie, *Say Her Name*; New York Civil Liberties Union, "Women Demand End to Discriminatory NYPD Stop-and-Frisk," press release, April 3, 2013; Women of Color Policy Network, *Women of Color: Two-Thirds of All Women in New York City Still Invisible in Policy—The 2nd Annual Report on The Status of Women of Color in NYC* (New York: New York University, Wagner Institute for Public Policy, 2003).

12. State of Missouri, *Racial Profiling Data/2013*, http://ago.mo.gov/docs/default -source/public-safety/2013agencyreports.pdf?sfvrsn=2, see "Agency: Ferguson Police Department."

13. US Department of Justice Civil Rights Division, *Investigation of the Ferguson Police Department* (Washington, DC: March 4, 2015).

14. Jessica McBride, "Breaion King: 5 Fast Facts You Need to Know," heavy.com, July 24, 2016; Phil Helsel, "Austin Police Chief 'Sickened, Saddened' by Violent Arrest," NBC News, July 22, 2016.

15. General Accounting Office, *Better Targeting of Passengers for Personal Searches Could Produce Better Results*, GAO/GGD 00-38 (Washington, DC: US General Accounting Office, 2000).

16. American Civil Liberties Union, Break the Chains, and the Brennan Center at New York University, *Caught in the Net: The Impact of Drug Policies on Women and Families* (New York, 2005), https://www.aclu.org/files/images/asset_upload_file431 _23513.pdf.

17. Women's Prison Association, "Quick Facts: Women and Criminal Justice 2009," http://www.wpaonline.org/wpaassets/Quick_Facts_Women_and_CJ_Sept09.pdf.

18. The Two-Spirit Society of Denver states: "The term Two-Spirit refers to another gender role believed to be common among most, if not all, first peoples of Turtle Island (North America), one that had a proper and accepted place within indigenous societies. This acceptance was rooted in the spiritual teachings that

say all life is sacred and that the Creator must have a reason for making someone different. This gender role was not based in sexual activities or practices, but rather the sacredness that comes from being different." The Native Youth Sexual Health Network adds, "There are many definitions and understandings that are nation-specific (Ex. Navajo, Cree, Diné, Anishinabe) and each individual person will have their own way of expressing their Two-Spirit-ness. Also, not all Indigenous people identify as Two-Spirit and have other ways and words to express their gender and sexual identity." For more information, visit www.nativeyouthsexualhealth.com /supportcircle.html.

19. I am mindful of critiques of the term "women of color" on the grounds that it "often supports racial hierarchies and doesn't fully allow for Black women to deal with the ever-present history and legacy of slavery, sexual and reproductive exploitation, and subsequent periods of holocaust." See Black Women's Blueprint, "Who We Are; Our Mission and History," www.blackwomensblueprint.org/mission.html. I also deeply appreciate Roxanne Dunbar-Ortiz's cautions about using the term "Native" or "Indigenous women": "Native peoples were colonized and deposed of their territories as distinct peoples—hundreds of nations—not as a racial or ethnic group" (*An Indigenous Peoples' History of the United States* [Boston: Beacon Press, 2015], xiii). As a result, "There is no such thing as a collective Indigenous peoples' perspective" (xiii, 13). Yet, Indigenous people were racialized "as targets of individual racial discrimination between the end of the Reconstruction in the South in the 1880s to the mid-twentieth century" (170).

20. Of course, this is not to say that men of color don't experience sexual harassment and assault by police officers and child-welfare enforcement agencies, as well as punishment for failure to comply with gender norms. It is simply to say that these types of experiences are both uniquely gendered and have disproportionate impacts on women of color.

CHAPTER 1: *Enduring Legacies*

1. Rebecca L. Robbins, "Self-Determination and Subordination: The Past, Present, and Future of American Indian Governance," in *The State of Native America: Genocide, Colonization and Resistance*, ed. M. Annette Jaimes (Boston: South End Press, 1992), 91; Luana Ross, *Inventing the Savage: The Social Construction of Native American Criminality* (Austin: University of Texas Press, 1998), 11.

2. See M. Annette Jaimes with Theresa Halsey, "American Indian Women: At the Center of Indigenous Resistance in Contemporary North America," in Jaimes, *The State of Native America*, 322, 311, 316; Andrea Smith and Luanna Ross, "Native Women and State Violence," *Social Justice* 31, no. 4 (2004): 1; Smith, *Conquest*, 3.

3. Dunbar-Ortiz, *An Indigenous Peoples' History of the United States*, quotes here and below from 10, 145, 60, 81–82, 83, 99, 58, 62, 68, 72, and 74–75.

4. Ibid., 137; Smith, *Conquest*, 15.

5. Smith and Ross, "Native Women and State Violence," 1.

6. Ross, *Inventing the Savage*, 15; Ortiz, *An Indigenous Peoples' History of the United States*, 80. See also Kristian Williams, *Our Enemies in Blue: Police and Power in America* (New York: Soft Skull Press, 2004), 40.

7. Dunbar-Ortiz, *An Indigenous Peoples' History of the United States*, 145–46.

8. Ibid., 154–55.

9. Joey Mogul, Andrea Ritchie, and Kay Whitlock, *Queer (In)Justice: The Criminalization of LGBT People in the United States* (Boston: Beacon Press, 2011), 4.

10. Mescalero Apache Tribe website, "Our Culture," http://mescaleroapachetribe.com/our-culture/; Barbara Tedlock, *Woman in the Shaman's Body: Reclaiming the Feminine in Religion and Medicine* (New York: Random House, 2009), 264.

11. Smith, *Conquest*, 8, 15–16.

12. Smith and Ross, "Native Women and State Violence," 2.

13. Albert L. Hurtado, *Indian Survival on the California Frontier* (New Haven, CT: Yale University Press, 1988), 170, 181.

14. Smith, *Conquest*, 25.

15. Hurtado, *Indian Survival*, 170, 181.

16. Cyndi Banks, "Ordering the Other: Reading Alaskan Native Culture Past and Present," in *Race, Gender, and Punishment: From Colonialism to the War on Terror*, ed. Mary Bosworth and Jeanne Flavin (New Brunswick, NJ: Rutgers University Press, 2007), 32–48, 42, 43.

17. Smith, *Conquest*, 1.

18. Ibid., 1, 8, 23; see also Jaimes, *State of Native America*, 318, 316; Scott Lauria Morgenson, *The Space Between Us: Queer Settler Colonialism and Indigenous Colonization* (Minneapolis: University of Minnesota Press, 2011).

19. Maria Lugones, "Heterosexualism and the Colonial/Modern Gender System," *Hypatia* 22, no. 1 (2007): 193, 197, 202.

20. Smith, *Conquest*, 23; see also Jaimes, *State of Native America*, 318, 316.

21. Vernetta D. Young and Zoe Spencer, "Multiple Jeopardy: The Impact of Race, Gender, and Slavery on the Punishment of Women in Antebellum America," in Bosworth and Flavin, *Race, Gender, and Punishment*, 65–77.

22. Smith, *Conquest*, 23; see also Jaimes, *State of Native America*, 318, 316.

23. Smith, *Conquest*, 178.

24. Deborah A. Miranda, "Extermination of the *Joyas*: Gendercide in Spanish California," *Gay and Lesbian Quarterly* 16, no. 1–2 (2010): 257–58.

25. Ibid., 264–66.

26. Smith, *Conquest*, 35–54; Ross, *Inventing the Savage*, 40, describing significant number of arrests of Indigenous people on the Flathead Reservation in Montana in 1927 "for resisting an officer, failure to attend school, failure to send children to school, and desertion from a nonreservation school."

27. Ross, *Inventing the Savage*, 15 (citing the 1850 California Act for the Government and Protection of Indians, which allowed whites to take Native children into indentured servitude when allegedly orphaned or with purported parental consent).

28. W. G. Bailey, ed., *The Encyclopedia of Police Science*, 2nd ed. (New York: Garland Press, 1995), s.v. National Constables Association, 114.

29. Ross, *Inventing the Savage*, 4, 6, 37–38. Kristian Williams suggests that Native people were required to carry passes much earlier, beginning in the seventeenth century (*Our Enemies in Blue*, 43).

30. Ross, *Inventing the Savage*, 16 (citing 1850 California Act for the Government and Protection of Indians).

31. Dunbar-Ortiz, *An Indigenous Peoples' History of the United States*, 170.
32. Ross, *Inventing the Savage*, 3.
33. See Smith, *Conquest*, 9; Dunbar-Ortiz, *An Indigenous Peoples' History of the United States*, 104.
34. Ross, *Inventing the Savage*, 168.
35. Ibid., 16, 25.
36. Dunbar-Ortiz, *An Indigenous Peoples' History of the United States*, 154.
37. See Smith, *Conquest*, 9–12, 20–21; Ross, *Inventing the Savage*, 55.
38. Ross, *Inventing the Savage*, 52.
39. bell hooks, *Ain't I a Woman: Black Women and Feminism* (Boston: South End Press, 1981).
40. David Baker, "Systemic White Racism and the Brutalization of Executed Black Women in the United States," in *It's a Crime: Women and Justice*, 4th ed., ed. Roslyn Muraskin (Upper Saddle River, NJ: Pearson, 2007), 398.
41. Ibid., 406.
42. Lawrence M. Friedman, *Crime and Punishment in American History* (New York: Basic Books, 1993), 86; Baker, "Systemic White Racism," 406.
43. William Craft, "Running a Thousand Miles for Freedom; or, the Escape of William and Ellen Craft from Slavery," in *The Long Walk to Freedom: Runaway Slave Narratives*, ed. Devon W. Carbado and Donald Weise (Boston: Beacon Press, 2012), 210; see also Coramae Richey Mann, *Unequal Justice: A Question of Color (Blacks in the Diaspora)* (Bloomington: Indiana University Press, 1993), 119.
44. Carbado and Weise, *Long Walk to Freedom*, 240.
45. Marcia Williams, ed., *Soul Survivors: The Definitive Anthology of Female Slave Narratives* (London: X Press, 1999), 141 (Linda Brent, "Incidents in the Life of a Slave Girl").
46. Williams, *Soul Survivors*, 52 (Elizabeth Keckley, "Behind the Scenes").
47. See, for example, Williams, *Soul Survivors*, 6 ("The Story of Mattie J. Jackson").
48. Work Projects Administration, *Born in Slavery, Oklahoma Narratives*, vol. 13, "Annie Hawkins, Age 90, Colbert, Okla.," image 131.
49. Williams, *Soul Survivors*, 54–56.
50. Ibid., 25 (Sylvia DuBois, "The Slave Who Whipped Her Mistress").
51. Ibid., 25, 35.
52. Williams, *Soul Survivors*, 70–71 ("History of Mary Prince, A West Indian Slave").
53. Gerda Lerner, ed., *Black Women in White America: A Documentary History* (New York: Vintage Books, 1992), 15.
54. Davis, *Women, Race & Class* (New York: Random House, 1981), 9 (citing Moses Grandy, *Narrative of the Life of Moses Grandy: Late a Slave in the United States of America* [Boston, 1844], 18).
55. Ibid. See also Williams, *Soul Survivors*, 25.
56. Williams, *Soul Survivors*, 141.
57. Ibid., 214.
58. Davis, *Women, Race & Class*, 175; see also Angela Y. Davis, "Reflections on the Black Woman's Role in the Community of Slaves," *Black Scholar* 12, no. 6 (November–December 1981): 2–15 ("In order to function as a slave, a black woman had to be annulled as a woman.").

59. Kathryn K. Russell, *The Color of Crime—Racial Hoaxes, White Fear, Black Protectionism, Police Harassment and Other Macroaggressions* (New York: New York University Press, 1999), 17.

60. Law professor Angela P. Harris, in "Race and Essentialism in Feminist Legal Theory," *Stanford Law Review* 42, no. 581 (1990), states, "As a legal matter, the experience of rape did not even exist for black women. During slavery, the rape of a black woman by any man, white or black, was simply not a crime" (15).

61. Williams, *Soul Survivors*, 162, 163.

62. Ibid., 82, 174.

63. Mann, *Unequal Justice*, 165; see also Williams, *Soul Survivors*, 38–39, 42. According to Williams, in Mississippi, the first slave patrols were federal troops (43). Sheriffs, constables, and night watches accompanied the arrival of colonists and performed policing duties including "keeping order," detaining "suspicious persons," making arrests, guarding prisoners, and serving warrants (38–39). Ultimately, according to Williams, "urban patrols, then, did not evolve from the watch system; rather adapted from the rural slave patrols, they came to supplant the watchmen" (45). See also H. M. Henry, *The Police Control of the Slave in South Carolina* (Emory, VA: Emory and Henry College, 1914), 28–50.

64. Mann, *Unequal Justice*, 165. See also Work Projects Administration, *Born in Slavery, Georgia Narratives*, vol. 4, part 4, "Slavery," 321–29.

65. Work Projects Administration, *Born in Slavery, Arkansas Narratives*, vol. 2, part 3, 375. Members of slave patrols were often referred to by enslaved persons as "patterollers" or "paddyrollers."

66. Work Projects Administration, *Born in Slavery, North Carolina Narratives*, vol. 11, part 2, "Interview with Lizzie Williams, Ex-Slave," 395.

67. Sally E. Hadden, *Slave Patrols: Law and Violence in Virginia and the Carolinas* (Cambridge, MA: Harvard University Press, 2001), 117.

68. Philip L. Reichel, "Southern Slave Patrols as a Transitional Police Type," in *Policing Perspectives: An Anthology*, ed. Larry K. Gaines and Gary W. Cordner (Los Angeles: Roxbury, 1999), 86.

69. See Stephanie Camp, *Closer to Freedom: Enslaved Women and Everyday Resistance in the Plantation South* (Durham: University of North Carolina Press, 2004); Deborah Gray White, *Ar'n't I a Woman? Female Slaves in the Plantation South* (New York: W. W. Norton, 1999); Davis, *Women, Race & Class*, 3, 21–22; Davis, "Reflections on the Black Woman's Role in the Community of Slaves."

70. Elsa Barkley Brown, "Negotiating and Transforming the Public Sphere," in *Women Transforming Politics: An Alternative Reader*, ed. Cathy Cohen (New York: New York University Press, 1997), 345–46.

71. Friedman, *Crime and Punishment in American History*, 94.

72. Talitha L. LeFlouria, *Chained in Silence: Black Women and Convict Labor in the New South* (Chapel Hill: University of North Carolina Press, 2015), 25.

73. Ibid., 24.

74. For quotes here and below, Sarah Haley, *No Mercy Here: Gender, Punishment, and the Making of Jim Crow Modernity* (Chapel Hill: University of North Carolina Press, 2016), 29, 34, 35, 30, 31; see also Jen Manion, *Liberty's Prisoners: Carceral Culture in Early America* (Philadelphia: University of Pennsylvania Press, 2015), 85–119.

75. See Manion, *Liberty's Prisoners*, 30–32; Ramona Brockett, "Conceptual Incarceration: A Thirteenth-Amendment Look at African Americans and Policing," in *The System in Black and White*, ed. Michael W. Markowitz and Delores D. Jones-Brown (Westport, CT: Praeger, 2000), 111.
76. LeFlouria, *Chained in Silence*, 15, 33, 34; see also Haley, *No Mercy Here*, 44.
77. LeFlouria, *Chained in Silence*, 14.
78. Ibid., 12–13.
79. Ibid., 32.
80. Ibid., 22, 46–48.
81. Ibid., 45.
82. Haley, *No Mercy Here*, 36, 51; see also Patricia Hill Collins, *Fighting Words: Black Women and the Search for Justice* (Minneapolis: University of Minnesota Press, 1998), 98–101.
83. Ibid., 2–3.
84. Ibid., 37–38.
85. Ibid., 38.
86. Jim Crow laws represented the embodiment of the doctrine of "separate but equal," which held that segregation did not violate the equal protection of laws required by the Fourteenth Amendment. In the words of Coramae Richey Mann, "Jim Crow laws regulated every dimension of social contact between blacks and whites. Separate building entrances and exits, seating arrangements in theatres (or separate theatres), public transportation, waiting rooms in railroad stations (and later, separate bus stations and airports), toilets, drinking fountains, hotels, restaurants and other accommodations were required for blacks" (*Unequal Justice*, 124).
87. See Russell, *Color of Crime*, 21, 23; Derrick Bell, *Race, Racism, and American Law*, 3rd ed. (Boston: Little, Brown, 1992), 38–89. See also Lerone Bennett, *Before the Mayflower: A History of Black America* (New York: Penguin, 1993), 255–96.
88. "We Charge Genocide: The Historic Petition to the United Nations for Relief from a Crime of the United States Government Against the Negro People," Civil Rights Congress, New York, 1951. Material cited in the following account can be found on pp. 55, 57–58, 81, 82, 85, 102, 103, 113, 116.
89. Danielle McGuire, *At the Dark End of the Street: Black Women, Rape, and Resistance—A New History of the Civil Rights Movement from Rosa Parks to the Rise of Black Power* (New York: Random House, 2010), 34–35, 45. In a highly unusual turn of events, the officers were tried, convicted of the rape, and sentenced to seven years in prison (61).
90. "We Charge Genocide," 82.
91. Ibid., 81.
92. McGuire, *At the Dark End of the Street*, 28, 49–50, 84–86. Ultimately, Claudette was convicted of assault and battery and violation of state segregation laws, despite proof that she had not violated the city laws she had been charged under and had been neither unruly nor abusive (89). Although community groups initially rallied around Claudette Colvin's case, civil rights leaders, including Rosa Parks, determined that her case could not serve as the spark for the Montgomery bus boycott because she was pregnant and unmarried, dark-skinned, lived in one of the poorest sections of town, and her parents worked as a maid and a laborer. These leaders ignored the fact that Colvin was a straight-A student and member

of the NAACP Youth Council (91–92). As McGuire writes, "Political respectability required middle-class decorum. Shining a spotlight on a pregnant black teenager would only fuel white stereotypes of black women's uninhibited sexuality. Colvin's swollen stomach could have become a stark reminder that desegregation would lead to sexual debauchery. . . . They risked evoking black stereotypes that could ultimately smother any movement for changes" (93). The politics of respectability which manifest in the movement's abandonment of Claudette Colvin's cause similarly shaped the choice and silencing of Rosa Parks as the standard-bearer of the civil rights movement (97–110).

93. Ibid., 218.

94. Angela Y. Davis, "Violence Against Women and the Ongoing Challenge to Racism," first published as a pamphlet in the Freedom Organizing Series by Kitchen Table: Women of Color Press (1985), reprinted in *The Angela Y. Davis Reader*, ed. Joy James (Malden, MA: Blackwell, 1998), 138, 147.

95. McGuire, *At the Dark End of the Street*, 195.

96. Ibid., 192–95.

97. Paula Johnson, "At the Intersection of Injustice: Experiences of African American Women in Crime and Sentencing," *Journal of Gender and the Law* 4, no. 1 (Fall 1995): 492; Collins, *Black Feminist Thought*, 924.

98. Baker, "Systemic White Racism," 407; see also Jennifer L. Morgan, "'Some Could Suckle over Their Shoulder': Male Travelers, Female Bodies, and the Gendering of Racial Ideology," *William and Mary Quarterly* 54, no. 1 (1997): 167–92, 171.

99. Mary Odem, *Delinquent Daughters: Protecting and Policing Adolescent Female Sexuality in the United States, 1885–1920* (Durham, NC: University of North Carolina Press, 1995), 33. See also Johnson, "At the Intersection of Injustice"; Linda L. Ammons, "Mules, Madonnas, Babies, Bath Water, Racial Imagery and Stereotypes: The African-American Woman and the Battered Woman Syndrome," *Wisconsin Literary Review* (1995): 1003, 1026–28. Ammons notes that "long after slavery had been abolished, in some courts the idea of rape and a black woman was inconceivable" (1025n104). For instance, in 1918 the Florida Supreme Court refused to extend the presumption of chastity to "another race that is largely immoral" (33–34, citing Dallas v. State, 79 So. 690, 691 [Fla. 1918]).

100. Baker, "Systemic White Racism," 407; Ammons, "Mules, Madonnas, Babies," 1050n172.

101. Cathy J. Cohen, "Punks, Bulldaggers, and Welfare Queens: The Radical Potential of Queer Politics?," *Gay and Lesbian Quarterly* 3 (1997): 437–65.

102. Collins, *Black Feminist Thought*, 83–84.

103. Ibid., 83.

104. Johnson, "At the Intersection of Injustice," 33–34.

105. Quoted in Ammons, "Mules, Madonnas, Babies," 173.

106. Ibid. The Moynihan Report essentially blamed the "deterioration of the fabric of Negro society" on the "dominant" role played by Black women in Black families. Paula Giddings, *When and Where I Enter: The Impact of Black Women on Race and Sex in America* (New York: Bantam, 1984), 325; see also Keeanga-Yamahtta Taylor, *From #BlackLivesMatter to Black Liberation* (Chicago: Haymarket Books, 2016), 40.

107. Johnson, "At the Intersection of Injustice," 33–34.

108. Haley, *No Mercy Here*, 25, 26.

109. Eithne Luibhéid, *Entry Denied: Controlling Sexuality at the Border* (Minneapolis: University of Minnesota Press, 2002), xi.

110. Ibid., x, xi, xii.

111. Ibid., xi, 3.

112. Ibid., x.

113. Ibid., xi, xii.

114. Ibid., xiii, xi.

115. Sess. 11, Chap. 141; 18 Stat. 477, 43rd Congress, March 3, 1875. Luibhéid, *Entry Denied*, xv; George Anthony Peffer, "Forbidden Families: Emigration Experiences of Chinese Women under Page Law 1875–1882," *Journal of American Ethnic History* 6, no. 1 (Fall 1986): 28–46.

116. The following section draws on Luibhéid, *Entry Denied*, 6, 31, 38, 41, xi, xii, xiv, xv, xvii, xviii, xvix, 77, 80–81, 207, 90, 78, 12, 9, 10, 26, 9, 7–8, 24, 27, 76, 16, 56, 62, 64, 67, 73, 75, 10, 48, 81, 48.

117. Clare Sears, *Arresting Dress: Cross-Dressing, Law, and Fascination in Nineteenth-Century San Francisco* (Durham, NC: Duke University Press, 2015), 121–33.

118. Ibid., 35, 37, 11. "The sexual labor of Chinese prostitutes was believed to be the nexus through which germs and disease could most easily be transmitted to white men. . . . Sex with Chinese prostitutes seemed to be the vector through which white supremacy and the perpetuity of 'the white race' was directly threatened" (37).

119. Luibhéid, *Entry Denied*, 44.

120. Yen Le Espiritu, "Race, Class, and Gender in Asian America," in *Making More Waves: New Writing by Asian American Women*, ed. Elaine H. Kim, Lilia V. Villanueva, and Asian Women United of California (Boston: Beacon Press, 1997), 135: Lisa C. Ikemoto, "Male Fraud," in *Critical Race Feminism: A Reader*, 2nd ed., ed. Adrien Katherine Wing (New York: New York University Press, 2003), 252–54.

121. Alicia Arrizón, "Latina Subjectivity, Sexuality and Sensuality," *Women & Performance: A Journal of Feminist Theory* 18, no. 3 (2009): 189–98; Juanita Díaz-Cotto, *Chicana Lives and Criminal Justice: Voices from El Barrio* (Austin: University of Texas Press, 2006), 11–12; see also Juanita Díaz-Cotto, "Latina Imprisonment and the War on Drugs," in Bosworth and Flavin, *Race, Gender, and Punishment*, 187.

122. Díaz-Cotto, *Chicana Lives and Criminal Justice*, xix.

123. Michael Bronski, *A Queer History of the United States* (Boston: Beacon Press, 2011), 13.

124. Sears, *Arresting Dress*, 10.

125. Nan Alamilla Boyd, *Wide Open Town: A Queer History of San Francisco* (Berkeley: University of California Press), 86–87, 90–91; Joan Nestle, "Lesbians and Prostitutes: A Historical Sisterhood," in Joan Nestle, *A Restricted Country* (Ithaca, NY: Firebrand, 1987), 157.

126. Collins, *Black Feminist Thought*, 920.

CHAPTER 2:*Policing Paradigms and Criminalizing Webs*

1. Sentencing Project, "Trends in U.S. Corrections: U.S. State and Federal Prison Population 1925–2014," fact sheet, http://sentencingproject.org/wp-content/uploads/2016/01/Trends-in-US-Corrections.pdf. "The number of women in prison has been increasing at a rate 50 percent higher than men since 1980" (4).

2. Sentencing Project, "Incarcerated Women and Girls," fact sheet, November 2015, http://www.sentencingproject.org/wp-content/uploads/2016/02/Incarcerated -Women-and-Girls.pdf.

3. Vera Institute, *Overlooked: Women and Jails in an Era of Reform* (New York, 2016), 6-7, 9.

4. Sentencing Project, "Trends in U.S. Corrections."

5. Vera Institute, *Overlooked*, 9.

6. Sentencing Project, "Incarcerated Women and Girls."

7. Mechthild Nagel, "Anti-Black Racism, Gender, and Abolitionist Politics," *Peace Review* 23, no. 3 (2011): 304–12; Barbara Bloom and Meda Chesney-Lind, "Women in Prison: Vengeful Equity," in Muraskin, *It's a Crime*, 544.

8. Christopher Hartney and Linh Vuong, *Created Equal: Racial and Ethnic Disparities in the U.S. Criminal Justice System* (Oakland, CA: National Council on Crime and Delinquency, March 2009). Native men were incarcerated at 4.2 times the rate of white men.

9. Black women are still between 1.6 and 4.1 times as likely to be incarcerated as white women of any age group. E. Ann Carson, "Prisoners in 2014," NCJ 248955, Bureau of Justice Statistics website, September 2015, https://www.bjs.gov/index .cfm?ty=pbdetail&iid=5387; see also Sentencing Project, "Incarcerated Women and Girls"; Marc Mauer, *The Changing Racial Dynamics of Women's Incarceration* (Washington, DC: Sentencing Project, 2013), http://sentencingproject.org /wp-content/uploads/2015/12/The-Changing-Racial-Dynamics-of-Womens -Incarceration.pdf.

10. Vera Institute, *Overlooked*, 11.

11. Federal Bureau of Investigation, *Crime in the United States—2014* (Washington, DC: FBI, 2015), https://ucr.fbi.gov/crime-in-the-u.s/2014/crime-in-the-u.s.-2014. Arrest data is not reported by both gender and race, so it is impossible to discern gendered racial disparities in arrest data. This figure represents an 8.5 percent increase since 2010, but is tapering off compared to previous decades: arrests of adult women increased by 36.5 percent between 1986 and 1995. FBI, *Crime in the United States—1995* (Washington, DC: FBI, 1996), https://ucr.fbi.gov/crime-in-the-u.s/1995.

12. Bloom and Chesney-Lind, "Women in Prison."

13. FBI, *Crime in the United States—2014*.

14. Sentencing Project, "Incarcerated Women and Girls."

15. Ibid. According to Bloom and Chesney-Lind, "Women in Prison," "When women do commit violent offenses, they often do so in self-defense and as a response to domestic violence. . . . Women prisoners are far more likely to kill intimates or relatives . . . than strangers" (548). According to Victoria Law, "In California, a study found that 93 percent of the women who had killed their significant others had been abused by them. That same study found that 67 percent of those women reported they had been attempting to protect themselves or their children. In New York State, 67 percent of women sent to prison for killing someone close to them were abused by this person." Victoria Law, "How Many Women are in Prison for Defending Themselves Against Domestic Violence?," *Bitch*, September 16, 2014, https://bitchmedia.org/post/women-in-prison-for-fighting-back-against-domestic -abuse-ray-rice.

16. Vera Institute, *Overlooked*, 9, 23.

17. Bloom and Chesney-Lind, "Women in Prison."

18. Center for American Progress, "Fact Sheet: The State of African American Women in the United States," November 7, 2013, https://www.americanprogress.org/issues/race/reports/2013/11/07/79165/fact-sheet-the-state-of-african-american-women-in -the-united-states/report.

19. "Poverty in Black America," Blackdemographics.com, http://blackdemographics .com/households/poverty/, accessed November 28, 2016.

20. National Women's Law Center; source: Census Bureau, Current Population Survey, 2012.

21. US Census Bureau, "American FactFinder: Poverty Status in the Past 12 Months of Families 2011-2015," http://factfinder.census.gov/faces/tableservices/jsf/pages /productview.xhtml?src=bkmk.

22. As Anannya Bhattacharjee puts it, "The supposed privacy and sanctity of the home is a very relative concept, whose application . . . [is] heavily conditioned by racial and economic status." Anannya Bhattacharjee, "Whose Safety? Women of Color and the Violence of Law Enforcement," working paper, American Friends Service Committee on Women, Population, and the Environment, 2001, 38.

23. Priscilla Ocen, "The New Racially Restrictive Covenant: Race, Welfare, and the Policing of Black Women in Subsidized Housing," *UCLA Law Review* 59 (2012): 1540, 1565, 1568–69, 1577–1581 (describing police profiling and discriminatory enforcement against Black women in public housing).

24. ACLU et al., *Caught in the Net.*

25. Ibid., 23.

26. Katherine Tate, James Lance Taylor, and Mark Q. Sawyer, *Something's in the Air: Race, Crime, and the Legalization of Marijuana* (New York: Routledge, 2013); ACLU et al., *Caught in the Net*, 24.

27. See Sentencing Project, *Disparity by Geography: The War on Drugs in America's Cities* (Washington, DC: Sentencing Project, May 1, 2008), 9–10, 16, 21–25, http:// www.sentencingproject.org/publications/disparity-by-geography-the-war-on -drugs-in-americas-cities; Patricia Allard, *Life Sentences: Denying Welfare Benefits to Women Convicted of Drug Offenses* (Washington, DC: Sentencing Project, 2002), https://www.opensocietyfoundations.org/sites/default/files/03-18-03atriciaAllard Report.pdf; ACLU et al., *Caught in the Net.*

28. Bloom and Chesney-Lind, "Women in Prison."

29. Drug Policy Alliance, "Fact Sheet: Women, Prison, and the Drug War," February 2016, http://www.drugpolicy.org/resource/women-prison-and-drug-war.

30. Sentencing Project, "Women in the Criminal Justice System: Briefing Sheets," May 2007, http://www.sentencingproject.org; Marc Mauer, Cathy Potler, and Richard Wolf, *Gender and Justice: Women, Drugs, and Sentencing Policy* (Washington, DC: Sentencing Project, 1999), 3, 4; Lisa D. Moore and Amy Elkavich, "Who's Using and Who's Doing Time: Incarceration, the War on Drugs, and Public Health," *American Journal of Public Health* 98, no. 5 (2008): 782–86.

31. Ross, *Inventing the Savage.*

32. FBI, *Crime in the United States—2014*. These numbers continue a long-standing trend; between 1999 and 2008, women's drug arrests increased by 19 percent, compared to 10 percent for men. Institute on Women and Criminal Justice, *Quick Facts: Women and Criminal Justice—2009* (New York: Women's Prison Association,

March 2009, http://www.wpaonline.org/wpaassets/Quick_Facts_Women_and_CJ
_Sept09.pdf (citing FBI, *Crime in the United States—2008*, tables 33 and 42.

33. Bloom and Chesney-Lind, "Women in Prison."

34. See, for instance, Harry G. Levine and Deborah Peterson Small, *Marijuana Arrest Crusade: Racial Bias and Police Policy in New York City* (New York: New York Civil Liberties Union, April 2008), http://www.nyclu.org; Katherine Beckett et al., "Drug Use, Drug Possession Arrests, and the Question of Race: Lessons from Seattle," *Social Problems* 52, no. 3 (2005): 419–41.

35. Debbie Nathan, "What Happened to Sandra Bland?," *Nation*, April 21, 2016.

36. Yvonne D. Newsome, "Border Patrol: The U.S. Customs Service and the Racial Profiling of African American Women," *Journal of African American Studies* 7, no. 3 (2003): 31–57.

37. ACLU et al., *Caught in the Net.*

38. Cathy Harris, *Flying While Black: A Whistleblower's Story* (Los Angeles: Milligan Books, 2001), 105.

39. Newsome, "Border Patrol."

40. ACLU et al., *Caught in the Net*, 29.

41. Ibid.; Newsome, "Border Patrol," 50.

42. Newsome, "Border Patrol," 54.

43. Ibid., 55.

44. Ibid., 33.

45. Ibid.

46. Ibid., 42–49 (citing Harris, *Flying While Black*).

47. Ibid.

48. American Civil Liberties Union of Arizona, *Driving While Black or Brown: An Analysis of Racial Profiling in Arizona* (Phoenix: ACLU Arizona, April 2008), https://www.acluaz.org/sites/default/files/documents/DrivingWhileBlackorBrown.pdf.

49. Díaz-Cotto, *Chicana Lives and Criminal Justice*, 134, 135, 137, 140, 141.

50. Geneva Horse Chief, "Amnesty International Hears Testimony on Racial Profiling," *Indian Country Today*, October 16, 2003.

51. Associated Press, "Los Angeles Police Officers Accused of Raping Women While on Duty," Fox News, February 18, 2016.

52. Crenshaw and Ritchie, *Say Her Name.*

53. See Sentencing Project, *Disparity by Geography*, 25.

54. Rebecca Maher, *Sexed Work: Gender, Race and Resistance in a Brooklyn Drug Market* (Oxford, UK: Oxford University Press, 1997), 2–3.

55. dream hampton, dir., *Treasure: From Tragedy to Transjustice, Mapping a Detroit Story*, 2015, www.treasuredoc.com.

56. Maher, *Sexed Work.*

57. ACLU et al., *Caught in the Net*, 30.

58. Maher, *Sexed Work.*

59. Ibid.

60. Ibid. For instance, Maher describes the issuance of 7,160 summons for minor offenses "aimed at deterring drug traffic in the area" by the Narcotics Division of the New York City Police Department within a six-month period in the early 1990s in a Brooklyn neighborhood.

61. Ellen M. Boylan, *Advocating for Reform of Zero Tolerance Student Discipline Policies: Lessons from the Field* (New York: Education Law Center, 2002); Andrea McArdle and Tanya Erzen, eds., *Zero Tolerance: Quality of Life and the New Police Brutality in New York City* (New York: New York University Press, 2001).

62. George L. Kelling and James Q. Wilson, "Broken Windows: The Police and Neighborhood Safety," *Atlantic*, March 1982, http://www.theatlantic.com/magazine /archive/1982/03/broken windows/304465.

63. Tanya Erzen, "Turnstile Jumpers and Broken Windows: Policing Disorder in New York City," in McArdle and Erzen, *Zero Tolerance*, 19–49.

64. Ibid.

65. Pete White, "Litigating Against Police Misconduct," plenary address, Critical Race Studies Symposium, UCLA, Los Angeles, October 17, 2015, citing early writings of James Q. Wilson.

66. Kelling and Wilson, "Broken Windows."

67. Bernard E. Harcourt, "Punitive Preventive Justice: A Critique," University of Chicago Public Law and Legal Theory Working Paper No. 386 / Coase-Sandor Institute for Law & Economics Working Paper No. 599 (2012), http://chicagounbound .uchicago.edu/law_and_economics/401, accessed January 15, 2016; see also Office of the Inspector General for the NYPD, *An Analysis of Quality-of-Life Summons, Quality-of-Life Misdemeanor Arrests, and Felony Crime in New York City, 2010-2015* (New York: New York City Department of Investigation, 2016), 3–5 (finding no empirical evidence of a link among summonses, misdemeanor-arrest activity, and felony crime).

68. National Law Center on Homelessness and Poverty, *No Safe Place: The Criminalization of Homelessness in U.S. Cities* (Washington, DC: 2014), 7–8.

69. K. Babe Howell, "Broken Lives from Broken Windows: The Hidden Costs of Aggressive Order-Maintenance Policing," *New York University Review of Law and Social Change* 33 (2009): 271, 274.

70. OIG-NYPD, *An Analysis of Quality-of-Life Summons*, 2.

71. NAACP, *Born Suspect: Stop and Frisk Abuses and the Continued Fight to End Racial Profiling in America* (Washington, DC: NAACP, 2014), 14; #SilentMarchNYC: Giselle, naacpconnect.org/video/entry/silentmarchnyc-giselle, June 14, 2012.

72. Dorothy E. Roberts, "Supreme Court Review, Foreword: Race, Vagueness and the Social Meaning of Order-Maintenance Policing," *Journal of Criminal Law and Criminology* 89, no.3 (Spring 1999): 775. See, generally, McArdle and Erzen, *Zero Tolerance*. Charles Reich, quoted in Phillip Beatty, Amanda Petteruti, and Jason Ziedenberg, *The Vortex: The Concentrated Racial Impact of Drug Imprisonment and the Characteristics of Punitive Counties* (Washington, DC: Justice Policy Institute, 2007), states, "Laws that are widely violated . . . especially lend themselves to selective and arbitrary enforcement" (14).

73. George Kelling, "Don't Blame My Broken Windows Theory for Poor Policing," *Politico*, August 11, 2015, http://www.politico.com/magazine/story/2015/08/broken -windows-theory-poor-policing-ferguson-kelling-121268.

74. Kelling and Wilson, "Broken Windows"

75. Rudolph W. Giuliani and William J. Bratton, *Police Strategy No. 5: Reclaiming the Public Spaces of New York*, July 6, 1994, http://marijuana-arrests.com/docs/Bratton -blueprint-1994—Reclaiming-the-public-spaces-of-NY.pdf, accessed April 4, 2016.

76. Ibid.
77. Kelling and Wilson, "Broken Windows."
78. Ibid.
79. Ibid.
80. Dayo F. Gore, Tamara Jones, Joo-Hyun Kang, "Organizing at the Intersections: A Roundtable Discussion of Police Brutality Through the Lens of Race, Class, and Sexual Identities," in McArdle and Erzen, *Zero Tolerance.*
81. Ibid.
82. Matt Lait and Scott Glover, "Killing of Homeless Woman Unjustified, Officer Says," *Los Angeles Times*, July 21, 2000; Nicholas Riccardi, "City to Pay $975,000 in Police Killing of Homeless Woman," *Los Angeles Times*, December 16, 2000; "L.A.—The Police Murder of Margaret Mitchell," *Revolutionary Worker* 1010 (June 13, 1999), http://revcom.us/a/v21/1010-019/1010/lapd.htm.
83. Smith, *Conquest*, 147.
84. Jim Hoffer, "Investigation: Woman Claims Brutality Against NYPD Officer," *Eyewitness News*, ABC 7 NY, August 1, 2014, http://abc7ny.com/news/investigation -woman-claims-police-brutality-against-nypd-officer/229978, accessed January 18, 2016.
85. Emma Lacey-Bordeaux, "Arizona Professor's Jay Walking Arrest Quickly Gets Out of Hand," CNN, June 30, 2014.
86. Mogul, Ritchie, and Whitlock, *Queer (In)Justice.*
87. Ibid.; Erzen, "Turnstile Jumpers," 19.
88. Mogul, Ritchie, and Whitlock, *Queer (In)Justice.*
89. Testimony of Veronica Garcia, Amnesty International hearing "One Nation, Many Faces: The State of Racial Profiling by Law Enforcement Today," October 2, 2003, transcript in author's collection. See, also, Roberta Spalter-Roth, "Street Vending in Washington, DC: Reassessing the Regulation of a 'Public Nuisance,'" occasional paper, Center for Washington Area Studies, George Washington University, 1985; Ana Muñiz, *Police, Power and the Production of Racial Boundaries* (New Brunswick, NJ: Rutgers University Press), 58, 62.
90. Center for American Progress, "Facts on Immigration Today," October 2014, https://www.americanprogress.org/issues/immigration/reports/2014/10/23/59040 /the-facts-on-immigration-today-3; Doris Meissner, Donald M. Kerwin, Muzzafar Chishti, and Claire Bergeron, *Immigration Enforcement in the United States: The Rise of a Formidable Machinery* (Washington, DC: Migration Policy Institute, 2013), 2, 9.
91. President Obama deported more than two million immigrants (Center for American Progress, "Facts on Immigration Today"); see also Meissner et al., *Immigration Enforcement in the United States*. Between 1892 and 1997, 2.1 million people were deported from the United States. See Tanya Golash-Boza, "Mapping the Shift from Border to Interior Enforcement of Immigration Laws During the Obama Presidency," Social Scientists on Immigration Policy, January 25, 2013, http://stopdeportationsnow.blogspot.com/2013/01/mapping-shift-from-border -to-interior_7232.html.
92. American Immigration Council, "The Growth of the U.S. Deportation Machine," fact sheet, March 2014, https://www.americanimmigrationcouncil.org/research /growth-us-deportation-machine, 3–4; Meissner et al., *Immigration Enforcement*

in the United States; Tanya Golash-Boza and Pierrette Hondagneu-Sotelo, "Latino Immigrant Men and the Deportation Crisis: A Gendered Racial Removal Program," *Latino Studies* 11, no. 3 (2013): 271, 276; Ken Dilanian, "Border Patrol Is Grappling with Misconduct Cases in Its Ranks," *Los Angeles Times*, September 7, 2010; National Network for Immigrant and Refugee Rights, *Over-Raided, Under Siege: U.S. Immigration Laws and Enforcement Destroy the Rights of Migrants* (Oakland, CA: National Network for Immigrant and Refugee Rights, 2008); H. Nimr, C. Tactaquin, and A. Garcia, *Human Rights & Human Security at Risk: The Consequences of Placing Immigration Enforcement and Services in the Department of Homeland Security* (Oakland, CA: National Network for Immigrant and Refugee Rights, 2003); National Network for Immigrant and Refugee Rights, *Preliminary Report and Findings of the Emergency National Border Justice and Solidarity Community Tour: Militarization and Impunity at the Border* (Oakland, CA: National Network for Immigrant and Refugee Rights, October 2006); T. Dunn, *The Militarization of the US-Mexico Border 1978–1992: Low-Intensity Conflict Doctrine Comes Home* (Austin: University of Texas, Center for Mexican American Studies, 1996).

93. American Immigration Council, "The Growth of the U.S. Deportation Machine," 2.

94. Tram Nguyen, *We Are All Suspects Now: Untold Stories from Immigrant Communities After 9/11* (Boston: Beacon Press, 2005), 100–101.

95. Coalición de Derechos Humanos, *Derechos Humanos: Alianza Indígena Sin Fronteras* 1, no. 1 (Summer 2004): 25, in author's collection.

96. Roberto Rodriguez, "'Never Again a World Without Us': The Many Tentacles of State Violence Against Black-Brown-Indigenous Communities," in *Who Do You Serve? Who Do You Protect?*, ed. Maya Schenwar, Joe Macaré, and Alana Yu-lan Price (Chicago: Haymarket Books, 2016), 65.

97. National Network for Immigrant and Refugee Rights, *Over-Raided, Under Siege*.

98. American Immigration Council, "The Growth of the U.S. Deportation Machine," 2; Golash-Boza and Hondagneu-Sotelo, "Latino Immigrant Men," 271, 276.

99. Eunice Hyunhye Cho and Lisa Graybill, *Families in Fear: The Atlanta Immigration Raids* (Montgomery, AL: Southern Poverty Law Center and Georgia Latino Alliance for Human Rights, 2016), 1.

100. Bhattacharjee, "Whose Safety?," 41–42.

101. American Immigration Council, "The Growth of the U.S. Deportation Machine," 6–7; Golash-Boza and Hondagneu-Sotelo, "Latino Immigrant Men," 271, 278–79, 281.

102. US Immigration and Customs Enforcement, "Priority Enforcement Program," https://www.ice.gov/pep, accessed January 14, 2017; Juliana Morgan-Trostle, Kexin Zheng and Carl Lipscombe, *State of Black Immigrants 2016* (New York: Black Alliance for Just Immigration and New York University School of Law Immigrant Rights Clinic, 2017), 14, 16–17. The Priority Enforcement Program replaced the earlier "Secure Communities" program, which was the subject of widespread opposition by states and localities.

103. Meissner et al., *Immigration Enforcement in the United States*, 7.

104. Morgan-Trostle et al., *State of Black Immigrants 2016*, 13, 15–19. William C. Anderson, "Killing Africa," in Schenwar, Macaré, and Price, *Who Do You Serve?*, 73.

105. Golash-Boza and Hondagneu-Sotelo, "Latino Immigrant Men," 271, 279.

106. National Network for Immigrant and Refugee Rights, *Over-Raided, Under Siege*.

107. Ibid.

108. Golash-Boza and Hondagneu-Sotelo, "Latino Immigrant Men." Fear of deportation was identified as the primary reason that 64 percent of undocumented women in a San Francisco study did not seek social services. See Chris Hogeland and Karen Rosen, *Dreams Lost, Dreams Found: Undocumented Women in the Land of Opportunity* (San Francisco: Coalition for Immigrant and Refugee Rights and Services, 1991), 63.

109. Rita E. Urquijo-Ruiz, "Alicia Sotero Vásquez: Police Brutality Against an Undocumented Mexican Woman," *Chicana/Latina Studies* 4, no. 1 (Fall 2004): 68–72, 74; see also Golash-Boza and Hondagneu-Sotelo, "Latino Immigrant Men."

110. Martha D. Escobar, *Captivity Beyond Prisons: Criminalization Experiences of Latina (Im)migrants* (Austin: University of Texas Press, 2016), 97, 105.

111. Nguyen, *We Are All Suspects Now*, xvii.

112. Ibid.

113. Ibid., 85.

114. Andrea J. Ritchie, "Law Enforcement Violence Against Women of Color," in *Color of Violence: The INCITE! Anthology* (2006; repr. ed., Durham, NC: Duke University Press, 2016).

115. Nina Bernstein, "Questions, Bitterness and Exile for Queens Girl in Terror Case," *New York Times*, June 17, 2005.

116. Luisita Lopez Torregrosa, "Life After Detention: 'I Was Definitely Cheated of a Future,'" *New York Times*, January 26, 2016.

117. Peter Hermann, "Baltimore's Transgender Community Mourns One of Their Own, Slain by Police," *Washington Post*, April 3, 2015, https://www.washingtonpost.com /local/crime/baltimores-transgender-community-mourns-one-of-their-own -slain-by-police/2015/04/03/2f657da4-d88f-11e4-8103-fa84725dbf9d_story.html.

118. "A Deadly U-Turn: Did Miriam Carey Need to Die After Wrong Car Move at White House Checkpoint?," *Democracy Now*, April 27, 2015; David Montgomery, "Her Name Was Miriam Carey," *Washington Post Magazine*, November 26, 2014.

119. Reena Flores, "White House Responds to Petition to Label Black Lives Matter a 'Terror' Group," *CBS News*, July 17, 2016, http://www.cbsnews.com/news/white -house-responds-to-petition-to-label-black-lives-matter-a-terror-group; Angela Davis, *Freedom Is a Constant Struggle* (Chicago: Haymarket Press, 2016), 140–41.

120. See Ritchie, "Law Enforcement Violence Against Women of Color," 155; Rights Working Group, *Faces of Racial Profiling: A Report from Communities Across America* (Washington, DC: 2010), 29.

121. Testimony of Sheila Mirza and Emira Habiby Browne, Amnesty International hearing "One Nation, Many Faces."

122. Louise A. Cainkar, *Homeland Insecurity: The Arab American and Muslim American Experience After 9/11* (New York: Russell Sage Foundation, 2009), 161.

123. Chaumtoli Huq, "American Devotion to Order over Justice Must End," *Al-Jazeera America*, August 25, 2015; see also Ben Fractenberg, "Mom Arrested for Blocking Sidewalk While Waiting for Family to Use Bathroom," *DNA Info*, September 2, 2014, https://www.dnainfo.com/new-york/20140902/midtown/mom -arrested-for-blocking-sidewalk-while-waiting-for-family-use-bathroom.

124. Chaumtoli Huq, "Stop Policing Gender Outlaws," *Al-Jazeera America*, October 14, 2015; Fractenberg, "Mom Arrested for Blocking Sidewalk."

125. Complaint, Itemid v. Borchardt, 16-cv-8033 (N.D. Ill. August 18, 2016).

126. "Muslim Woman Mistaken for Terrorist Sues Chicago Police," CBS News, August 12, 2016.

127. Shaista Patel, "Racing Madness," in *Disability Incarcerated: Imprisonment and Disability in the United States and Canada*, ed. Liat Ben-Moshe, Chris Chapman, and Allison C. Carey (New York: Palgrave Macmillan, 2014), 202.

128. Nadine Naber, Eman Desouky, and Lina Baroudi, "The Forgotten '-ism': An Arab American Women's Perspective on Zionism, Racism, and Sexism," in INCITE!, *Color of Violence*, 97, 104–6.

129. Nguyen, *We Are All Suspects Now*, 79–80.

130. Ibid., 79–80, 82.

131. Alexander quoted in ibid., 81.

132. Ibid., 140.

133. Bhattacharjee, "Whose Safety?," 9.

CHAPTER 3: *Policing Girls*

1. Naomi Martin, "Racist Comments Prompted McKinney Pool Party Fight, Host Says," *Dallas News*, June 2015; *MSNBC Talks with Teenage Eyewitness to McKinney TX Pool Party*, video, *All In with Chris Hayes*, June 9, 2015, https://www.youtube.com/watch?v=4zAnZA51Gjo; Sarah Mervosh, "McKinney Officer Eric Casebolt Resigns; Police Chief Calls Actions at Pool Party 'Indefensible,'" *Dallas News*, June 2015.

2. Martin, "Racist Comments Prompted McKinney Pool Party Fight."

3. Tristan Hallman, "Attorney Says Her Teenage Client's Treatment at McKinney Pool Party Was 'Inappropriate, Excessive and Without Cause,'" *Dallas News*, June 2015.

4. Martin, "Racist Comments Prompted McKinney Pool Party Fight."

5. Becton's case, and the prominent role of pool segregation during the Jim Crow era, were both highlighted a year later when Simone Manuels became the first African American to win gold in an Olympic swimming event. See Andray Domise, "Why Simone Manuel's Gold-Medal Swim in Rio Was So Historic," *MacLean's*, August 13, 2016.

6. Martin, "Racist Comments Prompted McKinney Pool Party Fight."

7. See, for example, Stacey Patton, "White Male Cops: Keep Your Hands off Black Women and Girls," *Dame Magazine*, June 20, 2015, http://www.damemagazine.com/2015/06/20/white-male-cops-keep-your-hands-black-women-and-girls.

8. Mervosh, "McKinney Officer Eric Casebolt Resigns."

9. Ibid.

10. "Texas Family Pursuing Civil Lawsuit in Pool Party Police Brutality Case," *Clutch*, June 2016.

11. David Love, "Her Name Is Shakara: Spring Valley High Victim Refused to Comply with Unfair Punishment," *Atlanta Black Star*, October 31, 2005; Eric Owens, "Fallout Continues over Viral Video of Slamming, Dragging High School Girl," *Daily Caller*, November 2, 2015; Thad Moore, Jason Silverstein, and Nancy Dillon, "South Carolina Student Who Was Assaulted by Deputy Ben Fields Is Living in Foster Care, Says Her Lawyer," *Daily News*, October 28, 2015.

12. Iyana Robertson, "Everything You Should Know About the Spring Valley High School Assault," *Vibe*, October 27, 2015.

13. Loren Thomas, "Student Arrested Says She Was Standing Up for Classmate," WLTX19, October 28, 2015.

14. Owens, "Fallout Continues over Viral Video."

15. Jamie Self, "Columbia Student Files Lawsuit to Void Law Used to Arrest Her," *State*, August 11, 2016.

16. Glen Luke Flanagan, "FBI Report on Spring Valley Causes New Court Date for Girl Charged," *State*, July 19, 2016, http://www.thestate.com/news/local/crime /article90476652.html.

17. Chris Sommerfeldt, "Disgraced South Carolina Officer Will Not Face Charges for Hurling Student Across Classroom," *New York Daily News*, September 3, 2016.

18. "Video Captures Police Handcuffing 5-Year-Old Girl," Associated Press, April 22, 2005; "A Current Affair to Show 5-Year-Old's Arrest Today," http://www .acurrentaffair.com/daily/todayshow/index.html, accessed April 24, 2005.

19. Monique W. Morris, *Pushout: The Criminalization of Black Girls in Schools* (New York: New Press, 2016), 4, 56–57.

20. New York Civil Liberties Union, *Criminalizing the Classroom: The Over-Policing of New York City Schools* (New York, 2007), 14, 15, 18. The report decries the evolution of "minor violations of school rules" into "violations of the penal law"—fighting in the hallway becomes "assault," taking a classmate's pencil case becomes a "property crime," talking back becomes "disorderly conduct" (18).

21. Ibid., 3.

22. INCITE!, Women of Color Against Violence, *Law Enforcement Violence Against Women of Color & Trans People of Color: A Critical Intersection of Gender Violence & State Violence; an Organizer's Resource and Tool Kit*, (Redmond, WA: INCITE! Women of Color Against Violence, 2008), 23 (hereafter INCITE!, *Organizer's Tool Kit on Law Enforcement Violence*); Ann Simmons, "Mothers Seek Action from Palmdale School; They Protest When Their Children Are Suspended After Allegedly Tussling with a Security Guard," *Los Angeles Times*, September 29, 2007.

23. Aidan McLaughlin, Thomas Tracy, and Dan Rivoli, "Hundreds of Harlem, Bronx Subway Riders Get Free MetroCard Swipes as Groups Protest Disproportionate Fare Beating Arrests," *New York Daily News*, May 11, 2016.

24. Morris, *Pushout*, 67; Remy Kharbanda and Andrea Ritchie, *Education Not Deportation: Impacts of New York City School Safety Policies on South Asian Immigrant Youth* (New York: Desis Rising Up and Moving, June 2006), 65–66.

25. See New York Civil Liberties Union, *Criminalizing the Classroom*, 20; Kharbanda and Ritchie, *Education Not Deportation*, 65–66, 70; Chino Hardin of Prison Moratorium Project, quoted in Elizabeth Hays, "Students United to Rip Patrol, Want Cops out of Schools," *New York Daily News*, February 18, 2004. Morris notes that although white men aged thirteen to eighteen are most likely to initiate a school shooting, police officers and metal detectors are more likely to be placed in schools where the student population is largely made up of youth of color (75).

26. Kharbanda and Ritchie, *Education Not Deportation*, 65–66.

27. Morris, *Pushout*, 69.

28. Ibid., 76.

29. Ibid., 77. In her study of police presence in a New York City school, Kathleen Nolan notes that generally offenses like "disorderly conduct" were charged for altercations between students in approximately 40 percent of cases, with the

remaining 60 percent arising from "insubordination during an exchange with an adult." Kathleen Nolan, *Police in the Hallways: Discipline in an Urban High School* (Minneapolis: University of Minnesota Press, 2011), 59. Nolan cites the following as examples of what she terms "the interplay between institutional demand for respect and the culture of penal control": "issued a summons . . . for misbehaving," "issued a [referral to the juvenile justice system] . . . for refusing to present her identification when asked to do so," "insubordinate towards a female [school safety officer] and used profanity towards her" (60–62).

30. *Disparities in Discipline: A Look at School Disciplinary Actions for Utah's American Indian Students* (Salt Lake City: University of Utah, SJ Quinney College of Law, Public Policy Clinic, 2014), 6.

31. Morris, *Pushout*, 76, 77.

32. Nolan, *Police in the Hallways*, 65, 66.

33. The Advancement Project, *Education on Lockdown: The Schoolhouse to Jailhouse Track*, March 2005, http://www.advancementproject.org/resources/entry/education-on-lockdown-the-schoolhouse-to-jailhouse-track; Tammy Johnson, Jennifer Emiko Boyden, and William J. Pittz, "Racial Profiling and Punishment in U.S. Public Schools," Applied Research Center, 2001, http://www.lausd.k12.ca.us/district_g/resources/small_lrn_com/files/profiling.pdf.

34. CSG Justice Center, in partnership with the Public Policy Research Institute at Texas A&M University, *Breaking Schools' Rules: A Statewide Study on How School Discipline Relates to Students' Success and Juvenile Justice Involvement* (July 2011).

35. Amanda Ripley, "How America Outlawed Adolescence," *Atlantic*, November 2016.

36. Morris, *Pushout*, 3, 68. From 2010 to 2014, young women, the vast majority Black, made up between 27 percent and 32 percent of arrests of youth in schools in Chicago. See Project NIA, *Policing Chicago Public Schools : A Gateway to the School-to-Prison Pipeline*, vol. 3, *2013–2014 Data on School Arrests*, 2015, http://cpdincps.com/new-page/; Project Nia, *Policing Public Schools in Chicago*, vol. 2, *2011–2012 Data on School Arrests*, 2014, http://cpdincps.com/downloadable-report; Mariame Kaba and Frank Edwards, "Policing Public Schools in Chicago 2," Project Nia, January 2012, https://policeinschools.files.wordpress.com/2011/12/policing-chicago-public-schools-final2.pdf. Young women were most frequently arrested for battery, disorderly conduct, and miscellaneous minor offenses (3, 5, 8, 11).

37. Morris, *Pushout*, 10, 34, 12.

38. Ibid., 70.

39. Ibid., 11, 19, 24, 58–59.

40. Ibid., 19, 58–59.

41. Ibid., 34.

42. *Disparities in Discipline*, 9–10.

43. Ibid.

44. Teresa Wiltz, "American Indian Girls Often Fall Through the Cracks," *Stateline*, Pew Charitable Trusts, March 4, 2016.

45. American Civil Liberties Union of South Dakota, *Profiles of Kids at Risk* (2005), https://www.aclu.org/other/profiles-kids-risk-winner-sd; see also Antoine v. Winner School District 59–2, no. CIV 06–3007, 2006 U.S. Dist. LEXIS 76910 (D.S.D. Oct. 19, 2006).

46. Lindsey Bever, "School Officer Fired After Video Showed Him Body Slamming a 12-Year-Old Girl," *Washington Post*, April 11, 2016.

47. "Police Review Policy After Tasers Used on Kids," CNN.com, November 15, 2004, http://www.cnn.com/2004/US/11/14/children.tasers/.

48. David Weber, "Records: Cops Used Tasers Against 24 Students Since 2003," *Sun Sentinel*, March 25, 2005; see also Ashley Swann, "Mom Upset After Officer Used Taser on Child During Fight," WSB-TV Atlanta, February 9, 2013.

49. Anne-Marie Cusac, "The Trouble with Tasers," *Progressive*, April 11, 2005.

50. Rebecca Kelin, "School Police Have Used Electroshock Weapons on At Least 4 Kids Since August," *Huffington Post*, September 29, 2016.

51. New York Civil Liberties Union, *Criminalizing the Classroom*, 16, 17.

52. Testimony witnessed by author.

53. New York Civil Liberties Union, *Criminalizing the Classroom*, 12.

54. Ibid., 16–17.

55. Elizabeth Sullivan, *Deprived of Dignity: Degrading Treatment and Abusive Discipline in New York City and Los Angeles Public Schools*, National Economic and Social Rights Initiative, 2007, https://www.nesri.org/sites/default/files/deprived_of _dignity_07.pdf.

56. Kharbanda and Ritchie, *Education Not Deportation*, 40.

57. Girls for Gender Equity, *Black Girls Breaking Silence on School Push-Out*, YouTube, https://www.youtube.com/watch?v=-yoAmxZMgpQ.

58. "Battery Charges Dropped Against Hercules High School Transgender Teen Who Had Been Bullied," CBSSF Bay Area, May 7, 2014; "Hercules Transgender Teen Charged with Battery After Fighting Back Against Bullies," CBSSF Bay Area, January 9, 2014.

59. Kharbarda and Ritchie, *Education Not Deportation*, 4, 7, 25, 28, 48, and 65–66; also see Letitia Miranda, "Undocumented Immigrants Fear Mass Deportation Under President Trump," *Buzzfeed*, November 10, 2016, https://www.buzzfeed.com /leticiamiranda/undocumented-immigrants-fear-mass-deportation-under -presiden?utm_term=.bpZOpb1OQ#.llkLzn2Ly.

60. Meg Wagner, "Washington Teen Sues Cop Who Dragged Her off Her Bike, Choked Her in Mall Parking Lot," *New York Daily News*, May 14, 2016.

61. Ibid.

62. Rod K. Brunson and Jody Miller, "Gender, Race, and Urban Policing: The Experience of African American Youths," *Gender and Society* 20, no. 4 (August 2006): 531–52, 532, 533, 539, 540, 541–42, 545, and 546.

63. Kathryn E. W. Himmelstein and Hannah Brückner, "Criminal Justice and School Sanctions Against Nonheterosexual Youth: A National Longitudinal Study," *Pediatrics* 127, no. 1 (January 2011): 54.

64. City Council, City of New York, transcript of the minutes of the Committee on Civil Rights, October 23, 2012; City Council, City of New York, transcript of the minutes of the Committee on Civil Rights, October 24, 2012.

65. See Taylor, *From #BlackLivesMatter to Black Liberation*, 190.

66. "Vivian Anderson: Community Activist, Global Advocate," http://www.vivian anderson.com.

67. Black Lives Matter website, "Every Black Girl Matters and Deserves to Grow into a Phenomenal Version of Themselves," http://blacklivesmatter.com/everyblack girlmatters.

68. EveryBlackGirl, press release, September 12, 2016, in author's collection.

69. Niya Kenny, *#EveryBlackGirl*, video, https://drive.google.com/file/d/0B6Pve1JkM3e3 WVAyZHlMdCoyVm8/view.

70. The Sadie Nash Leadership Project is a leadership-development program for young women twelve to twenty-one. For more information, go to www.sadienash.org. The video *Our Forgotten Voices from HIStory to HERstory*, YouTube, January 1, 2013, is at https://www.youtube.com/watch?v=F-T08_JPH-s.

CHAPTER 4: *Policing (Dis)Ability*

1. Terry Morris, *No Justice, No Peace: From Emmett Till To Rodney King* (Brooklyn, NY: Afrocentric Productions, 1993), 41; Selwyn Raab, "Officer Indicted in Bumpurs Case," *New York Times*, February 1, 1985; Davis, "Violence Against Women and the Ongoing Challenge to Racism," 138, 147; Selwyn Raab, "Ward Defends Police Actions in Bronx Death," *New York Times*, November 3, 1984; "Then, After the Killing," editorial, *New York Times*, November 2, 1984.

2. See, for example, Andrea J. Ritchie, "#SayHerName: Racial Profiling and Police Violence Against Black Women," *Harbinger* 41 (2016): 187.

3. Jackie Lacey, District Attorney of County of Los Angeles website, "District Attorney Declines to File Charges Against Former California Highway Patrol Officer," news release, December 3, 2015, http://da.lacounty.gov/sites/default/files/pdf /120315-da-decline-release-report.pdf.

4. Ibid.

5. Pinnock v. Farrow et al., First Amended Complaint, 14cv05551 (C.D. Ca, July 25, 2014); *California Highway Patrol Officer Beating Woman in the Head on Side of Road*, YouTube video, https://www.youtube.com/watch?v=DcCN5C7UBxo, July 5, 2014; "Beating Victim: CHP Officer 'Was Trying to Kill Me,'" *Crimesider*, August 11, 2014; "No Criminal Charges for Officer Seen Punching Woman on Video," *Los Angeles Times*, December 2, 2015; Artemis Moshtaghian and Sara Sidner, "$1.5 Million Settlement for Woman Beaten by California Patrol Officer," CNN, September 25, 2014; *Thug Cop Beats Homeless Black Woman (Support Rally & Fight for Justice)*, July 8, 2014, YouTube video, https://www.youtube.com/watch?v=sJ5lur3XWAc.

6. Alan Feuer, "Fatal Police Shooting in Bronx Echoes One from 32 Years Ago," *New York Times*, October 19, 2016; Alex Vitale, "Eleanor Bumpurs, Deborah Danner, and Finally Fixing Our Emergency Response," *Gotham Gazette*, October 20, 2016; Stephanie Pagonis, "NYPD Shooting of Mentally Ill Woman Invokes Memory of Eleanor Bumpurs," *New York Post*, October 20, 2016.

7. Deborah Danner, "Living with Schizophrenia," January 28, 2012, https://assets .documentcloud.org/documents/3146953/Living-With-Schizophrenia-by-Deborah -Danner.pdf.

8. Eli Rosenberg and Ashley Southall, "In Quick Response, de Blasio Calls Fatal Shooting of Mentally Ill Woman 'Unacceptable,'" *New York Times*, October 19, 2016.

9. Crenshaw and Ritchie, *Say Her Name*.

10. Haley, *No Mercy Here*, 18, 20.

11. See Chapman, Ben-Moshe, and Carey, "Preface," Ben-Moshe, Chapman, and Carey, *Disability Incarcerated*; Nirmala Erevelles, "Crippin' Jim Crow: Disability, Dis-Location, and the School-to-Prison Pipeline"; and Syrus Ware, Joan Ruzsa and Giselle Dias, "It Can't Be Fixed Because It's Not Broken," in Ben-Moshe,

Chapman, and Carey, *Disability Incarcerated*, 11, 85; and Camille A. Nelson, "Racializing Disability, Disabling Race: Policing Race and Mental Status," *Berkley Journal of Criminal Law* 15, no. 1 (2010): 13–17 (citing disability justice scholars).

12. E-mail to the author.

13. Immigrant women and other women of color were historically portrayed as the faces of "feeblemindedness" and "insanity" (Chapman, Ben-Moshe, and Carey, "Preface," Ben-Moshe, Chapman, and Carey, *Disability Incarcerated*, 8).

14. Vanessa Jackson, "An Early History—African American Mental Health," *Race, Healthcare, and the Law*, http://academic.udayton.edu/health/01status/mental01 .htm, 4, accessed April 11, 2016.

15. Pemina Yellow Bird, "Wild Indians: Native Perspectives on the Hiawatha Asylum for Insane Indians," at 3, 4, 5, http://www.power2u.org/downloads/Native PerspectivesPeminaYellowBird.pdf.

16. Sears, *Arresting Dress*, 42–43; see also Chapman, Ben-Moshe, and Carey, "Preface," Ben-Moshe, Chapman, and Carey, *Disability Incarcerated*; Erevelles, "Crippin' Jim Crow," 3, 4, 88.

17. Chapman, Ben-Moshe, and Carey, "Preface," Ben-Moshe, Chapman, and Carey, *Disability Incarcerated*, 9.

18. David M. Perry and Lawrence Carter-Long, "The Ruderman White Paper on Media Coverage of Law Enforcement Use of Force and Disability: A Media Study (2013–2015) and Overview," Ruderman Family Foundation, Boston, March 2016, 1, 8. See also Kimbriell Kelly et al., "Fatal Shootings by Police Remain Relatively Unchanged After Two Years," *Washington Post*, December 30, 2016, estimating that a quarter of police shootings in 2015 and 2016 involved people labeled with mental illness.

19. Doris A. Fuller, H. Richard Lamb, Michael Biasotti, and John Snook, *Overlooked in the Undercounted: The Role of Mental Illness in Fatal Law Enforcement Encounters* (Arlington, VA: Treatment Advocacy Center, Office of Research and Public Affairs, December 2015), http://www.treatmentadvocacycenter.org/storage/documents /overlooked-in-the-undercounted.pdf. The Treatment Advocacy Center has been criticized by mental health consumer rights organizations for its support of measures facilitating involuntary commitment.

20. Ibid., 1; Judge David L. Bazelon Center for Mental Health Law, letter to the President's Task Force on 21st-Century Policing, March 12, 2015, http://www.bazelon .org/LinkClick.aspx?fileticket=zGdyaep2AjI%3d; Rebecca Vallas and Shawn Fremstad, *Disability Is a Cause and Consequence of Poverty* (Washington, DC: Center for American Progress, 2014), write that the "poverty rate for working-age people with disabilities is nearly two and a half times higher than that for people without disabilities. Indeed, recent research finds that half of all working age adults who experience at least one year of poverty have a disability, and nearly two-thirds of those experiencing longer-term poverty have a disability"). See also Chapman, Ben-Moshe, and Carey, "Preface," Ben-Moshe, Chapman, and Carey, *Disability Incarcerated*, 12, 16; and Michael Rembis, "The New Asylums," in Ben-Moshe, Chapman, and Carey, *Disability Incarcerated*, 149–50.

21. New York City Department of Investigation, Office of the Inspector General for the NYPD, *Putting Training into Practice: A Review of the NYPD's Approach to Handling Interactions with People in Mental Crisis* (2017).

22. Fuller et al., *Overlooked in the Undercounted*, 5; Bazelon Center, letter to the President's Task Force on 21st-Century Policing.

23. Linda A. Teplin, "Keeping the Peace: Police Discretion and Mentally Ill Persons," *National Institute of Justice Journal* 11, no. 12 (July 2000): 9–15.

24. Jackson, "An Early History," writes: "In the late 1960s, Vernon Mark, William Sweet and Frank Ervin suggested that urban violence, which most African-Americans perceived as a reaction to oppression, poverty and state-sponsored economic and physical violence against us, was actually due to 'brain dysfunction,' and recommended the use of psychosurgery to prevent outbreaks of violence. . . . The issue of brain dysfunction as a cause of poor social conditions in African-American and Latino communities continues to crop up in the federally funded Violence Initiatives of the 1990s and current calls for psychiatric screening for all children entering juvenile justice facilities" (5). Such theories are reminiscent of diagnoses such as drapetomania (described as a mental disease causing slaves to run away that should be treated with whipping) and dysaethesia aethiopica (described as "rascality" that should also be treated with whipping) (ibid.). Similarly, women have historically been seen as prone to emotional disturbance because of their gender and defiance of gender norms and patriarchal authority—both embodying and causing psychiatric disability in others (ibid.); see also Gabriel Arkles, "Gun Control, Mental Illness, and Black Trans and Lesbian Survival," *Southwestern Law Journal* 42, no. 4 (2013): 876–98; James W. Hicks, "Ethnicity, Race, and Forensic Psychiatry: Are We Color-Blind?," *Journal of the American Academy of Psychiatry Law* 32 (2004): 31–33.

25. As part of this process, Nelson and others note the disabling effects of slavery, incarceration, and other racialized institutions such as Indian Residential Schools ("Racializing Disability, Disabling Race," 1, 5, 6); Chapman, Ben-Moshe, and Carey, "Preface," Ben-Moshe, Chapman, and Carey, *Disability Incarcerated*, 9; Erevelles, "Crippin' Jim Crow," 86–87.

26. Nelson, "Racializing Disability, Disabling Race," 45–47.

27. Arkles, "Gun Control"; Mogul, Ritchie, and Whitlock, *Queer (In)Justice*.

28. Rachel Anspaugh, "Police Violence Frequently Targets Disabled Black People—and We Hardly Ever Talk About It," *Fusion*, January 2, 2017; Emilie Raguso, "City Seeks Rejection of Wrongful Death Lawsuit Against Police; Celebrity Pathologist Disputes Cause of Death," *Berkeleyside*, September 23, 2016, http://www.berkeley side.com/2016/09/23/city-seeks-rejection-of-wrongful-death-lawsuit-against -berkeley-police-celebrity-pathologist-disputes-cause-of-death; Maria Moore, presentation at Say Her Name panel, National Lawyers Guild Conference, Oakland, California, October 2016; Kimberly Veklerov, "Leaked Documents Shed New Light on Kayla Moore's In-Custody Death," *Daily Californian*, May 7, 2014; Berkeley Cop Watch, "People's Investigation: In Custody Death of Kayla Moore," October 2013, in author's collection.

29. Moore, presentation; Veklerov, "Leaked Documents Shed New Light"; Berkeley Cop Watch, "People's Investigation."

30. See, for example, Veklerov, "Leaked Documents Shed New Light"; Toshio Meronek, "How Did Kayla Moore Die?" *East Bay Express*, March 4, 2013; Maria Moore, personal communications with the author.

31. Raguso, "City Seeks Rejection of Wrongful Death Lawsuit."

32. "Did Michelle Cusseaux Have to Die?" *Arizona Republic*, editorial, August 22, 2014; "Police Killing of Michelle Cusseaux Raises Questions of Wrongful Death & Handling of Mentally Ill," *Democracy Now*, May 20, 2015; Justin Sayers, "Phoenix Police Chief Agrees to Demote Sergeant in Michelle Cusseaux Killing," *Arizona Republic*, October 30, 2015.

33. Complaint, Garrett v. Dupra et al., 15cv1309 (D. Ariz., July 14, 2015).

34. Ibid.; "Police Killing of Michelle Cusseaux."

35. D. S. Woodfill, "Phoenix Police Introduce Mental-Health-Crisis Reforms," *Arizona Republic*, October 22, 2014.

36. Sayers, "Phoenix Police Chief Agrees to Demote Sergeant"; Miriam Wasser, "Phoenix Cop Who Killed Michelle Cusseaux Violated Department Policy, PPD Board Rules," *Phoenix New Times*, September 18, 2015.

37. Lauren Gold, "County Approves $1.8 Million Settlement in Shooting of Mentally Ill Rosemead Woman," *Pasadena Star News*, February 18, 2014.

38. "Woman, 62, Accuses Cops of Roughing Her Up Outside Church," *CBS News*, May 26, 2016.

39. K. Chandler, "Police Killings of Native Americans Is Out of Control," *Reverb Press*, September 30, 2015; John Lurie, "Native Lives Matter: A Solution to Police Violence in Indian Country," *Twin Cities Daily Planet*, January 14, 2015.

40. Lurie, "Native Lives Matter."

41. Yihyun Jeong, "7 Facts to Know About the Winslow Shooting," *Arizona Republic*, August 3, 2016; Dave Burke, "Bodycam Records the Moment Arizona Cop Shot a Native American Woman Dead as She Walked Towards Him with a Pair of Scissors," *Daily Mail*, July 28, 2016; Mark Hodge, "Killed for Holding Scissors," *Sun*, July 29, 2016.

42. Jeong, "7 Facts to Know"; Matt Agorist, "Disturbing Body Cam Shows Cop Execute Native American Woman for Holding Haircut Scissors," *freethoughtproject.com*, July 28, 2016.

43. Yihyun Jeong, "Winslow Officer Who Fatally Shot Loreal Tsingine Resigns," *Arizona Republic*, November 1, 2016.

44. Yihyun Jeong, "At Funeral, an Outpouring of Grief for Navajo Woman Killed by Winslow Police Officer," *Arizona Republic*, April 7, 2016.

45. James Fisher, "Disabled Couple Sues Delaware State Police over Raid Tactics," *USA Today*, September 29, 2015.

46. Complaint, Hayes vs. Popp et al., 15cv00872 (D. Del., September 28, 2015); Melissa Steele, "Rehoboth Couple Takes State Police to Court for Excessive Force," *Cape Gazette* (Delaware), October 2, 2015.

47. Chris Halsne, "Police Use Taser on Deaf Crime Victim," *KIRO 7*, August 5, 2012.

48. John Knicely, "Jury Agrees Deaf Woman's Rights Violated, but Refuses Huge Payout," *KIRO 7*, March 19, 2014.

49. Chapman, Carey, and Ben-Moshe, "Preface," Ben-Moshe, Chapman, and Carey, *Disability Incarcerated*, x.

50. Perry and Carter-Long, "Ruderman White Paper."

51. Ibid.

52. Ibid., 20–21.

53. Wesley Lowery, Kimberly Kindy, Keith L. Alexander, Julie Tate, Jennifer Jenkins, and Steven Rich, "Distraught People, Deadly Results," *Washington Post*, June 30, 2015.

54. In conversation with the author.

55. RIPPD, *Mental Illness Is Not a Crime in NYC*, August 19, 2010, YouTube, https://youtu.be/sEHSu8T1F0E; Lisa Ortega, "RIPPD: Diverting People Away from the Criminal Justice System: Police Procedure When It Comes to Mental Illness Must Change," *New York City Voices*, Spring 2006.

56. North Star Fund News, "Rights for Imprisoned People with Psychiatric Disabilities (RIPPD)," December 10, 2011, https://northstarfund.org/news/rights-for-imprisoned-people-with-psychiatric-disabilities-rippd#.dpuf; see also Rembis, "The New Asylums," 151.

57. Fuller et al., *Overlooked in the Undercounted*, 1.

58. Described by Candice Bernd in Schenwar, Macaré, and Price, *Who Do You Serve?*

59. Ibid.

60. Ibid., 157.

61. Ibid., 158.

62. See, generally, *Disability Incarcerated*; Arkles, "Gun Control," 888, 890.

CHAPTER 5: *Police Sexual Violence*

1. Black Women's Blueprint and Yolande M. S. Tomlinson, PhD, *Invisible Betrayal: Police Violence and the Rapes of Black Women in the United States* (September 22, 2014), http://tbinternet.ohchr.org/Treaties/CAT/Shared%20Documents/USA/INT_CAT_CSS_USA_18555_E.pdf.

2. Steven Yoder, "Cops Gone Wild," *American Prospect*, March 28, 2013. See also 2006 and 2008 UN reports, in author's collection.

3. Kirsten West Savali, "Dear President Obama, Mike Brown Is a 'Slain American,' Too," *Dame Magazine*, http://www.damemagazine.com/2014/08/25/dear-president-obama-mike-brown-slain-american-too.

4. See, for example, Michelle Denise Jackson, "A Painful Silence: What Daniel Holtzclaw Teaches Us About Black Women in America," *For Harriet*, http://www.forharriet.com/2014/09/a-painful-silence-what-daniel-holtzclaw.html#axzz4Pu TQxkIq; Eesha Pandit, "America's Disturbing Epidemic of Police Abuse Revealed: 'When the Person Who Sexually Assaults You Is a Police Officer, Who Do You Call?,'" *Salon*, November 13, 2015, http://www.salon.com/2015/11/13/americas_disturbing_epidemic_of_police_abuse_revealed_when_the_person_who_sexually_assaults_you_is_a_police_officer_who_do_you_call/; Darnell Moore, "While We Focus on Shootings, We Ignore Victims of Police Sexual Assault," Mic.com, April 23, 2015, https://mic.com/articles/116216/the-type-of-police-brutality-no-one-is-talking-about#.nooFJhymo. One notable exception was the NAACP, which called on the Department of Justice to press hate crime charges against Holtzclaw early on in the case. See Jessica Chasmar, "Oklahoma Cop Charged with Assaulting 8 Black Women; NAACP Seeks Hate Crime Charges," *Washington Times*, August 31, 2014, http://www.washingtontimes.com/news/2014/aug/31/okla-cop-charged-raping-8-black-women-naacp-seeks-/.

5. Sarah Larimer, "'I Was So Afraid': Ex-Oklahoma City Cop's Victims Speak Out After Rape Convictions," *Washington Post*, December 11, 2015, https://www.washingtonpost.com/news/morning-mix/wp/2015/12/11/i-was-so-afraid-ex-oklahoma-city-cops-victims-speak-out-after-rape-convictions/.

6. Jessica Testa, "The 13 Women Who Accused a Cop of Sexual Assault, in Their Own Words," *Buzzfeed*, December 9, 2015; see also Richard Eldredge, "Jannie Ligons, Who Helped Bring Former Police Officer Daniel Holtzclaw to Justice, Is Honored in Atlanta This Weekend," *Atlanta*, April 1, 2016, http://www.atlantamagazine.com /news-culture-articles/jannie-ligons-helped-bring-former-police-officer-daniel -holtzclaw-justice-honored-atlanta-weekend/.

7. "When Cops Rape: Daniel Holtzclaw & the Vulnerability of Black Women to Police Abuse," *Democracy Now*, December 15, 2015.

8. This account of the Holtzclaw rapes draws on Testa, "The 13 Women Who Accused a Cop of Sexual Assault."

9. Anna Merlan, "Daniel Holtzclaw's Defense Suggests Maybe His 13 Alleged Victims Are All Liars with an 'Agenda,'" *Jezebel*, December 7, 2015, http://jezebel.com/being -publicly-or-privately-accused-of-lying-about-bein-1746826142; Molly Redden and Lauren Gambino, "Oklahoma Officer's Trial Defense Attacks Credibility of Vulnerable Black Women," *Guardian*, November 27, 2015, https://www.theguardian .com/us-news/2015/nov/27/oklahoma-officer-daniel-holtzclaw-trial-defense -attacks-credibility-of-vulnerable-black-women.

10. Sarah Larimer, "Disgraced Ex-Cop Daniel Holtzclaw Sentenced to 263 Years for On-Duty Rapes, Sexual Assaults," *Washington Post,* January 22, 2016, https://www .washingtonpost.com/news/post-nation/wp/2016/01/21/disgraced-ex-officer-daniel -holtzclaw-to-be-sentenced-after-sex-crimes-conviction/.

11. Matt Sedensky and Nomaan Merchant, "Hundreds of Officers Lose Licenses over Sex Misconduct," Associated Press, November 1, 2015, http://bigstory.ap.org/article /fd1d4d05e561462a85abe50e7eaed4ec/ap-hundreds-officers-lose-licenses-over -sex-misconduct.

12. R. L. Goldman and S. Puro, "Revocation of Police Officer Certification," *Saint Louis University Law Journal* 45 (2001): 541, 563n142.

13. "Eugene, Oregon, Settles Two Suits with Women Abused by Cops," Associated Press, August 12, 2005; C. Stephens, "Magana Verdict," KVAL 13 News, June 30, 2004; "Trial Begins for Perverted Eugene Cop Roger Magana: Media Is Shut Out," Portland Independent Media Center, June 4, 2004, http://www.publish.portland. indiymedia.org/en/2004/06/290053.shtml, accessed August 25, 2005; C. Stephens, "Victim Speaks Out About Perverted Eugene Cop," KVAL 13 News, March 13, 2004; C. Stephens, "Magana Records Revealed," KVAL 13 News, March 4, 2004; "Four More Women Accuse Eugene Officer of Abuse," KATU 2 News, December 11, 2003.

14. US Department of Justice Civil Rights Division, *Investigation of the Baltimore City Police Department*, August 10, 2016, https://www.justice.gov/opa/file/883366/download.

15. Philip M. Stinson, John Liederbach, Steven L. Brewer, and Brooke E. Mathna, "Police Sexual Misconduct: A National Scale Study of Arrested Police Officers," Criminal Justice Faculty Publications, paper 30, 2014, http://scholarworks.bgsu.edu /cgi/viewcontent.cgi?article=1029&context=crim_just_pub; Samuel Walker and Dawn Irlbeck, *Driving While Female: A National Problem in Police Misconduct* (Omaha: Police Professionalism Initiative, University of Nebraska at Omaha, March 2002), 3–4.

16. Matthew Spina, "When a Protector Becomes a Predator," *Buffalo News*, November 22, 2015.

17. Philip Matthew Stinson, John Liederbach, Steven P. Lab, and Steven L. Brewer Jr., *Police Integrity Lost: A Study of Law Enforcement Officers Arrested* (Washington, DC: National Institutes of Justice, June 2016), 193, 104–5; see also Stinson et al., "Police Sexual Misconduct," 16.

18. Stinson et al., *Police Integrity Lost*, 191.

19. Cato Institute, National Police Misconduct Reporting Project, *2010 Annual Report* (Washington, DC: Cato Institute, 2010), http://www.policemisconduct.net /statistics/2010-annual-report.

20. See, for example, Allen Beck, Marcus Berzofsky, and Christopher Krebs, *Sexual Victimization in Prisons and Jails Reported by Inmates, 2011–2012* (Washington, DC: US Department of Justice, May 2013), https://www.bjs.gov/content/pub/pdf /svpjri1112.pdf.

21. Anannya Bhattacharjee, "Private Fists and Public Force," in *Policing the National Body: Race, Gender and Criminalization*, ed. Jael Silliman and Anannya Bhattacharjee (Boston: South End Press, 2002), 22.

22. Norm Stamper, *Breaking Rank: A Top Cop's Exposé of the Dark Side of American Policing* (New York: Nation Books, 2005), 123.

23. See Jennifer L. Truman and Michael Planty, *Criminal Victimization*, NCJ 239437 (Washington, DC: Bureau of Justice Statistics, October 2012); Callie Marie Rennison, *Rape and Sexual Assault: Reporting to Police and Medical Attention, 1992–2000*, NCJ 194530 (Washington, DC: Bureau of Justice Statistics, August 2002), reports that 74 percent of completed and attempted sexual assaults against women were not reported to the police.

24. See Peter B. Kraska and Victor E. Kappeler, "To Serve and Pursue: Exploring Police Sexual Violence Against Women," *Justice Quarterly* 12, no. 1 (1995): 85, 92.

25. Craig R. McCoy and Nancy Phillips, "Extorting Sex with a Badge," *Philadelphia Inquirer*, August 13, 2006, http://www.philly.com/philly/news/special_packages /inquirer/Extorting_sex_with_a_badge.html.

26. Cara E. Rabe-Hemp and Jeremy Braithwaite, "An Exploration of Recidivism and the Officer Shuffle in Police Sexual Violence," *Police Quarterly* 16, no. 2 (2012): 127–47, 129, 132.

27. Ibid., 85, 97.

28. Many have criticized this term as downplaying police rape and sexual assault, and the accompanying violence or threat of violence. Here it is included only where used by researchers.

29. "Voyeuristic actions" can include a number of violations, such as officers looking into homes without legal justification, or inappropriately taking or viewing sexually explicit videos. See International Association of Chiefs of Police, *Addressing Sexual Offenses and Misconduct by Law Enforcement: Executive Guide* (Alexandria, VA: 2011), 3; Kraska and Kappeler, "To Serve and Pursue," 85, 98–99.

30. International Association of Chiefs of Police, *Addressing Sexual Offenses and Misconduct by Law Enforcement*, 3–4.

31. Stinson, Liederbach, Lab, and Brewer, *Police Integrity Lost*; Rabe-Hemp and Braithwaite, "An Exploration of Recidivism," 130; Stinson et al., "Police Sexual Misconduct"; Kraska and Kappeler, "To Serve and Pursue," 85, 98.

32. Kraska and Kappeler, "To Serve and Pursue," 85, 103.

33. Ibid., 35, 190; Rabe-Hemp and Braithwaite, "An Exploration of Recidivism," 130–31; Stinson et al., "Police Sexual Misconduct," 2; Kraska and Kappeler, "To Serve and Pursue," 85, 89, 107.

34. A. Pittman, "Cop Crisis," *Eugene Weekly*, March 17, 2005. Similar conclusions were reached in connection with a rash of sexual assaults in the context of late-night traffic stops in Nassau and Suffolk Counties, New York, which came to light in 2001. See Shelly Feuer Domash, "A Few Bad Cops, or a Problem with the System," *New York Times*, February 11, 2001.

35. Steven Yoder, "Officers Who Rape: The Police Brutality Chiefs Ignore," *Al-Jazeera America*, January 19, 2016.

36. Spina, "When a Protector Becomes a Predator"; Philip M. Stinson, Zachary J. Calogeras, Natalie L. DiChiro, and Ryan K. Hunter, *California Police Sexual Misconduct Arrest Cases, 2005–2011*, Criminal Justice Faculty Publications no. 59 (2015), http://scholarworks.bgsu.edu/crim_just_pub/59; Linda B. Cottler et al., "Breaking the Blue Wall of Silence: Risk Factors for Experiencing Police Sexual Misconduct Among Female Offenders," *American Journal of Public Health* 104, no. 2 (2014): 338–44; Rabe-Hemp and Braithwaite, "An Exploration of Recidivism," 131, 132; Stinson et al., "Police Sexual Misconduct,"15; International Association of Chiefs of Police, *Addressing Sexual Offenses and Misconduct by Law Enforcement*; Sarah Eschholz and Michael S. Vaughn, "Police Sexual Violence and Rape Myths: Civil Liability Under Section 1983," *Journal of Criminal Justice* 29 (2001): 389–405. In a recent series of cases case involving Los Angeles police officers, civil complaints alleged: "The officers' modus operandi in each case was the same: find a vulnerable victim (usually a drug user), earn her trust, and then threaten her with arrest. Then, using the LAPD's vehicle and acting under color of authority, drive her to a secluded place and force her to perform a sexual act on one of the officers" (Matt Reynolds, "LA Settles Civil Case Against Officers Accused of Rape," Courthouse News Service, April 20, 2016, http://www.courthousenews.com/2016/04/20/la -settles-civil-case-against-officers-accused-of-rape).

37. Kraska and Kappeler, "To Serve and Pursue," 85, 104; Stinson et al., "Police Sexual Misconduct."

38. Michelle Fine et al., "Anything Can Happen with Police Around: Urban Youth Evaluate Strategies of Surveillance in Public Spaces," *Journal of Social Issues* 59, no. 1 (2003): 141–58, 151.

39. See Stinson et al., *California Police Sexual Misconduct Arrest Cases*, 9; Philip M. Stinson et al., "Police Sexual Misconduct"; Samuel Walker and Dawn Irlbeck, *Police Sexual Abuse of Teenage Girls: A 2003 Update on "Driving While Female"* (Omaha: Police Professionalism Initiative, University of Nebraska at Omaha, June 2003), 3; and Kraska and Kappeler, "To Serve and Pursue," 104.

40. Stinson et al., "Police Sexual Misconduct"; Walker and Irlbeck, *Police Sexual Abuse of Teenage Girls*, 2; Kraska and Kappeler, "To Serve and Pursue," 102, 103.

41. Spina, "When a Protector Becomes a Predator."

42. Walker and Irlbeck, *Police Sexual Abuse of Teenage Girls*.

43. Walker and Irlbeck, *Driving While Female*, 4.

44. Ibid.; "Driving While Female Report Launches UNO Police Professionalism Program," press release, University of Nebraska at Omaha, May 29, 2002, http://www .unomaha.edu/uac/releases/2002may29ppi.html.

45. Walker and Irlbeck, *Driving While Female*, 3.

46. Susan Montoya Brian, "$3M Settlement Reached in Police Sexual Assault Case," *Associated Press*, March 23, 2016.

47. Luibhéid, *Entry Denied*, 118, 120, 121; See Coalición de Derechos Humanos/Alianza Indigena Sin Fronteras, "Violence on the Border," press release, February 25, 2004; *Justice on the Line: The Unequal Impacts of Border Enforcement in Arizona Border Communities*, Border Action Network, on file with author; *In Our Own Backyard: A Community Report on Human Rights Abuses in Texas's Rio Grande Valley* (Valley Movement for Human Rights, 2004); Bhattacharjee, "Private Fists and Public Force," 23; Human Rights Watch/Americas, *Crossing the Line: Human Rights Abuses Along the U.S. Border with Mexico Persist Amid Climate of Impunity*, report 7, no. 4 (April 1995).

48. Dilanian, "Border Patrol Is Grappling with Misconduct Cases in Its Ranks"; see also Luibhéid, *Entry Denied*, 122-33; Julie Light, "Rape on the Border, Baiting Immigrants, Border Patrol Abuses, Anti-Immigrant Politics," *Progressive*, September 1996; Human Rights Watch, *Brutality Unchecked: Human Rights Abuses Along the U.S. Border with Mexico* (1992), 14.

49. Mark Karlin, "US Border Patrol Agent Sexually Assaults Undocumented Mother and Two Daughters: Who Are the Criminals?," *TruthOut*, March 19, 2014.

50. Nina Bernstein, "An Agent, a Green Card, and a Demand for Sex," *New York Times*, March 21, 2008.

51. Andrea Nill Sanchez, "Police Officer Found Guilty of Raping Undocumented Immigrant at Gunpoint Under Threat of Deportation," *ThinkProgress*, March 11, 2011.

52. Robert Lopez, "Former Anaheim Police Officer Convicted of Victimizing Women," *Los Angeles Times*, May 17, 2010, http://latimesblogs.latimes.com/lanow/2010/05/anaheim-sex-case-.html.

53. Frank H. Galvan and Mohsen Bazargen, *Interactions of Latina Transgender Women with Law Enforcement* (Los Angeles: Bienestar, 2012), http://williamsinstitute.law.ucla.edu/wp-content/uploads/Galvan-Bazargan-Interactions-April-2012.pdf.

54. Luibhéid, *Entry Denied*, 128.

55. Ibid., 128–30.

56. Ibid.

57. Joe Merusak, "Iredell Sheriff, Former Officer Settle Sexual Harassment Suit," *Charlotte Observer*, August 28, 2014.

58. Keri Blakinger, "Woman Sues After Upstate N.Y. Cop Avoids Rape Charges, Says She Was Forced into Having Sex," *New York Daily News*, May 16, 2016, http://www.nydailynews.com/new-york/woman-sues-upstate-n-y-avoids-rape-charges-article-1.2637913; Keri Blakinger and Reuven Blau, "Two More Women Claim They Were Sexually Abused by Former Syracuse Cop Who Was Fired After Complaints from Other Victims," *New York Daily News*, August 9, 2016, http://www.nydailynews.com/new-york/women-claim-syracuse-sexually-abused-article-1.2743535.

59. Blakinger, "Woman Sues"; Blakinger and Blau, "Two More Women."

60. Blakinger and Blau, "Two More Women."

61. Ibid.

62. Ibid.

63. Ibid.

64. Testimony of Andrea Ritchie before the US Prison Rape Elimination Commission, March 26, 2007, citing U.S. v. Guidry, 456 F.3d 493, 496–97 (5th Cir. 2006); see also Eschholz and Vaughn, "Police Sexual Violence and Rape Myths," 396–98.

65. Kraska and Kappeler, "To Serve and Pursue," 85, 104.

66. "Settlement in Kim Nguyen Case," *Korea Town News*, November 2, 2016, http://koreatownlanews.com/settlement-in-kim-nguyen-case/#more-1099; "Woman Caught on Camera Tumbling out of Police Car Says She Was Being Sexually Assaulted," CBS Los Angeles, January 9, 2014, http://losangeles.cbslocal.com/2014/01/09/woman-caught-on-camera-tumbling-out-of-police-car-says-she-was-being-sexually-assaulted/; Joel Rubin, "Handcuffed Woman Falls from Moving LAPD Patrol Car Video Indicates," *Los Angeles Times*, September 2, 2013, http://articles.latimes.com/2013/sep/02/local/la-me-ln-handcuffed-woman-falls-lapd-patrol-car-20130902; "Girl Dumped on Street from Moving Squad Car After Cop Sexually Assaults Her: Lawsuit," *Filming Cops*, http://filmingcops.com/girl-dumped-on-street-from-moving-squad-car-after-cop-sexually-assaults-her-lawsuit/.

67. See Amnesty International, *Stonewalled: Police Abuse and Misconduct Against Lesbian, Gay, Bisexual and Transgender People in the U.S.* (New York: Amnesty International, September 21, 2005), 40.

68. Stinson et al., "Police Sexual Misconduct."

69. BreakOUT!, *We Deserve Better!,* 2014, http://www.youthbreakout.org/sites/g/files/g189161/f/201410/WE%20DESERVE%20BETTER%20REPORT.pdf.

70. Ibid., 15.

71. Brandon Lowry, "El Monte Police Officer Accused of Raping Transgender Woman," NBC4 News, Los Angeles, October 25, 2013, http://www.nbclosangeles.com/news/local/El-Monte-Police-Officer-Accused-of-Raping-Transgender-Woman-229229431.html; Richard Winton, "El Monte Police Officer Suspected in Sexual Assault of Transsexual," *Los Angeles Times*, October 25, 2013, http://articles.latimes.com/2013/oct/25/local/la-me-1025-sex-assault-20131025; "Transgender Woman Claims She Was Raped By Police Officer," *Huffington Post*, October 29, 2013, http://www.huffingtonpost.com/2013/10/29/transgender-woman-rape-police_n_4174379.html.

72. INCITE!, *Organizer's Tool Kit on Law Enforcement Violence*, 45.

73. Amnesty International, *Stonewalled*, 41.

74. Gaurav Jashnani et al., "'From the time I leave my house, I'm under the gun': Trauma, Public Space and Order Maintenance Policing in New York City," 2017, forthcoming article, in author's collection.

75. Rabe-Hemp and Braithwaite, "An Exploration of Recidivism," 142; Tori Marlan, "Armed and Dangerous," *Chicago Reader*, August 31, 2001.

76. Rabe-Hemp and Braithwaite, "An Exploration of Recidivism," 136.

77. Ibid., 127–47, 128, 129, 138, 140; "Betrayed by the Badge," *Newsweek*, June 17, 2001.

78. Kraska and Kappeler, "To Serve and Pursue," 99.

79. Mary Beth G. v. City of Chicago, 723 F. 2d 1263, 1272 (7th Cir. 1983).

80. I first heard this term used to describe strip searches by Beverly Bain, a long-time mentor and antiviolence activist, now a professor at University of Toronto, in the context of the audit of the Toronto Police Service's response to sexual assault, for which she served as a special advisor. See also Andrea J. Ritchie, Deputation to Toronto Police Services Board Re: Draft Discussion Paper—"Search of Persons,"

December 15, 1998 (arguing that police searches meet legal definitions of sexual assault), in author's collection.

81. See also Arkles, "Regulating Prison Sexual Violence," 71–130.

82. Kraska and Kappeler, "To Serve and Pursue," 85, 101.

83. David Lohr, "Woman Says Gas Station Strip Search Was Like Sexual Assault," *Huffington Post*, August 10, 2015, http://www.huffingtonpost.com/entry/texas-strip -search-public_us_55c8f940e4b0923c12bdb903, Michael Zennie and Alex Greig, "Two Women Suing Police After They Were Subjected to Humiliating Roadside Cavity Search," *Daily Mail* (UK), July 5, 2013.

84. Minutes of March 21, 2006, meeting of the Maine Indian Tribal-State Commission, http://www.mitsc.org/meeting.php?do=viewMinutes&id=201.

85. Rodriques v. Furtado, 575 F. Suppl. 1439 (D. Mass 1991), cited in Kraska and Kappeler, "To Serve and Pursue," 85, 100, 101.

86. Bonds v. Utreas, 04 C 2617 (N.D. Ill. Judge Joan Lefkow).

87. Darnell Moore, "While We Focus on Shootings, We Ignore Victims of Police Sexual Assault," *Identities.Mic*, https://mic.com/articles/116216/the-type-of-police -brutality-no-one-is-talking-about#.nooFJhymo.

88. Kraska and Kappeler, "To Serve and Pursue," 85, 97.

89. Rabe-Hemp and Braithwaite, "An Exploration of Recidivism," 141; Andrea Ritchie testimony to Civilian Complaint Review Board, "Sexual Violence by Law Enforcement: The Case for CCRB Exercise of Jurisdiction over Complaints and Investigations," October 12, 2016, on file with author.

90. Testimony of Andrea J. Ritchie, director, Sex Workers Project at the Urban Justice Center Before the Committee on Public Safety of the Council of the City of New York, January 29, 2009, in author's collection; see also Spina, "When a Protector Becomes a Predator"; Stinson et al., "Police Sexual Misconduct," 2, 29; Walker and Irlbeck, "Police Sexual Abuse of Teenage Girls," 3; Walker and Irlbeck, *Driving While Female*, 6.

91. See, for example, M. Weiss, "Crooked-Cop Cases Surge," *New York Post*, October 22, 2007.

92. Rabe-Hemp and Braithwaite, "An Exploration of Recidivism," 141; Stinson et al., "Police Sexual Misconduct," 28; Kimberly Lonsway, "Preventing and Responding to Police Sexual Misconduct," *Law and Order* 52, no. 8 (August 2004): 82, 84–86, 88–90; Walker and Irlbeck, *Police Sexual Abuse of Teenage Girls*, 5; Walker and Irlbeck, *Driving While Female*, 3–4.

93. Candice Bernd, "Police Ignore Rampant Sexual Assault by Officers," *TruthOut*, July 2, 2014; Yoder, "Cops Gone Wild"; Rabe-Hemp and Braithwaite, "An Exploration of Recidivism," 142.

94. Andrea J. Ritchie and Delores Jones-Brown, "Policing Race, Gender and Sex: A Review of Law Enforcement Policies," *Women and Criminal Justice* 27, no. 1 (2017), dx.doi.org/10.1080/08974454.2016.1259599.

95. Steven Yoder, "Officers Who Rape: The Police Brutality Chiefs Ignore," *Al-Jazeera America*, January 19, 2016; see also Yoder, "Cops Gone Wild."

96. Yoder, "Officers Who Rape"; Yoder, "Cops Gone Wild."

97. Yoder, "Cops Gone Wild."

98. President's Task Force on 21st-Century Policing, *Final Report of the President's Task Force on 21st-Century Policing* (Washington, DC: Office of Community

Oriented Policing Services, 2015); James E. Copple and Patricia M. Dunn, *Gender, Sexuality, and 21st-Century Policing: Protecting the Rights of the LGBTQ+ Community* (Washington, DC: Office of Community Oriented Policing Services, 2017).

99. "Group Gathers in Protest of Accused Oklahoma City Officer Daniel Holtzclaw," *Oklahoman*, October 2, 2014.

100. Ebony Dallas, "OKC Artists for Justice Founders See Activism as Extension of Creativity," *Oklahoman*, December 2, 2015.

101. Black Women's Blueprint, "Call to Action: Visioning Justice in the Storm of Holtzclaw and Cosby," January 7, 2016, in author's collection.

CHAPTER 6: *Policing Gender Lines*

1. See, for example, Louise Westmarland, *Gender and Policing: Sex, Power and Police Culture* (Portland, OR: Willan Publishing, 2001); National Center for Women and Policing, http://www.womenandpolicing.org.

2. The term "gender binary" refers to the complex interplay of cultural and institutional ideas and practices that divide people into two rigidly defined genders, male and female. As Gabriel Arkles notes, there is a general assumption that all people are one of only two genders—male or female—and that these gender categories are natural, stable, distinct, and meaningful. This assumption leads to many more. For example, if an infant's genitals are interpreted as female, a range of expectations and interpretations follow about other physical characteristics as well as identity, behaviors, strengths, mannerisms, personality traits, choice of clothing, appearance, and sexual and romantic attractions. Gender divisions, identities, expressions, and roles, as well as gender-based hierarchies in distribution of power, violence, and wealth, are seen as the natural and politically neutral product of biological and social processes. However, the social construction of gender and the imposition of a binary gender system go beyond serving as neutral methods of social classification and organization to act as pillars of hierarchical power relations that must be defended as such. Within this construct, people who live in a manner deemed consistent with the gender they were assigned at birth are deemed to be "cisgender," and those who express and live in a manner deemed inconsistent with the gender they were assigned at birth are deemed "transgender." See also Dean Spade, *Normal Life: Critical Trans Politics* (Boston: South End Press, 2011); L'lerrét Jazelle Ailith, in "When Transness Is an Illusion," *L'lerrét*, January 30, 2016, http://www.llerret.com/when-transness-is-an-illusion/, urges wholesale abandonment of gender as a category and challenges conceptions of what it means to be cisgender: "Transness as radical thought requires us to realize that conceptualizations of what embodies cisness and transness are predicated on white narratives and logic. And furthermore, it requires us to rid ourselves of this lie that cisness (especially for black and brown people) has ever existed!"

3. Young and Spencer, "Multiple Jeopardy," 74.

4. Mogul, Ritchie, and Whitlock, *Queer (In)Justice*, 3.

5. Gary Bowen, "Living Our True Spirit: An Entire Rainbow of Possibilities" in *Trans Liberation: Beyond Pink or Blue*, ed. Leslie Feinberg (Boston: Beacon Press, 1998), 63, 64. Bowen also discusses white trans people misappropriating parts of Native culture.

6. Mogul, Ritchie, and Whitlock, *Queer (In)Justice*, 64–65.

7. I. Bennett Capers, "Cross Dressing and the Criminal," *Yale Journal of Law and the Humanities* 20, no. 1 (2008): 8–9; see also Katherine M. Franke, "The Central Mistake of Sex Discrimination Law: The Disaggregation of Sex from Gender," *University of Pennsylvania Law Review* 144, no. 1 (1995): 58.

8. Sears, *Arresting Dress*, quotes here and below from 60, 62, 65, and 80.

9. Ibid., 81; depositions taken in *Tikkun v. City of New York*, in author's collection.

10. Sears, *Arresting Dress*, 86.

11. Ibid., 5, 81, 139.

12. Ibid., 80–81, 94, 140. "According to arrest records, city police made ninety-nine cross-dressing arrests between 1863 and 1900, and local newspapers reported on forty-seven of these; all but one involved a person presumed to be white" (93).

13. Sears, *Arresting Dress*, 87, 90.

14. Ibid. Although the grounds for her deportation are unknown, Sears speculates that she could have been deemed to be suffering from "constitutional psychopathic inferiority," to be a "sexual pervert" "in constant conflict with social customs and constituted authorities," or suffering from "moral turpitude." Alternately, she may have been deemed to be "likely to become a public charge" because her gender deviance would lead to either unemployment or incarceration, both of which would render her dependent on the state (137–38).

15. Ibid., 95.

16. Jonathan Ned Katz, "Coming to Terms: Conceptualizing Men's Erotic and Affectional Relations with Men in the United States, 1820–1892," in *A Queer World: The Center for Gay and Lesbian Studies Reader*, ed. Martin Duberman (New York: New York University Press, 1997), 230.

17. Susan M. Schweik, *The Ugly Laws: Disability in Public* (New York: New York University Press, 2009), 163.

18. This term was used to describe people who had been assigned female identities at birth but successfully lived as men. It is unclear how Babe would have described Babe's own gender identity. All we know is that Babe lived as a man for much of Babe's life. Susan Stryker and Stephen Whittle, *The Transgender Studies Reader* (New York: Routledge, 2006), 423.

19. Sears, *Arresting Dress*, 122, 123.

20. Ibid.

21. Ibid., 87, 95, 122, 123, 141; see also Nayan Shah, *Stranger Intimacy: Contesting Race, Sexuality and the Law in the North American West* (Berkeley: University of California Press, 2011), 40–42, with respect to gender indeterminacy among South Asian immigrants.

22. Mogul, Ritchie, and Whitlock, *Queer (In)Justice*. Leslie Feinberg, in *Trans Liberation*, states, "I have been locked up in jail by cops because I was wearing a suit and tie. . . . The reality of why I was arrested was as cold as the cell's cement floor: I am considered a masculine female. That's a *gender* violation" (11).

23. Elizabeth Lapovsky Kennedy and Madeline Davis, "'They Was No One to Mess With': The Construction of the Butch Role in the Lesbian Community of the 1940s and 1950s," in *The Persistent Desire: A Femme-Butch Reader*, ed. Joan Nestle (Boston: Alyson Publications, 1992), 62, 69.

24. Audre Lorde, *Zami: A New Spelling of My Name; a Biomythography* (Berkeley, CA: Crossing Press, 1982), 187.

25. Feinberg, *Trans Liberation*: "My feminine drag queen sisters were in nearby cells, busted for wearing 'women's' clothing" (11).

26. Rey "Sylvia Lee" Rivera, "The Drag Queen," in *Making History: The Struggle for Gay and Lesbian Equal Rights*, ed. Eric Marcus (New York: HarperCollins, 1992), 189–90.

27. John D'Emilio, "History: Risky Business," *Windy City News*, September 10, 2008, http://windycitymediagroup.com/gay/lesbian/news/ARTICLE.php?AID=19336.

28. Kara Fox, "Maryland Lesbian Alleges Metro Police Abuse in Arrest," *Washington Blade*, April 26, 2002.

29. Personal communication, February 2004.

30. Sears writes, "Within nineteenth-century municipal codebooks, for example, cross-dressing, prostitute, and disabled bodies appeared alongside one another as (il)legal equivalents in public space, through general orders that banned the public appearance of a person wearing 'a dress not belonging to his or her sex,' in 'a state of nudity,' or 'deformed so as to be an unsightly or disgusting object'" (*Arresting Dress*, 2, 11). Sears also documents non-trans women's practice of cross-dressing in men's clothes to signal availability to trade sex, indicating transgressive sexuality through clothing transgressions (38, 42–43). Perceptions of Chinese women's attire as "masculine" no doubt contributed to the perception that they were engaged in prostitution (38).

31. Mogul, Ritchie, and Whitlock, *Queer (In)Justice*, 67; Gwen Smith, "Transsexual Terrorism," *Washington Blade*, October 3, 2003; see also Elaine Craig, "Transphobia and the Relational Production of Gender," *Hastings Women's Law Journal* 18, no. 137 (2007): 162.

32. Joanne Meyerowitz, *How Sex Changed: A History of Transsexuality in the United States* (Cambridge, MA: Harvard University Press, 2002), 87.

33. Meagan Taylor, "I Was Arrested Just for Being Who I Am," *Speak Freely* blog, ACLU website, November 10, 2015, https://www.aclu.org/blog/speak-freely/i-was-arrested-just-being-who-i-am.

34. See, for example, State v. Taylor, 122 Idaho 218, 220, 832 P.2d 1153, 1155 (Idaho Ct. App. 1992); People v. Martinez, 88 Cal. App. 4th 465, 486, 105 Cal. Rptr. 2d 841, 855 (Cal. Ct. App. 2001).

35. People v. Lomiller, 30 A.D.3d 276, 818 N.Y.S.2d 27 (N.Y. App. Div. 2006).

36. Sex-segregated facilities are physical spaces that are explicitly designated for members of only one gender and where people of another gender are not permitted. Many of these facilities—such as drug treatment programs, prisons, jails, hospitals, group homes, domestic violence shelters, and homeless shelters—disproportionately regulate the lives of low-income people, people of color, people with disabilities, women, and trans people.

37. Mandy Carter, "Southerners on New Ground," in *What Lies Beneath: Katrina, Race, and the State of the Nation*, ed. South End Press Collective (Cambridge, MA: South End Press, 2007).

38. North Carolina General Assembly, House Bill 2 ("An act to provide for single-sex multiple occupancy bathroom and changing facilities in schools and public agencies and to create statewide consistency in regulation of employment and public accommodations"), March 23, 2016; Katy Steinmetz, "Lawmakers in 6 More States Are Pursuing 'Bathroom Bills,'" Time.com, January 5, 2017; Anna Douglas

and Bristow Marchant, "NC's HB2 Law Inspires Others to Copy It Despite Tough Federal Stand," *McClatchy DC*, May 13, 2016, http://www.mcclatchydc.com/news /politics-government/article77505747.html; Mogul, Ritchie, and Whitlock, *Queer (In)Justice*, 66; Amnesty International, *Stonewalled*, 20; San Francisco Human Rights Commission, "Gender Neutral Bathroom Survey," Transgender Law Center, Summer 2001, cites instances of arrest and fear of arrest by private security and police for using the "wrong" restroom. HB2 prohibits municipalities from legislating access to restrooms according to gender identity. See Southerners on New Ground, "Unpacking HB2: What Happened in North Carolina?," http://southernersonnewground .org/wp-content/uploads/2016/04/SONG_FINALHB2flyer_BW.pdf; "The Fix That's a Farce: HB2 Is Still a Threat," June 30, 2016, http://southernersonnewground.org /2016/06/hb2farce.

39. Huda Jadallah, "Reflections of a Genderqueer Palestinian American Lesbian Mother," in *Arab and Arab American Feminisms: Gender, Violence and Belonging*, ed. Rabab Abdulhadi, Evelyn Alsultany, and Nadine Naber (Syracuse, NY: Syracuse University Press, 2011), 276.

40. Amnesty International, *Stonewalled*, 20.

41. Leslie Pearlman, "Transsexualism as Metaphor: The Collision of Sex and Gender," *Buffalo Law Review* 43 (1995): 835, 844; Marjorie Garber, *Vested Interests: Cross-Dressing and Cultural Anxiety* (New York: HarperPerennial, 1992), 13.

42. Mogul, Ritchie, and Whitlock, *Queer (In)Justice*, 67; INCITE!, *Organizer's Tool Kit on Law Enforcement Violence*, 19.

43. Ritchie, "Law Enforcement Violence," 143.

44. Galbreath v. City of Oklahoma, 568 F. App'x 534 (10th Cir. 2014); "Man Wearing High Heels, Giving Children Candy Arrested for Disorderly Conduct," News 9, June 9, 2010, http://www.news9.com/story/12622217/man-wearing-high-heels -giving-children-candy-arrested-for-disorderly-conduct.

45. Opinion, Galbreath v. City of Oklahoma City, 15cv6044 (10th Cir., Dec. 4, 2015).

46. Spade, *Normal Life*, 12, 137–69.

47. Ibid., 137–69; Amnesty International, *Stonewalled*, 18.

48. Hiibel v. Sixth Judicial Dist. Court of Nevada, Humboldt County, 542 U.S. 177, 124 S. Ct. 2451 (2004) upholds the law making it a crime not to identify oneself to a police officer when questioned.

49. See Spade, *Normal Life*, 150.

50. Spade, *Normal Life*, 11; Amnesty International, *Stonewalled*, 38–39, 43; see also Angela Irvine and BreakOUT! Members and Staff, "You Can't Run from the Police: Developing a Feminist Criminology That Incorporates Black Transgender Women," *Southwestern Law Review* 44 (2015): 101–9.

51. Ritchie, "Law Enforcement Violence," 142. Almost every time I've repeated this phrase during a workshop or presentation, I've observed at least one masculine-of-center Black woman in the room nod emphatically.

52. New York City Civilian Complaint Review Board, *Pride, Prejudice and Policing: An Evaluation of LGBTQ-Related Complaints from January 2010 through December 2015* (2016), 50.

53. *The Report of the 2015 US Transgender Survey* (Washington, DC: National Center for Transgender Equality, 2016), 12, 187–88 (hereafter the *2015 US Transgender Survey*).

54. M. S. Frazer and E. E. Howe, *Transgender Health and Economic Insecurity: A Report from the 2015 LGBT Health and Human Services Needs Assessment Survey*, Empire State Pride Agenda (2015), www.prideagenda.org/lgbtdata; Make the Road New York, *Transgressive Policing: Police Abuse of LGBTQ Communities in Jackson Heights* (October 2012), 5; Galvan and Bazargen, *Interactions of Latina Transgender Women with Law Enforcement*, 6; Human Rights Watch, *In Harm's Way: State Response to Sex Workers, Drug Users, and HIV in New Orleans* (December 2013); Human Rights Watch, *Sex Workers at Risk: Condoms as Evidence of Prostitution in Four U.S. Cities* (2012), http://www.hrw.org/sites/default/files/reports/us0712For Upload_1.pdf.

55. Frazer and Howe, *Transgender Health and Economic Insecurity*; Make the Road New York, *Transgressive Policing*, 5; Galvan and Mohsen, *Interactions of Latina Transgender Women*, 6.

56. Elijah Adiv Edelman et al., *Access Denied: Washington, DC, Trans Needs Assessment Report* (Washington, DC: DC Trans Coalition, 2015), https://dctranscoalition. files.wordpress.com/2015/11/dctc-access-denied-final.pdf; Jaime M. Grant, Lisa A. Mottet, and Justin Tanis, *Injustice at Every Turn: A Report of the National Transgender Discrimination Survey* (Washington, DC: National Center for Transgender Equality/National Gay and Lesbian Task Force, 2011), http://www.thetaskforce.org /static_html/downloads/reports/reports/ntds_full.pdf.

57. Make the Road New York, *Transgressive Policing*, 19.

58. Human Rights Watch, *Sex Workers at Risk*, 24.

59. FIERCE Cop Watch video.

60. See Adkins v. City of New York, 143 F. Supp. 3d 134 (S.D.N.Y. 2015).

61. Welfare Warriors Research Collaborative, *A Fabulous Attitude: Surviving and Thriving in New York City* (New York: Queers for Economic Justice, 2010), 39.

62. Audre Lorde Project website, Safe OUTside the System: The SOS Collective, http:// alp.org/community/sos.

63. Other members of the Coalition Against Police Brutality (CAPB) included the Justice Committee, the Malcolm X Grassroots Movement, CAAAV: Organizing Asian Communities, and Sista II Sista; see http://caaav.org/coalition-against-police -brutality.

64. Personal communication, September 15, 2008; Amnesty International, *Stonewalled*, 45; Lamot v. City of New York, No. 1:99-CV-11540 (S.D.N.Y. Nov. 23, 1999).

65. Sears, *Arresting Dress*, 75, 91.

66. Gore, Jones, and Kang, "Organizing at the Intersections," 267.

67. Mogul, Ritchie, and Whitlock, *Queer (In)Justice*, 147.

68. San Francisco Police Department Bulletin, *Rules of General Conduct*, 03-241 (2003); San Francisco Police Department Bulletin, *Standards for Interactions with Transgender Communities*, 03-243 (2003).

69. Washington, DC, Metropolitan Police Department, General Order 501-02, "Handling Interactions with Transgender Individuals," 2005.

70. Nicole Pasulka, "The Woman Who Helped Change How Police Treat Transgender People," *Buzzfeed*, July 10, 2014.

71. Amnesty International, *Stonewalled*, 54.

72. See New York City Young Women's Initiative, *Report and Recommendations* (May 2016), http://www.shewillbe.nyc/YWI-Report-and-Recommendations.pdf;

Communities United for Police Reform, *Priorities for the New NYPD Inspector General: Promoting Safety, Dignity and Rights for All New Yorkers* (2014), http://changethenypd.org/resources/priorities-new-nypd-inspector-general-promoting-safety-dignity-and-rights-all-new-yorkers. For more information on the campaign and organizations involved, please see BreakOUT! and Streetwise and Safe, *Get Yr Rights: A Toolkit for LGBTQS Youth and LGBTQS Youth-Serving Organizations* (2015), http://getyrrights.org/wp-content/uploads/2015/02/GYR-Toolkit-FINAL-02-05-2015.pdf.

73. BreakOUT! and Streetwise and Safe, *Get Yr Rights*.
74. See Spade, *Normal Life*, 123–24, 139.

CHAPTER 7: *Policing Sex*

1. Ritchie, "Law Enforcement Violence," 142, 143.
2. Mogul, Ritchie, and Whitlock, *Queer (In)Justice*.
3. The term "prostitution," rather than "sex work," is used in this chapter because it is the legal term for the offense most commonly used to criminalize people who are or are believed to be trading sex for money or something of value. The term "sex work" denotes a broader range of conduct, encompassing both legal and criminalized forms of sexual labor, including erotic dancing and massage, as well as commercial phone sex, bondage, domination, and submission. Additionally, while advanced as a term intended to recognize people in the sex trades as laborers entitled to workers' rights, it is not one that all people engaged in sexual exchange identify with. Accordingly, the terms "people in the sex trades" or "people who trade sex" are used to describe people who are involved in sexual exchange, whether by choice, circumstance, or coercion. The term "prostitute" is generally experienced as a slur, defining people with full identities as mothers, daughters, sisters, artists, students, etc. solely based on an act they are alleged to have committed. Accordingly, when used here it is placed in quotation marks.
4. Cynthia M. Blair, *I've Got to Make My Livin': Black Women's Sex Work in Turn-of-the-Century Chicago* (Chicago: University of Chicago Press, 2010), offers a welcome and refreshingly complex framing of Black women's involvement in the sex trades, which both takes into account "the communal memory of sexual abuse and the continuing centrality of facts of sexual violation to the structure of racial inequality" (6–7) and the reality that sex work offers Black women opportunities for economic self-reliance, avoidance of the predations and penury of domestic service, and escape from "the strictures of family and community," while simultaneously exposing women to violence, including police violence (10–12, 24, 25, 228).
5. Jessica R. Pliley, *Policing Sexuality: The Mann Act and the Making of the FBI* (Cambridge, MA: Harvard University Press, 2014), 17.
6. Shah, *Stranger*, 40–42, 222–23, 224, 225, 230.
7. Sears, *Arresting Dress*, 45.
8. Mogul, Ritchie, and Whitlock, *Queer (In)Justice*, 51, 62; Ritchie, "Law Enforcement Violence," 144.
9. Sears, *Arresting Dress*, 41, 42.
10. Ibid., 67–69.
11. Ibid., 71.

12. Ibid., 70–71; see also Boyd, *Wide Open Town*, 42.

13. Sears, *Arresting Dress*, 45, 46; see also Boyd, *Wide Open Town*, 42.

14. Sears, *Arresting Dress*, 50, 51.

15. Blair, *I've Got to Make My Livin'*, quotes here and below from 73, 78, 88, 89, 93, 94–95, 95–96, 97, 102, 103–4, 106, 127, 129, 163, 179, 184, 190, 214–15, 219, 221, 223, and 228.

16. Human Rights Watch, *Sex Workers at Risk*, 17.

17. Boyd, *Wide Open Town*, 216–18.

18. Ibid., 86.

19. Ibid., 213–14.

20. Nestle, "Lesbians and Prostitutes," 157; see also Sears, *Arresting Dress*. Boyd, *Wide Open Town*, notes the pseudo-scientific examination of both lesbian and sex-worker bodies for signs of sexual degeneracy, pervasive presence of lesbians in the sex trade in popular media, and shared experiences and strategies of resistance to police harassment (84, 85, 87, 89, 90, 137); Mindy Chateauvert, *Sex Workers Unite! A History of the Movement from Stonewall to Slutwalk* (Boston: Beacon Press, 2013), 8.

21. See Celia Williamson et al., "Police-Prostitute Interactions," *Journal of Progressive Human Services* 18, no. 2 (2007): 16–17.

22. Chateauvert, *Sex Workers Unite!*, 174.

23. *2015 US Transgender Survey*, 12, 187.

24. Human Rights Watch, *Sex Workers at Risk*, 50.

25. Meredith Dank et al., *Locked In: Interactions with the Criminal Justice and Child Welfare Systems for LGBTQ Youth, YMSM, and YWSW Who Engage in Survival Sex* (Washington, DC: Urban Institute, September 2015), 16, 20, 21.

26. Melissa Gira Grant, "The NYPD Arrests Women for Who They Are and Where They Go—Now They're Fighting Back," *Village Voice*, November 22, 2016.

27. See Shana M. Judge and Mariah Wood, "Racial Disparities in the Enforcement of Prostitution Laws," paper presented at Association for Public Policy Analysis and Management, November 6–8, 2014; https://appam.confex.com/appam/2014/webprogram/Paper11163.html; Chateauvert, *Sex Workers Unite!*, 62. San Francisco's Task Force on Prostitution noted that prostitution arrests targeted "the most visible, those working on the street, and those most vulnerable, including African American, transgender, and immigrant women" (150); see also NAACP, *Beyond the Rodney King Story: An Investigation of Police Conduct in Minority Communities* (Boston: Northeastern University Press, 1994), 22.

28. Chateauvert, *Sex Workers Unite!*, 62; Williamson et al., "Police-Prostitute Interactions," note that the underground nature of the sex trades facilitates police misconduct (18).

29. Judge and Wood, "Racial Disparities in the Enforcement of Prostitution Laws."

30. *2015 US Transgender Survey*, 163.

31. Chateauvert, *Sex Workers Unite!*, 64.

32. Grant, "NYPD Arrests Women"; see also Human Rights Watch, *Sex Workers at Risk*, 16–17.

33. Grant, "NYPD Arrests Women."

34. City Council, City of New York, transcript of the minutes of the Committee on Public Safety, October 10, 2012.

35. *2015 US Transgender Survey*, 163.

36. Dank et al., *Locked In*.

37. Human Rights Watch, *Sex Workers at Risk*.

38. See, for example, PROS Network and Leigh Tomppert, *Public Health Crisis: The Impact of Using Condoms as Evidence of Prostitution in New York City* (New York: PROS Network and Sex Workers Project, 2012), 68, http://sexworkersproject.org /downloads/2012/20120417-public-health-crisis.pdf.

39. PROS Network and Tomppert, *Public Health Crisis*, 22; see also Acacia Shields, *Criminalizing Condoms: How Policing Practices Put Sex Workers and HIV Services at Risk in Kenya, Namibia, Russia, South Africa, the United States, and Zimbabwe* (New York: Open Society Foundation, 2012), 4, 19, http://www.opensociety foundations.org/reports/criminalizing-condoms.

40. PROS Network and Tomppert, *Public Health Crisis*, 22; Shields, *Criminalizing Condoms*, 4, 19.

41. PROS, Network and Tomppert, *Public Health Crisis*, 21.

42. Shields, *Criminalizing Condoms*.

43. Human Rights Watch, *In Harm's Way*; Human Rights Watch, *Sex Workers at Risk*.

44. Florrie Burke, "Forced into Prostitution and Denied a Lifeline," *Huffington Post*, May 15, 2013; see also Memorandum in Support, http://sexworkersproject.org /downloads/2010/20100510-sign-on-memo-no-condoms-as-evidence.pdf; Legal Aid Society, Memorandum in Support, in author's collection; Safe Horizon, Memorandum in Support, in author's collection; Human Rights Watch, Memorandum in Support, in author's collection; New York Anti-Trafficking Network, Memorandum in Support, in author's collection.

45. Human Rights Watch, *Sex Workers at Risk*, 61, 66–67.

46. New York City Young Women's Initiative, *Report and Recommendations*.

47. President's Task Force on 21st-Century Policing, *Final Report of the President's Task Force on 21st-Century Policing*, 27–28.

48. Chateauvert, *Sex Workers Unite!*, 59.

49. *2015 US Transgender Survey*, 12.

50. Williamson et al., "Police-Prostitute Interactions," 22.

51. Sex Workers Project, *Behind Closed Doors* (New York: 2005); Sex Workers Project, *Revolving Door: An Analysis of Street-Based Prostitution in New York City*, (New York: 2003).

52. INCITE! *Organizer's Tool Kit on Law Enforcement Violence*, 25.

53. Mogul, Ritchie, and Whitlock, *Queer (In)Justice*, 141–42.

54. "Lawsuit: Girl, 12, Not Prostitute," *Brownsville Herald*, December 24, 2008; Chris Vogel, "Police Get the Wrong House in Galveston, Allegedly Assault 12-Year-Old Girl," *Houston Press*, December 17, 2008; Complaint, Milburn v. Gomez, et al., 08cv193 (S.D. Tex, December 2, 2008).

55. Memorandum and Order, Milburn v. Gomez et al., 08cv193 (S.D. Tex. November 17, 2010).

56. Young Women's Empowerment Project, *Girls Do What They Need to Do to Survive: Illuminating Methods Used by Girls in the Sex Trades and Street Economy to Fight Back and Heal* (2009), 30, 32.

57. C. Angel Torres and Naima Paz, *Denied Help: How Youth in the Sex Trade and Street Economy Are Turned Away from Systems Meant to Help Us and What We Are Doing to Fight Back* (Chicago: Young Women's Empowerment Project, 2012), 19, 27, 30.

58. Dank et al., *Locked In*.

59. Alliance for a Safe & Diverse DC, *Move Along: Policing Sex Work in Washington, D.C.* (Washington, DC: Different Avenues, 2008), 53.

60. Chateauvert, *Sex Workers Unite!*, 173.

61. Ibid., 155.

62. Sex Workers Project, *Behind Closed Doors*; Sex Workers Project, *Revolving Doors*.

63. Williamson et al., "Police-Prostitute Interactions," 24–25.

64. *2015 US Transgender Survey*, 163.

65. Mogul, Ritchie, and Whitlock, *Queer (In)Justice*, 63; Amnesty International, *Stonewalled*, 40.

66. Sex Workers Project, *Kicking Down the Door: The Use of Raids to Fight Trafficking in Persons* (New York: 2009), quotes here and below 3, 4, 5.

67. Eva Pendleton, "Domesticating Partnerships," in *Policing Public Sex*, ed. Dangerous Bedfellows (Boston: South End Press, 1986), 377.

68. Joan Nestle, "Voices from Lesbian Herstory," in Nestle, *A Restricted Country*, 111.

69. Chateauvert, *Sex Workers Unite!*, 79.

70. Solutions Not Punishment Coalition, *"The Most Dangerous Thing Out Here Is the Police": Trans Voices on Police Abuse and Profiling in Atlanta* (March 2016).

71. La. Rev. Stat. Ann. § 14:89 (2012).

72. See Doe v. Jindal, 851 F. Supp. 2d 995, 1000 n.12 (E.D. La. 2012).

73. Brendan M. Connor, Andrea J. Ritchie, and Women with a Vision, *"Just a Talking Crime": A Policy Brief in Support of the Repeal of Louisiana's Solicitation of a Crime Against Nature (SCAN) Statute* (2011), http://wwav-no.org/just-a-talking-crime -no-justice-policy-brief, 3.

74. Compare La. Rev. Stat. Ann. § 14:89(A)(2) (2010) and La. Rev. Stat. Ann. § 15:542 (2012) et seq., with La. R.S. 14:82.

75. Failure to comply with the registration requirements imposed on individuals convicted of a "crime against nature by solicitation" was punishable by terms of imprisonment of up to twenty years at hard labor, with no possibility of probation or parole. La. Rev. Stat. Ann. 15:542.1.4(A) (2012).

76. See Women with a Vision, "About" page, http://wwav-no.org/about, accessed April 1, 2013.

77. "Crimes Against Nature by Solicitation (CANS) Litigation," Center for Constitutional Rights, http://ccrjustice.org/home/get-involved/tools-resources/fact-sheets -and-faqs/louisiana-s-crime-against-nature-law-modern.

78. Complaint, Doe v. Jindal, 851 F. Supp. 2d 995 (E.D. La. 2012) (No. 11–388).

79. Plaintiff Hiroke Doe relates her experience (February 16, 2011); see http://ccrjustice .org/home/get-involved/tools-resources/fact-sheets-and-faqs/louisiana-s-crime -against-nature-law-modern.

80. Ibid.

81. Conner and Ritchie, *"Just a Talking Crime,"* 6.

82. Ibid., 1.

83. Ibid., 3

CHAPTER 8: *Policing Motherhood*

1. Hector Castro, "Pregnant Woman 'Tasered' by Police Is Convicted," *Seattle Intelligencer*, May 10, 2005.

2. Lisa Loving, "Seattle Settles Out of Court in Malaika Brooks Case," *Skanner News*, September 11, 2014; Bill Meares, "Justices Decline Case of Taser Use on Pregnant Woman," CNN, May 29, 2012.

3. Tonya McClary and Andrea J. Ritchie, *In the Shadows of the War on Terror: Persistent Police Brutality and Abuse in the United States*, unpublished report filed before UN Committee Against Torture, May 2006, author's collection.

4. Amnesty International, *Less Than Lethal? The Use of Stun Weapons in US Law Enforcement*, AMR 51/010/2008 (New York: 2008).

5. Dorothy Roberts, *Killing the Black Body: Race, Reproduction, and the Meaning of Liberty* (New York: Vintage Books, 1997).

6. Ibid.

7. See Dorothy E. Roberts, "Punishing Drug Addicts Who Have Babies: Women of Color, Equality, and the Right of Privacy," *Harvard Law Review* 104, no. 7 (1991): 1419.

8. Roberts, *Killing the Black Body*, 17.

9. Escobar, *Captivity Beyond Prisons*, 5, 11, 35, 46, 60, 63, 69–70, 94, 103, 109–110 (describing how "the merging of criminality and state dependency that occurs in relation to Black motherhood gets re-mapped onto Latina (im)migrants"); Cainkar, *Homeland Insecurity*, 242–43.

10. Victoria Law, "Your Pregnancy May Subject You to Even More Law Enforcement Violence," in Schenwar, Macaré, and Price, *Who Do You Serve?*, 92.

11. Amnesty International, *Less Than Lethal*.

12. "Chicago Cops Taser 8-Month-Pregnant Woman over Parking Violation," *RT News*, https://www.rt.com/usa/chicago-taser-pregnant-rent-324/.

13. "Chicago to Pay $55,000 to Tasered Pregnant Woman," NBC New York, April 6, 2013, http://www.nbcnewyork.com/news/nationalinternational/ChicagotoPay55 KtoTaseredPregnantWoman201792881.html.

14. Amnesty International, *Less Than Lethal.*.

15. Ritchie and Jones-Brown, "Policing Race, Gender and Sex."

16. "San Antonio Police Beat Pregnant Woman, a National Trend?," *Republic Magazine*, n.d., http://www.republicmagazine.com/news/san-antonio-police-beat -pregnant-woman-part-of-a-national-trend.html.

17. Patton, "White Male Cops."

18. S. Wooten and Reagan Ali, "Cop Punches Pregnant Woman in Stomach for Laughing at Him, Calls Her Black B*$#ch," *Countercurrent*, May 24, 2015; Brian Booker, "Cop Calls Pregnant Woman Racist Remark, Punches Her in the Stomach," *Digital Journal*, May 20, 2015.

19. Second Amended Complaint, McClennon v. City of Chicago, et. al, 14cv03233 (N.D. Ill. 2016).

20. See, for example, Patton, "White Male Cops"; Frank Donnelly, "Lawsuit: Woman Miscarried After Cops 'Battered' Her During 'False' Arrest," *Staten Island Advance*, February 1, 2016.

21. Patton, "White Male Cops."

22. Rob Johnson, "Harvey Cop Never Charged After 2 Pregnant Women Accused Him Of Misconduct," *CBSNewsChicago*, September 20, 2016, http://chicago .cbslocal.com/2016/09/20/harvey-cop-never-charged-after-2-pregnant-women -accused-him-of-misconduct/.

23. Complaint, Rios v. City of San Antonio, et al., 14cv590 (July 2, 2014); Marc Reagan, "Civil Rights: Woman Who Had Miscarriage Sues SAPD, City," *San Antonio Current*, October 7, 2014.

24. Nina Bernstein, "Protests Brew Over Attempt to Deport Woman," *New York Times*, February 14, 2006.

25. National Network for Immigrant and Refugee Rights, *Over-Raided, Under Siege*.

26. "Woman: Cops Ignored Pleas for Help at Arrest; Baby Died the Next Day," Fox News, January 31, 2007, http://www.foxnews.com/story/2007/01/31/womancops ignoredpleasforhelpatarrestbabydiednextday.html.

27. National Advocates for Pregnant Women, *Pregnant Women and Drug Use: Charles Condon and South Carolina's Policy of Punishment Not Treatment* (March 2006), http://advocatesforpregnantwomen.org/issues/criminal_cases_and_issues /pregnant_women_and_drug_use.php; see also Dorothy Roberts, "Unshackling Black Motherhood," *Michigan Law Review* 95 (1997–98): 938, 941.

28. Lynn Paltrow, "Background Concerning *Ferguson et al. v. City of Charleston*," National Advocates for Pregnant Women, http://www.advocatesforpregnantwomen .org/facts/ferguson_history.htm, accessed March 24, 2016; Roberts, *Killing the Black Body*, 164–67.

29. Roberts, "Unshackling Black Motherhood," 950; Roberts, *Killing the Black Body*, 10, 14.

30. Roberts, *Killing the Black Body*, 9.

31. Ferguson et al. v. City of Charleston, 532 U.S. 67 (2001). https://www.reproductive rights.org/sites/default/files/documents/fergusondecision.pdf.

32. Roberts, *Killing the Black Body*, 3.

33. Roberts, "Unshackling Black Motherhood," 943–44; ibid., 166.

34. *Ferguson et al. v. City of Charleston*.

35. Roberts, *Killing the Black Body*, 173.

36. Ibid., 175.

37. Bhattacharjee, "Private Fists and Public Force," 45.

38. Haley, *No Mercy Here*, 55–56.

39. Ibid. 33; Roberts, "Unshackling Black Motherhood," 954.

40. Roberts, *Killing the Black Body*, 183.

41. Ibid., 154.

42. Ibid., 180, 182.

43. Lynne Paltrow and Jeanne Flavin, "Arrests of and Forced Interventions on Pregnant Women in the United States, 1973–2005: Implications for Women's Legal Status and Public Health," *Journal of Health Politics, Policy and Law* 38, no. 2 (April 2013): 308.

44. Silliman and Bhattacharjee, *Policing the National Body*, xviii.

45. Ibid., 19.

46. Law, "Your Pregnancy May Subject You," 99–100, 101–2.

47. Paltrow and Flavin, "Arrests of and Forced Interventions."

48. Ibid., 334.

49. Bhattacharjee, "Private Fists and Public Force," 36.

50. Dorothy Roberts, *Shattered Bonds: The Color of Child Welfare* (New York: Basic Books, 2008), 33–46.

51. Ibid., 32, 59.

52. Ibid., 60–67; Dorothy Roberts, "Mothers Who Fail to Protect Their Children: Accounting for Private and Public Responsibility," in *Mother Troubles: Rethinking Contemporary Maternal Dilemmas*, ed. J. E. Hanigsberg and S. Rudder (Boston: Beacon Press 1999), 34; Roberts, "Unshackling Black Motherhood," 947–48.

53. David Love, "On the Criminalization of Black Motherhood," *Black Commentator*, May 8, 2008, http://blackcommentator.com/276/276_col_criminalization_of _black_motherhood_printer_friendly.html, accessed March 16, 2016.

54. Roberts, Mothers Who Fail to Protect Their Children, 41.

55. Roberts, *Shattered Bonds*, 61–67; Roberts, *Killing the Black Body*, 14.

56. Roberts, "Mothers Who Fail to Protect Their Children," 41.

57. Lakin Starling, "LAPD Officer Sentenced to 3 Years for Excessive Force in Alesia Thomas Case," *News One*, July 24, 2015; "Female LAPD Officer Guilty of Assault for Kicking Handcuffed Woman Who Died," *CBS News*, June 5, 2015.

58. Javier Panzar, "At Emotional Hearing, LAPD Officer Gets 36 Months in Jail in Assault Caught on Video," *Los Angeles Times*, July 23, 2015.

59. Mariame Kaba, *"Mistaken Identity": The Violent Un-Gendering of Black Women and the NYPD*, http://www.usprisonculture.com/blog/2014/08/04/mistaken -identity-the-violent-un-gendering-of-black-women-and-the-nypd/; John Marzulli, Laura Dimon, and Ginger Adams Otis, "Naked Brooklyn Woman Dragged from Apartment, Left Topless in Hallway for Minutes by NYPD Officers Who Say She Beat 12-Year-Old Daughter," *New York Daily News*, August 1, 2014, http:// www.nydailynews.com/new-york/brooklyn/nypd-officers-drag-naked-brooklyn -woman-apartment-video-article-1.1889292.

60. Jessica Miller et al., "Utah Attorneys Shocked That Violence in 2014 Police Video Was Never Investigated," *Salt Lake Tribune*, July 7, 2016.

61. Roberts, *Shattered Bonds*, 77–79.

62. Ibid., 78–79.

63. Roberts, *Shattered Bonds*, 31.

64. Black Youth Project 100, *Agenda for Black Futures*, http://agendatobuildblack futures.org; Sarah Jarvis, "Mom Who Left Kids in Car Sentenced to 18 Years' Probation," *Arizona Republic*, May 15, 2015; Kay Steigler, "Mom Gets Arrested for 'Abandoning' Kids in Nearby Food Court While at Job Interview," *ThinkProgress*, July 18, 2015; Sara Jaffe, Mariame Kaba, Randy Abelda, and Kathleen Geier, "How to End the Criminalization of America's Mothers," *Nation*, August 21, 2014.

65. Roberts, *Shattered Bonds*.

66. Bhattacharjee, "Private Fists and Public Force," 44.

67. Jaffe et al., "How to End the Criminalization of America's Mothers"; "Where School Boundary-Hopping Can Mean Time in Jail," *Al-Jazeera Tonight*, January 21, 2014; Daniel Tepfer, "Tanya McDowell Sentenced to 5 Years in Prison," *Connecticut Post*, March 27, 2012; John Nickerson, "Mom Accused of Stealing Education Pleads Guilty," *Stamford Advocate*, February 22, 2012; Khadijah Z. Ali-Coleman, "Mom Jailed for Enrolling Kids in School Tells Her Story in New Book, Film," *Ebony*, March 20, 2014; "Mother Who Put Kids in Wrong School Released from Jail Early," CNN, January 27, 2011; "Kelley Williams-Bolar, Ohio Mother, Convicted of Felony for Lying to Get Kids into Better School," *Huffington Post Education*, January 27, 2011.

68. Noam Cohen, "New Jersey Daily Briefing; Officer's Suspension Ends," *New York Times*, September 12, 1997; Ronald Smothers, "Newark Officer Is Cleared in Shooting During Arrest," *New York Times*, September 5, 1997; Kit Roane, "Police Changes Promised," *New York Times*, July 8, 1997.

69. Roberts, *Shattered Bonds*.

70. See Kenrya Rankin, "Black Lives Matter Partners with Reproductive Justice Groups to Fight for Black Women," *RHReality Check*, February 9, 2016.

CHAPTER 9: *Police Responses to Violence*

1. Andrea Ritchie, "Black Feminism Enters the New Millennium," *New Barrister*, March 2000.

2. Greg Smith and Tara George, "Officers Accused of Beating Woman," *New York Times*, March 2, 2000; Juan Forero, "Two Officers Are Accused of Beating Woman Who Asked for Their Names and Badge Numbers," *New York Times*, March 2, 2000; J. Zamgba Browne, "Two Officers Sentenced in Assault of Black Woman," *Amsterdam News*, November 15, 2001.

3. Forero, "Two Officers Are Accused."

4. Smith and George, "Officers Accused of Beating Woman"; Forero "Two Officers Are Accused"; National Briefs, *Pittsburgh Post Gazette*, March 2, 2000.

5. Smith and George, "Officers Accused of Beating Woman."

6. Angela Y. Davis, Keynote Address, Color of Violence conference, *Colorlines*, http://www.colorlines.com/articles/color-violence-against-women. Davis also invoked the name of LaTanya Haggerty during her remarks, asking the audience to consider what might have prevented her death. See also Davis, "Violence Against Women," 146, 148.

7. Andrea J. Ritchie, "Policy and Oversight: Women of Color's Experiences of Policing," January 28, 2015, submission to the President's Task Force on 21st-Century Policing, http://changethenypd.org.

8. Julie Goldscheid, Donna Coker, Sandra Park, Tara Neal, and Valerie Halstead, *Responses from the Field: Sexual Assault, Domestic Violence, and Policing* (New York: CUNY Academic Works, 2015), 18, http://academicworks.cuny.edu/cl_pubs/76. Perhaps this is not surprising given the high incidence of domestic violence among male police officers—for instance, in 2006, it was reported that the head of the NYPD domestic violence unit on Staten Island abused his partner, once beating her for getting him the "wrong" birthday cake. Two studies have found that at least 40 percent of police officer families experience domestic violence, in contrast to 10 percent of families in the general population. See P. H. Neidig et al., "Interspousal Aggression in Law Enforcement Families: A Preliminary Investigation," *Police Studies* 15, no. 1 (1992): 30–38; Leanor Boulin Johnson, testimony before the House Select Committee on Children, Youth, and Families, 102nd Congress, 1st Sess., May 1991, in *On the Front Lines: Police Stress and Family Well-Being* (Washington, DC: Government Printing Office, 1991), 32–48; M. Straus and R. Gelles, *Physical Violence in American Families—Risk Factors and Adaptations to Violence in 8,145 Families* (New Brunswick, NJ: Transaction, 1990). A third study of older and more experienced officers found domestic violence occurring in 24 percent of these families, indicating that domestic violence is two to four times

more common among police families than American families in general (Neidig et al., "Interspousal Aggression," 25–28); Goldscheid et al., *Responses from the Field*, 12, 15.

9. Crenshaw and Ritchie, *Say Her Name*, 24–25; Ritchie, "Law Enforcement Violence," 151.

10. Marjua Estevez, "#MelissaVentura's Extrajudicial Execution Protested in Harlem," *Vibe*, January 3, 2017, vibe.com/2017/01/melissa-ventura-killed-by-cops; Rosalie Chan, "Police Are Investigating a Fatal Shooting of a Woman in Arizona," Time.com, July 7, 2016.

11. Fred Clasen-Kelly, "The Seconds Before the Shots," *Charlotte Observer*, March 21, 2015.

12. Crenshaw and Ritchie, *Say Her Name*, 25; Dawn Rhodes, "Friends, Family Say Goodbye to Woman Accidentally Killed by Chicago Police," *Chicago Tribune*, January 6, 2016.

13. Kwame Dixon and Patricia E. Allard, *Police Brutality and International Human Rights in the United States: The Report on Hearings Held in Los Angeles, California, Chicago, Illinois, and Pittsburgh, Pennsylvania, Fall 1999* (New York: Amnesty International USA, February 2000), 18.

14. "Four More Women Accuse Eugene Officer of Abuse," KATU News, December 11, 2003; Rebecca Nolan, "Police Sex Case Victim Found Dead at Residence," *Oregon Register-Guard*, September 29, 2004.

15. Phillips and McCoy, "Extorting Sex with a Badge."

16. Ibid.

17. Mariame Kaba in conversation with the author.

18. Michael Lansu, "Woman Acquitted of Eavesdropping Charges for Recording Cops Sues City," *Chicago Sun-Times*, January 14, 2012.

19. See Jessica Shaw et al., "Beyond Surveys and Scales: How Rape Myths Manifest in Sexual Assault Police Records," *Psychology of Violence* (2016), advance online publication, http://dx.doi.org/10.1037/vio0000072; M. Haviland, V. Frye, V. Rajah, J. Thukral, and M. Trinity, *The Family Protection and Domestic Violence Intervention Act of 1995: Examining the Effects of Mandatory Arrest in New York City* (New York: Urban Justice Center, Family Violence Project, 2001), 67.

20. Haviland et al., *The Family Protection and Domestic Violence Act of 1995*, 17–18, 21, 23–25.

21. Ibid., 19–20.

22. Ibid., 75, 75–77.

23. Amnesty International, *Stonewalled*, 78.

24. Mogul, Ritchie, and Whitlock, *Queer (In)Justice*, 130.

25. Ibid., 137–38.

26. National Coalition of Anti-Violence Programs, *Lesbian, Gay, Bisexual, Transgender, Queer and HIV-Affected Intimate Partner Violence in 2015* (2016 Release Edition), 10. This represents a decrease in percentage of survivors who reported to police over previous years—55 percent in 2014 and 35 percent in 2013. National Coalition of Anti-Violence Programs, *Lesbian, Gay, Bisexual, Transgender, Queer and HIV-Affected Intimate Partner Violence in 2014* (2015 Release Edition), 26.

27. National Coalition of Anti-Violence Programs (2016), 11.

28. National Coalition of Anti-Violence Programs (2014), 52.

29. Haviland et al., *The Family Protection and Domestic Violence Intervention Act of 1995.*

30. See Safe House Progressive Alliance for Nonviolence, *Victim-Defendant Toolkit,* 2001, in author's collection.

31. Shaw et al., "Beyond Surveys and Scales."

32. Nina Strochlich, "'Out in the Night' and the Redemption of the 'Killer Lesbian Gang,'" *Daily Beast,* June 21, 2014, http://www.thedailybeast.com/articles/2014 /06/21/out-in-the-night-and-the-redemption-of-the-killer-lesbian-gang.html.

33. INCITE! Women of Color Against Violence & FIERCE!. "Re-Thinking 'The Norm' in Police/Prison Violence and Gender Violence: Critical Lessons from the New Jersey 7," *LeftTurn Magazine,* September 2008, http://incite-national.org/sites /default/files/incite_files/resource_docs/9908_toolkitrev-nj7.pdf.

34. A video and description of the exhibit, and of the publication that accompanies it, can be found at *No Selves to Defend,* http://noselves2defend.tumblr.com/; see also Arkles, "Gun Control," 855–99.

35. *Survived and Punished: End the Criminalization of Survivors of Sexual and Domestic Violence,* http://www.survivedandpunished.org.

36. Goldscheid et al., "Responses from the Field." Similarly, historic and present-day factors, including distrust of the police, have been found to play a role in Black women's willingness to report sexual violence to the police. Helen A. Neville and Aalece Pugh, "General and Culture-Specific Factors Influencing African American Women's Reporting Patterns and Perceived Social Support Following Sexual Assault," *Violence Against Women* 3, no. 4 (1997): 361–90. See also Nawal Ammar et al., "Experiences of Muslim and Non-Muslim Battered Immigrant Women with the Police in the United States: A Closer Understanding of Commonalities and Differences," *Violence Against Women* 19, no. 12 (2014): 1449–71; Nawal Ammar et al., "Calls to Police And Police Response: A Case Study Of Latina Immigrant Women in the USA," *International Journal of Police Science & Management* 7, no. 4 (2005): 230–44.

37. Goldscheid et al., 28.

38. Amnesty International, *Maze of Injustice: The Failure to Protect Indigenous Women from Sexual Violence in the USA* (New York, 2007), 2, 4, 8, 27–30, 47–49.

39. H. N. Bui, "Help-Seeking Behavior Among Abused Immigrant Women," *Violence Against Women* 9, no. 2 (2003): 207–39.

40. *2015 US Transgender Survey,* 12.

41. See Susan L. Miller, "Unintended Consequences of Mandatory Arrest: Policy Problems and Possibilities," presentation at Mandatory Arrest: Original Intentions, Outcomes in our Communities, and Future Directions, Columbia University School of Law, New York, NY, June 17, 2005; Jessica Dayton, "Intimate Violence: The Silencing of a Woman's Choice: Mandatory Arrest and No Drop Prosecution Policies in Domestic Violence Cases," *Cardozo Women's Law Journal* 9 (2003), 281, 288.

42. Miller, "Unintended Consequences."

43. John Johnson, "A New Side to Domestic Violence: Arrests of Women Have Risen Sharply Since Passage of Tougher Laws," *Los Angeles Times,* April 27, 1996.

44. Ibid.

45. Meda Chesney-Lind, "Criminalizing Victimization: The Unintended Consequences of Mandatory Arrest Policies for Girls and Women," *Criminology and Public Policy* 2, no. 1 (2002): 81–90.

46. Susan L. Miller and Michelle L. Malloy, "Women's Use of Force: Voices of Women Arrested for Domestic Violence," *Violence Against Women* 12, no. 1 (2006): 89–115; Susan Miller, "The Paradox of Women Arrested for Domestic Violence," *Violence Against Women* 7, no. 12 (2001).

47. Haviland et al. *The Family Protection and Domestic Violence Intervention Act of 1995.*

48. Ibid.

49. National Coalition of Anti-Violence Programs, *Lesbian, Gay, Bisexual, Transgender and Queer Domestic/Intimate Partner Violence in the United States in 2009* (New York: National Coalition of Anti-Violence Programs, 2010), 4.

50. National Coalition of Anti-Violence Programs, *Lesbian, Gay, Bisexual, Transgender and Queer Domestic/Intimate Partner Violence in the United States in 2015* (New York: National Coalition of Anti-Violence Programs, 2016), 10.

51. Johnson, "A New Side to Domestic Violence."

52. Escobar, *Captivity Beyond Prisons*, 111–13.

53. Haviland et al., *The Family Protection and Domestic Violence Intervention Act of 1995.*

54. Ibid.

55. Ibid.

56. See Kavitha Sreeharsha, "Victims' Rights Unraveling: The Impact of Local Immigration Enforcement Policies on the Violence Against Women Act," *Georgetown Journal of Gender and the Law* 11 (2010): 649. Women's dependent or undocumented status is often manipulated by batterers, who use the threat of deportation as part of a matrix of domination and control. In addition, women arrested under mandatory arrest laws could themselves face deportation. See Anita Raj and Jay Silverman, "Violence Against Immigrant Women: The Role of Culture, Context and Legal Immigrant Status on Intimate Partner Violence," *Violence Against Women* 8, no. 3 (March 2002): 367–98; Deena Jang, Len Marin, and Gail Pendleton, *Domestic Violence in Immigrant and Refugee Communities: Assessing the Rights of Battered Women*, 2nd ed. (San Francisco: Family Violence Prevention Fund, 1997).

57. Ann Arbor for Black Lives, *Organizing Against Police Brutality and Mass Incarceration in Washtenaw County* (2015), in author's collection.

58. Anonymous, *People's Retort to the Prosecutor's Report* (2016), in author's collection.

59. Austin McCoy, "Ann Arbor Is America: The Police Kill Aura Rosser and the System Exonerates Itself—Again," Medium.com, January 2015.

60. Sunnivie Brydum and Mitch Kellaway, "This Black Trans Man Is in Prison for Killing His Rapist," *Advocate*, April 8, 2015; Justice for Ky Peterson!, https://action network.org/petitions/justice-for-ky-peterson-black-transgender-man-sentenced -to-20-years-in-prison-for-defending-himself-against-sexual-assault.

61. Francine Sherman and Annie Balck, *Gender Injustice: System-Level Juvenile Justice Reform for Girls* (Washington, DC: National Crittenton Foundation and the National Women's Law Center, 2015).

62. Movement for Black Lives, *Vision for Black Lives: Policy Demands for Black Power, Freedom and Justice* (New York: Movement for Black Lives, 2016), https://policy. m4bl.org/platform.

63. This toolkit is available for download at www.creative-interventions.org/tools /toolkit, accessed January 23, 2017.

64. Critical Resistance and INCITE!, "Statement on Gender-Based Violence and the Prison Industrial Complex," 2001, incite-national.org/page/incite-critical -resistance-statement.

CHAPTER 10: *Resistance*

1. Kate Abbe-Lambertz, "These 15 Black Women Were Killed During Police Encounters. Their Lives Matter, Too," *Huffington Post*, February 13, 2015; James Thilman, "Did the NYPD Suffocate A Mentally Ill Woman To Death While Trying To Cuff Her?," *Gothamist*, April 3, 2012. The family won a $1.1 million settlement.
2. James McKinley, "Man Sentenced to 12 Years in Beating Death of Transgender Woman," *New York Times*, April 19, 2016.
3. Jeff Mays, "Transgender Groups Protest Handling of Islan Nettles' Death," *DNA. Info*, January 21, 2014.
4. Justice for Shantel Davis!, https://justice4shantel.com.
5. Carmen Dixon, testimony submitted to the New York City Council Executive Budget Hearing Jointly with the Committee on Public Safety, May 21, 2015, on behalf of Black Lives Matter NYC and Safety Beyond Policing Coalition.
6. Kevin Tarr, "Who Was Kyam Livingston?" *Brooklyn Ink*, August 28, 2014, http://thebrooklynink.com/2014/08/28/54070-who-was-kyam-livingston.
7. For more information on the First National Day of Action to End State Violence Against Black Women and Girls, please visit http://byp100.org/justice-for-rekia.
8. This project can be seen at #SayHerName x #InHerHonor at http://sayhername .blacklivesmatter.com.
9. Lizzie Johnson, "SFPD Sergeant Identified in Woman's Fatal Shooting," Sfgate.com, May 31, 2016.
10. Davis, *Freedom Is a Constant Struggle*, 18–19.
11. See, for example, Angela Y. Davis, "Political Prisoners, Prisons, and Black Liberation," "Race and Criminalization: Black Americans in the Punishment Industry," "Rape, Racism, and the Capitalist Setting," "Violence Against Women and the Ongoing Challenge to Racism," "Joan Little: The Dialectics of Rape," "Surrogates and Outcast Mothers: Racism and Reproductive Politics in the Nineties," "Reflections on Race, Class and Gender in the U.S.A.," all in James, *The Angela Y. Davis Reader*.
12. Joy James, *Resisting State Violence* (Minneapolis: University of Minnesota Press, 1996), 30–31.
13. INCITE!, *Organizer's Tool Kit on Law Enforcement Violence*, 19.
14. Beth Richie, "Queering Antiprison Work: African American Lesbians in the Juvenile Justice System," in *Global Lockdown: Race, Gender, and the Prison-Industrial Complex*, ed. Julia Sudbury (New York: Routledge, 2005), 80.
15. Critical Resistance and INCITE!, "Statement on Gender-Based Violence."
16. Anannya Bhattacharjee, "Women of Color and the Violence of Law Enforcement," Justice Visions working paper, American Friends Service Committee and Committee on Women, Population and the Environment, 2001.
17. Audre Lorde Project, "Statement: Open Letter to LGBTST Communities Opposing War," January 27, 2003, http://alp.org/whatwedo/statements/antiwar.
18. Audre Lorde Project, "Statement: For All the Ways They Say We Are, No One Is Illegal," April 21, 2006, http://alp.org/whatwedo/statements/nooneisillegal.

19. Davis, *Women, Race & Class*, 3. See also Manion, *Liberty's Prisoners*, 126–32.

20. McGuire, *At the Dark End of the Street*, 35; Ida B. Wells-Barnett, *The Red Record: Tabulated Statistics and Alleged Causes of Lynching in the United States* (1895).

21. McGuire, *At the Dark End of the Street*, quotes here and below from 137–39, 75–76, 78, 63–69, 195–201, and 249.

22. Ibid. 253–75; Angela Y. Davis, "JoAnne Little: The Dialectics of Rape," *Ms.*, June 1975. There is some question as to whether Little had in fact been arrested for prostitution in the past. According to Mindy Chateauvert, Little had, a fact that was denied by Angela Davis as profiling and buried by defense counsel as vestiges of the politics of respectability that would have precluded defense of a woman in the sex trades who charged rape. See Chateauvert, *Sex Workers Unite!*, 159–60.

23. Kimberly Springer, *Living for the Revolution: Black Feminist Organizations, 1968–1980* (Durham, NC: Duke University Press, 2005), 88; Combahee River Collective, *Six Black Women, Why Did They Die?*, http://library.brown.edu/pdfs/1124979008226934.pdf.

24. Davis, "Violence Against Women," 147.

25. Richie, *Arrested Justice*; Mimi E. Kim, *Dancing the Carceral Creep: The Anti-Domestic Violence Movement and the Paradoxical Pursuit of Criminalization, 1973–1986* (Berkeley: UC Berkeley Institute for the Study of Societal Issues, 2015). Retrieved from http://eprints.cdlib.org/uc/item/804227k6; INCITE!, *Color of Violence*.

26. Mogul, Ritchie, and Whitlock, *Queer (In)Justice*, 54.

27. Susan Stryker, *Transgender History* (Berkeley: Seal Press, 2008), 60–61.

28. Ibid., 72–73; Jennifer Worley, "Street Power and the Claiming of Public Space: San Francisco's 'Vanguard' and Pre-Stonewall Queer Radicalism," in *Captive Genders: Trans Embodiment and the Prison Industrial Complex*, ed. Eric A. Stanley and Nat Smith (San Francisco: AK Press, 2011).

29. See Stryker, *Transgender History*, 96–97, on the film.

30. Che Gossett, Reina Gossett, and A. J. Lewis, "Reclaiming Our Lineage: Organized Queer, Gender Nonconforming, and Transgender Resistance to Police Violence," *SF Online*, October 1–2, 2012; see also Regina Kunzel, *Criminal Intimacy: Prison and the Unusual History of Modern American Sexuality* (Chicago: University of Chicago Press, 2008), 191.

31. Nestle, "Voices from Lesbian Herstory," 111; "Fight Police Abuse! Remember Blues!," flyer, undated (c. 1984), Lesbian Herstory Archives, New York City.

32. Mogul, Ritchie, and Whitlock, *Queer (In)Justice*.

33. William Rashbaum, "Woman Dies After Police Mistakenly Raid Her Apartment," *New York Times*, May 17, 2003.

34. Coalition for Justice and Accountability, *Tasers: A Reassessment* (San Jose, CA: Coalition for Justice and Accountability, March 10, 2005).

35. Best Practices Policy Project, "Washington, D.C. Passes Bill to Repeal Discredited "Prostitution Free Zones," October 8, 2014, http://www.bestpracticespolicy.org/2014/10/08/washington-d-c-passes-bill-to-repeal-discredited-prostitution-free-zones; David Grosso, "Time to Repeal 'Prostitution Free Zones,'" *Washington Blade*, April 3, 2014; Tim Craig, "D.C. 'Prostitution-Free Zones' Probably Unconstitutional, Attorney General's Office Says," *Washington Post*, January 24, 2012; *Prostitution Free Zone*, https://vimeo.com/4652102 (2009); Alliance for a Safe and Diverse DC, *Move Along*.

36. Mitch Kellaway, "Arizona Appeals Court Overturns Monica Jones's Conviction for 'Walking While Trans,'" *Advocate*, January 27, 2015; Gretchen Rachel Blickensderfer, "Monica Jones Found Guilty Under Prostitution Ordinance," *Windy City Times*, April 11, 2014.

37. "Yvonne McNeal, Homeless Lesbian Woman, Shot and Killed by New York Police," *Huffington Post*, October 7, 2011; Welfare Warriors Research Collaborative, *A Fabulous Attitude*.

38. See Kirsten West Savali, "Black Women Are Killed by Police, Too," *Dame Magazine*, August 18, 2014; Mariame Kaba, "Erasing Fannie Lou, and Other Black Women Victimized by Police," *Prison Culture* blog, August 22, 2014, usprisonculture.com/blog/2014/08/22/erasing-fannie-lou-and-other-black-women-victimized-by-police; Evette Dion, "You Know Police Kill Black Women Too, You Just Don't Hear About It," *Bustle*, December 8, 2014; "The Conversation: Women of Color Speak Out on Police Violence," *Ravishly*, February 2015, http://www.ravishly.com/conversation/women-color-speak-out-police-violence; "A Deadly U-Turn," *Democracy Now*; Montgomery, "Her Name Was Miriam Carey"; Tom Dart, "Former Texas Officer Who Fatally Shot Unarmed Woman Found Not Guilty, *Guardian*, April 8, 2016; Christopher Maag, "Police Shooting of Mother and Infant Exposes a City's Racial Tension," *New York Times*, January 30, 2008.

39. SNaPCo, *Wrongful Arrest*, YouTube, uploaded October 27, 2014, https://www.youtube.com/watch?v=BHnV5q3LwMI.

40. Dyana Bagby, "East Point Mayor Apologizes to Trans Man After Alleged Police Discrimination," *Georgia Voice*, October 31, 2014, http://thegavoice.com/east-point-mayor-apologizes-trans-man-alleged-police-discrimination.

41. Racial Justice Action Center, "Victory! East Point Police Department to Adopt Most Progressive Trans Policies in the Nation," press release, April 9, 2015, http://www.rjactioncenter.org/EastPointVictory.

42. Democracy Now, *Denver Police Killing of LGBT Teen Jessica Hernandez Sparks Outcry as Officers' Claims Disputed*, February 13, 2015. Video available at https://www.youtube.com/watch?v=Narncvd9anw.

43. Nat Stein, "Buried Seedz of Resistance Uproots Denver Pride with Protest Against Police Violence," *Colorado Independent*, June 22, 2015.

44. Project Nia, *We Are Rekia's Haven*, YouTube, posted March 18, 2016, https://www.youtube.com/watch?v=SDC5vgDPFtU.

45. Mariame Kaba, "#FireDanteServin: An Abolitionist Campaign in Chicago," *Prison Culture* blog, September 19, 2015, http://www.usprisonculture.com/blog/tag/rekia-boyd.

46. Aishwarya Kumar, "#DontPayDante, Activists Say After Rekia Boyd Killer Quits CPD With Pension," *DNAinfo*, May 17, 2016. For more information about #Don't Pay Dante, #Save CSU, go to https://rememberrekia.wordpress.com.

47. For more information about the Second National Day of Action to End State Violence Against Black Women, Girls, and Femmes, go to http://blackyouthproject.com/national-sayhername-day-acknowledging-injustice-against-black-women-girls-and-femmes.

48. "Alexia Christian: Shot 10 Times by Atlanta Police," Blackgirltragic.com, accessed January 20, 2017; "Activists, Mother Demand Video in Alexia Christian Police

Killing," *Atlanta Progressive News*, September 4, 2015; "It's Bigger Than You Holds One Year Anniversary March," *Atlanta Progressive News*, August 22, 2015; Gloria Tatum, "Atlanta Citizens Review Board Gets on Activists' Last Nerve," *Atlanta Progressive News*, May 15, 2015.

49. Sameer Rao, "Activists Gather Around the Country to #SayHerName," *Colorlines*, May 20, 2016.

50. "Oakland Residents Still Seeking Police Accountability for the Shooting Death of Yuvette Henderson," KGNU, February 8, 2016.

51. Reniqua Adams, "Jasmine Abdullah: 'If I Don't Do This, I'm Going to Die,'" *Nation*, June 20, 2016; Orie Givens, "Lesbian Black Lives Matter Leader Will Spend 72 More Days in Jail for 'Lynching,'" *Advocate*, June 7, 2016; "Black Lives Matter Activist Convicted of 'Felony Lynching': It's More Than Ironic, It's Disgusting," *Democracy Now*, June 2, 2016; Black Lives Matter, "Black Lives Matter Organizer, Jasmine Abdullah AKA Jasmine Richards Targeted and Convicted of 'Attempted Lynching,'" June 2, 2016, http://blacklivesmatter.com/black-lives-matter-organizer -jasmine-abdullah-aka-jasmine-richards-targeted-and-convicted-of-attempted -lynching.

52. Yezmin Villareal, "Day 50, and BLM's Los Angeles Protest Is Still Going Strong," *Advocate*, August 31, 2016; Kate Mather, James Queally, and Ruben Vives, "Amid Protests, Panel Finds That LAPD Did Not Violate Deadly Force Rules in Shooting of Black Woman in South L.A.," *Los Angeles Times*, July 12, 2016.

53. Black Feminist Futures, *Defending Black Womanhood: A Toolkit for a Community Altar Building Project for Black Women and Girls*, https://docs.google.com/document /d/1TEGGoiINCdBSm5aNYa-9LQJBseDzEIoErUZM8lCskSo/edit.

54. Defend Black Womanhood, http://www.blackfeministfuture.org/defend-black -womanhood.

55. Walker Orenstein, "Is Compromise Possible on Changing Police Use of Deadly Force Law?," *Bellingham (WA) Herald*, January 17, 2017; Matt Nagle, "Justice for Jackie Efforts Move Forward," *Tacoma (WA) Weekly*, April 21, 2016.

56. National Queer Asian Pacific Islander Alliance, "LGBTQ Asian Groups to Protest Policing in 8 Cities Nationwide," press release, May 7–15, 2016, http://www.nqapia .org/beta/wp-content/uploads/2016/04/Week-of-Action-Media-Advisory.pdf.

57. Mark Tseng-Putterman, "10 Times Asian Americans Took on Systemic Racism in 2016," Medium.com, December 23, 2016; Sandra Allen, "The Trials of Teresa Sheehan," *Buzzfeed*, July 9, 2015.

58. Southerners on New Ground, "Free from Fear: From the Community Safety Act to Standard Operating Procedures in Bull City," June 1, 2016, http://southernerson newground.org/2016/06/community-safety-act-standard-operating-procedures -bull-city/; Southerners on New Ground, "SONG Launches Free from Fear," January 16, 2015, http://southernersonnewground.org/2015/01/freefromfear.

59. See Black Lives Matter, "Black Lives Matter Stands In Solidarity with Water Protectors at Standing Rock," http://blacklivesmatter.com/solidarity-with-standing -rock/; Kelly Hayes, "Our History and Our Dreams: Building Black and Native Solidarity," in *Who Do You Serve?*, 133.

60. See Taylor, *From #BlackLivesMatter to Black Liberation*, 180 (describing the work of Mothers Against Police Brutality in Houston).

61. For more information on Families United for Justice, please visit https://fu4j.org.
62. Eli Saslow, "For Diamond Reynolds, Trying to Move Past 10 Tragic Minutes of Video," *Washington Post*, September 10, 2016.
63. Taylor, *From #BlackLivesMatter to Black Liberation*, 53.
64. Elaine Woo, "Rena Price Dies at 97; Her and Son's Arrests Sparked Watts Riots," *Los Angeles Times*, June 22, 2013. Rumors that police had also assaulted a Black pregnant woman also fueled the outrage of community residents.
65. Christopher Mathias, "Cop Who Gunned Down Ramarley Graham Gets a Raise," *Huffington Post*, December 21, 2015, http://www.huffingtonpost.com/entry/ramarley -graham-nypd-richard-haste_us_567455d4e4b0b958f6567aa0.
66. Matt Taibbi, "Why Baltimore Blew Up," *Rolling Stone*, May 26, 2015.
67. Taylor, *From #BlackLivesMatter to Black Liberation*, 161, 166.
68. Andrea J. Ritchie, "As We #SayHerName, 7 Policy Paths to Stop Police Violence Against Black Girls and Women," *Colorlines*, May 19, 2016.
69. Movement for Black Lives, *A Vision for Black Lives*.

CONCLUSION

1. Davis, *Freedom Is a Constant Struggle*, 87.
2. Angela Y. Davis, "Race and Criminalization," in James, *The Angela Y. Davis Reader*, 64.
3. Davis, *Freedom Is a Constant Struggle*, 105.
4. Ibid., 70.
5. Charlene A. Carruthers, "In Defense of Korryn Gaines, Black Women and Children," *Colorlines*, August 5, 2016.
6. Taylor, *From #BlackLivesMatter to Black Liberation*, 108.
7. Rachel Herzing, "Big Dreams and Bold Steps Toward a Police-Free Future," in *Who Do You Serve?*
8. See Maya Dukmasova, "Abolish the Police? Organizers Say It's Less Crazy Than It Sounds," *Chicago Reader*, August 25, 2016.
9. Critical Resistance and INCITE!, "Statement on Gender-Based Violence."

INDEX

Abdullah, Jasmine, 225

abolition: abolition feminism, 241; of policing, xv, 103, 124, 126, 200–202, 238, 240–241, 243; as praxis, xv

Acosta, Karina, 62

Adams, Sarah, 117

African American Policy Forum, 9, 125, 205, 209, 220

Aikins, Jaisha, 73–74, 76, 77, 78

Alexander, Marissa, 68, 193, 203

Al-Matar, Itemid "Angel," 67–68

Almodovar, Denise, 117

Alwysh, Sourette, 179

AMEMSA (Arab, Middle Eastern, Muslim, and South Asian) women: Arab women, 2, 40, 46, 63–69, 134–35, 168, 190–91; arrests and incarceration rates, 62; controlling narratives and, 40, 68, 81, 97–98, 144–45, 185–86, 190–91, 227, 237; domestic violence and, 185–86; gender nonconformity and, 39, 86, 97; gender policing and, 134; as immigrants, 2–3, 14, 37–38, 39, 62, 168, 190–91, 216; Middle Eastern women, 116, 168, 190–91, 195, 197; motherhood and, 168; police response to violence and, 186, 190–91, 197; police sexual violence against, 113, 117, 149; pregnancy and, 168; as queer people of color, 134, 227; racial profiling and, 40, 46, 63–69; religious profiling, 46, 63–69, 81, 168, 190–91, 216, 227; in school settings, 81; sexuality and, 134, 227; war on terror and, 63–69. See also Muslim women; South Asian women; war on terror; *individual identities*

Ammons, Linda, 260n99

Amnesty International, 9, 51, 59, 66, 105, 168, 188

Anderson, Michelle Siguenza, 178

Anderson, Tanisha, 91, 101, 203, 205, 219, 220, 229. See also Johnson, Cassandra

Anderson, Vivian, 85–86

Ann Arbor Alliance for Black Lives, 198–99

anti-Blackness, 4, 56–57

antiviolence movements, 16–17, 106, 110, 124–25, 183–88, 192, 199–201, 212–13

Antor, Sandra, 1

Arab women, 2, 40, 46, 63–69, 134–35, 168, 190–91. See also AMEMSA (Arab, Middle Eastern, Muslim, and South Asian) women; war on terror

Arkles, Gabriel, 133, 284n2

Arnwine, Barbara, 125

Arrested Justice (Richie), 122

arrests: of Black women, 10, 29, 30, 43–46, 47–48, 51–53, 76–78, 147, 149–50, 262n9; child welfare law enforcement, 176–80, 190, 198; crimes of poverty, 45; domestic violence, 196; for domestic violence, 45, 195–98, 262n15; drug use, 45, 47, 51–53, 263n32; gendered racial disparities, 10, 44, 262n11; gender policing arrests, 285n12; immigration and, 299n56; increases over time, 44–45; Latinx women, 149–50; mandatory arrest policies, 186, 195–98, 200–201, 240, 299n56; for noncompliance, 72–73, 82–83, 165–66; poverty-related offenses, 45; queer people of color, 196; racial profiling and, 10,

305

44, 262n11; resisting arrest, 72–73; in school settings, 76–77, 78–79, 271n36; self-defense and, 45, 191, 194, 196–97, 212, 262n15; sex work/prostitution, 147, 149–50, 290n27; theft and other property crimes, 29, 30, 44–45
Asians for Black Lives, 227
Asian women: Asian trans women, 149, 191, 207; Black Lives Matter and, 227; controlling narratives and, 14, 23, 40, 81, 97–98, 144–45, 227; drug laws and, 46, 48; gender nonconformity and, 39, 86, 97, 130; as immigrants, 14, 37–38, 39, 168; as LGBTQ people, 130, 149, 191, 227; motherhood and, 168; police killing of, 96–97, 97–98, 215–16; pregnancy and, 168; racial profiling and, 40, 45; rates of engagement in sex work, 149; resistance, 227; response to police violence against, 195, 197; sex work/prostitution, 37–38, 39, 144–46, 149; strip searches, 48, 80–81; trafficking and, 157–58. *See also* Asian women, police physical violence against; Asian women, police sexual violence against; Asian women, racial profiling of; Chinese women
Asian women, police physical violence against: Asian mothers, 171; controlling narratives and, 96–97; as immigrants, 97–98, 157–58; response to police violence against, 189, 195; searches, 189; sex work/prostitution and, 157–58. *See also* Asian women; Asian women, police sexual violence against; Asian women, racial profiling of
Asian women, police sexual violence against: controlling narratives and, 145; gender policing and, 118; as immigrants, 115; sexuality policing and, 145–46. *See also* Asian women; Asian women, police physical violence against; Asian women, racial profiling of
Asian women, racial profiling of: controlling narratives, 236; gender policing and, 130–31; girls/youth and, 80–81; as

immigrants, 37–38, 39, 130–31; police response to violence and, 191, 195; pregnancy and, 39; school systems and, 80–81; sexuality policing and, 191; sex work/prostitution and, 37–38, 39; strip searches and, 48. *See also* Asian women; Asian women, police physical violence against; Asian women, police sexual violence against
Assata's Daughters, 224
Audre Lorde Project (ALP), 57, 139–40, 159, 201, 208, 209, 216

Baez, Iris, 228
Bah, Adama, 65
Bah, Hawa, 228
Bain, Beverly, 88, 282n80
Baker, Ella, 244
Baldwin, Dara, 99, 101
Banks, Korneisha, 187
Banks, Rosie, 93
Bates, Daisy, 211
Bean, Babe, 130
Becton, Dajerria, 70–72, 73, 206
Beltran, Alicia, 175
Berkeley Copwatch, 94–95
Bhattacharjee, Annanya, 61, 69, 174, 180, 182, 200, 263n22
Black Feminist Futures, 226
Black Lives Matter, 2, 72, 85, 122–23, 199, 203–5, 209, 222–23, 225–27. *See also* Movement for Black Lives
Black women: arrest and incarceration rates, 10, 29, 30, 43–46, 47–48, 51–53, 76–78, 147, 149–50, 262n9; Black lesbians, 137–38, 158–59, 193–94, 214; controlling narratives and, 35, 49–50, 74, 81, 89, 144–45, 146–47, 190–91; criminalization of, 29–37, 43–46; death by community members, 238–39; drug law enforcement, 11, 45–46, 47–50, 172–76; incarceration rates, 44, 47, 262n9; lesbians, 137–38, 158–59, 193–94, 214; motherhood and, 27, 57, 165–68, 170, 172–81, 260n106, 293n9; Movement for Black Lives and, 2, 199, 209, 222, 231–32, 237; police physical

violence and, 112–13, 114; resistance and, xii–xiii, xv, 78, 84–87, 156, 201, 216, 273nn69–70; school discipline and, 76–77; sexual nonconformity and, 77–78, 84; status offenses, 83–84, 87; stop and frisk and, 84–85. *See also* school systems; youth of color
Girls Rock Charleston, 73
Giselle, 55
Global North/Global South, 236, 253n6
Golden, Pearlie, 91
Goldschied, Julie, 186
Gore, Dayo, 140
Gossett, Che, 217
Gossett, Reina, 214
Graham, Ramarley, 229. *See also* Hartley, Patricia; Malcolm, Constance
Gray, Freddie, 1, 101
Grey, Jeanette, 158–59
Grey, Kimani, 229–30
Greywind, Martina, 175
Grissom, Tiffaney, 150–51
Groves, Kim, 65, 215
Guerrero, Diana, 114
Guidance on Gender Bias in Policing (US Department of Justice), 125
Gullikson, Sharon, 58
Gunn Allen, Paula, 22
Gutierrez, Jewlyes, 81

Haggerty, LaTanya, 183, 215, 296n6
Haley, Sarah, xii, 29–30, 31, 36–37, 91, 174
Hall, Mya, 1, 65, 203, 228
Hamer, Fannie Lou, 34–35, 211
Hamilton, Brandi, 121
Hansen-Singthong, Anothai, 189
Harcourt, Bernard, 54
Harm Free Zones, 201
Harriet's Apothecary, 203
Harrington, Penny, 110, 112
Harris, Cathy, 50
Harris-Dawson, Marqueece, 68
Hartley, Patricia, 229. *See also* Graham, Ramarley
Hawkins, Annie, 26
Hayder, Tashnuba, 64

Hayes, Lisa, 99–100
Haywood, Deon, 162
Height, Dorothy, 34, 211
Helping Individual Prostitutes Survive (HIPS), 149
Henderson, Yuvette, 225
Hernandez, Jessie, 222
Hernandez, Jo, 223
Hernandez, Vivianna, 132
Herzing, Rachel, 240
Hill, Renata, 193. *See also* New Jersey 7
Holmes, Billie Moton, 32
Holtzclaw, Daniel, 105–8, 110, 116, 125–26, 188, 206, 213, 222, 277n4
homelessness: broken windows policing and, 54–55, 57, 58; police violence and, 45–46, 54–58, 89–90, 92–93, 133–34, 156, 179–80, 190, 214
hooks, bell, 25, 36, 78
Howell, Cynthia, 228. *See also* Spruill, Alberta
Human Rights Watch, 138, 149, 151, 152–53, 216
Huq, Chaumtoli, 66–67

immigrants/immigration and law enforcement: AMEMSA women and, 14, 62, 168; arrests rates, 82, 299n56; border control and, 13, 14, 49–51, 115–16; broken windows policing and, 57, 67; Chinese women and, 37–38, 39; collaboration with local law enforcement, 61–62; colonialism/colonization and, 14, 15, 36, 37–40, 210, 216; controlling narratives and, 37–40, 115–16, 274n13; criminalization of, 115–16; deportation, 45, 59, 60, 61, 62, 69, 114–15, 115–16, 140, 171, 266n91, 285n14, 299n56; disability and, 274n13; domestic violence and, 97–98, 195, 197, 198, 299n56; enforcement as policing paradigm, 14, 59–63; exclusions of, 17, 37–38, 39, 161, 268n108, 285n14; extortion of sex, 114–15, 116; gender nonconformity and, 39; gender policing and, 40–41, 130, 140, 285n14; incarceration rates, 46;